ON EMPIRE, LIBERTY, AND REFORM

THE LEWIS WALPOLE SERIES IN
EIGHTEENTH-CENTURY CULTURE AND HISTORY

ON EMPIRE, LIBERTY, AND REFORM

Speeches and Letters

Edmund Burke

Edited by

DAVID BROMWICH

Yale University Press   New Haven & London

Published with assistance from the Annie Burr Lewis Fund.

Designed by James J. Johnson and set in Bulmer and Baskerville types by Keystone Typesetting Inc., Orwigsburg, Pennsylvania.
Printed in the United States of America.

Library of Congress Cataloging-in-Publication Data

Burke, Edmund, 1729–1797.
On empire, liberty, and reform : speeches and letters / Edmund Burke ; edited by David Bromwich.
p.cm. — (The Lewis Walpole series in eighteenth-century culture and history)
A collection of speeches.
Includes bibliographical references and index.
ISBN 0–300–08146–4 (alk. paper)

1. Great Britain — Colonies — History — 18th century — Sources. 2. Indigenous peoples — Great Britain — Colonies — History — 18th century — Sources. I. Bromwich, David, 1951– . II. Title. III. Series.
JV1016.B87 2000
941.07′3′092 — dc21 99–045105

A catalogue record for this book is available from the British Library.

1   3   5   7   9   10   8   6   4   2

Contents

Editorial Note and Acknowledgments

This is a reader's not a scholar's edition. "Speeches and Letters" indicates a principle of selection that emerged by accident: almost all the desired selections turned out to be public speeches, public letters, or private letters on public affairs. Except for the great four-day "Speech in Opening the Impeachment of Warren Hastings," I have chosen works suitable to reprint without abridgment. The texts are from the Rivington edition of the *Works of the Right Honourable Edmund Burke*, 16 vols. (London, 1792–1827), edited by French Laurence and Walker King, a production begun in collaboration with Burke himself during his last years. The eight volumes of 1803, my source for most of the selections here, are described in William B. Todd's *Bibliography of Edmund Burke* as "for that time the 'definitive edition.' " Laurence and King were among the best-informed and most loyal of Burke's younger followers; a modern scholar is not likely to outguess them as to his ultimate intention, though his original aims are projectable by other means. The *Works* laid the foundation for the later nineteenth-century collected editions that made Burke known to the architects of Whig history and liberal constitutionalism: Macaulay, Lecky, Dicey, and others. The degree of my sympathy with their view will be evident in the commentary and perhaps also in the choice of works to print.

I thank the Lewis Walpole Library and the Beinecke Rare Book and Manuscript Library of Yale University for the use of their copies of the *Works*. For private letters, I have relied on the *Correspondence of the Right Honourable Edmund Burke*, 4 vols. (London, 1844), and the Bohn edition of Burke's *Works*, 8 vols. (London, 1883–90). The letter to Miss Mary Palmer is reprinted here by permission of the Huntington Library, Art Collections, and Botanical Gardens, San Marino, California (HM 22523). When paraphrasing Burke's arguments, I have tried to preserve his language (e.g., men of honor, not persons of honor) where it is archaic but intelligible, rather than impose on the reader a peculiar amalgam of late eighteenth-century and late twentieth-century usage. I have brought punctuation and capitalization in the letters into conformity with Burke's normal practice, and have silently corrected a few errors after comparison with the versions in Thomas Copeland's definitive edition, *The Correspondence of Edmund Burke*, 10 vols. (Chicago, 1958–78). I should like to acknowledge a larger debt to the work Copeland supervised, one of the true monuments of modern scholarship, and to the *The Writings and Speeches of Edmund Burke* (Oxford, 1981–) edited by Paul Langford, whose published volumes have been an indispensable resource. I owe more particular thanks to three scholars of the eighteenth century: Jenny Davidson, who traced the allusions and made the translations to produce a draft of page notes for this edition, while assisting also with suggestions on the headnotes and introduction; Ian Harris, who answered queries and offered encouragement from an expert knowledge of the texts; and John Faulkner, who brought to the entire manuscript his candid judgment and generous understanding of Burke's career. It is a different and a better book than it would have been without their help.

Introduction

Edmund Burke, the greatest political writer in English, and one of the most inspired orators in the history of representative government, was born on New Year's Day, 1729, on Arran Quay, Dublin. His father, Richard Burke, a successful attorney in the Irish Court of Exchequer, had married a Catholic, Mary Nagle. Their daughter, Juliana, would be raised a Catholic; the sons of the marriage, Garrett, Edmund, and Richard, were guided into the established Church of Ireland, of which their father was a member. This division in the avowed faith of Burke's family was to be the germ of a career peculiarly marked by ambivalence. A promising son of the professional classes, destined for the middle station of life, he would come to define himself by connection with an aristocracy he knew from a wary distance. A sympathizer with a suppressed minority, he would praise the existing order that preserved a society at peace, and yet would urge the necessity of reform to uproot the causes of bitter discontents.

His early childhood was spent at Ballyduff, with his Catholic relatives; at eleven, he returned to Dublin, and from twelve to fifteen was educated at an independent school run by a Quaker, Abraham Shackleton — "a man," as Burke would describe him, of "a native elegance of manners which nothing but good-nature and unaffected simplicity of heart can give." The son of the schoolmaster, Richard Shackleton, was an early friend who later became one of Burke's most devoted admirers. From these fortunate beginnings, Burke acquired a solid foundation of learning in history and literature, and at the age of fifteen entered Trinity College, Dublin. He was already writing a good deal of verse, and hoping to make a literary career. At Trinity his love of poetry deepened. There he also started a debating club, and wrote most of the thirteen issues of a magazine, *The Reformer,* whose preferred topics were theatre and the relation between taste and morals.

The Burke of these early years is a prodigy—a man of extraordinary gifts but one whose field of action is far from settled. The period between his graduation from Trinity in 1748 and his emergence as an author in London in 1757 is all-important to his development; yet concerning these years we have almost no firsthand testimony, and the seven letters that survive are extremely reticent. We know that at the age of twenty-one, Burke enrolled in the study of law in the Middle Temple, in accord with his father's expectations. But he had not forgotten his ambition to be a writer. The genres of sentimental drama, political pamphlet, and verse-satire (at which he was proficient) were at this time fairly porous to each other; anonymous as many literary productions were, a coffee-house bravo with talent and pluck might try his hand at almost anything. On the internal evidence of character and aspiration, and the external evidence of connections that a few years later seem to materialize from thin air, there is reason to suppose that Burke in the early 1750s was active in the world of letters.

At some point he definitively gave up the study of law, and caused a breach with his father that would never be repaired. We catch a glimpse of him in the mid-1750s from an anecdote by Joseph Emin, another young man out of sorts with fate, who had come from India to seek his fortune in England. Seeing Burke in St. James's Park with an acquaintance he knew from Calcutta, Emin fell into conversation with them and that evening was invited to Burke's rooms near the Temple. "Sir, my name is Edmund Burke, at your service. I am a runaway son from a father, as you are." He offered Emin money and, being refused, paid him to copy two works still in manuscript, *A Vindication of Natural*

Society and *A Philosophical Enquiry into the Origin of Our Ideas of the Sublime and Beautiful.* In 1757, Burke married Jane Nugent — a marriage that would prosper. He has left one memorial of their courtship, a marveling description of her grace, sympathy, and gentleness, written apparently for himself.

His most durable success in bookmaking came from his arrangement with Dodsley to publish the *Annual Register of the Year's Events.* Starting with the first issue in 1758, Burke undertook to write the historical narrative for several issues in succession. When other obligations called him away in the late 1760s, the compiling of the *Register* would be handed over to trusted disciples; but throughout his career, the enterprise gave him a valuable instrument for shaping the public view of contemporary politics and literature. Meanwhile, in 1756 he had published anonymously the *Vindication of Natural Society,* and in 1757 the *Sublime and Beautiful.* The former is a work of history and theory, or rather of history factitiously informed by theory, which speculates that human nature might free itself from all the ills of ordinary life by destroying the artifice of social order: rules, laws, governments, every normative and customary arrangement. The latter is a discussion of the premises of taste, which argues that the strongest passions, including those produced by works of art, spring from a fear of power beyond the limits of human imagining, and an unfathomable instinct for staying close to the source of the fear. Both books are reductive and experimental — the *Vindication,* to the point of consistent if not quite transparent absurdity — and both if taken literally would foreclose certain motives of learning: the hope of a regulated society on which the science of politics is founded; and the hope of serene judgment on which the discipline of aesthetics is founded. Of course, these productions are in different ways theoretical romances, which test the depth of common sense by the force of a limiting case. Yet together they leave a strange impression. One feels that for their author, an impartial sense of mischief, and a fascination with moral enquiry for its own sake, have become the visible signs of a crisis of doubt. The stability of life (Burke seems to say) itself rests on nothing but the persistence of the human faith in stability. And the confidence of that faith is assaulted on every side: by utopian speculation in politics, but also and more generally by the human craving for exposure to scenes of risk on the largest scale.

These early books enjoyed a considerable influence. The *Vindication* was absorbed into the rationalist political literature of the next generation: its official status as a parody did not stop it from being read as a credible indictment of the injustices of society. The *Sublime and Beautiful* had reverberations both more immediate and more lasting. It launched in earnest the discussion of taste and judgment which would preoccupy the literature of Europe in the second half of the eighteenth century. Burke was to be known hereafter as "the sublime and beautiful Mr. Burke" or "Burke with his sublime and beautiful," an allusion that would become as hackneyed an element of caricatures as the monkish robe signifying his supposed allegiance to Catholicism. But effects like these lie in the future, and are mere crosscurrents, eddies of disputation propelled by words that have no proper name to back them. A figure we can identify as the Edmund Burke of political biography enters our view for the first time in 1759.

He came to the attention of the House of Commons as the private secretary of William Gerard Hamilton — "single-speech Hamilton" as he was called, for reasons that require no exegesis. In 1761 Hamilton took Burke with him to Ireland, where he himself was chief secretary to the lord lieutenant, Lord Halifax; and the circumstances may have encouraged Burke's labor on the *Tracts on the Popery Laws,* a work never published in his lifetime, which he used as a source and point of departure for his later writings on the subject. In the early 1760s Burke was a witness of the Whiteboy disturbances that led to the hanging of Catholic agrarian rebels as Jacobite conspirators. One may suppose he was looking back to this period, and further back to his childhood, in the remarkable confession of a speech two decades later: "When, indeed, the smallest rights of the poorest people in the kingdom are in question, I would set my face against any act of pride and power countenanced by the highest that are in it; and if it should come to the last extremity, and to a contest of blood — God forbid! God forbid! — my part is taken: I would take my fate with the poor and low and feeble." He seems to have learned from the outbreaks of the 1760s a hatred of violence even in the name of liberation, and a horror of punishments and proscriptions directed against whole classes of persons. Probably it was about this time that Burke began to think of himself as a reformer. The term *reform* he would always use favorably and in connection with his own activity. He defined it by contrast with two other words, *innovation* and *despotism*.

By 1763, his relations with Hamilton were growing frayed, and in 1765 the two men broke irreparably. Burke complained that the terms of service Hamilton now stipulated would close every other avenue. The implication seems to be that after the success of the *Sublime and Beautiful,* he would have liked to write more for the public and for himself; and that, by an overbearing contractual exclusiveness, Hamilton was trying to crush his legitimate ambitions. It was an ordinary wrangle and blowout — the eighteenth century is full of muffled screams from the warmly patronized — and one need not suppose that Hamilton was acting with malice. Still, the grounds of Burke's appeal warrant a careful hearing, for they show his awareness of his precarious status as a man of talent. "What you blame," he told his patron in a letter of February 1765, "is only this: That I will not consent to bind myself to you for no less a term than my whole life: in a sort of domestick situation, for a consideration to be taken out of your private fortune, that is, to circumscribe my hopes, to give up even the possibility of liberty, and absolutely to annihilate myself for ever. I beseech you, is the demand, or the refusal the act of unkindness?" Still distraught, he raked up irritable memories of the affair a few months later when writing to a friend: "Not to value myself (as a gentleman a freeman a man of Education; and one pretending to Literature) is there any situation in Life so low or even so criminal, that can subject a man to the possibility of such an engagement?" Burke's severing of his ties with Hamilton came from an angry and incorrigible self-trust. To the end of his career he would feel the pressure that such a reaction implies, and even under the irony of *A Letter to a Noble Lord,* written in his sixty-seventh year, one can see him work to preserve a decorum still taxed near to breaking: "I have strained every nerve to keep the noble lord in that situation, which alone makes him my superiour." The passion of his advocacy of an aristocratic society, and the passion of his criticism of it, issued from a single complex consciousness. A more complacent man or a more simply rebellious one would never have written as Burke wrote.

He did not lack a patron for long. In 1765 he was appointed private secretary to the Marquess of Rockingham — a man almost his exact contemporary, as Hamilton also had been. Through the skill of Burke's arrangement with another benefactor, Lord Verney, the job soon brought with it a seat in Parliament from the closed borough of Wendover, in Buckinghamshire. The victory celebrations were of a kind not always to be associated with the name of Burke: "in a few minutes the room was cleared of smoke and full of — Liberty, Wilkes and Liberty, Burke and Wilkes, Freedom and Wendover; empty bottles, broken bottles, rivers of wine, brooks of brandy." The Rockingham Whigs had emerged in British politics at the moment to catch a confused reflected glory from the popular cause of Wilkes. They presented themselves as a respectable alternative to the "patriotism" of the elder Pitt, with its high-handed contempt for party; and their belief in the authority of the House of Commons made them tactical allies of the protests against the ministerial attempt to keep Wilkes out of Parliament. Burke's delicate task in the two decades that lay ahead would be to exploit this association where useful, while preserving the distinct identity of the Rockinghamites as a party of high and dry anti-monarchists.

The first Rockingham administration began in 1765, near the start of Burke's service in the Commons, but it was founded on an unstable coalition and would end in 1766, after one year and twenty days. Its major achievement was the repeal of the

Stamp Act. Burke wrote its history in "A Short Account of a Late Short Administration," employing a style of impersonal humility and flatly declarative pride, a mixed manner that suited his role and that he would come to favor in subsequent narratives of the Rockingham Whigs. If Lord Rockingham was the party's banner and pedigree, Burke was already its nerves and its brain. Much of the burden of negotiations had fallen on him, and in the late 1760s he appears to have suffered a spell of nervous prostration, the first of several that would afflict him after intervals of heavy absorption in the business of party or government. Meanwhile, his fame had begun to be a separate thing from that of the party. His maiden speech in the House of Commons drew the admiration of the most discriminating judges. Burke had "gained more reputation," observed Dr. Johnson at the time, "than perhaps any man at his [first] appearance ever gained before. He made two speeches in the House for repealing the Stamp-act, which were publickly commended by Mr Pitt, and have filled the town with wonder."

Dr. Johnson's vicarious interest serves as a reminder of a second milieu that Burke inhabited. Together with Johnson and Joshua Reynolds, and with his father-in-law, Dr. Nugent, he had founded The Club in 1764, for discussion of moral and literary topics, and kept up attendance thereafter as steadily as he could. In the early 1760s, he was the patron of the republican painter James Barry, whom he advised on general matters of craft and training. He later gave substantial assistance to George Crabbe, who would attest that his first major poem, "The Library," was partly "written in [Burke's] presence, and the whole submitted to his judgment; receiving, in its progress, the benefit of his correction." In advance of his political success, Burke had achieved high standing as a man of letters; and there was affection as well as regret in Goldsmith's description of him as the man, of all his generation, "Who, born for the universe, narrowed his mind, / And to party gave up what was meant for mankind."

But party, as Burke understood it, was a broader and more generous principle of association than such a criticism presumes.

The word, to him, denoted a voluntary association bound by principles and loyalty, which could serve as a counterweight to ministerial or monarchical authority and at the same time curb the egotism of day-to-day political bargaining. A party is a corporate artifice that makes an impression as distinct as that of an individual; and *character* is the word Burke often uses to describe at once the leader of a party and the coloring a party gives to a leader. A given party's emphasis is bound to be selective, but its objects are not therefore partial. It is not synonymous with faction, or with the conventional loyalty that opportunists like to denounce as "partisanship." At the center of the mixed constitutional system, Burke believed, was an aristocratic part (the assembly), which took the dominant role in making and modifying policy. Its aggrandizement was held in check by a democratic part (the people) and by a monarchical part (the king). To assure the stability of the system, the virtues of the statesman must be prudence, moderation, and humility, the last defined as a gregarious seeking for qualified advice and assistance. Yet statesmen are not born but made by experience and the performance of duties; and association with a party must shape any leader who aims to be representative. That such a leader is answerable to a certain interest is wholly compatible with his dignity and consistent with his claim to act for the public good. By contrast, it is the leader answerable to no interest, or to a shifting amalgamation of interests, who is dangerous to constitutional government. The members of a party agree to act together even in rare cases of disagreement, and thus, by the influence of principle and character, a party adds to the available stock of public wisdom and virtue. Such groups naturally begin in opposition. "When bad men combine, the good must associate; else they will fall, one by one, an unpitied sacrifice in a contemptible struggle." The words have acquired a separate fame, but they were written by Burke in 1770, in *Thoughts on the Cause of the Present Discontents,* a party manifesto in defense of the idea of party.

The book-length pamphlet was circulated in manuscript, among the Old Whigs whom Burke once called the "stamina" of the Rockingham party, and it was revised and adjusted in keeping with their sense of political exigency. It would remain Burke's only full-scale attempt at political theory until the *Reflections on the Revolution in France*. Otherwise, he composed and published speeches, of a new order of exactingness; and, more rarely, speeches revised for print from the memory of extemporaneous performance. The tenor of the *Thoughts* is moderate, but its argument hangs on a conspiratorial hypothesis, namely that the king has long kept a "double cabinet." Certain members of the government, Burke believed, were reporting back to George III in secret, and by serving two masters were betraying their constitutional loyalty. It was the first of several real or conjectured designs of usurpation that would call forth all his fury of reproach. (A Machiavellian writer in no other way, Burke did consistently have a Machiavellian eye for conspiracy.) After the agitations over Wilkes, the theory of the double cabinet whatever its degree of truth was a plausible charge, and the pamphlet served its purpose. It conferred a distinct identity on the Rockingham Whigs as a party of opposition.

This would be their chief claim to public honor in the 1770s, during the debates on American policy and throughout the American war. They argued against the imposition of new taxes on Americans, against the punitive acts that followed the Boston Tea Party, against fighting the war itself once the colonies had declared their independence, and in favor of early termination of the war even when a British victory seemed likely. They would be known as the party that got the American question right. In spite of the reputation that Burke's efforts gained, he found the years of debate against the administration of Lord North a serial torture. Rockingham (a diffident and retiring man) preserved a detachment from daily politics that discouraged any proper concerting of tactics, whether by secession from parliamentary debates on America or the fomenting of extra-parliamentary opposition. Burke for his part never gave a sign of preferring the way of life he saw beginning in the colonies. He seems to have discerned, without rapture, the elements of constitutional democracy in the colonial assemblies; certain of his utterances suggest that a regime of equal representation might be practicable, for Americans. But the worst danger of the fight to suppress America was that it was a domestic conflict within the empire. In the fever of civil war, the English were forfeiting the civil liberties they cherished as their inheritance. Stripped of his customary prudence, Burke's demonstrations of antipathy toward Lord North and George III were exorbitant, and well noted by his enemies. He did not deplore American victories. If one may invoke a distinction between the intentions of a political actor and his dramatic stance, Burke's intentions at this time were those of a moderate who believed his government had launched irrevocably a campaign that would hasten the loss of the empire. But his stance was that of a dissident. Someone who so radically questioned the policy of the king left grounds for speculation that he might later question the premises of monarchy. However embarrassing the admission would become on both sides, the truth is that Burke was a hero to radicals through most of his parliamentary career.

Yet to call Burke a dissident suggests too narrow a reading of his politics. It is no better than the usual error of treating him as the founder of modern conservatism. For he was always a believer in political and constitutional balance. When he saw it veer to the side of monarchical aggrandizement, as it did on American affairs in the 1770s, he was capable of siding with republicans against the tyranny of an empire that had turned from magnanimity. When he believed it had swung too far against all established institutions, as it did on French affairs with the enthusiasm of the "revolution societies" in the 1790s, he opposed the French Revolution as a betrayal of the spirit of 1688 and spoke of privilege and prescription as the bulwark of the social order. Political terms like *left* and *right* are an intellectual labor-saving device, and we should not suppose that a name for a character as intricate as Burke's will capture the truth about him; but with provisional accuracy it may be said that he was a Whig who became, by a slow process of self-identification, the last of the Old Whigs. He would come to believe that revolution is the ultimate enemy of reform. Yet Burke emerged as an independent voice during the late 1760s, and at this period, as he considered the interests of the empire, the greatest threat to British liberty did not come from people calling themselves revolutionists. His eloquence in debate against the policy of taxation and coercion made him known by the mid-1770s as an authority on American affairs: a public recognition enhanced by his employment as agent for the New York assembly, which required him to argue cases regularly before the Board of Trade. In 1774, these obvious qualifications drew the interest of a set of Bristol merchants who were seeking a candidate for Parliament. Burke accepted their invitation to stand for election, and he was returned to the House of Commons at the end of the year.

Bristol was a major constituency. The opinions of one of its two representatives could therefore be expected to carry a weight apart from the identity of his party. Burke knew this well, and one can feel him rise to the dignity of his stature in March 1775, in the "Speech on Conciliation with the American Colonies." A strong self-confidence is audible in the opening, in the deliberate and sustained exposition, in the authoritative urgency of the "warning voice" that closes this magnificent speech. It was by every mark a Burkean performance, but above anything he had yet achieved. Burke lost the vote and England went to war. But the lucidity of his argument set a standard that remains — for historical and circumstantial enquiry as the basis of present policy, and for a searching self-inquest concerning the responsibilities of government. Like certain of his other defeats, it invigorated him as no temporizing victory could have done, and it seems to have hardened his sense of purpose. *Happy* is a word one does not easily apply to Burke, but if one reads the public writings and the letters of his Bristol years, which lasted until 1780, one has an impression of continuous satisfaction — the thriving of a public man in public discussion, out of power it is true, but close to the center of policy and always assured of his grasp. At no other period does he exhibit the same unforced deployment of a generous-spirited energy. And yet this was a time at which Burke inwardly despaired. Long before the war was over, he realized in dismay that the commonwealth would now be vastly shrunk. The pattern established by the empire in its treatment of America, the attempt to enforce self-interest through commercial and political domination, far from being renounced in principle had never once come under serious scrutiny.

Burke in 1780 was admired locally in Bristol as well as nationally. But the merchants and artisans who formed so large a portion of his constituency had their own interests to protect. They disagreed with him on many issues, as he recounts in the "Speech at Bristol Guildhall": his support for reducing the severity of penalties against debtors; his advocacy of trading opportunities for Ireland; above all, his fight for the relief of Catholic disabilities. The last difference of judgment ran deeper than the others, and would cost Burke the votes he needed to win the election that fall. He must have guessed it, and his choice at this moment to affirm his support of Lord Savile's bill, which repealed the law that excluded Catholics from the common rights of property, exhibits a singular triumph of courage over expedience. For the summer of 1780 had brought the Gordon Riots. During the long first week of June, all London was at the mercy of the violent mob that thronged the streets, the incendiary tens of thousands whose only intelligible cry was a bigoted resentment. The march with which the riots began — led by Lord George Gordon, a half-crazed demagogue and Protestant fanatic — had been explicitly directed against Catholic rights. Throughout this sobering episode, which shook the peace of the kingdom, Burke helped to hold the authority of Parliament against the demands of the mob. In the aftermath of the terror, he urged clemency for all but the instigators and the most savage of the offenders. It seems a consistent trait, with Burke, that he is apt to be calm when others are stirred to enthusiasm or panic. Yet, equally, he has a capacity to excite himself and his listeners by obscure portents, about which the minds of those in authority remain impassive. His self-possession was widely remarked at the time, but the spectacle of the Gordon Riots left a deep impression, which the resumption of order could never entirely efface. It may have been a hidden cause of his first astonished response when news arrived of the actions of the Paris crowd of July 1789.

Never having held a cabinet position, Burke was made paymaster of forces in the second Rockingham administration, to which the king reluctantly assented in March 1782, after the failure of the American war and the breakup of Lord North's government. This was to be an even shorter administration than the earlier one of 1765–66: the party was already split on American affairs and parliamentary reform when Lord Rockingham died on 1 July. Burke's labors at this time were given over to the economic reforms he saw as a remedy for the discontents that were simmering before the riots. "In that period of difficulty and danger," he would write of himself in *A Letter to a Noble Lord,* "I consulted, and sincerely co-operated with men of all parties, who seemed disposed to the same ends, or to any part of them. Nothing, to prevent disorder, was omitted: when it appeared, nothing to subdue it was left uncounselled, nor unexecuted, as far as I could prevail. At the time I speak of, and having a momentary lead, so aided and so encouraged, and as a feeble instrument in a mighty hand—I do not say, I saved my country; I am sure I did my country important service." Yet, almost from the moment of his rejection at Bristol, he had been absorbed in another concern: the injustices of the East India Company's government of India and the necessity of regulating the company by some authority outside itself. To Burke, this was not a case chiefly of the misappropriation of funds, or the irregular use of power by a company acting in place of a constituted government. What was in question was the bond of humanity that linked him with the natives of a country at the outermost edge of the empire.

In Burke's writings on India of the 1780s and 1790s, the urgency of the moral judgment outpaces any conceivable party advantage. His severity is detectable from his first letters on the subject in 1780 and 1781, where he has begun to discern a criminal consistency in the policies of the company, and a criminal abuse of the law in the whole temper of English justice in India. But a report of a speech of July 1784 shows the tremendous change that came over him in just three years. He now recounts the exploits of the company as part of the catastrophic history of the empire itself:

> [Laying his hand on a volume of Reports which lay on the table] I swear, said he, by this book, that the wrongs done to humanity in the eastern world, shall be avenged on those who have inflicted them: They will find, when the measure of their iniquity is full, that Providence was not asleep. The wrath of Heaven would sooner or later fall upon a nation, that suffers, with impunity, its rulers thus to oppress the weak and innocent. We had already lost one empire, perhaps, as a punishment for the cruelties authorized in another. And men might exert their ingenuities in qualifying facts as they pleased, but there was only one standard by which the Judge of all the earth would try them. It was not whether the interest of the East India Company made them necessary, but whether they coincided with the prior interests of humanity, of substantial justice, with those rights which were *paramount to all others.*

Burke's campaign for the reform of the company would continue through his authorship of the ninth and eleventh reports of the Select Committee on India, and would eventually lead to the impeachment of its governor-general, Warren Hastings. By his own account, "this India business" absorbed most of his energy for fourteen years. The evidence is in his collected writings, one-third of which are devoted to India, but the human exertion thereby encompassed can hardly be understood in calculations of quantity. Burke spoke of the white people in India as *they* — as if the human race alone now mattered to him.

This self-sacrifice for the welfare of an alien people was a source of genuine bewilderment to his contemporaries. It is responsible for the larger number of anecdotal reports that describe him at this period as deranged or mad. A typically brilliant and unsympathetic print by Gillray (*Opposition,* 1788) shows him driving the fashionable coach-and-four of the Rock-

ingham Whigs, with Charles Fox riding shotgun. The horses
(party worthies) are on a downward path half-sunk in the
"Slough of Despond" that is Indian affairs, a trunk brimming
with parchments is seen to contain the "Bill of Rights," "Magna
Charta," and "Impeachment of W. Hastings," and over the ful-
some caption "O Liberty! O Virtue! O my Country!" the un-
shaven Fox and jesuitical Burke seem a grotesque and delusively
mismatched pair. This had become his public profile by 1788;
the trial dragged him further down with every forward step.
Why, asked many observers, did Burke invest so much in a hopeless cause that concerned a remote and unalluring portion of
the empire? Even supposing that Hastings did extort illegal trib-
utes for the company, procure the judicial murder of a witness
against him, and approve or countenance the torture of prisoners, what made Burke commit himself to a pursuit that would
hold him captive the better part of two decades? It was a sensible
and prudent question. The favorable view of Hastings taken by
Lord Thurlow, who presided over the impeachment, and the
growing influence of company money in domestic politics, had
rendered a conviction improbable from the first. Burke went
forward anyway because the exemplary power of such a proceeding was more important to him than any immediate result.

He had touched a profound self-contradiction in the aims
and methods of imperial rule, as he recognized in a draft note for
a speech on India (possibly Dundas's bill of regulation of 1782–
83): "I do not wonder, that we find the greatest difficulties in the
exclusive administration of that vast, heterogeneous, intricate
Mass of Interests, which at this day forms the Body of the British
Power. Under any form of government, this would be difficult;
under ours, it comes to be a matter of the greatest complexity;
because, in an hundred instances, the Interest of our Empire is
scarcely to be reconciled to the Interest of our Constitution."
Down to his last months of life, Burke dwelt on India and the
English failure there of moral courage and attention. He asked
his young friend French Laurence to be sure after he was dead to
remember his defiance "of the judgments of those, who consider

the dominion of the glorious Empire given by an incomprehensible dispensation of Divine providence into our hands as nothing more than an opportunity of gratifying for the lowest of their purposes, the lowest of their passions. . . . Above all make out the cruelty of this pretended acquittal, but in reality this barbarous and inhuman condemnation of whole Tribes and nations, and of all the abuses they contain. If Europe recovers its civilization that work will be useful." Civilization itself depended on the preservation of a human trust which the empire in India had betrayed.

It would be an exaggeration to say that beside the reform of British India, the French Revolution was comparatively a distraction for Burke. Yet that was how he described it in the final paragraph of the *Reflections on the Revolution in France:* he writes (he tells the French correspondent to whom that book is addressed) as one "who snatches from his share in the endeavours which are used by good men to discredit opulent oppression the hours he has employed on your affairs." In fact, he had persuaded himself by 1790 that a revolution was poised to descend on all of Europe. The revolution in France was only its first episode. Once the established powers understood things in this light, their duty was to consider France as "expunged out of the system of Europe." Who then were the revolutionists? A combination, said Burke, of "turbulent, discontented men of quality," "political men of letters," and politicians whose shallow craft would be overwhelmed in wave after wave of innovation. All that these men did was supposed to be done on behalf of "the people." Yet the people were hustled onto the stage of the revolution as a credulous mob whose bodies packed the barricades, whose voices drowned out sense in the political clubs, whose very presence rendered all the proceedings of the assembly giddy and capricious. Burke's initial response to the event in a letter of August 1789 had suggested the detachment of an aesthete: "what Spectators, and what actors!" But the two registers of judgment are not as separate as they appear. For Burke, art was never merely art. In one of his late writings, the *Appeal from the New to the Old Whigs,* he would assert that "art is man's nature." He meant that we learn to sympathize by practice in the occasions of sympathy. Art supplies such occasions more readily, and with more time for reflection, than life can be trusted to do, but the work of imagination is the same in both cases. That is why he would say in the *Reflections* that the theatre is often a better school of moral sentiments than churches.

None of us is born human. We are made so by the knowledge we acquire from the responses we feel and show to human things. People associated for a public purpose naturally cultivate what they love, so that their politics may take "a tincture from their character." Yet a total revolution changes this utterly. The greed for rights, like the greed of empire — so hot that it would destroy a society rather than relax its importuning for one moment — suggested to Burke a fanaticism in the new order that rendered its converts monstrous. He had two names for the political threat he placed under this description in the 1790s. He called it "Jacobinism," and he called it "Indianism." These names were metaphors for each other, as Burke showed plainly in *Thoughts on French Affairs* when he said the wielders of sudden fortunes from East India were revolutionists "almost to a man, who cannot bear to find that their present importance does not bear a proportion to their wealth." He went on to connect Indianism with Jacobinism in a curious intuition: "The fact is, that as money increases and circulates, and as the circulation of news, in politics and letters, becomes more and more diffused, the persons who diffuse this money, and this intelligence, become more and more important." Under a modern capitalist regime, mobility of wealth fosters mobility of ideas and thereby the rise of a class of speculative investors, politicians, and pamphleteers whose moral commitments are as unstable as their property is unfixed. This train of thought is developed explicitly in Burke's writings on France, but it draws on premises already familiar from his writings on India.

The *Reflections* is a masterly performance in a genre that evades classification. A treatise on pragmatic statesmanship, an aesthetic guide to the ceremony of government, a history of European morals with an implicit reading of the Reformation as well as the Glorious Revolution, it closes with a detailed criticism of the French economic policies of 1789–90 and some hints for putting the new government on a sound financial basis. What stays in the minds of most readers is Burke's portrayal of the revolution as a tragedy — "the most astonishing" event, the most prodigious change in Europe since the coming of Christianity, and unlike its predecessor a bringer of radical evil — "the worst, the second fall of man," as his disciple Windham called it. An important clue to Burke's reaction may be that his political ideas had always been more practical and less theoretical than those of the Jacobins. He said it best in the "Speech on Conciliation":

> We Englishmen stop very short of the principles upon which we support any given part of our Constitution; or even the whole of it together. . . . All government, indeed every human benefit and enjoyment, every virtue, and every prudent act, is founded on compromise and barter. We balance inconveniences; we give and take; we remit some rights, that we may enjoy others; and, we choose rather to be happy citizens, than subtle disputants. . . . In every arduous enterprise, we consider what we are to lose, as well as what we are to gain; and the more and better stake of liberty every people possess, the less they will hazard in a vain attempt to make it more. These are *the cords of man.* Man acts from adequate motives relative to his interest; and not on metaphysical speculations.

Burke thought that the revolutionists were in this sense metaphysicians. They aimed at the termination, once and for all, of an enlightened regime of trust, a politics founded on necessary barter and compromise. From the moment they took power, all the effective government their country had was suspect in their eyes. If they performed what they promised, the revolution would end with the abolition of property and the extinction of common liberty.

In his sequence of writings on France, especially the *Appeal from the New to the Old Whigs* (1791) and the *Letters on a Regicide Peace* (1796–97), Burke became a consistently penetrating, determinedly uncharitable critic of the democratic principles associated with "the rights of man." Yet the speeches on India contemporary with these writings leave no doubt that he was still a believer in human rights; and in the *Reflections,* he offered a list of the ordinary rights that any decent society should guard among its members: "They have a right to the fruits of their industry; and to the means of making their industry fruitful. They have a right to the acquisitions of their parents; to the nourishment and improvement of their offspring; to instruction in life, and to consolation in death. Whatever each man can separately do, without trespassing upon others, he has a right to do for himself; and he has a right to a fair portion of all which society, with all its combinations of skill and force, can do in his favour." The passage suggests how far Burke's principles set him against the perpetuation of slavery. His *Sketch for a Negro Code* written in the early 1780s, with its practical design for putting slavery on a course of extinction, would give a strong impetus to the campaign by which Wilberforce and others eventually brought about its abolition in England. His list of rights says almost as much as can be said without resorting to the language of a social contract.

The tenacity of Burke's prejudice against the very idea of contract has surprised many readers. After all, modernization itself has often been described as a progress from status to contract. Yet Burke believed that this meant, in practice, a transformation of every tacit agreement into a matter of constant bargaining and negotiation. His writing accordingly keeps up a principled resistance to what believers in contract have come to call progress. We ought, Burke thinks, to seek to preserve a good deal of the presumptive authority of status, which depends on trust much more than on contract. Status makes for a variety in the social order, because it can assume different shapes in different walks of life, but the reductive medium of contract changes every transaction into the single currency of performance and reward. The sense of inward worth comes to be defined by cash value alone, and the realm of human things is assimilated to the realm of things. By contrast, the older trust in status, which implied a sense of merit regardless of use and reward, taught that there were objects of admiration quite apart from the money calculus. From this point of view, it was the ancient morality of chivalry that truly refined and civilized; whereas a modern morality founded on sheer utility coarsens the affections of social life. Without some reasonless devotion to a standard of virtue — a standard that is beyond the reach of immediate reward — we give up along with presumptive status the very possibility of honor. To ask, as merchants, lawyers, and revolutionists do of every tacit agreement, "What is it worth to me?" is to interrogate every duty of life at the bar of self-interest. This observation, already implicit in the "Speech on Conciliation" and the "Speech on Fox's East India Bill," is fully expounded as an argument in the *Reflections*. Its originality marks Burke as the earliest and perhaps the greatest critic of utilitarianism. His intuition about the non-rational character of virtue, and his attack on the psychology of commercial and scientific reason-giving, also curiously suggest a common ground with Rousseau — another profound critic of the Enlightenment, whom Burke when young had admired with reservations and only gradually came to detest as a "professor of vanity."

Reflections on the Revolution in France was as important at the time for what it did as for what it said. It split the Whig party. On one side thereafter were those, like Fox, who embraced the revolution as the latest resting place of the march of liberty, and on the other those who followed Burke in opposing it as a new species of tyranny. At the king's levee in February 1791, George III told Burke that his book had rendered a service for which all gentlemen must feel obliged to him. Burke was so amazed that the words had to be repeated in person by a messenger — the king's son, William Duke of Clarence — before he took them in sufficiently to convey an acknowledgment. This compliment from the king was an informed piece of praise. Burke had in fact devoted a paragraph of the *Reflections* to the importance of "the spirit of religion" and "the spirit of a gentleman," which he said were the core of a chivalric feeling that kept alive ideas of honor and duty in modern Europe. His book also drew compliments of a different kind. Revolution societies in England made it a custom of their Bastille Day celebrations to toast Burke for having begun the great debate on the French Revolution. The most famous of the replies he provoked, Tom Paine's *Rights of Man,* quickly outsold the *Reflections* by a ratio of ten to one, and the pamphlet war that followed, with more than a hundred further replies, helped to create a democratic readership that did not exist before. Burke had invented the French Revolution as a world-historical event for the English mind. The radical orator and poet John Thelwall reckoned that in this way the *Reflections* "made more democrats, among the thinking part of mankind, than all the works ever written in answer to it."

Burke must have grown used to such ironies. In 1791, he became for practical purposes an independent in the House of Commons; his frequent ally was now the same William Pitt he once had feared as a stalking-horse for tyranny, and who had said of Burke's vehement manner in debate: "I seldom think it worth my while to call him to order, or indeed to make him any answer." On his retirement in 1794, the king and Pitt would award him a pension of twenty-five hundred pounds — an amount that was possible only because, falling under the crown's reserved revenue, it was not subject to the restrictions of the Civil List Act passed by the House of Commons at the insistence of Burke a decade earlier.

As for the impeachment of Warren Hastings, it was finally brought to a close in 1794. Throughout the seven-year process, Burke's reputation as a pragmatic statesman was dwindling. The decline had begun in the Regency crisis of 1788–89, when, at the first onset of the madness of George III, he made an argument — entirely cogent from a constitutional point of view, but delivered with an almost uncontrolled passion — urging the institution of a Regency to allow the Prince of Wales to reign as surrogate for the ailing king. The alternative, Burke said, was to leave the throne virtually empty and invite aggrandizement from an energetic and unscrupulous ministerial power: a description well adapted to the younger Pitt, then enjoying undisputed authority in the House of Commons and serving as ostensible protector of the interests of George III. Burke in these debates became notorious for having drawn a pathetic and degrading picture of a king bereft of sense. His manner in the impeachment had grown just as intractable. Convinced by evidence outside the purview of the trial that Warren Hastings, to parry an accusation of bribery, had ordered the judicial murder of a native servant of the company, Burke unloosed his suspicions in May 1789 by declaring that Hastings "murdered this man by the hands of Sir Elijah Impey" (the judge who pronounced the death sentence). He was reprimanded by the House of Commons, but even when apologizing for the lapse, he spoke with a ferocity hardly consistent with the costume of public repentance. He repeated the word *murder* as often as possible, now wrapped in quotation marks, and added in defense of the statement that incurred the rebuke: "What led me into that error? Nine years' meditation upon that subject." Hastings's acquittal by the House of Lords in 1795 concluded what had become more and more a solitary pursuit of justice — justice of the dramatically arresting kind that Burke once referred to as "sympathetic revenge."

His son, Richard, whom he had brought up to be his political successor, died suddenly in August 1794. From that moment Burke considered his life at an end, as he remarks in many letters of the time. Yet his last years did not find him dwelling wholly in retrospect. He urged Pitt to take the initiative in launching a full-scale war against France; he made new converts such as James Mackintosh among the younger talents who had attacked the *Reflections;* he sponsored and found the patronage to support a school for the sons of the émigré nobility. The energy he could spare from fomenting a counter-revolution in France, he devoted to fostering reforms that might prevent a revolution in Ireland, and arguing for the passage of repressive laws to obstruct the growth of a radical movement in England. Fear of violence had been a leading motive of his thought, as far back as the *Sublime and Beautiful*. Now to a large extent his conduct and thought alike became a defense against that fear. He believed the way of life that had matured in Europe since the Reformation — a practice of trust that was a consequence but also a cause of mixed constitutional government — was on the point of being driven out by a regime based on abstract rights and confiscation. The revolution was stronger than those caught up in it could possibly know. It had come to India, it had come to France, and now it threatened Ireland and England: its menace to the civilized order of Europe was more encompassing than any set of reforms that might be derived from its principles. Yet the Burke of the posthumous *Letters on a Regicide Peace*, which occupied his final years, is still recognizably the Burke of *Thoughts on the Cause of the Present Discontents*. The pamphleteer adroit at ferreting out domestic conspiracy, the prophet against the abuses of the British Empire, and the preserver of a political trust against the tide of thoughtless innovation, here at last are joined in a single character.

It has been said that Burke was a critic of totalitarianism at the first appearance of the phenomenon, indeed at the first tremors that betokened its possible appearance. This is so far accurate that what he says against the revolutionists in France becomes still truer when applied to twentieth-century revolutionists: "Their humanity is not dissolved. They only give it a long prorogation. They are ready to declare, that they do not think two thousand years too long a period for the good that they pursue. It is remarkable, that they never see any way to their projected good but by the road of some evil. Their imagination is not fatigued with the contemplation of human suffering through the wild waste of centuries added to centuries of misery and desolation. Their humanity is at their horizon — and, like the horizon, it always flies before them." He observed of the Jacobins, "They unplumb the dead for bullets to assassinate the living," and he took his own warning with literal force. Burke died on 9 July 1797. He lies buried in an unmarked plot — a

tactic he requested to prevent the Jacobins from digging up his
tomb if their politics should triumph.

A skeptic of enlightenment, of the all-sufficing power of rational design to regulate society and politics, Burke was nevertheless a hero of the eighteenth-century Enlightenment. He
earned the gratitude and admiration of its greatest minds,
Hume and Kant among them, and was a steady though often a
hidden influence on the liberalism of their successors, Benjamin
Constant and John Stuart Mill. The speeches of his Bristol years
were among the political writings most favored by the constitutional founders of the United States. And yet, for a generation or
so after his death, Burke ceased to be a celebrated name in
English politics. Between 1806 and 1829 he is scarcely quoted,
alluded to, or evoked as a distinguished predecessor in parliamentary debates or in the quarterly reviews. He did not make a
suitable icon for the Tories any more than he did for the Whigs.
His incomprehensible obsession with India, the excessive and
premature distaste he showed for nineteenth-century France,
and the unpleasantness of his Catholic affiliations: these things
stood in the way. During this interval of neglect, his fame and
works were kept in the public mind chiefly by the romantic poets
and critics — Wordsworth, Hazlitt, and Coleridge — and secon-
darily by the early utilitarians, who found his defenses of custom
an indispensable foil to their arguments for legal and political
reform.

By the time Macaulay wrote his *History of England,* Lecky his
History of England in the Eighteenth Century, Leslie Stephen his
History of English Thought in the Eighteenth Century, and Lord Ac-
ton his *Lectures on the French Revolution,* Burke seems to have
become a classic without any intervening phase of inquiry into
the proper basis for his acceptance. He could now be mentioned. But what was meant when people spoke of a Burkean
judgment, or of Burkean constitutionalism? Matthew Arnold
gave the best description of the power by which his writings keep
their hold on readers when he praised Burke as an example of

living by ideas. "Burke is so great because, almost alone in England, he brings thought to bear on politics, he saturates politics with thought." The absorbing political question of the nineteenth century was how to accommodate society to the advance of democracy — a question on which we can look back now, for practical wisdom and psychological insight, to a great theorist, Tocqueville, and a great statesman, Lincoln, both of them readers of Burke. Yet Burke remains unique in the way he combines the discrete kinds of authority that belong to the statesman and the theorist. As a commentator on the strengths and weaknesses of democracy, the uses of political suffrage, and the need for checks against popular sovereignty, he stands as a sentinel over all the discussions that have followed.

The first thing apt to strike a reader of Burke is the weight of command with which he can assert a policy: "You ought not, in reason, to trifle with so large a mass of the interests and feelings of the human race. You could at no time do so without guilt; and be assured that you will not be able to do it long with impunity." Hardly separable from the muscularity is an instinctive delicacy, a savoring of the climactic or incongruous detail. Burke has an unfeigned pleasure in toying with his antagonists, and he can show the gravity of a connoisseur when allowing a well-laid trap to be sprung. Consider the metaphor by which a political adventurer, Lord Chatham, is shown to become the captive of his own contrivances:

> He made an administration so checkered and speckled, he put together a piece of joinery so crossly indented and whimsically dovetailed, a cabinet so variously inlaid, such a piece of diversified mosaic, such a tesselated pavement without cement — here a bit of black stone and there a bit of white, patriots and courtiers, king's friends and republicans, whigs and tories, treacherous friends and open enemies, — that it was indeed a very curious show, but utterly unsafe to touch and unsure to stand on. The colleagues whom he had assorted at the same boards stared at each other, and were obliged to ask, — "Sir, your name?" — "Sir, you have the advantage of me." — "Mr. Such a one." — "I

beg a thousand pardons." I venture to say, it did so happen that persons had a single office divided between them, who had never spoke to each other in their lives, until they found themselves, they knew not how, pigging together, heads and points, in the same truckle-bed.

But just as naturally, Burke's characterizations may come to life in a sudden cartoon, with staring particulars of horror or hilarity; as in the celebrated sentence of *A Letter to a Noble Lord* about the Jacobins and their aristocratic well-wisher: "Whatever his Grace may think of himself, they look upon him, and every thing that belongs to him, with no more regard than they do upon the whiskers of that little long-tailed animal, that has been long the game of the grave, demure, insidious, spring-nailed, velvet-pawed, green-eyed philosophers, whether going upon two legs, or upon four." It is a smashing stroke of satire, and deliberately indecorous — an explosive charge with a long fuse timed to go off at the word *philosophers*.

Fear of the damage he can inflict is among the calculated effects of Burke's writing. Side by side with this goes an utterly different source of authority, a pragmatic ease in calling the bluff of political tools and profiteers. "Anarchy is found tolerable," he dryly says of the failure of the Intolerable Acts in Massachusetts, when the empire's abrogation of colonial government has only led to a demonstration of the colony's self-sufficiency. In the same way, throughout the "Speech on Conciliation" he reminds his listeners of the century of prosperity they are preparing to squander in war: "I, for one, protest against compounding our demands: I declare against compounding, for a poor limited sum, the immense, evergrowing, eternal debt which is due to generous government from protected freedom." These examples serve as sufficient testimony against the received idea that Burke was an ornate writer. His usual style on the contrary proves him to be, as Hazlitt said, "one of the severest writers we have," the one "whose words are the most like things." His aphorisms tend to be short-winded. They may issue from a play on words ("To make us love our country, our country ought to be lovely") or a passing thought clinched by generalization ("Virtue will catch as well as vice by contact") or the sententious rounding of a maxim ("The situation of man is the preceptor of his duty"). Burke is prolific of such utterances, which anthologists have long been fond of pruning from context; but it is always a particular setting that gathers the force of a saying for Burke; so that when he writes, for example, "We are not made at once to pity the oppressor and the oppressed," the statement has a pertinence to the ordering of sympathies between the Jacobins and their victims which it cannot have and does not wish to have alone.

Nobody ever found out Burke's meaning by excerpts. To infer his sense from a few planted observations is equally to miss the enchantment of his prose; for the most casual remark may open on the resounding cadences of the grand style:

> They enter the capital of America only to abandon it; and these assertors and representatives of the dignity of England, at the tail of a flying army, let fly their Parthian shafts of memorials and remonstrances at random behind them. Their promises and their officers, their flatteries and their menaces, were all despised; and we were saved the disgrace of their formal reception, only because the Congress scorned to receive them; whilst the state-house of independent Philadelphia opened her doors to the public entry of the ambassador of France. From war and blood we went to submission; and from submission plunged back again to war and blood; to desolate and be desolated, without measure, hope, or end. I am a Royalist, I blushed for this degradation of the crown. I am a Whig, I blushed for the dishonor of Parliament. I am a true Englishman, I felt to the quick for the disgrace of England. I am a man, I felt for the melancholy reverse of human affairs, in the fall of the first power of the world.

In such remarkable passages, the writer becomes a historical narrator; and yet not an impartial narrator, whatever that may be. He includes himself in the picture among the characters who

took an active part. Yet Burke seems to have felt that one of his
functions was also to bear witness, to acknowledge that he was a
man who felt what must be felt on such an occasion.

Burke's language, especially in the 1780s and 1790s, draws
on two strains of eloquence very difficult to hold together. He
remains, as he was in the debates on America, the voice of conciliatory statesmanship, but he has become also the voice of retribution. In the speeches on India, his words are alive with es-
trangement, and with a clarity in speaking of the unpardonable
for which there could never have been a correlative in policy, or
any way back to common parliamentary politics. He writing has
become an extended proof that every profit has a more than
financial cost. When a company agent squeezes money from an
Indian "bribe-factor" to pay for tea from China, he is shown to
have started a train of acts whose cruelty defies comprehension:

> My Lords, they began by winding cords round the fingers of the
> unhappy freeholders of those provinces, until they clung to and
> were almost incorporated with one another; and then they ham-
> mered wedges of iron between them, until, regardless of the
> cries of the sufferers, they had bruised to pieces and forever
> crippled those poor, honest, innocent, laborious hands, which
> had never been raised to their mouths but with a penurious and
> scanty proportion of the fruits of their own soil; but those fruits
> (denied to the wants of their own children) have for more than
> fifteen years furnished the investment for our trade with China,
> and been annually sent out, and without recompense, to pur-
> chase for us that delicate meal which your Lordships, and all
> this auditory, and all this country, have begun every day for
> these fifteen years at their expense. To those beneficent hands
> that labor for our benefit the return of the British government
> has been cords and hammers and wedges. But there is a place
> where those crippled and disabled hands will act with resistless
> power. What is it that they will not pull down, when they are
> lifted to heaven against their oppressors?

This sense of a retribution fearfully earned by the empire
comes to touch every detail of his writings on India. His passing

allegories bristle with contempt: the East India Company set up "an exchequer, wherein extortion was the assessor, fraud the cashier, confusion the accountant, concealment the reporter, and oblivion the remembrancer." And the descriptions of Warren Hastings rise in a torrent of unremitting fury: "He is also never corrupt but he is cruel; he never dines without creating a famine; he does not take from the loose superfluity of standing greatness, but falls upon the indigent, the oppressed, and ruined." In these speeches, as in the *Reflections,* where he is trying to salvage the last of Britain's pre-capitalist morality of governance, Burke stands against a system of reckless innovation and pleads for calm and gradual reform. Yet his manner is anything but calm. He works his audience up to a pitch of indignation, in order to work them down to a generous acceptance of an ancient way of life. The strategy can make for a paradoxical tension between the tactics and the apparent ends of persuasion.

A similar tension may be observed between his rhetoric and his aims in the American policy of the mid-1770s. There Burke struck an attitude of reason and magnanimity in order to permit a rebellion to conclude itself in peace. For such was the practical meaning of his offer of conciliation: America was to be allowed to form its own government and remain in the empire only as a partner. Burke spoke of the arguments over taxation that had become the subject of careless demagogy and of the good that would now be served by consigning them to a "wise and salutary neglect." The ironic phrase deserves some elaboration. The soundest guide, he believed, to political practice was common utility—utility, that is, in an older sense which implies the long-term benefit of an entire people, and calls for a disposition to preserve as well as an ability to improve. "A true politican always considers how he shall make the most of the existing materials of his country," and to make the most of the existing materials will sometimes mean to make the least of the grounds of present grievance. Did the parent country have a right, in the nature of the imperial constitution, to tax the American colonies as it pleased? Possibly so. But it would be foolish to inquire curiously into the origins of that right, because to do so could only raise the disputants to a new ferocity of contention.

For the same reason, all enquiry into the origins of governments is to be discouraged. Governments derive their legitimacy from their effects. "If the people are happy, united, wealthy, and powerful, we presume the rest." Besides, all governments without exception have begun in violence. An admirer surprised at Burke's antipathy to the French Revolution, Captain Thomas Mercer, argued with him that violence was justified in overthrowing a regime that had itself begun in violence. Burke replied in a letter of February 1790: "It is possible that many estates about you were originally obtained by arms, that is, by violence, a thing almost as bad as superstition, and not much short of ignorance: but it is *old violence;* and that which might be wrong in the beginning, is consecrated by time, and becomes lawful." The old violence may be metaphysically as wicked as the new, but if I do not want new violence, I will require no metaphysical warrant to discountenance violent talk. First principles are a favorite stimulant of revolutionists. By contrast, salutary neglect may embody a statesman's readiness to be satisfied when the parties to an old dispute at last agree. It is as superfluous as it is impolitic to insist that they agree on why they agree.

Burke stood out wherever possible as an advocate of pragmatic compromise. Does this mean that his various appeals to principle may be dismissed as sophistry? The charge was made often enough in his lifetime, and it seems credible when we consider a famous case, the difference between his stance on the American and on the French Revolution. There is an even stronger appearance of contradiction between his reluctance to tamper with prescription in France and his insistence on radically altering the charter of the East India Company. One can begin to make out a consistency between these positions by remarking that Burke in every case stood for a traditional or a habitual or a precedented way of life against the encroachments of those who would uproot it. On this point America is the hardest test. Was its claim of independence really founded on a traditional understanding? Yet Burke's idea of tradition is more flexible than many of his commentators imply. He remarked in his "Speech on Conciliation" that for the colonists, a republican way of life now seemed to have become customary. Theirs was a natural growth of English liberty over a century and a half, beyond the borders of England. The argument serves as a reminder that Burke never confused the use of reason in politics with mere obedience to a theory. On India, a man of theory could have argued either way. Here was a traditional society torn apart by a commercial regime of modernization. Even so, it would have been plausible to hold up the company's charter as the inviolable bond of a sacred trust. Burke chose less predictably to condemn the company itself and to prosecute its governor-general as the greatest of innovators.

In pursuing constitutional justice for India, Burke was driven in 1783 to propose a design of thoroughgoing reform. The moderate reform measure adopted by Pitt in 1784 was of so little interest to him that he never commented on it. "In this situation," Frederick G. Whelan sums up in an excellent recent study, "he had to make a choice, and his choice was unambiguous: the rights of the Indians were to be defended, even though this meant dismantling the established legal and customary prerogatives of the company and remodeling imperial government." Burke realized that events change the meaning of the situation that is the preceptor of man's duty. Reluctant to allow the government to run the company, out of respect for the traditional separation of politics and trade, he was finally persuaded that the charter must be revised, the authority of the company weakened, and many of its activities overseen by a power external to itself.

By contrast, his design to limit the prerogatives of the king was gradually tempered. From the *Thoughts on the Present Discontents* in 1770 to the "Speech on Economical Reform" of 1780, Burke believed that the power of the crown had increased, was increasing, and ought to be diminished. But starting in 1789 he becomes an out-and-out defender of monarchy as an institution that ought to be perpetuated—not only because it is good in itself but because its abolition cannot be reconciled with the survival of mixed constitutional government. Here again, it was historical contingency that altered the direction of his warnings. Never since the Interregnum had monarchy itself seemed on the verge of being overthrown. Still, the warmest advocate of Burke must allow that he shows a dangerous ease in recruiting the same words on both sides of a question. He wrote in the *Reflections* of the terror of an age when "kings are hurl'd from their thrones by the Supreme Director of this great drama." He had uttered nearly the same phrase with a degree of satisfaction in the Regency debates, but now it is yoked into a solemn lament of the fall of Louis XVI and Marie Antoinette, an elegy on the impermanence of all earthly greatness. One of his critics, Mary Wollstonecraft, was attuned enough to hear the echo and chided Burke for his rhetorical thrift: he was painting a different picture "without having troubled yourself to clean your palette." Not his principles but his deftness in their defense sometimes lays him open to the charge of versatility.

More than a tactical shift may be in question when one compares Burke's several general views of the nature of morality. At times, and prominently in the India prosecution, he argues that moral duties are derived from a natural law written in our hearts and therefore must remain the same for all people in all situations. Yet he had written earlier that such duties are only to be induced from habits of conduct inseparable from their environment. Burke appears as just such a theorist of morality-as-adaptation in the *Letter to the Sheriffs of Bristol,* where he says that "for any practical purpose" free government "is what the people think so." This contextualist view of morals may seem hardly different from the "geographical morality" proposed by the East India Company's defenders, according to which the tyrannical practices the company employed in Asia were suitable to Asian expectations. Yet Burke in the Indian context surely meant to turn once and for all from what people or governors may "think so" and appeal instead to "the natural equality of mankind at large."

These occasionally divergent views of the nature of moral judgment can be traced to a single guiding maxim from which Burke never departed. In every case, he warns his listeners not to interpret the rules of politics and morality in their own favor, and not to contravene the clear sense of right and wrong in the people they presume to govern. *One must never be the judge in one's own cause:* the principle is invoked centrally in the "Speech on Conciliation" and again in the *Reflections.* If, to argue effectively for your cause, you have to draw up an indictment of a whole people, it is you who are wrong in your jurisdiction and not they in their protest. Burke is a great unmasker of the self-deception that involves itself with every attempt at domination. What holds true in civil law he has the psychological acuteness to extend to matters of constitutional propriety and balance. The maxim against being judge in one's own cause applies to the king in a monarchy, and in the same way it applies to the majority of the people in a democracy.

Attentive as he is to the local texture of politics, Burke is the major theorist who seems least assured of the good of political activity. This trait sets him apart from the long line of classic and modern republican writers. He believed that politics should be carried on as a steady business to protect it from becoming a constant imperative. The motto of Jonathan Swift, "Party is the madness of many for the gain of a few," was the antithesis of Burke's belief and practice. As he understood it, politics could never be a natural interest to more than a few. The people should be encouraged to guard against abuses by politicians, but should not concern themselves in the overhaul of government: to do so only creates a "distemper of remedy," by which popular feeling can be manipulated behind the scenes. Who then decides the adjustments of policy for the common good? Burke's answer is, a deliberative body of representatives. If asked how the people can be sure that their will is adequately felt, he replies that when they are doubtful, they can plant doubts among the mediating representatives of public opinion; when they are swindled or cheated, they can circulate petitions or appeals that exhibit a threat to the established order; and when policy has rendered them miserable, they can show it by tumults, by desperate and destructive actions, and by "the very last resource of the thinking and the good," a revolution.

Early in his career, Burke was known as a champion of rights of representation for the disfranchised: Catholics and Dissenters, the voters for Wilkes in Middlesex, the American colonists. But he had never treated civil life as a continuous wrangle whose only rule was an ever-expanding creation of rights, and he worked hard in his later years to discourage the English from adopting that pattern of idealism. In the absence of positive rights, an enlightened politics might still revolve around an ideal of trust. Admittedly trust is an elusive good, nothing but an idea with a correlative sentiment, and the results it can bring in practice depend on its remaining mostly tacit. To judge the adequacy of the idea as Burke presents it, one needs to look at the response of the Rockingham party to popular opinion in times of crisis. It faced two such challenges inescapably, from the supporters of Wilkes in the late 1760s and from the Yorkshire County movement led by Christopher Wyvill in 1779–80, and its posture was what might have been expected: the party listened, it negotiated, and meditated action on its own; it did not execute the commands of the people. This record of prudential withdrawal may lead to various inferences about Burke and his associates, some of them awkward, some flattering. It does not indicate that they believed in the sovereignty of the king. The whole testimony of Burke's career goes the other way: most of his energy for two and a half decades was given to increasing the power of the House of Commons at the expense of the crown.

This complex stationing of Burke in regard to public opinion is a vivid clue to his politics, and its doctrine is broached as early as his speech of 1774 at the conclusion of the polls in Bristol. Walter Bagehot had in mind the peculiarly Burkean sense of active representation on behalf of a people whose characteristic virtue is passive vigilance, when he remarked that Burke himself "had the passions of more ordinary men in a degree, and of an intensity, which ordinary men may be most thankful that they have not." Ordinary men and women serve best in their station as a check on the complacency or the incapacity of a party. Or, as Burke put it once, the people are there to give the alarm at emergencies. The party, in turn, devises a plan to restore tranquillity and to remove the inequities that have made the existing order unjust. The danger of a party acting alone is that it easily degenerates into a system of favorites. The danger of the people acting alone is that they are liable to be drawn by the flattery of a charlatan they take for a true leader — someone impossible to regulate because answerable to no interest beyond the approval of the moment.

Many parties, from the free-trade liberals of nineteenth-century England to the American right in the Cold War, have wanted to claim Burke as one of their own. None of their programs answers in any measure to a candid description of his. Burke believed that there should be a ruling elite, composed in some part by the hereditary aristocracy and in some part by a natural aristocracy of intellect and talents; that it should accommodate, without encouraging, reform of the existing arrangements of property and the franchise; that it should inculcate and seek to spread the manners of a restrained liberty to the parts of the empire and the trading world whose interests it controlled or bartered with; that it should fix a pattern of religious belief, with tolerance toward other beliefs; above all, that its members should be capable of self-sacrifice: a generous surrender of their private interest and even their lives for the sake of perpetuating the order to which their loyalty belonged. These ideas are untimely, and it is often argued that Burke now belongs to the eighteenth century. The present anthology has been compiled in the belief that this is not so. His certainties put him at a distance from us; his anxieties bring him closer.

A Hungarian political theorist, G. M. Tamás, surveying the fortunes of Eastern Europe in 1993, remarked that the emancipation brought by the fall of communism had left political thought in Europe oddly impoverished. Educated citizens now

fell back on a contempt for the state and all its works as the sum
total of the practical wisdom they required. What had been lost
was a sense of the complex and admirable thing that public life
can be. Tamás went on to cite Burke, Hegel, and Tocqueville as
thinkers from whom the people of the former communist republics might seek edification. These theorists recognized the
dignity of the public good as an achievement distinct from the
accumulation of private benefits; yet they did so from a perspective that scorned neither privacy as such nor individuality. To
read Burke today is just as chastening an experience for the
citizen of a commercial democracy. He offers none of the consolations we know well. He does not believe that prosperity in
commerce is an all-sufficing good, or that the profit it brings can
repair the political decay of society. In certain circumstances,
it does the reverse. Financial innovation, he says, may be the
enemy of social stability, just as technological innovation may
be the enemy of natural stability. Nothing would have repelled
Burke more than the idea that the market runs society. Indeed,
if an emphasis can be claimed as original with him, it lies in the
suggestion that society is a work of art without a maker. The fact
that society is not a work of science, that its rules of operation are
not written down anywhere, not even in the intentions of its
founders — none of this, he thought, should make us less careful
or protective of its benefits. Social practices have usually grown
up for a reason, and there is a use in many things that seem on
their face archaic and absurd. We may suppose we cherish and
preserve these things; but it is they that cherish and preserve us.
In searching out reasons to justify an existing practice, Burke was
always willing to err on the side of charity.

The most uncontroversial part of his legacy and the part now
hardest to betray may be his naturalism. "I do not like to see any
thing destroyed; any void produced in society; any ruin on the
face of the land." He did not believe with Locke that things were
necessarily improved by "mixing our labour" with them; and he
often wrote as if the transition from nature to commodity were a
passage in the depravation of human nature itself. We are hu-

manized by the time it takes to grow used to our own responses to things, and we do not have enough time if the stimuli change at too rapid a rate. No single person made society, nor has the latest generation; and by seeking to change it quickly and efficiently, we risk the creation of a mechanism void of the conditions that made us possible. The self-contempt that is latent in such a policy will be legible in its effects. Readers have long been puzzled when asked to sympathize with Burke's defense of "prescription," or with his sense of the psychological disposition that makes this possible, which he called "presumption." Yet at the bottom of his thinking is a faith that is not fanatical. He believed that the long habituation of people to certain customs and practices yields a presumption in favor of continuing those customs and practices, and that this fact ought to be taken into account by any politician who does not treat his country as a field of conquest. The making of sudden fortunes, the coming to power of a new set of persons without gratitude to the old, the wish to extirpate a whole way of life and reorganize all experience for the sake of money or efficiency or abstract rights: these are the tendencies of modern life that Burke most fears. He seldom speaks of one without showing that the others are in his mind.

What used to obstruct an appreciation of Burke was his unembarrassed apology for high politics. But the face of things has changed tremendously in our democratic politics in the past decade. The prevalence of leaders who declare, with neither pride nor humility, that they are utterly bound by popular mandates, is one sign of the change but there are others more ominous. Politicians and lawyers together have gone far to set the vocation of politics on the usual trajectory from status to contract. In keeping with that pressure, and obedient to the tendency of all contracts, political interest is on the way to being swallowed up by mercantile interest. The political elite in the two centuries preceding ours kept up a nervous suspicion — if never entirely antagonistic, still powerfully self-defensive — toward the ambitious and increasing power of the commercial elite. That suspicion is dying out at a time when the facade of democracy becomes more and more an affair of plebiscitary temperature-takings and polls. At this crisis in the survival of politics, Burke may warn us that political and mercantile interest are not two names for a single thing. The real subject of his writings on France is the ruin of deliberative representation by a frenzied reliance on the popular will. The real subject of his writings on India is the ruin of constitutional government by the usurping power of a commercial empire. It is possible that democracy based in the global market is now approaching a transition in which for the first time these two sources of instability will be seen to converge.

On being shown a passage from Burke's *Reflections* that he had ridiculed on its first publication, Fox is reported to have said, "Burke is right after all; but Burke is often right — only he is right too soon." That impression has been shared by many later readers. It is true that the age of high politics Burke lived for and helped to invent is gone; and equality of rights has proved compatible with social order to a degree he would have found unimaginable. But in quite another realm, the bearings of his thought have been unexpectedly vindicated. Through most of the twentieth century, the theorists of government who seemed most adequate were those who placed close to the center of discussion the question of labor. Political science, for them, grew out of a distinct and premised relation with economics, and Burke seemed slightly out of place in their company because he spoke of politics in so close a relation with morality and culture. Yet we seem to be passing from an age when human beings were chiefly defined as laboring animals to an age in which they are defined by the forms they choose of self-regard and voluntary association.

Democratic theorists have long been occupied with distributive justice and the minimum satisfaction of economic needs, but political thought is being drawn again to reflect on the sources of honor, or the appreciable and immaterial evidence of a life well lived. If this change of direction persists, the philosophers and economists from Locke to Smith to Marx, who founded the self-image of human beings on labor, will command less interest in the future than those like Burke who wrote about the duties of persons in a community bound by a non-negotiable trust. "Manners," he remarks in the *Regicide Peace,* "are of more importance than the laws. Upon them, in a great measure, the laws depend. The law touches us but here and there, and now and then. Manners are what vex or soothe, corrupt or purify, exalt or debase, barbarize or refine us, by a constant, steady, uniform insensible operation." He was a psychologist of representation, in both the political and aesthetic senses of the word, which he refused to keep separate. We are left therefore with a question that belongs at once to an old and a new kind of thinker. How shall we represent ourselves? Burke gives the beginning of an answer with his persistent reminder to take stock of what we already have. We inherit a liberal society as effortlessly as a feeling and ought to revise it as parsimoniously as a story.

ON EMPIRE, LIBERTY, AND REFORM

Speech at His Arrival at Bristol (1774)

A set of Bristol Whigs invited Burke in 1774 to stand as a candidate for Parliament. They chose him on the strength of reports of his "Speech on American Taxation" and the general tenor of his actions during eight years of service with the Rockingham party. They could hardly have picked a more resourceful advocate of English commercial interests and American liberty—two goods that then appeared compatible to the merchants of Bristol. The approach was made through the Reverend Dr. Thomas Wilson, a radical, who in a letter of 28 June 1774 asked Burke, on behalf of "a few friends at Bristol, merchants of fortune and character," whether "if they find themselves strong enough, you will be ready to serve them, if they put you up as a candidate to represent them."

From Burke's point of view the proposition was both timely and risky. Bristol was the second city of the kingdom, a prosperous and politically active constituency, more prestigious than any except London and Westminster. A member representing its interests in the House of Commons would draw all eyes. Victory here would offer Burke an incomparable platform for arguments and proposals on domestic and foreign policy, and it would bring an independent source of authority to distinguish him from the aristocratic circle around Lord Rockingham. Besides, after his eight years as member from the pocket borough of Wendover, the seat had been withdrawn from him; Lord Verney, who allowed him to occupy it as a gift, was now in financial difficulties and preferred a holder who could pay his way.

By the time he received word of satisfactory support at Bristol,

Burke had already been elected for the pocket borough of Malton. Yet he chose to stand for the contested seat with the knowledge that precisely because Bristol was politically alive — a place where issues of national importance were debated by industrious citizens, a center for the worst and best pamphleteering, perhaps the city outside London where the democratic spirit pulsed strongest — the actions of its members were sure to be scrutinized from every angle. The utter ease of the Wendover seat, on the score of local responsibility, would be gone forever. With the dignity of republican service would come an exposure to the force of republican criticism. Burke accepted the invitation, and made this speech to welcome the chance.

Mr. Burke's Speech
at His Arrival at Bristol

GENTLEMEN,

I am come hither to solicit in person, that favour which my friends have hitherto endeavoured to procure for me, by the most obliging, and to me the most honourable, exertions.

I have so high an opinion of the great trust which you have to confer on this occasion; and, by long experience, so just a diffidence in my abilities, to fill it in a manner adequate even to my own ideas, that I should never have ventured of myself to intrude into that awful situation. But since I am called upon by the desire of several respectable fellow-subjects, as I have done at other times, I give up my fears to their wishes. Whatever my other deficiencies may be, I do not know what it is to be wanting to my friends.

I am not fond of attempting to raise publick expectations by great promises. At this time, there is much cause to consider, and very little to presume. We seem to be approaching to a great crisis in our affairs, which calls for the whole wisdom of the wisest among us, without being able to assure ourselves, that any wisdom can preserve us from many and great inconveniencies. You know I speak of our unhappy contest with America. I confess, it is a matter on which I look down as from a precipice. It is difficult in itself, and it is rendered more intricate by a great variety of plans of conduct. I do not mean to enter into them. I will not suspect a want of good intention in framing them. But however pure the intentions of their authors may have been, we all know that the event has been unfortunate. The means of recovering our affairs are not obvious. So many great questions of commerce, of finance, of constitution, and of policy, are involved in this American deliberation, that I dare engage for nothing, but that I shall give it, without any predilection to former opinions, or any sinister bias whatsoever, the most honest and impartial consideration of which I am capable. The publick has a full right to it; and this great city, a main pillar in the commercial interest of Great Britain, must totter on its base by the slightest mistake with regard to our American measures.

Thus much, however, I think it not amiss to lay before you; That I am not, I hope, apt to take up or lay down my opinions lightly. I have held, and ever shall maintain, to the best of my power, unimpaired and undiminished, the just, wise, and necessary constitutional superiority of Great Britain. This is necessary for America, as well as for us. I never mean to depart from it. Whatever may be lost by it, I avow it. The forfeiture even of your favour, if by such a declaration I could forfeit it, though the first object of my ambition, never will make me disguise my sentiments on this subject.

But, — I have ever had a clear opinion, and have ever held a constant correspondent conduct, that this superiority is consistent with all the liberties a sober and spirited American ought to desire. I never mean to put any colonist, or any human creature, in a situation, not becoming a free-man. To reconcile British superiority with American liberty shall be my great object, as far as my little faculties extend. I am far from thinking that both, even yet, may not be preserved.

When I first devoted myself to the publick service, I considered how I should render myself fit for it; and this I did by endeavouring to discover what it was, that gave this country the rank it holds in the world. I found that our prosperity and dignity arose principally, if not solely, from two sources; our constitution and commerce. Both these I have spared no study to understand, and no endeavour to support.

The distinguishing part of our constitution is its liberty. To preserve that liberty inviolate, seems the particular duty and proper trust of a member of the House of Commons. But the liberty, the only liberty I mean, is a liberty connected with order; that not only exists along with order and virtue, but which cannot exist at all without them. It inheres in good and steady government, as in its substance and vital principle.

The other source of our power is commerce, of which you are so large a part, and which cannot exist, no more than your liberty, without a connection with many virtues. It has ever been a very particular and a very favourite object of my study, in its principles, and in its details. I think many here are acquainted with the truth of what I say. This I know, that I have ever had my house open, and my poor services ready, for traders and manufacturers of every denomination. My favourite ambition is to have those services acknowledged. I now appear before you to make trial, whether my earnest endeavours have been so wholly oppressed by the weakness of my abilities, as to be rendered insignificant in the eyes of a great trading city; or whether you chuse to give a weight to humble abilities, for the sake of the honest exertions with which they are accompanied. This is my trial to-day. My industry is not on trial. Of my industry I am sure, as far as my constitution of mind and body admitted.

When I was invited by many respectable merchants, freeholders, and freemen of this city, to offer them my services, I had just received the honour of an election at another place, at a very great distance from this. I immediately opened the matter to those of my worthy constituents who were with me, and they unanimously advised me not to decline it. They told me, that they had elected me with a view to the publick service; and as great questions relative to our commerce and colonies were imminent, that in such matters I might derive authority and support from the representation of this great commecial city; they desired me therefore to set off without delay, very well persuaded that I never could forget my obligations to them, or to my friends, for the choice they had made of me. From that time to this instant I have not slept; and if I should have the honour of being freely chosen by you, I hope I shall be as far from slumbering or sleeping when your service requires me to be awake, as I have been in coming to offer myself a candidate for your favour.

Speech at the Conclusion of the Poll (1774)

Early in the century, the city of Bristol had recognized a tradition of two Tory members; it had lately shifted to one Tory and one Whig; but in 1774 the city returned two Whigs to Parliament, Henry Cruger and Edmund Burke. Cruger came from a distinguished colonial family of New York. An articulate opponent of the Stamp Act, and a friend to the cause of Wilkes and Liberty, he drew much of his support from the artisan classes. Alongside Cruger, certain traits of Burke's political character were thrown into relief: his comparative moderation, his independence, and his aristocratic connections. These were, of course, the very qualifications that had buoyed his candidacy, but he showed early signs of defining his stance more rigorously than expected.

To the audience that had come to celebrate the victory, Burke declared at the conclusion of the polls that he would not be bound by mandates. A statement of principle, this was also a polemical response to an utterance of reflex gratitude by Cruger, who had affirmed "the legality and propriety of the people's instructing their representatives in Parliament," and described himself as "the servant of my constituents, not their master, subservient to their will, not superiour to it." Burke refused any such vow of compliance: "It ought to be the happiness and glory of a representative to live in the strictest union, the closest correspondence, and the most unreserved communication with his constituents. Their wishes ought to have great weight with him; their opinion, high respect; their business, unremitted attention. . . . But *authoritative* instructions; *mandates* issued, which the member is bound blindly and implicitly to obey, to vote, and to argue for, though contrary to the clearest conviction of his judgment and conscience; these are things utterly unknown to the laws of this land, and which arise from a fundamental mistake of the whole order and tenour of our constitution." He would recur to the sentiment, with variations, in many subsequent speeches.

Burke's strictures here contain the germ of a theory of representation that would later be invested with much authority by the American authors of the *Federalist Papers*. The theory holds that a legislator may gain, from experience in making laws, a knowledge hardly available to those who elect him. The people remain the source of ultimate power since they can turn a representative out of office. Meanwhile, the representative is to follow the public good, and bring to bear his understanding of the pragmatic means to attain that good. Answerable to the suffrage of opinion, he should be its guide and not its follower.

This dignified sense of the relation between a leader and his constituents is strengthened by a clear idea of Parliament as a deliberative body. The representative does not merely represent a city, but a nation and an empire. The interests of a large and various commonwealth are best served by those who possess the competence only a knowledge of politics and exposure to sustained discussion can give. Burke incidentally declined to participate with Cruger in a victory parade.

Mr. Burke's Speech
to the Electors of Bristol,

On his being declared by the Sheriffs,
duly elected one of the Representatives
in Parliament for that City.

On Thursday the third of November, 1774.

GENTLEMEN,

I cannot avoid sympathizing strongly with the feelings of the gentleman who has received the same honour that you have conferred on me. If he, who was bred and passed his whole life amongst you; if he, who through the easy gradations of acquaintance, friendship, and esteem, has obtained the honour, which seems of itself, naturally and almost insensibly, to meet with those, who, by the even tenour of pleasing manners and social virtues, slide into the love and confidence of their fellow-citizens; — if he cannot speak but with great emotion on this subject, surrounded as he is on all sides with his old friends; you will have the goodness to excuse me, if my real, unaffected embarrassment prevents me from expressing my gratitude to you as I ought.

I was brought hither under the disadvantage of being unknown, even by sight, to any of you. No previous canvass was made for me. I was put in nomination after the poll was opened. I did not appear until it was far advanced. If, under all these accumulated disadvantages, your good opinion has carried me to this happy point of success; you will pardon me, if I can only say to you collectively, as I said to you individually, simply and plainly, I thank you — I am obliged to you — I am not insensible of your kindness.

This is all that I am able to say for the inestimable favour you have conferred upon me. But I cannot be satisfied, without saying a little more in defence of the right you have to confer such a favour. The person that appeared here as counsel for the candidate, who so long and so earnestly solicited your votes, thinks proper to deny, that a very great part of you have any votes to give. He fixes a standard period of time in his own imagination, not what the law defines, but merely what the convenience of his client suggests, by which he would cut off, at one stroke, all those freedoms, which are the dearest privileges of your corporation; which the common law authorizes; which your magistrates are compelled to grant; which come duly authenticated into this court; and are saved in the clearest words, and with the most religious care and tenderness, in that very act of parliament, which was made to regulate the elections by freemen, and to prevent all possible abuses in making them.

I do not intend to argue the matter here. My learned counsel has supported your cause with his usual ability; the worthy sheriffs have acted with their usual equity, and I have no doubt, that the same equity, which dictates the return, will guide the final determination. I had the honour, in conjunction with many far wiser men, to contribute a very small assistance, but however some assistance, to the forming the judicature which is to try such questions. It would be unnatural in me, to doubt the justice of that court, in the trial of my own cause, to which I have been so active to give jurisdiction over every other.

I assure the worthy freemen, and this corporation, that, if the gentleman perseveres in the intentions, which his present warmth dictates to him, I will attend their cause with diligence, and I hope with effect. For, if I know any thing of myself, it is not my own interest in it, but my full conviction, that induces me to tell you — *I think there is not a shadow of doubt in the case.*

I do not imagine that you find me rash in declaring myself, or very forward in troubling you. From the beginning to the end of the election, I have kept silence in all matters of discussion. I have never asked a question of a voter on the other side, or supported a doubtful vote on my own. I respected the abilities of my managers; I relied on the candour of the court. I think the worthy sheriffs will bear me witness, that I have never once made an attempt to impose upon their reason, to surprise their justice, or to ruffle their temper. I stood on the hustings (except when I gave my thanks to those who favoured me with their votes) less like a candidate, than an unconcerned spectator of a publick proceeding. But here the face of things is altered. Here is an attempt for a general *massacre* of suffrages; an attempt, by a promiscuous carnage of *friends* and *foes*, to exterminate above two thousand votes, including *seven hundred polled for the gentleman himself, who now complains*, and who would destroy the friends whom he has obtained, only because he cannot obtain as many of them as he wishes.

How he will be permitted, in another place, to stultify and disable himself, and to plead against his own acts, is another question. The law will decide it. I shall only speak of it as it concerns the propriety of publick conduct in this city. I do not pretend to lay down rules of decorum for other gentlemen. They are best judges of the mode of proceeding that will recommend them to the favour of their fellow-citizens. But I confess, I should look rather awkward, if I had been the *very first to produce the new copies of freedom*, if I had persisted in producing them to the last; if I had ransacked, with the most unremitting industry, and the most penetrating research, the remotest corners of the kingdom to discover them; if I were then, all at once, to turn short, and declare, that I had been sporting all this while with the right of election; and that I had been drawing out a poll, upon no sort of rational grounds, which disturbed the peace of my fellow-citizens for a month together — I really, for my part, should appear awkward under such circumstances.

It would be still more awkward in me, if I were gravely to look the sheriffs in the face, and to tell them, they were not to determine my cause on my own principles; nor to make the return upon those votes, upon which I had rested my election. Such would be my appearance to the court and magistrates.

But how should I appear to the *voters* themselves? if I had gone round to the citizens intitled to freedom, and squeezed them by the hand — "Sir, I humbly beg your vote — I shall be eternally thankful — may I hope for the honour of your support? — Well! — come — we shall see you at the council-house." — If I were then to deliver them to my managers, pack them into tallies, vote them off in court, and when I heard from the bar — "Such a one only! and such a one for ever! — he's my man!" — "Thank you, good Sir — Hah! my worthy friend! thank you kindly — that's an honest fellow — how is your good family?" — Whilst these words were hardly out of my mouth, if I should have wheeled round at once, and told them — "Get you gone, you pack of worthless fellows! you have no votes — you are usurpers! you are intruders on the rights of real freemen! I will have nothing to do with you! you ought never to have been produced at this election, and the sheriffs ought not to have admitted you to poll."

Gentlemen, I should make a strange figure, if my conduct had been of this sort. I am not so old an acquaintance of yours as the worthy gentleman. Indeed I could not have ventured on such kind of freedoms with you. But I am bound, and I will endeavour, to have justice done to the rights of freemen; even though I should, at the same time, be obliged to vindicate the former[1] part of my antagonist's conduct against his own present inclinations.

I owe myself, in all things, to *all* the freemen of this city. My particular friends have a demand on me, that I should not deceive their expectations. Never was cause or man supported with more constancy, more activity, more spirit. I have been supported with a zeal indeed and heartiness in my friends, which (if their object had been at all proportioned to their endeavours) could never be sufficiently commended. They supported me upon the most liberal principles. They wished that the members for Bristol should be chosen for the city, and for their country at large, and not for themselves.

So far they are not disappointed. If I possess nothing else, I am sure I possess the temper that is fit for your service. I know

---

1 Mr. Brickdale opened his poll, it seems, with a tally of those very kind of freemen, and voted many hundreds of them [*Burke's note*].

nothing of Bristol, but by the favours I have received, and the virtues I have seen exerted in it.

I shall ever retain, what I now feel, the most perfect and grateful attachment to my friends — and I have no enmities; no resentment. I never can consider fidelity to engagements, and constancy in friendships, but with the highest approbation; even when those noble qualities are employed against my own pretensions. The gentleman, who is not fortunate as I have been in this contest, enjoys, in this respect, a consolation full of honour both to himself and to his friends. They have certainly left nothing undone for his service.

As for the trifling petulance, which the rage of party stirs up in little minds, though it should shew itself even in this court, it has not made the slightest impression on me. The highest flight of such clamorous birds is winged in an inferiour region of the air. We hear them, and we look upon them, just as you, gentlemen, when you enjoy the serene air on your lofty rocks, look down upon the gulls, that skim the mud of your river, when it is exhausted of its tide.

I am sorry I cannot conclude, without saying a word on a topick touched upon by my worthy colleague. I wish that topick had been passed by; at a time when I have so little leisure to discuss it. But since he has thought proper to throw it out, I owe you a clear explanation of my poor sentiments on that subject.

He tells you, that "the topick of instructions has occasioned much altercation and uneasiness in this city;" and he expresses himself (if I understand him rightly) in favour of the coercive authority of such instructions.

Certainly, gentlemen, it ought to be the happiness and glory of a representative, to live in the strictest union, the closest correspondence, and the most unreserved communication with his constituents. Their wishes ought to have great weight with him; their opinion high respect; their business unremitted attention. It is his duty to sacrifice his repose, his pleasures, his satisfactions, to theirs; and, above all, ever, and in all cases, to prefer their interest to his own. But, his unbiassed opinion, his mature judgment, his enlightened conscience, he ought not to sacrifice to you; to any man, or to any set of men living. These he does not derive from your pleasure; no, nor from the law and the constitution. They are a trust from Providence, for the abuse of which he is deeply answerable. Your representative owes you, not his industry only, but his judgment; and he betrays, instead of serving you, if he sacrifices it to your opinion.

My worthy colleague says, his will ought to be subservient to yours. If that be all, the thing is innocent. If government were a matter of will upon any side, yours, without question, ought to be superiour. But government and legislation are matters of reason and judgment, and not of inclination; and, what sort of reason is that, in which the determination precedes the discussion; in which one set of men deliberate, and another decide; and where those who form the conclusion are perhaps three hundred miles distant from those who hear the arguments?

To deliver an opinion, is the right of all men; that of constituents is a weighty and respectable opinion, which a representative ought always to rejoice to hear; and which he ought always most seriously to consider. But *authoritative* instructions; *mandates* issued, which the member is bound blindly and implicitly to obey, to vote, and to argue for, though contrary to the clearest conviction of his judgment and conscience; these are things utterly unknown to the laws of this land, and which arise from a fundamental mistake of the whole order and tenour of our constitution.

Parliament is not a *congress* of ambassadors from different and hostile interests; which interests each must maintain, as an agent and advocate, against other agents and advocates; but parliament is a *deliberative* assembly of *one* nation, with *one* interest, that of the whole; where, not local purposes, not local prejudices ought to guide, but the general good, resulting from the general reason of the whole. You chuse a member indeed; but when you have chosen him, he is not member of Bristol, but he is a member of *parliament*. If the local constituent should have an interest, or should form an hasty opinion, evidently opposite to the real good of the rest of the community, the member for that place

ought to be as far, as any other, from any endeavour to give it
effect. I beg pardon for saying so much on this subject. I have
been unwillingly drawn into it; but I shall ever use a respectful
frankness of communication with you. Your faithful friend, your
devoted servant, I shall be to the end of my life: a flatterer you do
not wish for. On this point of instructions, however, I think it
scarcely possible, we ever can have any sort of difference. Perhaps I may give you too much, rather than too little trouble.

From the first hour I was encouraged to court your favour to
this happy day of obtaining it, I have never promised you any
thing, but humble and persevering endeavours to do my duty.
The weight of that duty, I confess, makes me tremble; and whoever well considers what it is, of all things in the world will fly
from what has the least likeness to a positive and precipitate
engagement. To be a good member of parliament, is, let me tell
you, no easy task; especially at this time, when there is so strong a
disposition to run into the perilous extremes of servile compliance or wild popularity. To unite circumspection with vigour,
is absolutely necessary; but it is extremely difficult. We are now
members for a rich commercial *city*; this city, however, is but a
part of a rich commercial *nation*, the interests of which are various, multiform, and intricate. We are members for that great
nation, which however is itself but part of a great *empire*, extended by our virtue and our fortune to the farthest limits of the
east and of the west. All these wide-spread interests must be
considered; must be compared; must be reconciled if possible.
We are members for a *free* country; and surely we all know, that
the machine of a free constitution is no simple thing; but as
intricate and as delicate, as it is valuable. We are members in a
great and ancient *monarchy*; and we must preserve religiously,
the true legal rights of the sovereign, which form the key-stone
that binds together the noble and well-constructed arch of our
empire and our constitution. A constitution made up of balanced powers must ever be a critical thing. As such I mean to
touch that part of it which comes within my reach. I know my
inability, and I wish for support from every quarter. In particular

I shall aim at the friendship, and shall cultivate the best correspondence, of the worthy colleague you have given me.

I trouble you no farther than once more to thank you all; you,
gentlemen, for your favours; the candidates, for their temperate
and polite behaviour; and the sheriffs, for a conduct which may
give a model for all who are in publick stations.

To William Burgh (9 February 1775)

William Burgh, twelve years Burke's junior, was a member of the Irish House of Commons and a politician with theological interests. His orthodox *Scriptural Confutation of the Arguments against the One Godhead* was published anonymously in June 1774, and evidently was read by Burke, who asked to meet the author. Burgh wrote a letter disclosing his identity and recalling a kindness Burke had shown him as a boy; when, in 1775, he brought out a second edition of the pamphlet, he asked to dedicate it to Burke and sent a proof sheet of the dedication page. From Burke's belief in the good of a church establishment, Burgh had wrongly inferred a settled hostility toward religious toleration. This letter politely corrects him.

To William Burgh

(9 February 1775)

DEAR SIR,

I beg you will not think that my delay in returning you the proof sheet of your most ingenious and most obliging dedication could proceed from a want of the liveliest sensibility to the great honour you have done me. I now return the proof, with my sincerest and most grateful acknowledgments.

Some topicks are touched in that dedication, on which I could wish to explain myself to you. I should have been glad to do it through Mr Mason; but to my great loss, on this, and many other accounts, he left town suddenly. Indeed, at that time and ever since, the pressure of American business on one hand and a petition against my election on the other, left me not a single minute at my disposal — and I have now little leisure enough to explain myself clearly on some points in that dedication, which I either misunderstood, or they go upon a misapprehension of some part of my publick conduct. For which reason I wish, if I might presume to interfere, that they may be a little altered.

It is certain that I have, to the best of my power, supported the establishment of the Church, upon grounds and principles, which I am happy to find countenanced by your approbation. This you have been told; but you have not heard that I supported also the petition of the dissenters, for a larger toleration than they enjoy at present, and under the letter of the act of King William. In fact my opinion in favour of toleration goes far beyond the limits of that act; which was no more than a provision for certain sets of men, under certain circumstances; and by no means, what is commonly called, an act of toleration. I am greatly deceived if my opinions on this subject are not consistent with the strictest, and the best supported Church-establishment. I cannot consider our dissenters, of almost any kind, as schismaticks;

whatever some of their leaders might originally have been in the eye of him, who alone knows, whether they acted under the direction of such conscience as they had, or at the instigation of pride and passion. There are many things among most of them, which I rather *dislike*, than dare to *condemn*. My ideas of toleration go far beyond even theirs. I would give a full civil protection, in which I include an immunity from all disturbance of their pub-lick religious worship, and a power of teaching in schools, as well as temples, to Jews, Mahometans, and even Pagans; especially if they are already possessed of any of those advantages by long and prescriptive usage; which is as sacred in this exercise of rights, as in any other. Much more am I inclined to tolerate those, whom I look upon as our brethren; I mean all those who profess our common hope; extending to all the reformed and unreformed churches, both at home and abroad; in none of whom I find any thing capitally amiss, but their mutual hatred of each other. I can never think any man an heretick, or schismatick by *education*. It must be, as I conceive, by an act in which his *own choice*, (influ-enced by blamable passions), is more concerned than it can be by his early prejudices, and his being aggregated to bodies, for whom men naturally form a great degree of reverence and affec-tion. This is my opinion; and my conduct has been conformable to it. Another age will see it more general; and I think that this general affection to religion will never introduce indifference; but will rather increase real zeal, Christian fervour, and pious emulation; that it will make a common cause against Epicurism, and every thing that corrupts the mind, and renders it unworthy of its family. But toleration does not exclude rational preference, either as to modes, or opinions; and all the lawful and honest means which may be used for the support of that preference.

I should be happy to converse with you, and such as you, on these subjects, and to unlearn my mistaken opinions; if such they should be; for however erroneous, I believe there is no evil ingre-dient in them. In looking over that dedication, if you should agree with me, that there are some expressions that carry with them an idea of my pushing my ideas of Church establishment further than I do, you will naturally soften or change them accordingly. I do not very well know how to excuse the great liberty I take in troubling you with observations, where I ought to speak only my obligations. Be assured that I feel myself extremely honoured by your good opinion, and shall be made very happy by your friendship. I am, with the greatest esteem, &c.

Speech on Conciliation with America (1775)

Burke's association with the American colonies went back to his maiden speech on resistance to the Stamp Act, in January 1766. His attempt to secure their status as equal trading partners with England was based on the principle of parliamentary control over America and the policy of withholding any conspicuous assertion of that control. Though the Rockingham administration counted the repeal of the Stamp Act as its major accomplishment, this had been achieved at the cost of passing the Declaratory Act, which reaffirmed the sovereignty of the House of Commons and the continuing dependence of the colonies. It was an unsatisfactory compromise. If George Grenville overestimated the power of the imperial center to enforce its will across a distance of three thousand miles, Burke and his party underrated the ferocity of the resentment driving the movement for independence in America.

Between 1771 and 1775, Burke was agent for the province of New York at the Court of Great Britain, a position that required him to explain the interests and justify the actions of the New York assembly before the Board of Trade. This practical experience, along with the knowledge he acquired as a scholar of American affairs, made him among the best-informed authorities in the House of Commons and perhaps the most influential of all those sympathetic to the American side. Later, he would maintain friendly contacts with several of the leading spirits of American independence, among them Benjamin Franklin and (until 1790) Tom Paine.

By 1774, Burke seems to have decided that a separate American interest in the empire was an established fact, which no assertion of control by Parliament could change. Yet his party never pressed for independence. Rather, the Rockingham Whigs attempted to explain and justify the American stirrings for freedom and to remove the grounds of discontent. The speech on taxation of 1774 is the greatest of Burke's extemporaneous performances of which a record has been preserved; and yet, in substance, it was a policy speech and not particularly original. It leaned heavily on his arguments for the "principle" and "character" of a political party in *Thoughts on the Cause of the Present Discontents,* and deplored the want of principle and character that had produced the inconsistent policies of Charles Townshend and Lord Chatham.

By contrast, the "Speech on Conciliation" is a written speech, with both words stressed. Together with the "Speech at Guildhall" (1780) and the "Speech on Fox's East India Bill" (1783), it is among Burke's unrivaled masterpieces of eloquent reasoning. Much of its argument is prudential in the classical sense. The speech moves for conciliation — a peaceful bringing together of divergent interests by an appeal to the broader aims they share. But its path of exposition is strikingly innovative: as much as any political work of the eighteenth century, this speech deploys the historical method of the Enlightenment. Burke asks, What sort of people are the Americans? By what conditions have they been formed, and to what ends is their environment now shaping them? Finally, given what we know of their circumstances, what conduct may we fairly expect from them in the present controversy? Distance, extent, the manners of Protestant radicalism in the northern colonies and of slavery in the southern colonies, the ascendancy of lawyers and a lawyerlike way of thinking among the colonists: all these have a place for Burke among the social causes that make for a spirit of resistance.

A parallel question is asked of his English listeners about themselves. How much of the American experience have they shared, though at some remove, in their own national education in liberty? To what premises could an English statesman appeal in asking the Americans to be satisfied with less liberty? The largest common inheritance of the English and American people, Burke concludes, is the history of liberty itself. So while urging a prudential wisdom — "The question with me is not, whether you have a right to render your people miserable, but whether it is not your interest to make them happy" — he now adds a practical corollary: "An Englishman is the unfittest person on earth to argue another Englishman into slavery." There is an underlying irony characteristic of Burke, for he sees that the spirit of liberty may be proportionately stronger in a people who savor it daily in contrast with its opposite. The presence of slavery has if anything sharpened the feeling among the colonists of the priceless good of freedom.

The advice to recognize common interests, and to recognize by analogy a shared ground of experience, proceeds from a deep conviction of Burke's. He believed — it is a view he shares with Montesquieu and Hume — that a political order is governed not by asserted rights or positive laws or an "original contract" but rather by interest and opinion. He does not pause to ask whether the House of Commons actually has a right to enforce a regulation of trade against the will of the colonists. Metaphysically, it may have such a right. But of what use is the right, except as it serves the interest of peace and a prosperous conduct of the business of the empire? An abstract good might be served by the colonial governors sticking to the letter of the imperial charter. More is gained by preserving the colonists as trading partners, and as continuing allies in time of war.

In proposing "not peace through the medium of war," but peace as a resumption of ordinary relations, Burke makes this policy follow from the nature of both the colonies and the mother country. The pragmatic case is argued here with massive support and modulation, and it carries conviction in itself. Yet Burke's words imply that something larger than a pragmatic motive has brought him to speak as he does. The generosity, or magnanimity, that can be felt in the very tones of the speech, may spring from a sense that the spirit of liberty is a kind of miracle, an astonishing fact of life that had better be witnessed and accepted and not tampered with. In the face of the progress of the colonies over the past seventy years, says Burke, "my rigor relents. I pardon something to the spirit of liberty."

A consideration of principle, as well, goes beyond the urging of mere political expediency. Burke speaks of his horror of acting as the judge in his own cause. Yet this is what he fears the English have become in their dealings with the colonies. The result, when such deep moral feelings are joined to the case for prudence, can be gauged by the tenor of his peroration:

> Deny them this participation of freedom, and you break that sole bond, which originally made, and must still preserve, the unity of the empire. . . . Do not dream that your letters of office, and your instructions, and your suspending clauses, are the things that hold together the great contexture of this mysterious whole. These things do not make your government. . . . It is the spirit of the English Constitution, which, infused through the mighty mass, pervades, feeds, unites, invigorates, vivifies, every part of the empire, even down to the minutest member.

It is as if participation in the idea of a human commonwealth, itself constituted by various smaller societies, has become for Burke a blessing that stands in the place of religious communion.

The speech was delivered on 22 March 1775.

Mr. Burke's Speech on Moving His Resolutions for Conciliation with the Colonies

I hope, Sir, that notwithstanding the austerity of the Chair, your good-nature will incline you to some degree of indulgence towards human frailty. You will not think it unnatural, that those who have an object depending, which strongly engages their hopes and fears, should be somewhat inclined to superstition. As I came into the house full of anxiety about the event of my motion, I found to my infinite surprise, that the grand penal Bill, by which we had passed sentence on the trade and sustenance of America, is to be returned to us from the other house.[1] I do confess, I could not help looking on this event as a fortunate omen. I look upon it as a sort of providential favour; by which we are put once more in possession of our deliberative capacity, upon a business so very questionable in its nature, so very uncertain in its issue. By the return of this Bill, which seemed to have taken its flight for ever, we are at this very instant nearly as free to choose a plan for our American government, as we were on the first day of the session. If, Sir, we incline to the side of conciliation, we are not at all embarrassed (unless we please to make ourselves so) by any incongruous mixture of coercion and restraint. We are therefore called upon, as it were by a superiour warning voice, again to attend to America; to attend to the whole of it together; and to review the subject with an unusual degree of care and calmness.

Surely it is an awful subject; or there is none so on this side of the grave. When I first had the honour of a seat in this house, the

---

1 The Act to restrain the trade and commerce of the provinces of Massachuset's-Bay and New Hampshire, and colonies of Connecticut and Rhode Island, and Providence Plantation, in North America, to Great Britain, Ireland, and the British Islands in the West Indies; and to prohibit such provinces and colonies from carrying on any fishery on the banks of Newfoundland, and other places therein mentioned, under certain conditions and limitations [*Burke's note*].

affairs of that continent pressed themselves upon us, as the most important and most delicate object of parliamentary attention. My little share in this great deliberation oppressed me. I found myself a partaker in a very high trust; and having no sort of reason to rely on the strength of my natural abilities for the proper execution of that trust, I was obliged to take more than common pains, to instruct myself in every thing which relates to our colonies. I was not less under the necessity of forming some fixed ideas, concerning the general policy of the British empire. Something of this sort seemed to be indispensable; in order, amidst so vast a fluctuation of passions and opinions, to concenter my thoughts; to ballast my conduct; to preserve me from being blown about by every wind of fashionable doctrine. I really did not think it safe, or manly, to have fresh principles to seek upon every fresh mail which should arrive from America.

At that period, I had the fortune to find myself in perfect concurrence with a large majority in this House. Bowing under that high authority, and penetrated with the sharpness and strength of that early impression, I have continued ever since, without the least deviation in my original sentiments. Whether this be owing to an obstinate perserverance in errour, or to a religious adherence to what appears to me truth and reason, it is in your equity to judge.

Sir, Parliament having an enlarged view of objects, made, during this interval, more frequent changes in their sentiments and their conduct, than could be justified in a particular person upon the contracted scale of private information. But though I do not hazard any thing approaching to a censure on the motives of former parliaments to all those alterations, one fact is undoubted; that under them the state of America has been kept in continual agitation. Every thing administered as remedy to the publick complaint, if it did not produce, was at least followed by, an heightening of the distemper; until, by a variety of experiments, that important country has been brought into her present situation; — a situation which I will not miscall, which I dare not name; which I scarcely know how to comprehend in the terms of any description.

In this posture, Sir, things stood at the beginning of the session. About that time, a worthy member[2] of great parliamentary experience, who, in the year 1766, filled the chair of the American committee with much ability, took me aside; and, lamenting the present aspect of our politicks, told me, things were come to such a pass, that our former methods of proceeding in the house would be no longer tolerated. That the publick tribunal (never too indulgent to a long and unsuccessful opposition) would now scrutinize our conduct with unusual severity. That the very vicissitudes and shiftings of ministerial measures, instead of convicting their authors of inconstancy and want of system, would be taken as an occasion of charging us with a predetermined discontent, which nothing could satisfy; whilst we accused every measure of vigour as cruel, and every proposal of lenity as weak and irresolute. The publick, he said, would not have patience to see us play the game out with our adversaries: we must produce our hand. It would be expected, that those who for many years had been active in such affairs should shew, that they had formed some clear and decided idea of the principles of colony government; and were capable of drawing out something like a platform of the ground, which might be laid for future and permanent tranquillity.

I felt the truth of what my hon. friend represented; but I felt my situation too. His application might have been made with far greater propriety to many other gentlemen. No man was indeed ever better disposed, or worse qualified, for such an undertaking than myself. Though I gave so far into his opinion, that I immediately threw my thoughts into a sort of parliamentary form, I was by no means equally ready to produce them. It generally argues some degree of natural impotence of mind, or some want of knowledge of the world, to hazard plans of government, except from a seat of authority. Propositions are made, not only

2 Mr. Rose Fuller [*Burke's note*]. A Sussex landowner, ironmaster, and Jamaica planter, Rose Fuller opposed punitive measures against the Americans in the early 1770s.

ineffectually, but somewhat disreputably, when the minds of men are not properly disposed for their reception; and for my part, I am not ambitious of ridicule; not absolutely a candidate for disgrace.

Besides, Sir, to speak the plain truth, I have in general no very exalted opinion of the virtue of paper government; nor of any politicks, in which the plan is to be wholly separated from the execution. But when I saw, that anger and violence prevailed every day more and more; and that things were hastening towards an incurable alienation of our colonies; I confess my caution gave way. I felt this, as one of those few moments in which decorum yields to an higher duty. Publick calamity is a mighty leveller; and there are occasions when any, even the slightest, chance of doing good, must be laid hold on, even by the most inconsiderable person.

To restore order and repose to an empire so great and so distracted as ours, is, merely in the attempt, an undertaking that would ennoble the flights of the highest genius, and obtain pardon for the efforts of the meanest understanding. Struggling a good while with these thoughts, by degrees I felt myself more firm. I derived, at length, some confidence from what in other circumstances usually produces timidity. I grew less anxious, even from the idea of my own insignificance. For, judging of what you are, by what you ought to be, I persuaded myself, that you would not reject a reasonable proposition, because it had nothing but its reason to recommend it. On the other hand, being totally destitute of all shadow of influence, natural or adventitious, I was very sure, that, if my proposition were futile or dangerous; if it were weakly conceived, or improperly timed, there was nothing exterior to it, of power to awe, dazzle, or delude you. You will see it just as it is; and you will treat it just as it deserves.

The proposition is peace. Not peace through the medium of war; not peace to be hunted through the labyrinth of intricate and endless negotiations; not peace to arise out of universal discord, fomented from principle, in all parts of the empire; not peace to depend on the juridical determination of perplexing questions; or the precise marking the shadowy boundaries of a complex government. It is simple peace; sought in its natural course, and in its ordinary haunts. — It is peace sought in the spirit of peace; and laid in principles purely pacifick. I propose, by removing the ground of the difference, and by restoring the *former unsuspecting confidence of the colonies in the mother country*, to give permanent satisfaction to your people; and (far from a scheme of ruling by discord) to reconcile them to each other in the same act, and by the bond of the very same interest, which reconciles them to British government.

My idea is nothing more. Refined policy ever has been the parent of confusion; and ever will be so, as long as the world endures. Plain good intention, which is as easily discovered at the first view, as fraud is surely detected at last, is, let me say, of no mean force in the government of mankind. Genuine simplicity of heart is an healing and cementing principle. My plan, therefore, being formed upon the most simple grounds imaginable, may disappoint some people, when they hear it. It has nothing to recommend it, to the pruriency of curious ears. There is nothing at all new and captivating in it. It has nothing of the splendour of the project, which has been lately laid upon your table by the noble lord in the blue ribband.[3] It does not propose to fill

---

3 "That when the governor, council, or assembly, or general court, of any of his majesty's provinces or colonies in America, shall *propose* to make provision, *according to the condition, circumstances,* and *situation,* of such province or colony, for contributing their *proportion* to the *common defence* (such *proportion* to be raised under the authority of the general court, or general assembly, of such province or colony, and disposable by parliament) and shall engage to make provision also for the support of the civil government, and the administration of justice, in such province or colony, it will be proper, *if such proposal shall be approved by his majesty, and the two houses of parliament,* and for so long as such provision shall be made accordingly, to forbear, *in respect of such province or colony,* to levy any duty, tax, or assessment, or to impose any farther duty, tax, or asssessment, except such duties as it may be expedient to continue to levy or impose, for the regulation of commerce; the nett produce of the duties last mentioned to be carried to the account of such province or colony respectively." Resolution moved by Lord North in the committee; and agreed to by the house, 27th Feb. 1775 [*Burke's note*]. Frederick North, Lord North (1732–92), as prime minister a reluctant but obedient instrument of the king's colonial policy,

your lobby with squabbling colony agents, who will require the interposition of your mace, at every instant, to keep the peace amongst them. It does not institute a magnificent auction of finance, where captivated provinces come to general ransom by bidding against each other, until you knock down the hammer, and determine a proportion of payments, beyond all the powers of algebra to equalize and settle.

The plan, which I shall presume to suggest, derives, however, one great advantage from the proposition and registry of that noble lord's project. The idea of conciliation is admissible. First, the house in accepting the resolution moved by the noble lord, has admitted, notwithstanding the menacing front of our address, notwithstanding our heavy bill of pains and penalties — that we do not think ourselves precluded from all ideas of free grace and bounty.

The house has gone farther; it has declared conciliation admissible, *previous* to any submission on the part of America. It has even shot a good deal beyond that mark, and has admitted, that the complaints of our former mode of exerting the right of taxation were not wholly unfounded. That right thus exerted is allowed to have had something reprehensible in it; something unwise, or something grievous; since, in the midst of our heat and resentment, we, of ourselves, have proposed a capital alteration; and, in order to get rid of what seemed so very exceptionable, have instituted a mode that is altogether new; one that is, indeed, wholly alien from all the ancient methods and forms of parliament.

The *principle* of this proceeding is large enough for my purpose. The means proposed by the noble lord for carrying his ideas into execution, I think indeed, are very indifferently suited to the end; and this I shall endeavour to shew you before I sit down. But, for the present, I take my ground on the admitted principle. I mean to give peace. Peace implies reconciliation;

had the Order of the Garter (the blue ribbon) conferred on him by George III in 1772.

and where there has been a material dispute, reconciliation does in a manner always imply concession on the one part or on the other. In this state of things I make no difficulty in affirming, that the proposal ought to originate from us. Great and acknowledged force is not impaired, either in effect or in opinion, by an unwillingness to exert itself. The superiour power may offer peace with honour and with safety. Such an offer from such a power will be attributed to magnanimity. But the concessions of the weak are the concessions of fear. When such a one is disarmed, he is wholly at the mercy of his superiour; and he loses for ever that time and those chances, which, as they happen to all men, are the strength and resources of all inferiour power.

The capital leading questions on which you must this day decide, are these two. First, whether you ought to concede; and secondly, what your concession ought to be. On the first of these questions we have gained (as I have just taken the liberty of observing to you) some ground. But I am sensible that a good deal more is still to be done. Indeed, Sir, to enable us to determine both on the one and the other of these great questions with a firm and precise judgment, I think it may be necessary to consider distinctly the true nature and the peculiar circumstances of the object which we have before us. Because after all our struggle, whether we will or not, we must govern America, according to that nature, and to those circumstances; and not according to our own imaginations; not according to abstract ideas of right; by no means according to mere general theories of government, the resort to which appears to me, in our present situation, no better than arrant trifling. I shall therefore endeavour, with your leave, to lay before you some of the most material of these circumstances in as full and as clear a manner as I am able to state them.

The first thing that we have to consider with regard to the nature of the object is — the number of people in the colonies. I have taken for some years a good deal of pains on that point. I can by no calculation justify myself in placing the number below two millions of inhabitants of our own European blood and colour; besides at least 500,000 others, who form no inconsiderable part of the strength and opulence of the whole. This, Sir, is, I believe, about the true number. There is no occasion to exaggerate, where plain truth is of so much weight and importance. But whether I put the present numbers too high or too low, is a matter of little moment. Such is the strength with which population shoots in that part of the world, that state the numbers as high as we will, whilst the dispute continues, the exaggeration ends. Whilst we are discussing any given magnitude, they are grown to it. Whilst we spend our time in deliberating on the mode of governing two millions, we shall find we have millions more to manage. Your children do not grow faster from infancy to manhood, than they spread from families to communities, and from villages to nations.

I put this consideration of the present and the growing numbers in the front of our deliberation; because, Sir, this consideration will make it evident to a blunter discernment than yours, that no partial, narrow, contracted, pinched, occasional system will be at all suitable to such an object. It will shew you, that it is not to be considered as one of those *minima*[4] which are out of the eye and consideration of the law; not a paltry excrescence of the state; not a mean dependant, who may be neglected with little damage, and provoked with little danger. It will prove, that some degree of care and caution is required in the handling such an object; it will shew that you ought not, in reason, to trifle with so large a mass of the interests and feelings of the human race. You could at no time do so without guilt; and be assured you will not be able to do it long with impunity.

But the population of this country, the great and growing population, though a very important consideration, will lose much of its weight, if not combined with other circumstances. The commerce of your colonies is out of all proportion beyond the numbers of the people. This ground of their commerce

---

4 From the legal maxim *De minimis non curat lex* ("The law does not concern itself with trifles").

indeed has been trod some days ago, and with great ability, by a distinguished person,[5] at your bar. This gentleman, after thirty-five years — it is so long since he first appeared at the same place to plead for the commerce of Great Britain — has come again before you to plead the same cause, without any other effect of time, than, that to the fire of imagination and extent of erudition, which even then marked him as one of the first literary characters of his age, he has added a consummate knowledge in the commercial interest of his country, formed by a long course of enlightened and discriminating experience.

Sir, I should be inexcusable in coming after such a person with any detail; if a great part of the members who now fill the house had not the misfortune to be absent when he appeared at your bar. Besides, Sir, I propose to take the matter at periods of time somewhat different from his. There is, if I mistake not, a point of view, from whence if you will look at this subject, it is impossible that it should not make an impression upon you.

I have in my hand two accounts; one a comparative state of the export trade of England to its colonies, as it stood in the year 1704, and as it stood in the year 1772. The other a state of the export trade of this country to its colonies alone, as it stood in 1772, compared with the whole trade of England to all parts of the world (the colonies included) in the year 1704. They are from good vouchers; the latter period from the accounts on your table, the earlier from an original manuscript of Davenant, who first established the inspector general's office, which has been ever since his time so abundant a source of parliamentary information.

The export trade to the colonies consists of three great branches. The African, which, terminating almost wholly in the colonies, must be put to the account of their commerce; the West Indian; and the North American. All these are so interwoven, that the attempt to separate them, would tear to pieces

5 Mr. Glover [*Burke's note*]. Richard Glover (1712–85), poet and merchant, who had addressed Parliament on 16 March.

the contexture of the whole; and if not entirely destroy, would very much depreciate the value of all the parts. I therefore consider these three denominations to be, what in effect they are, one trade.

The trade to the colonies, taken on the export side, at the beginning of this century, that is, in the year 1704, stood thus:

Exports to North America, and the West Indies . . . . £.483,265
To Africa. 86,665
                                                     569,930

In the year 1772, which I take as a middle year between the highest and lowest of those lately laid on your table, the account was as follows:

To North America, and the West Indies. . . . . . . £.4,791,734
To Africa 866,398
To which if you add the export trade from Scotland,
    which had in 1704 no existence 364,000
                                                     6,022,132

From five hundred and odd thousand, it has grown to six millions. It has increased no less than twelve-fold. This is the state of the colony trade, as compared with itself at these two periods, within this century; — and this is matter for meditation. But this is not all. Examine my second account. See how the export trade to the colonies alone in 1772 stood in the other point of view, that is, as compared to the whole trade of England in 1704.

The whole export trade of England,
    including that to the colonies, in 1704 . . . . . .£.6,509,000
Export to the colonies alone, in 1772. 6,024,000
    Difference 485,000

The trade with America alone is now within less than 500,000l. of being equal to what this great commercial nation, England, carried on at the beginning of this century with the whole world! If I had taken the largest year of those on your table, it would rather have exceeded. But, it will be said, is not this American trade an unnatural protuberance, that has drawn the juices from the rest of the body? The reverse. It is the very food that has nourished every other part into its present magnitude. Our general trade has been greatly augmented; and augmented more or less in almost every part to which it ever extended; but with this material difference; that of the six millions which in the beginning of the century constituted the whole mass of our export commerce, the colony trade was but one twelfth part; it is now (as a part of sixteen millions) considerably more than a third of the whole. This is the relative proportion of the importance of the colonies at these two periods: and all reasoning concerning our mode of treating them must have this proportion as its basis; or it is a reasoning weak, rotten, and sophistical.

Mr. Speaker, I cannot prevail on myself to hurry over this great consideration. It is good for us to be here. We stand where we have an immense view of what is, and what is past. Clouds indeed, and darkness, rest upon the future. Let us, however, before we descend from this noble eminence, reflect that this growth of our national prosperity has happened within the short period of the life of man. It has happened within sixty-eight years. There are those alive whose memory might touch the two extremities. For instance, my Lord Bathurst[6] might remember all the stages of the progress. He was in 1704 of an age at least to be made to comprehend such things. He was then old enough *acta parentum jam legere, et quæ sit poterit cognoscere virtus*[7] — Suppose, Sir, that the angel of this auspicious youth, foreseeing the many virtues, which made him one of the most amiable, as he is one of the most fortunate men of his age, had opened to him in vision, that, when, in the fourth generation,[8] the third prince of the house of

6 Allen Bathurst (1684–1775), first Earl Bathurst, Tory statesman and friend of Lord North, whose son was in the North ministry.

7 Virgil *Eclogues* 4.26–27: "to read of the acts of his father, and to know what virtue is."

8 George III was the grandson not the son of George II, and thus the fourth generation of the Hanoverian succession.

Brunswick had sat twelve years on the throne of that nation, which (by the happy issue of moderate and healing councils) was to be made Great Britain,[9] he should see his son, Lord Chancellor of England, turn back the current of hereditary dignity to its fountain, and raise him to an higher rank of peerage, whilst he enriched the family with a new one [10] — If amidst these bright and happy scenes of domestick honour and prosperity, that angel should have drawn up the curtain, and unfolded the rising glories of his country, and whilst he was gazing with admiration on the then commercial grandeur of England, the genius should point out to him a little speck, scarce visible in the mass of the national interest, a small seminal principle, rather than a formed body, and should tell him — "Young man, there is America — which at this day serves for little more than to amuse you with stories of savage men, and uncouth manners; yet shall, before you taste of death, shew itself equal to the whole of that commerce which now attracts the envy of the world. Whatever England has been growing to by a progressive increase of improvement, brought in by varieties of people, by succession of civilising conquests and civilising settlements in a series of seventeen hundred years, you shall see as much added to her by America in the course of a single life!" If this state of his country had been foretold to him, would it not require all the sanguine credulity of youth, and all the fervid glow of enthusiasm, to make him believe it? Fortunate man, he has lived to see it! Fortunate indeed, if he lives to see nothing that shall vary the prospect, and cloud the setting of his day!

Excuse me, Sir, if turning from such thoughts I resume this comparative view once more. You have seen it on a large scale; look at it on a small one. I will point out to your attention a particular instance of it in the single province of Pensylvania. In the year 1704 that province called for 11,459*l.* in value of your

9 The Act for the Union of England and Scotland passed in 1707.
10 Bathurst's son was Henry Bathurst (1714–94), Baron Apsley, appointed Lord Chancellor in 1771.

commodities, native and foreign. This was the whole. What did it demand in 1772? Why nearly fifty times as much; for in that year the export to Pensylvania was 507,909*l.* nearly equal to the export to all the colonies together in the first period.

I choose, Sir, to enter into these minute and particular details; because generalities, which, in all other cases are apt to heighten and raise the subject, have here a tendency to sink it. When we speak of the commerce with our colonies, fiction lags after truth; invention is unfruitful, and imagination cold and barren.

So far, Sir, as to the importance of the object in the view of its commerce, as concerned in the exports from England. If I were to detail the imports, I could shew how many enjoyments they procure, which deceive the burthen of life; how many materials which invigorate the springs of national industry, and extend and animate every part of our foreign and domestick commerce. This could be a curious subject indeed — but I must prescribe bounds to myself in a matter so vast and various.

I pass therefore to the colonies in another point of view, their agriculture. This they have prosecuted with such a spirit, that, besides feeding plentifully their own growing multitude, their annual export of grain, comprehending rice, has some years ago exceeded a million in value. Of their last harvest, I am persuaded, they will export much more. At the beginning of the century, some of these colonies imported corn from the mother country. For some time past, the old world has been fed from the new. The scarcity which you have felt would have been a desolating famine, if this child of your old age, with a true filial piety, with a Roman charity, had not put the full breast of its youthful exuberance to the mouth of its exhausted parent.

As to the wealth which the colonies have drawn from the sea by their fisheries, you had all that matter fully opened at your bar. You surely thought those acquisitions of value, for they seemed even to excite your envy; and yet the spirit, by which that enterprising employment has been exercised, ought rather, in my opinion, to have raised your esteem and admiration. And pray,

Sir, what in the world is equal to it? Pass by the other parts, and look at the manner in which the people of New England have of late carried on the whale fishery. Whilst we follow them among the tumbling mountains of ice, and behold them penetrating into the deepest frozen recesses of Hudson's Bay and Davis's Streights, whilst we are looking for them beneath the arctick circle, we hear that they have pierced into the opposite region of polar cold, that they are at the antipodes, and engaged under the frozen serpent of the south. Falkland Island, which seemed too remote and romantick an object for the grasp of national ambition, is but a stage and resting-place in the progress of their victorious industry. Nor is the equinoctial heat more discouraging to them, than the accumulated winter of both the poles. We know that whilst some of them draw the line and strike the harpoon on the coast of Africa, others run the longitude, and pursue their gigantick game along the coast of Brazil. No sea but what is vexed by their fisheries. No climate that is not witness to their toils. Neither the perseverance of Holland, nor the activity of France, nor the dexterous and firm sagacity of English enterprise, ever carried this most perilous mode of hardy industry to the extent to which it has been pushed by this recent people; a people who are still, as it were, but in the gristle, and not yet hardened into the bone of manhood. When I contemplate these things; when I know that the colonies in general owe little or nothing to any care of ours, and that they are not squeezed into this happy form by the constraints of watchful and suspicious government, but that through a wise and salutary neglect, a generous nature has been suffered to take her own way to perfection; when I reflect upon these effects, when I see how profitable they have been to us, I feel all the pride of power sink, and all presumption in the wisdom of human contrivances melt, and die away within me. My rigour relents. I pardon something to the spirit of liberty.

I am sensible, Sir, that all which I have asserted, in my detail, is admitted in the gross; but that quite a different conclusion is drawn from it. America, gentlemen say, is a noble object. It is an object well worth fighting for. Certainly it is, if fighting a people be the best way of gaining them. Gentlemen in this respect will be led to their choice of means by their complexions and their habits. Those who understand the military art, will of course have some predilection for it. Those who wield the thunder of the state, may have more confidence in the efficacy of arms. But I confess, possibly for want of this knowledge, my opinion is much more in favour of prudent management, than of force; considering force not as an odious, but a feeble instrument, for preserving a people so numerous, so active, so growing, so spirited as this, in a profitable and subordinate connection with us.

First, Sir, permit me to observe, that the use of force alone is but *temporary*. It may subdue for a moment; but it does not remove the necessity of subduing again: and a nation is not governed, which is perpetually to be conquered.

My next objection is its *uncertainty*. Terrour is not always the effect of force; and an armament is not a victory. If you do not succeed, you are without resource; for, conciliation failing, force remains; but, force failing, no further hope of reconciliation is left. Power and authority are sometimes bought by kindness; but they can never be begged as alms, by an impoverished and defeated violence.

A further objection to force is, that you *impair the object* by your very endeavours to preserve it. The thing you fought for is not the thing which you recover; but depreciated, sunk, wasted, and consumed in the contest. Nothing less will content me, than *whole America*. I do not choose to consume its strength along with our own; because in all parts it is the British strength that I consume. I do not choose to be caught by a foreign enemy at the end of this exhausting conflict; and still less in the midst of it. I may escape; but I can make no insurance against such an event. Let me add, that I do not choose wholly to break the American spirit, because it is the spirit that has made the country.

Lastly, we have no sort of *experience* in favour of force as an instrument in the rule of our colonies. Their growth and their utility has been owing to methods altogether different. Our ancient indulgence has been said to be pursued to a fault. It may be so. But we know, if feeling is evidence, that our fault was more tolerable than our attempt to mend it; and our sin far more salutary than our penitence.

These, Sir, are my reasons for not entertaining that high opinion of untried force, by which many gentlemen, for whose sentiments in other particulars I have great respect, seem to be so greatly captivated. But there is still behind a third consideration concerning this object, which serves to determine my opinion on the sort of policy which ought to be pursued in the management of America, even more than its population and its commerce, I mean its *temper and character.*

In this character of the Americans, a love of freedom is the predominating feature which marks and distinguishes the whole: and as an ardent is always a jealous affection, your colonies become suspicious, restive, and untractable, whenever they see the least attempt to wrest from them by force, or shuffle from them by chicane, what they think the only advantage worth living for. This fierce spirit of liberty is stronger in the English colonies probably than in any other people of the earth; and this from a great variety of powerful causes; which, to understand the true temper of their minds, and the direction which this spirit takes, it will not be amiss to lay open somewhat more largely.

First, the people of the colonies are descendents of Englishmen. England, Sir, is a nation, which still I hope respects, and formerly adored, her freedom. The colonists emigrated from you, when this part of your character was most predominant; and they took this bias and direction the moment they parted from your hands. They are therefore not only devoted to liberty, but to liberty according to English ideas, and on English principles. Abstract liberty, like other mere abstractions, is not to be found. Liberty inheres in some sensible object; and every nation has formed to itself some favourite point, which by way of eminence becomes the criterion of their happiness. It happened, you know, Sir, that the great contests for freedom in this country were from the earliest times chiefly upon the question of taxing.

Most of the contests in the ancient commonwealths turned primarily on the right of election of magistrates; or on the balance among the several orders of the state. The question of money was not with them so immediate. But in England it was otherwise. On this point of taxes the ablest pens, and most eloquent tongues, have been exercised; the greatest spirits have acted and suffered. In order to give the fullest satisfaction concerning the importance of this point, it was not only necessary for those who in argument defended the excellence of the English constitution, to insist on this privilege of granting money as a dry point of fact, and to prove, that the right had been acknowledged in ancient parchments, and blind usages, to reside in a certain body called an house of commons. They went much further; they attempted to prove, and they succeeded, that in theory it ought to be so, from the particular nature of a house of commons, as an immediate representative of the people; whether the old records had delivered this oracle or not. They took infinite pains to inculcate, as a fundamental principle, that, in all monarchies, the people must in effect themselves mediately or immediately possess the power of granting their own money, or no shadow of liberty could subsist. The colonies draw from you, as with their life-blood, these ideas and principles. Their love of liberty, as with you, fixed and attached on this specifick point of taxing. Liberty might be safe, or might be endangered in twenty other particulars, without their being much pleased or alarmed. Here they felt its pulse; and as they found that beat, they thought themselves sick or sound. I do not say whether they were right or wrong in applying your general arguments to their own case. It is not easy indeed to make a monopoly of theorems and corollaries. The fact is, that they did thus apply those general arguments; and your mode of governing them, whether through lenity or indolence, through wisdom or mistake, confirmed them in the imagination, that they, as well as you, had an interest in these common principles.

They were further confirmed in this pleasing errour, by the form of their provincial legislative assemblies. Their governments are popular in an high degree; some are merely popular; in all, the popular representative is the most weighty; and this share of the people in their ordinary government never fails to inspire them with lofty sentiments, and with a strong aversion from whatever tends to deprive them of their chief importance.

If any thing were wanting to this necessary operation of the form of government, religion would have given it a complete effect. Religion, always a principle of energy, in this new people, is no way worn out or impaired; and their mode of professing it is also one main cause of this free spirit. The people are protestants; and of that kind, which is the most adverse to all implicit submission of mind and opinion. This is a persuasion not only favourable to liberty, but built upon it. I do not think, Sir, that the reason of this averseness in the dissenting churches from all that looks like absolute government is so much to be sought in their religious tenets, as in their history. Every one knows that the Roman Catholick religion is at least coeval with most of the governments where it prevails; that it has generally gone hand in hand with them; and received great favour and every kind of support from authority. The church of England too was formed from her cradle under the nursing care of regular government. But the dissenting interests have sprung up in direct opposition to all the ordinary powers of the world; and could justify that opposition only on a strong claim to natural liberty. Their very existence depended on the powerful and unremitted assertion of that claim. All protestantism, even the most cold and passive, is a sort of dissent. But the religion most prevalent in our northern colonies is a refinement on the principle of resistance; it is the dissidence of dissent; and the protestantism of the protestant religion. This religion, under a variety of denominations, agreeing in nothing but in the communion of the spirit of liberty, is predominant in most of the northern provinces; where the church of England, notwithstanding its legal rights, is in reality no more than a sort of private sect, not composing most probably the tenth of the people. The colonists left England when this spirit was high; and in the emigrants was the highest of all: and even that stream of foreigners, which has been constantly flowing into these colonies, has, for the greatest part, been composed of dissenters from the establishments of their several countries, and have brought with them a temper and character far from alien to that of the people with whom they mixed.

Sir, I can perceive by their manner, that some gentlemen object to the latitude of this description; because in the southern colonies the church of England forms a large body, and has a regular establishment. It is certainly true. There is however a circumstance attending these colonies, which, in my opinion, fully counterbalances this difference, and makes the spirit of liberty still more high and haughty than in those to the northward. It is that in Virginia and the Carolinas, they have a vast multitude of slaves. Where this is the case in any part of the world, those who are free, are by far the most proud and jealous of their freedom. Freedom is to them not only an enjoyment, but a kind of rank and privilege. Not seeing there, that freedom, as in countries where it is a common blessing, and as broad and general as the air, may be united with much abject toil, with great misery, with all the exterior of servitude, liberty looks, amongst them, like something that is more noble and liberal. I do not mean, Sir, to commend the superiour morality of this sentiment, which has at least as much pride as virtue in it; but I cannot alter the nature of man. The fact is so; and these people of the southern colonies are much more strongly, and with an higher and more stubborn spirit, attached to liberty than those to the northward. Such were all the ancient commonwealths; such were our Gothick ancestors; such in our days were the Poles; and such will be all masters of slaves, who are not slaves themselves. In such a people the haughtiness of domination combines with the spirit of freedom, fortifies it, and renders it invincible.

Permit me, Sir, to add another circumstance in our colonies, which contributes no mean part towards the growth and effect of this untractable spirit. I mean their education. In no country perhaps in the world is the law so general a study. The profession itself is numerous and powerful; and in most provinces it takes the lead. The greater number of the deputies sent to the congress were lawyers. But all who read, and most do read, endeavour to obtain some smattering in that science. I have been told by an eminent bookseller, that in no branch of his business, after tracts of popular devotion, were so many books as those on the law exported to the plantations. The colonists have now fallen into the way of printing them for their own use. I hear that they have sold nearly as many of Blackstone's Commentaries in America as in England. General Gage marks out this disposition very particularly in a letter on your table. He states, that all the people in his government are lawyers, or smatterers in law; and that in Boston they have been enabled, by successful chicane, wholly to evade many parts of one of your capital penal constitutions. The smartness of debate will say, that this knowledge ought to teach them more clearly the rights of legislature, their obligations to obedience, and the penalties of rebellion. All this is mighty well. But my[11] honourable and learned friend on the floor, who condescends to mark what I say for animadversion, will disdain that ground. He has heard, as well as I, that when great honours and great emoluments do not win over this knowledge to the service of the state, it is a formidable adversary to government. If the spirit be not tamed and broken by these happy methods, it is stubborn and litigious. *Abeunt studia in mores.*[12] This study renders men acute, inquisitive, dexterous, prompt in attack, ready in defence, full of resources. In other countries, the people, more simple, and of a less mercurial cast, judge of an ill principle in government only by an actual grievance; here they anticipate the evil, and judge of the pressure of the grievance by the badness of the principle. They augur misgovernment at a distance; and snuff the approach of tyranny in every tainted breeze.

The last cause of this disobedient spirit in the colonies is hardly less powerful than the rest, as it is not merely moral, but

11 The Attorney General [*Burke's note*]. Edward Thurlow (1731–1806), later first Baron Thurlow, had voted against the repeal of the Stamp Act and favored taxing the Americans. He would be appointed lord chancellor in 1778.

12 Ovid *Heroides* 15.83: "Studies go to form manners."

laid deep in the natural constitution of things. Three thousand miles of ocean lie between you and them. No contrivance can prevent the effect of this distance, in weakening government. Seas roll, and months pass, between the order and the execution: and the want of a speedy explanation of a single point, is enough to defeat a whole system. You have, indeed, winged ministers of vengeance, who carry your bolts in their pounces to the remotest verge of the sea. But there a power steps in, that limits the arrogance of raging passions and furious elements, and says, "So far shalt thou go, and no farther."[13] Who are you, that should fret and rage, and bite the chains of nature? — Nothing worse happens to you, than does to all nations, who have extensive empire; and it happens in all the forms into which empire can be thrown. In large bodies, the circulation of power must be less vigorous at the extremities. Nature has said it. The Turk cannot govern Ægypt, and Arabia, and Curdistan, as he governs Thrace; nor has he the same dominion in Crimea and Algiers, which he has at Brusa and Smyrna. Despotism itself is obliged to truck and huckster. The Sultan gets such obedience as he can. He governs with a loose rein, that he may govern at all; and the whole of the force and vigour of his authority in his centre, is derived from a prudent relaxation in all his borders. Spain, in her provinces, is, perhaps, not so well obeyed, as you are in yours. She complies too; she submits; she watches times. This is the immutable condition, the eternal law, of extensive and detached empire.

Then, Sir, from these six capital forces; of descent; of form of government; of religion in the northern provinces; of manners in the southern; of education; of the remoteness of situation from the first mover of government; from all these causes a fierce spirit of liberty has grown up. It has grown with the growth of the people in your colonies, and increased with the increase of their wealth; a spirit, that unhappily meeting with an exercise of power

13 *King Lear* 3.7.63–64: "The winged vengeance overtake such children"; Job 38.11: "Hitherto shalt thou come."

in England, which, however lawful, is not reconcileable to any ideas of liberty, much less with theirs, has kindled this flame, that is ready to consume us.

I do not mean to commend either the spirit in this excess, or the moral causes which produce it. Perhaps a more smooth and accommodating spirit of freedom in them would be more acceptable to us. Perhaps ideas of liberty might be desired, more reconcileable with an arbitrary and boundless authority. Perhaps we might wish the colonists to be persuaded, that their liberty is more secure when held in trust for them by us (as their guardians during a perpetual minority) than with any part of it in their own hands. But the question is, not whether their spirit deserves praise or blame; — what, in the name of God, shall we do with it? You have before you the object; such as it is, with all its glories, with all its imperfections on its head. You see the magnitude; the importance; the temper; the habits; the disorders. By all these considerations, we are strongly urged to determine something concerning it. We are called upon to fix some rule and line for our future conduct, which may give a little stability to our politicks, and prevent the return of such unhappy deliberations as the present. Every such return will bring the matter before us in a still more untractable form. For, what astonishing and incredible things have we not seen already? What monsters have not been generated from this unnatural contention? Whilst every principle of authority and resistance has been pushed, upon both sides, as far as it would go, there is nothing so solid and certain, either in reasoning or in practice, that has not been shaken. Until very lately, all authority in America seemed to be nothing but an emanation from yours. Even the popular part of the colony constitution derived all its activity, and its first vital movement, from the pleasure of the crown. We thought, Sir, that the utmost which the discontented colonists could do, was to disturb authority; we never dreamt they could of themselves supply it; knowing in general what an operose business it is, to establish a government absolutely new. But having, for our purposes in this contention, resolved, that none but an obedient assembly should sit, the humours of the people there, finding all passage through the legal channel stopped, with great violence broke out another way. Some provinces have tried their experiment, as we have tried ours; and theirs has succeeded. They have formed a government sufficient for its purposes, without the bustle of a revolution, or the troublesome formality of an election. Evident necessity, and tacit consent, have done the business in an instant. So well they have done it, that Lord Dunmore (the account is among the fragments on your table) tells you, that the new institution is infinitely better obeyed than the ancient government ever was in its most fortunate periods. Obedience is what makes government, and not the names by which it is called; not the name of governour, as formerly, or committee, as at present. This new government has originated directly from the people; and was not transmitted through any of the ordinary artificial media of a positive constitution. It was not a manufacture ready formed, and transmitted to them in that condition from England. The evil arising from hence is this; that the colonists having once found the possibility of enjoying the advantages of order, in the midst of a struggle for liberty, such struggles will not henceforward seem so terrible to the settled and sober part of mankind, as they had appeared before the trial.

Pursuing the same plan of punishing by the denial of the exercise of government to still greater lengths, we wholly abrogated the ancient government of Massachuset. We were confident, that the first feeling, if not the very prospect of anarchy, would instantly enforce a complete submission. The experiment was tried. A new, strange, unexpected face of things appeared. Anarchy is found tolerable. A vast province has now subsisted, and subsisted in a considerable degree of health and vigour, for near a twelvemonth, without governour, without publick council, without judges, without executive magistrates. How long it will continue in this state, or what may arise out of this unheard-of situation, how can the wisest of us conjecture? Our late experience has taught us, that many of those fundamental principles, formerly believed infallible, are either not of the importance they were imagined to be; or that we have not at all adverted to some other far more important, and far more powerful principles, which entirely over-rule those we had considered as omnipotent. I am much against any further experiments, which tend to put to the proof any more of these allowed opinions, which contribute so much to the publick tranquillity. In effect, we suffer as much at home, by this loosening of all ties, and this concussion of all established opinions, as we do abroad. For, in order to prove that the Americans have no right to their liberties, we are every day endeavouring to subvert the maxims which preserve the whole spirit of our own. To prove that the Americans ought not to be free, we are obliged to depreciate the value of freedom itself; and we never seem to gain a paltry advantage over them in debate, without attacking some of those principles, or deriding some of those feelings, for which our ancestors have shed their blood.

But, Sir, in wishing to put an end to pernicious experiments, I do not mean to preclude the fullest inquiry. Far from it. Far from deciding on a sudden or partial view, I would patiently go round and round the subject, and survey it minutely in every possible aspect. Sir, if I were capable of engaging you to an equal attention, I would state, that, as far as I am capable of discerning, there are but three ways of proceeding relative to this stubborn spirit, which prevails in your colonies, and disturbs your government. These are — To change that spirit, as inconvenient, by removing the causes. To prosecute it as criminal. Or, to comply with it as necessary. I would not be guilty of an imperfect enumeration; I can think of but these three. Another has indeed been started, that of giving up the colonies; but it met so slight a reception, that I do not think myself obliged to dwell a great while upon it. It is nothing but a little sally of anger, like the frowardness of peevish children, who, when they cannot get all they would have, are resolved to take nothing.

The first of these plans, to change the spirit as inconvenient, by removing the causes, I think is the most like a systematick proceeding. It is radical in its principle; but it is attended with

great difficulties, some of them little short, as I conceive, of im-
possibilities. This will appear by examining into the plans which
have been proposed.

As the growing population of the colonies is evidently one
cause of their resistance, it was last session mentioned in both
houses, by men of weight, and received not without applause,
that, in order to check this evil, it would be proper for the crown
to make no further grants of land. But to this scheme there are
two objections. The first, that there is already so much unsettled
land in private hands, as to afford room for immense future
population, although the crown not only withheld its grants, but
annihilated its soil. If this be the case, then the only effect of this
avarice of desolation, this hoarding of a royal wilderness, would
be to raise the value of the possessions in the hands of the great
private monopolists, without any adequate check to the growing
and alarming mischief of population.

But if you stopped your grants, what would be the consequence? The people would occupy without grants. They have
already so occupied in many places. You cannot station garrisons in every part of these deserts. If you drive the people from
one place, they will carry on their annual tillage, and remove
with their flocks and herds to another. Many of the people in the
back settlements are already little attached to particular situations. Already they have topped the Apalachian mountains. From
thence they behold before them an immense plain, one vast,
rich, level meadow; a square of five hundred miles. Over this
they would wander, without a possibility of restraint; they would
change their manners with the habits of their life; would soon
forget a government, by which they were disowned; would become hordes of English Tartars; and, pouring down upon your
unfortified frontiers a fierce and irresistible cavalry, become masters of your governours and your counsellors, your collectors and
comptrollers, and of all the slaves that adhered to them. Such
would, and, in no long time, must be, the effect of attempting to
forbid as a crime, and to suppress as an evil, the command and

blessing of Providence, "Increase and multiply." Such would be the happy result of an endeavour to keep as a lair of wild beasts, that earth, which God, by an express charter, has given to the children of men. Far different, and surely much wiser, has been our policy hitherto. Hitherto we have invited our people by every kind of bounty, to fixed establishments. We have invited the husbandman to look to authority for his title. We have taught him piously to believe in the mysterious virtue of wax and parchment. We have thrown each tract of land, as it was peopled, into districts; that the ruling power should never be wholly out of sight. We have settled all we could; and we have carefully attended every settlement with government.

Adhering, Sir, as I do, to this policy, as well as for the reasons I have just given, I think this new project of hedging-in population to be neither prudent nor practicable.

To impoverish the colonies in general, and in particular to arrest the noble course of their marine enterprises, would be a more easy task. I freely confess it. We have shewn a disposition to a system of this kind; a disposition even to continue the restraint after the offence; looking on ourselves as rivals to our colonies, and persuaded that of course we must gain all that they shall lose. Much mischief we may certainly do. The power inadequate to all other things is often more than sufficient for this. I do not look on the direct and immediate power of the colonies to resist our violence, as very formidable. In this, however, I may be mistaken. But when I consider, that we have colonies for no purpose but to be serviceable to us, it seems to my poor understanding a little preposterous, to make them unserviceable, in order to keep them obedient. It is, in truth, nothing more than the old, and, as I thought, exploded problem of tyranny, which proposes to beggar its subjects into submission. But remember, when you have completed your system of impoverishment, that nature still proceeds in her ordinary course; that discontent will increase with misery; and that there are critical moments in the fortune of all states, when they who are too weak to contribute to your prosperity, may be strong enough to complete your ruin. *Spoliatis arma supersunt.*[14]

The temper and character, which prevail in our colonies, are, I am afraid, unalterable by any human art. We cannot, I fear, falsify the pedigree of this fierce people, and persuade them that they are not sprung from a nation, in whose veins the blood of freedom circulates. The language in which they would hear you tell them this tale, would detect the imposition; your speech would betray you. An Englishman is the unfittest person on earth to argue another Englishman into slavery.

I think it is nearly as little in our power to change their republican religion, as their free descent; or to substitute the Roman Catholick, as a penalty; or the Church of England, as an improvement. The mode of inquisition and dragooning is going out of fashion in the old world; and I should not confide much to their efficacy in the new. The education of the Americans is also on the same unalterable bottom with their religion. You cannot persuade them to burn their books of curious science; to banish their lawyers from the courts of law; or to quench the lights of their assemblies, by refusing to choose those persons who are best read in their privileges. It would be no less impracticable to think of wholly annihilating the popular assemblies, in which these lawyers sit. The army, by which we must govern in their place, would be far more chargeable to us; not quite so effectual; and perhaps, in the end, full as difficult to be kept in obedience.

With regard to the high aristocratick spirit of Virginia and the southern colonies, it has been proposed, I know, to reduce it, by declaring a general enfranchisement of their slaves. This project has had its advocates and panegyrists; yet I never could argue myself into any opinion of it. Slaves are often much attached to their masters. A general wild offer of liberty, would not always be accepted. History furnishes few instances of it. It is sometimes as hard to persuade slaves to be free, as it is to compel freemen to

14 Juvenal *Satires* 8.124: "Though plundered, they will still have their arms."

be slaves: and in this auspicious scheme, we should have both these pleasing tasks on our hands at once. But when we talk of enfranchisement, do we not perceive that the American master may enfranchise too; and arm servile hands in defence of freedom? A measure to which other people have had recourse more than once, and not without success, in a desperate situation of their affairs.

Slaves as these unfortunate black people are, and dull as all men are from slavery, must they not a little suspect the offer of freedom from that very nation which has sold them to their present masters? From that nation, one of whose causes of quarrel with those masters, is their refusal to deal any more in that inhuman traffick? An offer of freedom from England, would come rather oddly, shipped to them in an African vessel, which is refused an entry into the ports of Virginia or Carolina, with a cargo of three hundred Angola negroes. It would be curious to see the Guinea captain attempting at the same instant to publish his proclamation of liberty, and to advertise his sale of slaves.

But let us suppose all these moral difficulties got over. The ocean remains. You cannot pump this dry; and as long as it continues in its present bed, so long all the causes which weaken authority by distance will continue. "Ye gods, annihilate but space and time, and make two lovers happy!" [15] — was a pious and passionate prayer; — but just as reasonable, as many of the serious wishes of very grave and solemn politicians.

If then, Sir, it seems almost desperate to think of any alterative course, for changing the moral causes (and not quite easy to remove the natural) which produce prejudices irreconcileable to the late exercise of our authority; but that the spirit infallibly will continue; and, continuing, will produce such effects, as now embarrass us; the second mode under consideration is, to prosecute that spirit in its overt acts, as *criminal.*

At this proposition, I must pause a moment. The thing seems

---

15 Pope, *Peri Bathous*, ch. 11; a parody of Herculean bombast in the manner of Dryden's tragedies.

a great deal too big for my ideas of jurisprudence. It should seem, to my way of conceiving such matters, that there is a very wide difference in reason and policy, between the mode of proceeding on the irregular conduct of scattered individuals, or even of bands of men, who disturb order within the state, and the civil dissentions which may, from time to time, on great questions, agitate the several communities which compose a great empire. It looks to me to be narrow and pedantick, to apply the ordinary ideas of criminal justice to this great publick contest. I do not know the method of drawing up an indictment against an whole people. I cannot insult and ridicule the feelings of millions of my fellow creatures, as Sir Edward Coke insulted one excellent individual (Sir Walter Raleigh) at the bar. I am not ripe to pass sentence on the gravest publick bodies, entrusted with magistracies of great authority and dignity, and charged with the safety of their fellow-citizens, upon the very same title that I am. I really think, that for wise men this is not judicious; for sober men, not decent; for minds tinctured with humanity, not mild and merciful.

Perhaps, Sir, I am mistaken in my idea of an empire, as distinguished from a single state or kingdom. But my idea of it is this; that an empire is the aggregate of many states, under one common head; whether this head be a monarch, or a presiding republick. It does, in such constitutions, frequently happen (and nothing but the dismal, cold, dead uniformity of servitude can prevent its happening) that the subordinate parts have many local privileges and immunities. Between these privileges, and the supreme common authority, the line may be extremely nice. Of course disputes, often too, very bitter disputes, and much ill blood, will arise. But though every privilege is an exemption (in the case) from the ordinary exercise of the supreme authority, it is no denial of it. The claim of a privilege seems rather *ex vi termini*,[16] to imply a superiour power. For to talk of the privileges of a state or of a person, who has no superiour, is hardly any

16 "From the very meaning of the word."

better than speaking nonsense. Now, in such unfortunate quarrels, among the component parts of a great political union of communities, I can scarcely conceive any thing more completely imprudent, than for the head of the empire to insist, that, if any privilege is pleaded against his will, or his acts, that his whole authority is denied; instantly to proclaim rebellion, to beat to arms, and to put the offending provinces under the ban. Will not this, Sir, very soon teach the provinces to make no distinctions on their part? Will it not teach them that the government, against which a claim of liberty is tantamount to high treason, is a government to which submission is equivalent to slavery? It may not always be quite convenient to impress dependent communities with such an idea.

We are indeed, in all disputes with the colonies, by the necessity of things, the judge. It is true, Sir. But I confess, that the character of judge in my own cause, is a thing that frightens me. Instead of filling me with pride, I am exceedingly humbled by it. I cannot proceed with a stern, assured, judicial confidence, until I find myself in something more like a judicial character. I must have these hesitations as long as I am compelled to recollect, that, in my little reading upon such contests as these, the sense of mankind has, at least, as often decided against the superiour as the subordinate power. Sir, let me add too, that the opinion of my having some abstract right in my favour would not put me much at my ease in passing sentence; unless I could be sure, that there were no rights which, in their exercise under certain circumstances, were not the most odious of all wrongs, and the most vexatious of all injustice. Sir, these considerations have great weight with me, when I find things so circumstanced, that I see the same party, at once a civil litigant against me in point of right, and a culprit before me; while I sit as criminal judge, on acts of his, whose moral quality is to be decided upon the merits of that very litigation. Men are every now and then put, by the complexity of human affairs, into strange situations; but justice is the same, let the judge be in what situation he will.

There is, Sir, also a circumstance which convinces me, that

this mode of criminal proceeding is not (at least in the present stage of our contest) altogether expedient; which is nothing less than the conduct of those very persons who have seemed to adopt that mode, by lately declaring a rebellion in Massachuset's Bay, as they had formerly addressed to have traitors brought hither under an act of Henry the Eighth, for trial. For though rebellion is declared, it is not proceeded against as such; nor have any steps been taken towards the apprehension or conviction of any individual offender, either on our late or our former address; but modes of public coercion have been adopted, and such as have much more resemblance to a sort of qualified hostility towards an independent power than the punishment of rebellious subjects. All this seems rather inconsistent; but it shews how difficult it is to apply these juridical ideas to our present case.

In this situation, let us seriously and coolly ponder. What is it we have got by all our menaces, which have been many and ferocious? What advantage have we derived from the penal laws we have passed, and which, for the time, have been severe and numerous? What advances have we made towards our object, by the sending of a force, which, by land and sea, is no contemptible strength? Has the disorder abated? Nothing less.—When I see things in this situation, after such confident hopes, bold promises, and active exertions, I cannot, for my life, avoid a suspicion, that the plan itself is not correctly right.

If then the removal of the causes of this spirit of American liberty be, for the greater part, or rather entirely, impracticable; if the ideas of criminal process be inapplicable, or, if applicable, are in the highest degree inexpedient, what way yet remains? No way is open, but the third and last—to comply with the American spirit as necessary; or, if you please to submit to it, as a necessary evil.

If we adopt this mode, if we mean to conciliate and concede; let us see of what nature the concession ought to be: to ascertain the nature of our concession, we must look at their complaint. The colonies complain, that they have not the characteristick mark and seal of British freedom. They complain, that they are taxed in a parliament, in which they are not represented. If you mean to satisfy them at all, you must satisfy them with regard to this complaint. If you mean to please any people, you must give them the boon which they ask; not what you may think better for them, but of a kind totally different. Such an act may be a wise regulation, but it is no concession; whereas our present theme is the mode of giving satisfaction.

Sir, I think you must perceive, that I am resolved this day to have nothing at all to do with the question of the right of taxation. Some gentlemen startle — but it is true: I put it totally out of the question. It is less than nothing in my consideration. I do not indeed wonder, nor will you, Sir, that gentlemen of profound learning are fond of displaying it on this profound subject. But my consideration is narrow, confined, and wholly limited to the policy of the question. I do not examine, whether the giving away a man's money be a power excepted and reserved out of the general trust of government; and how far all mankind, in all forms of polity, are entitled to an exercise of that right by the charter of nature. Or whether, on the contrary, a right of taxation is necessarily involved in the general principle of legislation, and inseparable from the ordinary supreme power. These are deep questions, where great names militate against each other; where reason is perplexed; and an appeal to authorities only thickens the confusion. For high and reverend authorities lift up their heads on both sides; and there is no sure footing in the middle. This point is the *great Serbonian bog, betwixt Damiata and Mount Casius old, where armies whole have sunk.*[17] I do not intend to be overwhelmed in that bog, though in such respectable company. The question with me is, not whether you have a right to render your people miserable; but whether it is not your interest to make them happy. It is not, what a lawyer tells me, I *may* do; but what humanity, reason, and justice, tell me, I ought to do. Is a politick act the worse for being a generous one? Is no concession proper, but that which is made from your want of right to

17 *Paradise Lost* 2.592–94.

keep what you grant? Or does it lessen the grace or dignity of relaxing in the exercise of an odious claim, because you have your evidence-room full of titles, and your magazines stuffed with arms to enforce them? What signify all those titles, and all those arms? Of what avail are they, when the reason of the thing tells me, that the assertion of my title is the loss of my suit; and that I could do nothing but wound myself by the use of my own weapons?

Such is stedfastly my opinion of the absolute necessity of keeping up the concord of this empire by a unity of spirit, though in a diversity of operations, that, if I were sure the colonists had, at their leaving this country, sealed a regular compact of servitude; that they had solemnly abjured all the rights of citizens; that they had made a vow to renounce all ideas of liberty for them and their posterity, to all generations, yet I should hold myself obliged to conform to the temper I found universally prevalent in my own day, and to govern two million of men, impatient of servitude, on the principles of freedom. I am not determining a point of law; I am restoring tranquillity; and the general character and situation of a people must determine what sort of government is fitted for them. That point nothing else can or ought to determine.

My idea therefore, without considering whether we yield as matter of right, or grant as matter of favour, is *to admit the people of our colonies into an interest in the constitution*; and, by recording that admission in the journals of parliament, to give them as strong an assurance as the nature of the thing will admit, that we mean for ever to adhere to that solemn declaration of systematick indulgence.

Some years ago, the repeal of a revenue act, upon its understood principle, might have served to shew, that we intended an unconditional abatement of the exercise of a taxing power. Such a measure was then sufficient to remove all suspicion, and to give perfect content.[18] But unfortunate events, since that time, may

---

18   Referring to the repeal of the Stamp Act (1766); the Declaratory Act simultaneously reaffirmed the right of Parliament to tax the colonies.

make something further necessary; and not more necessary for the satisfaction of the colonies, than for the dignity and consistency of our own future proceedings.

I have taken a very incorrect measure of the disposition of the house, if this proposal in itself would be received with dislike. I think, Sir, we have few American financiers. But our misfortune is, we are too acute; we are too exquisite in our conjectures of the future, for men oppressed with such great and present evils. The more moderate among the opposers of parliamentary concession freely confess, that they hope no good from taxation; but they apprehend the colonists have further views; and if this point were conceded, they would instantly attack the trade-laws. These gentlemen are convinced, that this was the intention from the beginning; and the quarrel of the Americans with taxation was no more than a cloke and cover to this design. Such has been the language even of a[19] gentleman of real moderation, and of a natural temper so well adjusted to fair and equal government. I am, however, Sir, not a little surprised at this kind of discourse, whenever I hear it; and I am the more surprised, on account of the arguments which I constantly find in company with it, and which are often urged from the same mouths, and on the same day.

For instance, when we allege, that it is against reason to tax a people under so many restraints in trade as the Americans, the[20] noble Lord in the blue ribband shall tell you, that the restraints on trade are futile and useless; of no advantage to us, and of no burthen to those on whom they are imposed; that the trade to America is not secured by the acts of navigation, but by the natural and irresistible advantage of a commercial preference.

Such is the merit of the trade laws in this posture of the debate. But when strong internal circumstances are urged against

19 Mr. Rice [*Burke's note*]. George Rice (ca. 1724–79), who had voted against the repeal of the Stamp Act and opposed concessions to the colonies, said on 6 March that he would favor a lightening of taxation if he could be sure it would not lead to fiercer resistance.

20 Lord North [*Burke's note*].

the taxes; when the scheme is dissected; when experience and the nature of things are brought to prove, and do prove, the utter impossibility of obtaining an effective revenue from the colonies; when these things are pressed, or rather press themselves, so as to drive the advocates of colony taxes to a clear admission of the futility of the scheme; then, Sir, the sleeping trade laws revive from their trance; and this useless taxation is to be kept sacred, not for its own sake, but as a counter-guard and security of the laws of trade.

Then, Sir, you keep up revenue laws which are mischievous, in order to preserve trade laws that are useless. Such is the wisdom of our plan in both its members. They are separately given up as of no value, and yet one is always to be defended for the sake of the other. But I cannot agree with the noble lord, nor with the pamphlet from whence he seems to have borrowed these ideas, concerning the inutility of the trade laws. For without idolizing them, I am sure they are still, in many ways, of great use to us; and in former times, they have been of the greatest. They do confine, and they do greatly narrow, the market for the Americans. But my perfect conviction of this, does not help me in the least to discern how the revenue laws form any security whatsoever to the commercial regulations; or that these commercial regulations are the true ground of the quarrel; or, that the giving way in any one instance of authority, is to lose all that may remain unconceded.

One fact is clear and indisputable. The publick and avowed origin of this quarrel, was on taxation. This quarrel has indeed brought on new disputes on new questions; but certainly the least bitter, and the fewest of all, on the trade laws. To judge which of the two be the real radical cause of quarrel, we have to see whether the commercial dispute did, in order of time, precede the dispute on taxation? There is not a shadow of evidence for it. Next, to enable us to judge whether at this moment a dislike to the trade laws be the real cause of quarrel, it is absolutely necessary to put the taxes out of the question by a repeal. See how the Americans act in this position, and then you will be able to discern correctly what is the true object of the controversy, or whether any controversy at all will remain? Unless you consent to remove this cause of difference, it is impossible, with decency, to assert that the dispute is not upon what it is avowed to be. And I would, Sir, recommend to your serious consideration, whether it be prudent to form a rule for punishing people, not on their own acts, but on your conjectures? Surely it is preposterous at the very best. It is not justifying your anger, by their misconduct; but it is converting your ill-will into their delinquency.

But the colonies will go further. —Alas! alas! when will this speculating against fact and reason end? —What will quiet these panick fears which we entertain of the hostile effect of a conciliatory conduct? Is it true, that no case can exist, in which it is proper for the sovereign to accede to the desires of his discontented subjects? Is there any thing peculiar in this case, to make a rule for itself? Is all authority of course lost, when it is not pushed to the extreme? Is it a certain maxim, that, the fewer causes of dissatisfaction are left by government, the more the subject will be inclined to resist and rebel?

All these objections being in fact no more than suspicions, conjectures, divinations, formed in defiance of fact and experience; they did not, Sir, discourage me from entertaining the idea of a conciliatory concession, founded on the principles which I have just stated.

In forming a plan for this purpose, I endeavoured to put myself in that frame of mind, which was the most natural, and the most reasonable; and which was certainly the most probable means of securing me from all errour. I set out with a perfect distrust of my own abilities; a total renunciation of every speculation of my own; and with a profound reverence for the wisdom of our ancestors, who have left us the inheritance of so happy a constitution, and so flourishing an empire, and what is a thousand times more valuable, the treasury of the maxims and principles which formed the one, and obtained the other.

During the reigns of the kings of Spain of the Austrian family, whenever they were at a loss in the Spanish councils, it was common for their statesmen to say, that they ought to consult the genius of Philip the Second. The genius of Philip the Second might mislead them; and the issue of their affairs shewed, that they had not chosen the most perfect standard. But, Sir, I am sure that I shall not be misled, when, in a case of constitutional difficulty, I consult the genius of the English constitution. Consulting at that oracle (it was with all due humility and piety) I found four capital examples in a similar case before me: those of Ireland, Wales, Chester, and Durham.

Ireland, before the English conquest, though never governed by a despotick power, had no parliament. How far the English parliament itself was at that time modelled according to the present form, is disputed among antiquaries. But we have all the reason in the world to be assured, that a form of parliament, such as England then enjoyed, she instantly communicated to Ireland; and we are equally sure that almost every successive improvement in constitutional liberty, as fast as it was made here, was transmitted thither. The feudal baronage, and the feudal knighthood, the roots of our primitive constitution, were early transplanted into that soil; and grew and flourished there. Magna Charta, if it did not give us originally the house of commons, gave us at least a house of commons of weight and consequence. But your ancestors did not churlishly sit down alone to the feast of Magna Charta. Ireland was made immediately a partaker. This benefit of English laws and liberties, I confess, was not at first extended to *all* Ireland. Mark the consequence. English authority and English liberty had exactly the same boundaries. Your standard could never be advanced an inch before your privileges. Sir John Davis shews beyond a doubt, that the refusal of a general communication of these rights, was the true cause why Ireland was five hundred years in subduing; and after the vain projects of a military government, attempted in the reign of Queen Elizabeth, it was soon discovered, that nothing could make that country English, in civility and allegiance, but your laws and your forms of legislature. It was not English arms, but the English constitution, that conquered Ireland. From that time, Ireland has ever had a general parliament, as she had before a partial parliament. You changed the people; you altered the religion; but you never touched the form or the vital substance of free government in that kingdom. You deposed kings; you restored them; you altered the succession to theirs, as well as to your own crown; but you never altered their constitution; the principle of which was respected by usurpation; restored with the restoration of monarchy, and established, I trust, for ever, by the glorious Revolution. This has made Ireland the great and flourishing kingdom that it is; and from a disgrace and a burthen intolerable to this nation, has rendered her a principal part of our strength and ornament. This country cannot be said to have ever formally taxed her. The irregular things done in the confusion of mighty troubles, and on the hinge of great revolutions, even if all were done that is said to have been done, form no example. If they have any effect in argument, they make an exception to prove the rule. None of your own liberties could stand a moment if the casual deviations from them, at such times, were suffered to be used as proofs of their nullity. By the lucrative amount of such casual breaches in the constitution, judge what the stated and fixed rule of supply has been in that kingdom. Your Irish pensioners would starve, if they had no other fund to live on than taxes granted by English authority. Turn your eyes to those popular grants from whence all your great supplies are come; and learn to respect that only source of publick wealth in the British empire.

My next example is Wales. This country was said to be reduced by Henry the Third. It was said more truly to be so by Edward the First. But though then conquered, it was not looked upon as any part of the realm of England. Its old constitution, whatever that might have been, was destroyed; and no good one was substituted in its place. The care of that tract was put into the hands of lords marchers — a form of government of a very singular kind; a strange heterogeneous monster, something between hostility and government; perhaps it has a sort of resemblance, according to the modes of those times, to that of commander in chief at present, to whom all civil power is granted as secondary. The manners of the Welsh nation followed the genius of the government; the people were ferocious, restive, savage, and uncultivated; sometimes composed, never pacified. Wales within itself, was in perpetual disorder; and it kept the frontier of England in perpetual alarm. Benefits from it to the state, there were none. Wales was only known to England by incursion and invasion.

Sir, during that state of things, parliament was not idle. They attempted to subdue the fierce spirit of the Welsh by all sorts of rigorous laws. They prohibited by statute the sending all sorts of arms into Wales, as you prohibit by proclamation (with something more of doubt on the legality) the sending arms to America. They disarmed the Welsh by statute, as you attempted, (but still with more question on the legality) to disarm New England by an instruction. They made an act to drag offenders from Wales into England for trial, as you have done (but with more hardship) with regard to America. By another act, where one of the parties was an Englishman, they ordained, that his trial should be always by English. They made acts to restrain trade, as you do; and they prevented the Welsh from the use of fairs and markets, as you do the Americans from fisheries and foreign ports. In short, when the statute-book was not quite so much swelled as it is now, you find no less than fifteen acts of penal regulation on the subject of Wales.

Here we rub our hands—A fine body of precedents for the authority of parliament and the use of it!—I admit it fully; and pray add likewise to these precedents, that all the while, Wales rid this kingdom like an *incubus*; that it was an unprofitable and oppressive burthen; and that an Englishman travelling in that country could not go six yards from the high road without being murdered.

The march of the human mind is slow. Sir, it was not, until after two hundred years, discovered, that by an eternal law, Providence had decreed vexation to violence; and poverty to rapine.

Your ancestors did however at length open their eyes to the ill husbandry of injustice. They found that the tyranny of a free people could of all tyrannies the least be endured; and that laws made against a whole nation were not the most effectual methods for securing its obedience. Accordingly, in the twenty-seventh year of Henry VIII. the course was entirely altered. With a preamble stating the entire and perfect rights of the crown of England, it gave to the Welsh all the rights and privileges of English subjects. A political order was established; the military power gave way to the civil; the marches were turned into counties. But that a nation should have a right to English liberties, and yet no share at all in the fundamental security of these liberties, the grant of their own property, seemed a thing so incongruous; that eight years after, that is, in the thirty-fifth of that reign, a complete and not ill-proportioned representation by counties and boroughs was bestowed upon Wales, by act of parliament. From that moment, as by a charm, the tumults subsided; obedience was restored; peace, order, and civilization, followed in the train of liberty—When the day-star of the English constitution had arisen in their hearts, all was harmony within and without—

> *Simul alba nautis*
> *Stella refulsit,*
> *Defluit saxis agitatus humor:*
> *Concidunt venti, fugiúntque nubes:*
> *Et minax (quòd sic voluere) ponto*
> *Unda recumbit.*[21]

The very same year the county palatine of Chester received the same relief from its oppressions, and the same remedy to its disorders. Before this time Chester was little less distempered than Wales. The inhabitants, without rights themselves, were the fittest to destroy the rights of others; and from thence Richard II.

---

21 Horace *Odes* 1.12.27–32: "As soon their clear star [Castor and Pollux] shines out for sailors, the crashing water is sucked back from the rocks: the winds die down, the clouds depart at once: and the threatening wave (because they have willed it so) falls gently into the sea."

drew the standing army of archers, with which for a time he oppressed England. The people of Chester applied to parliament in a petition penned as I shall read to you.

"To the king our sovereign lord, in most humble wise shewn unto your excellent majesty, the inhabitants of your grace's county palatine of Chester; That where the said county palatine of Chester is and hath been always hitherto exempt, excluded and separated out and from your high court of parliament, to have any knights and burgesses within the said court; by reason whereof the said inhabitants have hitherto sustained manifold disherisons, losses, and damages, as well in their lands, goods, and bodies, as in the good, civil, and politick governance and maintenance of the commonwealth of their said country: (2.) And for as much as the said inhabitants have always hitherto been bound by the acts and statutes made and ordained by your said highness, and your most noble progenitors, by authority of the said court, as far forth as other counties, cities, and boroughs have been, that have had their knights and burgesses within your said court of parliament, and yet have had neither knight ne burgess there for the said county palatine; the said inhabitants, for lack thereof, have been oftentimes touched and grieved with acts and statutes made within the said court, as well derogatory unto the most ancient jurisdictions, liberties and privileges of your said county palatine, as prejudicial unto the common wealth, quietness, rest, and peace of your grace's most bounden subjects inhabiting within the same."

What did parliament with this audacious address? — Reject it as a libel? Treat it as an affront to government? Spurn it as a derogation from the rights of legislature? Did they toss it over the table? Did they burn it by the hands of the common hangman? — They took the petition of grievance, all rugged as it was, without softening or temperament, unpurged of the original bitterness and indignation of complaint; they made it the very preamble to their act of redress; and consecrated its principle to all ages in the sanctuary of legislation.

Here is my third example. It was attended with the success of the two former. Chester, civilised as well as Wales, has demonstrated that freedom and not servitude is the cure of anarchy; as religion, and not atheism, is the true remedy for superstition. Sir, this pattern of Chester was followed in the reign of Charles II. with regard to the county palatine of Durham, which is my fourth example. This county had long lain out of the pale of free legislation. So scrupulously was the example of Chester followed, that the style of the preamble is nearly the same with that of the Chester act; and without affecting the abstract extent of the authority of parliament, it recognizes the equity of not suffering any considerable district in which the British subjects may act as a body, to be taxed without their own voice in the grant.

Now if the doctrines of policy contained in these preambles, and the force of these examples in the acts of parliament, avail any thing, what can be said against applying them with regard to America? Are not the people of America as much Englishmen as the Welsh? The preamble of the act of Henry VIII. says, the Welsh speak a language no way resembling that of his majesty's English subjects. Are the Americans not as numerous? If we may trust the learned and accurate Judge Barrington's account of North Wales, and take that as a standard to measure the rest, there is no comparison. The people cannot amount to above 200,000; not a tenth part of the number in the colonies. Is America in rebellion? Wales was hardly ever free from it. Have you attempted to govern America by penal statutes? You made fifteen for Wales. But your legislative authority is perfect with regard to America; was it less perfect in Wales, Chester, and Durham? But America is virtually represented. What! does the electrick force of virtual representation more easily pass over the Atlantick, than pervade Wales, which lies in your neighbourhood; or than Chester and Durham, surrounded by abundance of representation that is actual and palpable? But, Sir, your ancestors thought this sort of virtual representation, however ample, to be totally insufficient for the freedom of the inhabitants of territories that are so near, and

comparatively so inconsiderable. How then can I think it sufficient for those which are infinitely greater, and infinitely more
remote?

You will now, Sir, perhaps imagine, that I am on the point of
proposing to you a scheme for a representation of the colonies
in parliament. Perhaps I might be inclined to entertain some
such thought; but a great flood stops me in my course. *Opposuit
natura*[22] — I cannot remove the eternal barriers of the creation.
The thing in that mode, I do not know to be possible. As I
meddle with no theory, I do not absolutely assert the imprac-
ticability of such a representation. But I do not see my way to it;
and those who have been more confident, have not been more
successful. However, the arm of publick benevolence is not
shortened; and there are often several means to the same end.
What nature has disjoined in one way, wisdom may unite in another. When we cannot give the benefit as we would wish, let us
not refuse it altogether. If we cannot give the principal, let us
find a substitute. But how? Where? What substitute?

Fortunately I am not obliged for the ways and means of this
substitute to tax my own unproductive invention. I am not even
obliged to go to the rich treasury of the fertile framers of imaginary commonwealths; not to the Republick of Plato, not to the
Utopia of More; not to the Oceana of Harrington. It is before
me — It is at my feet, *and the rude swain treads daily on it with his
clouted shoon.*[23] I only wish you to recognize, for the theory, the
ancient constitutional policy of this kingdom with regard to representation, as that policy has been declared in acts of parliament; and, as to the practice, to return to that mode which an
uniform experience has marked out to you, as best; and in which
you walked with security, advantage, and honour, until the year
1763.[24]

22 Juvenal *Satires* 10.152: "Nature stands in the way."
23 Milton *Comus* 634–35.
24 Marking the end of the Seven Years War, after which the Sugar Act and
Stamp Act were passed, in 1764, to secure revenues independently of the colonial
assemblies.

My resolutions therefore mean to establish the equity, and justice of a taxation of America, by *grant*, and not by *imposition*. To mark the *legal competency* of the colony assemblies for the support of their government in peace, and for publick aids in time of war. To acknowledge that this legal competency has had *a dutiful and beneficial exercise*; and that experience has shewn the *benefit of their grants*, and the *futility of parliamentary taxation as a method of supply*.

These solid truths compose six fundamental propositions. There are three more resolutions corollary to these. If you admit the first set, you can hardly reject the others. But if you admit the first, I shall be far from solicitous whether you accept or refuse the last. I think these six massive pillars will be of strength sufficient to support the temple of British concord. I have no more doubt than I entertain of my existence, that, if you admitted these, you would command an immediate peace, and with but tolerable future management, a lasting obedience in America. I am not arrogant in this confident assurance. The propositions are all mere matters of fact; and if they are such facts as draw irresistible conclusions even in the stating, this is the power of truth, and not any management of mine.

Sir, I shall open the whole plan to you together, with such observations on the motions as may tend to illustrate them where they may want explanation. The first is a resolution — "That the colonies and plantations of Great Britain in North America, consisting of fourteen separate governments, and containing two millions and upwards of free inhabitants, have not had the liberty and privilege of electing and sending any knights and burgesses, or others to represent them in the high court of parliament." — This is a plain matter of fact, necessary to be laid down, and (excepting the description) it is laid down in the language of the constitution; it is taken nearly *verbatim* from acts of parliament.

The second is like unto the first — "That the said colonies and plantations have been liable to, and bounden by, several subsidies, payments, rates, and taxes, given and granted by parliament, though the said colonies and plantations have not their knights and burgesses, in the said high court of parliament, of their own election, to represent the condition of their country; by lack whereof they have been oftentimes touched and grieved by subsidies given, granted, and assented to, in the said court, in a manner prejudicial to the common wealth, quietness, rest, and peace of the subjects inhabiting within the same."

Is this description too hot, or too cold, too strong, or too weak? Does it arrogate too much to the supreme legislature? Does it lean too much to the claims of the people? If it runs into any of these errours, the fault is not mine. It is the language of your own ancient acts of parliament. *Non meus hic sermo, sed quæ præcepit Ofellus, rusticus, abnormis sapiens.*[25] It is the genuine produce of the ancient, rustick, manly, home-bred sense of this country. — I did not dare to rub off a particle of the venerable rust that rather adorns and preserves, than destroys the metal. It would be a profanation to touch with a tool the stones which construct the sacred altar of peace. I would not violate with modern polish the ingenuous and noble roughness of these truly constitutional materials. Above all things, I was resolved not to be guilty of tampering, the odious vice of restless and unstable minds. I put my foot in the tracks of our forefathers; where I can neither wander nor stumble. Determining to fix articles of peace, I was resolved not to be wise beyond what was written; I was resolved to use nothing else than the form of found words; to let others abound in their own sense; and carefully to abstain from all expressions of my own. What the law has said, I say. In all things else I am silent. I have no organ but for her words. This, if it be not ingenious, I am sure is safe.

There are indeed words expressive of grievance in this second resolution, which those who are resolved always to be in the right, will deny to contain matter of fact, as applied to the present case; although parliament thought them true, with regard to the counties of Chester and Durham. They will deny that the Ameri-

---

25 Horace *Satires* 2.2.2–3: "This is not my talk, but the teaching of Ofellus, a peasant full of shrewd practical wisdom."

cans were ever "touched and grieved" with the taxes. If they consider nothing in taxes but their weight as pecuniary impositions, there might be some pretence for this denial. But men may be sorely touched and deeply grieved in their privileges, as well as in their purses. Men may lose little in property by the act which takes away all their freedom. When a man is robbed of a trifle on the highway, it is not the two-pence lost that constitutes the capital outrage. This is not confined to privileges. Even ancient indulgences withdrawn, without offence on the part of those who enjoyed such favours, operate as grievances. But were the Americans then not touched and grieved by the taxes, in some measure, merely as taxes? If so, why were they almost all, either wholly repealed or exceedingly reduced? Were they not touched and grieved, even by the regulating duties of the sixth of George II? Else why were the duties first reduced to one third in 1764, and afterwards to a third of that third in the year 1766? Were they not touched and grieved by the stamp act? I shall say they were, until that tax is revived. Were they not touched and grieved by the duties of 1767, which were likewise repealed, and which, Lord Hillsborough tells you (for the ministry) were laid contrary to the true principle of commerce? Is not the assurance given by that noble person to the colonies of a resolution to lay no more taxes on them, an admission that taxes would touch and grieve them? Is not the resolution of the noble lord in the blue ribband, now standing on your journals, the strongest of all proofs that parliamentary subsidies really touched and grieved them? Else why all these changes, modifications, repeals, assurances, and resolutions?

The next proposition is — "That, from the distance of the said colonies, and from other circumstances, no method hath hitherto been devised for procuring a representation in parliament for the said colonies." This is an assertion of a fact. I go no further on the paper; though in my private judgment, an useful representation is impossible; I am sure it is not desired by them; nor ought it perhaps by us; but I abstain from opinions.

The fourth resolution is — "That each of the said colonies

hath within itself a body, chosen in part, or in the whole, by the freemen, freeholders, ,or other free inhabitants thereof, commonly called the General Assembly, or General Court, with powers legally to raise, levy, and assess, according to the several usage of such colonies, duties and taxes towards defraying all sorts of publick services."

This competence in the colony assemblies is certain. It is proved by the whole tenour of their acts of supply in all the assemblies, in which the constant style of granting is, "an aid to his majesty;" and acts granting to the crown have regularly for near a century passed the publick offices without dispute. Those who have been pleased paradoxically to deny this right, holding that none but the British parliament can grant to the crown, are wished to look to what is done, not only in the colonies, but in Ireland, in one uniform unbroken tenour every session. Sir, I am surprised, that this doctrine should come from some of the law servants of the crown. I say, that if the crown could be responsible, his majesty — but certainly the ministers, and even these law officers themselves, through whose hands the acts pass biennially in Ireland, or annually in the colonies, are in an habitual course of committing impeachable offences. What habitual offenders have been all presidents of the council, all secretaries of state, all first lords of trade, all attornies and all solicitors general! However, they are safe; as no one impeaches them; and there is no ground of charge against them, except in their unfounded theories.

The fifth resolution is also a resolution of fact — "That the said general assemblies, general courts, or other bodies legally qualified as aforesaid, have at sundry times freely granted several large subsidies and publick aids for his majesty's service, according to their abilities, when required thereto by letter from one of his majesty's principal secretaries of state; and that their right to grant the same, and their cheerfulness and sufficiency in the said grants, have been at sundry times acknowledged by parliament."
To say nothing of their great expences in the Indian wars; and not to take their exertion in foreign ones, so high as the supplies in

the year 1695; not to go back to their publick contributions in the year 1710; I shall begin to travel only where the journals give me light; resolving to deal in nothing but fact, authenticated by parliamentary record; and to build myself wholly on that solid basis.

On the fourth of April, 1748,[26] a committee of this house came to the following resolution:

"Resolved,

That it is the opinion of this committee, *That it is just and reasonable* that the several provinces and colonies of Massachuset's Bay, New Hampshire, Connecticut, and Rhode Island, be reimbursed the expenses they have been at in taking and securing to the crown of Great Britain, the island of Cape Breton and its dependencies."

These expences were immense for such colonies. They were above 200,000*l.* sterling; money first raised and advanced on their publick credit.

On the 28th of January, 1756,[27] a message from the king came to us, to this effect — "His majesty, being sensible of the zeal and vigour with which his faithful subjects of certain colonies in North America have exerted themselves in defence of his majesty's just rights and possessions, recommends it to this house to take the same into their consideration, and to enable his majesty to give them such assistance as may be a *proper reward and encouragement.*"

On the 3d of February, 1756,[28] the house came to a suitable resolution, expressed in words nearly the same as those of the message: but with the further addition, that the money then voted was as an *encouragement* to the colonies to exert themselves with vigour. It will not be necessary to go through all the testimonies which your own records have given to the truth of my resolutions. I will only refer you to the places in the journals:

26 Journals of the House, Vol. xxv [*Burke's note*].
27 Ibid. Vol. xxvii [*Burke's note*].
28 Ibid. [*Burke's note*].

Vol. xxvii.— 16th and 19th May, 1757.
Vol. xxviii.—June 1st, 1758—April 26th and 30th, 1759—March
            26th and 31st, and April 28th, 1760—Jan. 9th and
            20th, 1761.
Vol. xxix.— Jan. 22d and 26th, 1762—March 14th and 17th,
            1763.

Sir, here is the repeated acknowledgment of parliament, that
the colonies not only gave, but gave to satiety. This nation has
formally acknowledged two things; first, that the colonies had
gone beyond their abilities, parliament having thought it necessary to reimburse them; secondly, that they had acted legally and
laudably in their grants of money, and their maintenance of
troops, since the compensation is expressly given as reward and
encouragement. Reward is not bestowed for acts that are unlaw-
ful; and encouragement is not held out to things that deserve
reprehension. My resolution therefore does nothing more than
collect into one proposition, what is scattered through your journals. I give you nothing but your own; and you cannot refuse in
the gross, what you have so often acknowledged in detail. The
admission of this, which will be so honourable to them and to
you, will, indeed, be mortal to all the miserable stories, by which
the passions of the misguided people have been engaged in an
unhappy system. The people heard, indeed, from the beginning
of these disputes, one thing continually dinned in their ears, that
reason and justice demanded, that the Americans, who paid no
taxes, should be compelled to contribute. How did that fact
of their paying nothing, stand, when the taxing system began?
When Mr. Grenville began to form his system of American revenue, he stated in this house, that the colonies were then in debt
two million six hundred thousand pounds sterling money; and
was of opinion they would discharge that debt in four years. On
this state, those untaxed people were actually subject to the payment of taxes to the amount of six hundred and fifty thousand a
year. In fact, however, Mr. Grenville was mistaken. The funds
given for sinking the debt did not prove quite so ample as both
the colonies and he expected. The calculation was too sanguine:

the reduction was not completed till some years after, and at different times in different colonies. However, the taxes after the war continued too great to bear any addition, with prudence or propriety; and when the burthens imposed in consequence of former requisitions were discharged, our tone became too high to resort again to requisition. No colony, since that time, ever has had any requisition whatsoever made to it.

We see the sense of the crown, and the sense of parliament, on the productive nature of a *revenue by grant*. Now search the same journals for the produce of the *revenue by imposition*—Where is it?—let us know the volume and the page—what is the gross, what is the net produce?—to what service is it applied?—how have you appropriated its surplus?—What, can none of the many skilful index-makers, that we are now employing, find any trace of it?—Well, let them and that rest together.—But are the journals, which say nothing of the revenue, as silent on the discontent? Oh no! a child may find it. It is the melancholy burthen and blot of every page.

I think then I am, from those journals, justified in the sixth and last resolution, which is—"That it hath been found by experience, that the manner of granting the said supplies and aids, by the said general assemblies, hath been more agreeable to the said colonies, and more beneficial, and conducive to the publick service, than the mode of giving and granting aids in parliament, to be raised and paid in the said colonies." This makes the whole of the fundamental part of the plan. The conclusion is irresistible. You cannot say, that you were driven by any necessity to an exercise of the utmost rights of legislature. You cannot assert, that you took on yourselves the task of imposing colony taxes, from the want of another legal body, that is competent to the purpose of supplying the exigencies of the state without wounding the prejudices of the people. Neither is it true that the body so qualified, and having that competence, had neglected the duty.

The question now, on all this accumulated matter, is;— whether you will chuse to abide by a profitable experience, or a mischievous theory; whether you chuse to build on imagination or fact; whether you prefer enjoyment or hope; satisfaction in your subjects, or discontent?

If these propositions are accepted, every thing which has been made to enforce a contrary system, must, I take it for granted, fall along with it. On that ground, I have drawn the following resolution, which, when it comes to be moved, will naturally be divided in a proper manner: "That it may be proper to repeal an act, made in the seventh year of the reign of his present majesty, intituled, An act for granting certain duties in the British colonies and plantations in America; for allowing a drawback of the duties of customs upon the exportation from this kingdom, of coffee and cocoa-nuts of the produce of the said colonies or plantations; for discontinuing the drawbacks payable on China earthenware exported to America; and for more effectually preventing the clandestine running of goods in the said colonies and plantations. — And that it may be proper to repeal an act, made in the fourteenth year of the reign of his present majesty, intituled, An act to discontinue, in such manner, and for such time, as are therein mentioned, the landing and discharging, lading or shipping, of goods, wares, and merchandize, at the town and within the harbour of Boston, in the province of Massachuset's Bay, in North America. — And that it may be proper to repeal an act, made in the fourteenth year of the reign of his present majesty, intituled, An act for the impartial administration of justice, in the cases of persons questioned for any acts done by them, in the execution of the law, or for the suppression of riots and tumults, in the province of Massachuset's Bay, in New England. — And that it may be proper to repeal an act, made in the fourteenth year of the reign of his present majesty, intituled, An act for the better regulating the government of the province of Massachuset's Bay, in New England. — And, also, that it may be proper to explain and amend an act, made in the thirty-fifth year of the reign of King Henry the Eighth, intituled, An act for the trial of treasons committed out of the king's dominions."

I wish, Sir, to repeal the Boston Port Bill, because (independently of the dangerous precedent of suspending the rights of the subject during the king's pleasure) it was passed, as I apprehend, with less regularity, and on more partial principles, than it ought. The corporation of Boston was not heard before it was condemned. Other towns, full as guilty as she was, have not had their ports blocked up. Even the restraining bill of the present session does not go to the length of the Boston Port Act. The same ideas of prudence, which induced you not to extend equal punishment to equal guilt, even when you were punishing, induce me, who mean not to chastise, but to reconcile, to be satisfied with the punishment already partially inflicted.

Ideas of prudence, and accommodation to circumstances, prevent you from taking away the charters of Connecticut and Rhode Island, as you have taken away that of Massachuset's Colony, though the crown has far less power in the two former provinces than it enjoyed in the latter; and though the abuses have been full as great, and as flagrant, in the exempted as in the punished. The same reasons of prudence and accommodation have weight with me in restoring the charter of Massachuset's Bay. Besides, Sir, the act which changes the charter of Massachuset's is in many particulars so exceptionable, that if I did not wish absolutely to repeal, I would by all means desire to alter it; as several of its provisions tend to the subversion of all publick and private justice. Such, among others, is the power in the governour to change the sheriff at his pleasure; and to make a new returning officer for every special cause. It is shameful to behold such a regulation standing among English laws.

The act for bringing persons accused of committing murder under the orders of government to England for trial, is but temporary. That act has calculated the probable duration of our quarrel with the colonies; and is accommodated to that supposed duration. I would hasten the happy moment of reconciliation; and therefore must, on my principle, get rid of that most justly obnoxious act.

The act of Henry the Eighth, for the trial of treasons, I do not mean to take away, but to confine it to its proper bounds and original intention; to make it expressly for trial of treasons (and the greatest treasons may be committed) in places where the jurisdiction of the crown does not extend.

Having guarded the privileges of local legislature, I would next secure to the colonies a fair and unbiassed judicature; for which purpose, Sir, I propose the following resolution: "That, from the time when the general assembly or general court of any colony or plantation in North America, shall have appointed by act of assembly, duly confirmed, a settled salary to the offices of the chief justice and other judges of the superiour court, it may be proper, that the said chief justice and other judges of the superiour courts of such colony, shall hold his and their office and offices during their good behaviour; and shall not be removed therefrom, but when the said removal shall be adjudged by his majesty in council, upon a hearing on complaint from the general assembly, or on a complaint from the governour, or council, or the house of representatives severally, of the colony in which the said chief justice and other judges have exercised the said offices."

The next resolution relates to the courts of admiralty.

It is this: — "That it may be proper to regulate the courts of admiralty, or vice admiralty, authorized by the 15th chap. of the 4th of George the Third, in such a manner as to make the same more commodious to those who sue, or are sued, in the said courts, and to provide for the more decent maintenance of the judges in the same."

These courts I do not wish to take away; they are in themselves proper establishments. This court is one of the capital securities of the act of navigation. The extent of its jurisdiction, indeed, has been increased; but this is altogether as proper, and is, indeed, on many accounts, more eligible, where new powers were wanted, than a court absolutely new. But courts incommodiously situated, in effect, deny justice; and a court, partaking in the fruits of its own condemnation, is a robber. The congress complain, and complain justly of this grievance.[29]

These are the three consequential propositions. I have thought of two or three more; but they came rather too near detail, and to the province of executive government, which I wish parliament always to superintend, never to assume. If the first six are granted, congruity will carry the latter three. If not, the things that remain unrepealed, will be, I hope, rather unseemly incumbrances on the building, than very materially detrimental to its strength and stability.

Here, Sir, I should close; but that I plainly perceive some objections remain, which I ought, if possible, to remove. The first will be, that, in resorting to the doctrine of our ancestors, as contained in the preamble to the Chester act, I prove too much; that the grievance from a want of representation stated in that preamble, goes to the whole of legislation as well as to taxation. And that the colonies grounding themselves upon that doctrine, will apply it to all parts of legislative authority.

To this objection with all possible deference and humility, and wishing as little as any man living to impair the smallest particle of our supreme authority, I answer, that *the words are the words of parliament, and not mine*; and, that all false and inconclusive inferences, drawn from them, are not mine; for I heartily disclaim any such inference. I have chosen the words of an act of parliament, which Mr. Grenville, surely a tolerably zealous and very judicious advocate for the sovereignty of parliament, formerly moved to have read at your table, in confirmation of his tenets. It is true, that Lord Chatham considered these preambles

29 The Solicitor-General informed Mr. B. when the resolutions were separately moved, that the grievance of the judges partaking of the profits of the seizure had been redressed by office; accordingly the resolution was amended [*Burke's note*]. The solicitor-general, Alexander Wedderburn (1733–1805), once a violent opponent of Lord North, had been turned by his appointment into an enforcer and defender of the administration's policy. On 3 December 1777 friends of both would intervene to avert a duel between Burke and Wedderburn after a heated debate on the defeat at Saratoga.

as declaring strongly in favour of his opinions. He was a no less powerful advocate for the privileges of the Americans. Ought I not from hence to presume, that these preambles are as favourable as possible to both, when properly understood; favourable both to the rights of parliament, and to the privilege of the dependencies of this crown? But, Sir, the object of grievance in my resolution, I have not taken from the Chester, but from the Durham act, which confines the hardship of want of representation to the case of subsidies; and which therefore falls in exactly with the case of the colonies. But whether the unrepresented counties were *de jure*, or *de facto*, bound, the preambles do not accurately distinguish; nor indeed was it necessary; for whether *de jure*, or *de facto*, the legislature thought the exercise of the power of taxing, as of right, or as of fact without right, equally a grievance, and equally oppressive.

I do not know, that the colonies have, in any general way, or in any cool hour, gone much beyond the demand of immunity in relation to taxes. It is not fair to judge of the temper or dispositions of any man, or any set of men, when they are composed and at rest, from their conduct, or their expressions, in a state of disturbance and irritation. It is besides a very great mistake to imagine, that mankind follow up practically any speculative principle, either of government or of freedom, as far as it will go in argument and logical illation. We Englishmen stop very short of the principles upon which we support any given part of our constitution; or even the whole of it together. I could easily, if I had not already tired you, give you very striking and convincing instances of it. This is nothing but what is natural and proper. All government, indeed every human benefit and enjoyment, every virtue, and every prudent act, is founded on compromise and barter. We balance inconveniences; we give and take; we remit some rights, that we may enjoy others; and, we choose rather to be happy citizens, than subtle disputants. As we must give away some natural liberty, to enjoy civil advantages; so we must sacrifice some civil liberties, for the advantages to be derived from the communion and fellowship of a great empire. But in all fair dealings the thing bought, must bear some proportion to the purchase paid. None will barter away the immediate jewel of his soul. Though a great house is apt to make slaves haughty, yet it is purchasing a part of the artificial importance of a great empire too dear, to pay for it all essential rights, and all the intrinsick dignity of human nature. None of us who would not risk his life, rather than fall under a government purely arbitrary. But, although there are some amongst us who think our constitution wants many improvements, to make it a complete system of liberty, perhaps none who are of that opinion would think it right to aim at such improvement, by disturbing his country, and risking every thing that is dear to him. In every arduous enterprise, we consider what we are to lose, as well as what we are to gain; and the more and better stake of liberty every people possess, the less they will hazard in a vain attempt to make it more. These are *the cords of man.* Man acts from adequate motives relative to his interest; and not on metaphysical speculations. Aristotle, the great master of reasoning, cautions us, and with great weight and propriety, against this species of delusive geometrical accuracy in moral arguments, as the most fallacious of all sophistry.

The Americans will have no interest contrary to the grandeur and glory of England, when they are not oppressed by the weight of it; and they will rather be inclined to respect the acts of a superintending legislature; when they see them the acts of that power, which is itself the security, not the rival, of their secondary importance. In this assurance, my mind most perfectly acquiesces; and I confess, I feel not the least alarm, from the discontents which are to arise, from putting people at their ease; nor do I apprehend the destruction of this empire, from giving, by an act of free grace and indulgence, to two millions of my fellow citizens, some share of those rights, upon which I have always been taught to value myself.

It is said indeed, that this power of granting, vested in American assemblies, would dissolve the unity of the empire; which was preserved, entire, although Wales, and Chester, and Durham, were added to it. Truly, Mr. Speaker, I do not know what this unity means; nor has it ever been heard of, that I know, in the constitutional policy of this country. The very idea of subordination of parts, excludes this notion of simple and undivided unity. England is the head; but she is not the head and the members too. Ireland has ever had from the beginning a separate, but not an independent, legislature; which, far from distracting, promoted the union of the whole. Every thing was sweetly and harmoniously disposed through both islands for the conservation of English dominion, and the communication of English liberties. I do not see that the same principles might not be carried into twenty islands, and with the same good effect. This is my model with regard to America, as far as the internal circumstances of the two countries are the same. I know no other unity of this empire, than I can draw from its example during these periods, when it seemed to my poor understanding more united than it is now, or than it is likely to be by the present methods.

But since I speak of these methods, I recollect, Mr. Speaker, almost too late, that I promised, before I finished, to say something of the proposition of the noble lord on the floor,[30] which has been so lately received, and stands on your journals. I must be deeply concerned, whenever it is my misfortune to continue a difference with the majority of this house. But as the reasons for that difference are my apology for thus troubling you, suffer me to state them in a very few words. I shall compress them into as small a body as I possibly can, having already debated that matter at large, when the question was before the committee.

First, then, I cannot admit that proposition of a ransom by auction; — because it is a meer project. It is a thing new; unheard of; supported by no experience; justified by no analogy; without example of our ancestors, or root in the constitution.

It is neither regular parliamentary taxation, nor colony grant. *Experimentum in corpore vili*,[31] is a good rule, which will ever make

30 Lord North [*Burke's note*].

31 "An experiment on a worthless body" is preferable to an experiment on a valuable one.

me adverse to any trial of experiments on what is certainly the most valuable of all subjects; the peace of this empire.

Secondly, it is an experiment which must be fatal in the end to our constitution. For what is it but a scheme for taxing the colonies in the antichamber of the noble lord and his successors? To settle the quotas and proportions in this house, is clearly impossible. You, Sir, may flatter yourself, you shall sit a state auctioneer, with your hammer in your hand, and knock down to each colony as it bids. But to settle (on the plan laid down by the noble lord) the true proportional payment for four or five and twenty governments, according to the absolute and the relative wealth of each, and according to the British proportion of wealth and burthen, is a wild and chimerical notion. This new taxation must therefore come in by the back-door of the constitution. Each quota must be brought to this house ready formed; you can neither add nor alter. You must register it. You can do nothing further. For on what grounds can you deliberate either before or after the proposition? You cannot hear the counsel for all these provinces, quarrelling each on its own quantity of payment, and its proportion to others. If you should attempt it, the committee of provincial ways and means, or by whatever other name it will delight to be called, must swallow up all the time of parliament.

Thirdly, it does not give satisfaction to the complaint of the colonies. They complain, that they are taxed without their consent; you answer, that you will fix the sum at which they shall be taxed. That is, you give them the very grievance for the remedy. You tell them indeed, that you will leave the mode to themselves. I really beg pardon: it gives me pain to mention it; but you must be sensible that you will not perform this part of the compact. For, suppose the colonies were to lay the duties which furnished their contingent, upon the importation of your manufactures; you know you would never suffer such a tax to be laid. You know too, that you would not suffer many other modes of taxation. So that, when you come to explain yourself, it will be found, that you will neither leave to themselves the quantum nor the mode; nor indeed any thing. The whole is delusion from one end to the other.

Fourthly, this method of ransom by auction, unless it be *universally* accepted, will plunge you into great and inextricable difficulties. In what year of our Lord are the proportions of payments to be settled? To say nothing of the impossibility that colony agents should have general powers of taxing the colonies at their discretion; consider, I implore you, that the communication by special messages, and orders between these agents and their constituents on each variation of the case, when the parties come to contend together, and to dispute on their relative proportions, will be a matter of delay, perplexity, and confusion, that never can have an end.

If all the colonies do not appear at the outcry, what is the condition of those assemblies, who offer, by themselves or their agents, to tax themselves up to your ideas of their proportion? The refractory colonies, who refuse all composition, will remain taxed only to your old impositions, which, however grievous in principle, are trifling as to production. The obedient colonies in this scheme are heavily taxed; the refractory remain unburthened. What will you do? Will you lay new and heavier taxes by parliament on the disobedient? Pray consider in what way you can do it. You are perfectly convinced that in the way of taxing, you can do nothing but at the ports. Now suppose it is Virginia that refuses to appear at your auction, while Maryland and North Carolina bid handsomely for their ransom, and are taxed to your quota; How will you put these colonies on a par? Will you tax the tobacco of Virginia? If you do, you give its death-wound to your English revenue at home, and to one of the very greatest articles of your own foreign trade. If you tax the import of that rebellious colony, what do you tax but your own manufactures, or the goods of some other obedient, and already well taxed colony? Who has said one word on this labyrinth of detail, which bewilders you more and more as you enter into it? Who has presented, who can present you, with a clue, to lead you out of it? I think, Sir, it is impossible, that you should not recollect that the colony bounds are so implicated in one another (you know it by your other experiments in the bill for prohibiting the New-England fishery) that you can lay no possible restraints on almost any of them which may not be presently eluded, if you do not confound the innocent with the guilty, and burthen those whom upon every principle, you ought to exonerate. He must be grossly ignorant of America, who thinks, that, without falling into this confusion of all rules of equity and policy, you can restrain any single colony, especially Virginia and Maryland, the central, and most important of them all.

Let it also be considered, that, either in the present confusion you settle a permanent contingent, which will and must be trifling; and then you have no effectual revenue: or you change the quota at every exigency; and then on every new repartition you will have a new quarrel.

Reflect besides, that when you have fixed a quota for every colony, you have not provided for prompt and punctual payment. Suppose one, two, five, ten years arrears. You cannot issue a treasury extent against the failing colony. You must make new Boston port bills, new restraining laws, new acts for dragging men to England for trial. You must send out new fleets, new armies. All is to begin again. From this day forward the empire is never to know an hour's tranquillity. An intestine fire will be kept alive in the bowels of the colonies, which one time or other must consume this whole empire. I allow indeed that the empire of Germany raises her revenue and her troops by quotas and contingents; but the revenue of the empire, and the army of the empire, is the worst revenue, and the worst army, in the world.

Instead of a standing revenue, you will therefore have a perpetual quarrel. Indeed the noble lord, who proposed this project of a ransom by auction, seemed himself to be of that opinion. His project was rather designed for breaking the union of the colonies, than for establishing a revenue. He confessed, he apprehended that his proposal would not be to *their taste*. I say, this scheme of disunion seems to be at the bottom of the project; for I will not suspect that the noble lord meant nothing but merely to delude the nation by an airy phantom which he never intended to realize. But whatever his views may be; as I propose the peace and union of the colonies as the very foundation of my plan, it cannot accord with one whose foundation is perpetual discord.

Compare the two. This I offer to give you is plain and simple. The other full of perplexed and intricate mazes. This is mild; that harsh. This is found by experience effectual for its purposes; the other is a new project. This is universal; the other calculated for certain colonies only. This is immediate in its conciliatory operation; the other remote, contingent, full of hazard. Mine is what becomes the dignity of a ruling people; gratuitous, unconditional, and not held out as matter of bargain and sale. I have done my duty in proposing it to you. I have indeed tired you by a long discourse; but this is the misfortune of those to whose influence nothing will be conceded, and who must win every inch of their ground by argument. You have heard me with goodness. May you decide with wisdom! For my part, I feel my mind greatly disburthened by what I have done to-day. I have been the less fearful of trying your patience, because on this subject I mean to spare it altogether in future. I have this comfort, that in every stage of the American affairs, I have steadily opposed the measures that have produced the confusion, and may bring on the destruction, of this empire. I now go so far as to risk a proposal of my own. If I cannot give peace to my country; I give it to my conscience.

But what (says the financier) is peace to us without money? Your plan gives us no revenue. No! But it does — For it secures to the subject the power of REFUSAL; the first of all revenues. Experience is a cheat, and fact a liar, if this power in the subject of proportioning his grant, or of not granting at all, has not been found the richest mine of revenue ever discovered by the skill or by the fortune of man. It does not indeed vote you £152,750: 11: 2¾ths, nor any other paltry limited sum. — But it gives the strong box itself, the fund, the bank, from whence only revenues can arise amongst a people sensible of freedom: *Posita luditur arca.*[32] Cannot you in England; cannot you at this time of day; cannot you, a house of commons, trust to the principle which has raised so mighty a revenue, and accumulated a debt of near 140 millions in this country? Is this principle to be true in England, and false every where else? Is it not true in Ireland? Has it not hitherto been true in the colonies? Why should you presume, that, in any country, a body duly constituted for any function, will neglect to perform its duty, and abdicate its trust? Such a presumption would go against all governments in all modes. But, in truth, this dread of penury of supply, from a free assembly, has no foundation in nature. For first observe, that, besides the desire which all men have naturally of supporting the honour of their own government; that sense of dignity, and that security to property, which ever attends freedom, has a tendency to increase the stock of the free community. Most may be taken where most is accumulated. And what is the soil or climate where experience has not uniformly proved, that the voluntary flow of heaped-up plenty, bursting from the weight of its own rich luxuriance, has ever run with a more copious stream of revenue, than could be squeezed from the dry husks of oppressed indigence, by the straining of all the politick machinery in the world.

Next we know, that parties must ever exist in a free country. We know too, that the emulations of such parties, their contradictions, their reciprocal necessities, their hopes, and their fears, must send them all in their turns to him that holds the balance of the state. The parties are the gamesters; but government keeps the table, and is sure to be the winner in the end. When this game is played, I really think it is more to be feared, that the people will be exhausted, than that government will not be supplied. Whereas, whatever is got by acts of absolute power ill obeyed,

32 Adapting a passage from Juvenal, *Satires* 1.89–90, here paraphrased to mean "play the game with your real resources," but in its original context suggesting that men gamble with "all their hoard beside them."

because odious, or by contracts ill kept, because constrained; will be narrow, feeble, uncertain, and precarious. *"Ease would retract vows made in pain, as violent and void."*[33]

I, for one, protest against compounding our demands: I declare against compounding, for a poor limited sum, the immense, evergrowing, eternal debt, which is due to generous government from protected freedom. And so may I speed in the great object I propose to you, as I think it would not only be an act of injustice, but would be the worst œconomy in the world, to compel the colonies to a sum certain, either in the way of ransom, or in the way of compulsory compact.

But to clear up my ideas on this subject—a revenue from America transmitted hither—do not delude yourselves—you never can receive it—No, not a shilling. We have experience that from remote countries it is not to be expected. If, when you attempted to extract revenue from Bengal, you were obliged to return in loan what you had taken in imposition; what can you expect from North America? for certainly, if ever there was a country qualified to produce wealth, it is India; or an institution fit for the transmission, it is the East-India Company. America has none of these aptitudes. If America gives you taxable objects, on which you lay your duties here, and gives you, at the same time, a surplus by a foreign sale of her commodities to pay the duties on these objects which you tax at home, she has performed her part to the British revenue. But with regard to her own internal establishments; she may, I doubt not she will, contribute in moderation. I say in moderation; for she ought not to be permitted to exhaust herself. She ought to be reserved to a war; the weight of which, with the enemies that we are most likely to have, must be considerable in her quarter of the globe. There she may serve you, and serve you essentially.

For that service, for all service, whether of revenue, trade, or empire, my trust is in her interest in the British constitution. My hold of the colonies is in the close affection which grows from

33 *Paradise Lost* 4.96–97.

common names, from kindred blood, from similar privileges, and equal protection. These are ties, which, though light as air, are as strong as links of iron. Let the colonies always keep the idea of their civil rights associated with your government; — they will cling and grapple to you; and no force under heaven will be of power to tear them from their allegiance. But let it be once understood, that your government may be one thing, and their privileges another; that these two things may exist without any mutual relation; the cement is gone; the cohesion is loosened; and every thing hastens to decay and dissolution. As long as you have the wisdom to keep the sovereign authority of this country as the sanctuary of liberty, the sacred temple consecrated to our common faith, wherever the chosen race and sons of England worship freedom, they will turn their faces towards you. The more they multiply, the more friends you will have; the more ardently they love liberty, the more perfect will be their obedience. Slavery they can have any where. It is a weed that grows in every soil. They may have it from Spain, they may have it from Prussia. But until you become lost to all feeling of your true interest and your natural dignity, freedom, they can have from none but you. This is the commodity of price, of which you have the monopoly. This is the true act of navigation, which binds to you the commerce of the colonies, and through them secures to you the wealth of the world. Deny them this participation of freedom, and you break that sole bond, which originally made, and must still preserve, the unity of the empire. Do not entertain so weak an imagination, as that your registers and your bonds, your affidavits and your sufferances, your cockets and your clearances, are what form the great securities of your commerce. Do not dream that your letters of office, and your instructions, and your suspending clauses, are the things that hold together the great contexture of this mysterious whole. These things do not make your government. Dead instruments, passive tools as they are, it is the spirit of the English communion, that gives all their life and efficacy to them. It is the spirit of the English constitution, which, infused through the mighty mass, pervades, feeds, unites, invigorates, vivifies, every part of the empire, even down to the minutest member.

Is it not the same virtue which does every thing for us here in England? Do you imagine then, that it is the land tax act which raises your revenue? that it is the annual vote in the committee of supply, which gives you your army? or that it is the mutiny bill which inspires it with bravery and discipline? No! surely no! It is the love of the people; it is their attachment to their government from the sense of the deep stake they have in such a glorious institution, which gives you your army and your navy, and infuses into both that liberal obedience, without which your army would be a base rabble, and your navy nothing but rotten timber.

All this, I know well enough, will sound wild and chimerical to the profane herd of those vulgar and mechanical politicians, who have no place among us; a sort of people who think that nothing exists but what is gross and material; and who therefore, far from being qualified to be directors of the great movement of empire, are not fit to turn a wheel in the machine. But to men truly initiated and rightly taught, these ruling and master princi- ples, which, in the opinion of such men as I have mentioned, have no substantial existence, are in truth every thing, and all in all. Magnanimity in politicks is not seldom the truest wisdom; and a great empire and little minds go ill together. If we are conscious of our situation, and glow with zeal to fill our places as becomes our station and ourselves, we ought to auspicate all our publick proceedings on America, with the old warning of the church, *Sursum corda!*[34] We ought to elevate our minds to the greatness of that trust to which the order of Providence has called us. By adverting to the dignity of this high calling, our ancestors have turned a savage wilderness into a glorious em- pire; and have made the most extensive, and the only honour- able conquests; not by destroying, but by promoting, the wealth, the number, the happiness, of the human race. Let us get an American revenue as we have got an American empire. English

34 "Lift up your hearts," from the Latin mass.

privileges have made it all that it is; English privileges alone will make it all it can be.

In full confidence of this unalterable truth, I now (*quod felix faustumque sit*)[35] — lay the first stone of the temple of peace; and I move you,

"That the colonies and plantations of Great Britain in North America, consisting of fourteen separate governments, and containing two millions and upwards of free inhabitants, have not had the liberty and privilege of electing and sending any knights and burgesses, or others, to represent them in the high court of parliament."

* * * * *

Upon this resolution, the previous question was put, and carried; — for the previous question 270, against it 78.

* * * * *

As the propositions were opened separately in the body of the speech, the reader perhaps may wish to see the whole of them together, in the form in which they were moved for.

"MOVED,

That the colonies and plantations of Great Britain in North America, consisting of fourteen separate governments, and containing two millions and upwards of free inhabitants, have not had the liberty and privilege of electing and sending any knights and burgesses, or others, to represent them in the high court of parliament.

"That the said colonies and plantations have been made liable to, and bounden by, several subsidies, payments, rates, and taxes, given and granted by parliament; though the said colonies and plantations have not their knights and burgesses, in the said high court of parliament, of their own election, to represent the condition of their country, *by lack whereof, they have been oftentimes*

---

35 "May it be happy and auspicious."

touched and grieved by subsidies given, granted, and assented to, in the
said court, in a manner prejudicial to the common wealth, quietness,
rest, and peace, of the subjects inhabiting within the same.

"That, from the distance of the said colonies, and from other circumstances, no method hath hitherto been devised for procuring a representation in parliament for the said colonies.

"That each of the said colonies hath within itself a body, chosen, in part or in the whole, by the freemen, freeholders, or other free inhabitants thereof, commonly called the general assembly, or general court; with powers legally to raise, levy, and assess, according to the several usage of such colonies, duties and taxes towards defraying all sorts of publick services.[36]

"That the said general assemblies, general courts, or other bodies, legally qualified as aforesaid, have at sundry times freely granted several large subsidies and publick aids for his majesty's service, according to their abilities, when required thereto by letter from one of his majesty's principal secretaries of state; and that their right to grant the same, and their cheerfulness and sufficiency in the said grants, have been at sundry times acknowledged by parliament.

"That it hath been found by experience, that the manner of granting the said supplies and aids, by the said general assemblies, hath been more agreeable to the inhabitants of the said colonies, and more beneficial and conducive to the publick service, than the mode of giving and granting aids and subsidies in parliament to be raised and paid in the said colonies.

"That it may be proper to repeal an act, made in the 7th year of the reign of his present majesty, intituled, An act for granting certain duties in the British colonies and plantations in America; for allowing a drawback of the duties of customs, upon the expor-

36 The first four motions and the last had the previous question put on them. The others were negatived.

The words in Italicks were, by an amendment that was carried, left out of the motion; which will appear in the journals, though it is not the practice to insert such amendments in the votes [*Burke's note*].

tation from this kingdom, of coffee and cocoa-nuts, of the produce of the said colonies or plantations; for discontinuing the drawbacks payable on China earthen-ware exported to America; and for more effectually preventing the clandestine running of goods in the said colonies and plantations.

"That it may be proper to repeal an act, made in the 14th year of the reign of his present majesty, intituled, An act to discontinue, in such manner, and for such time, as are therein mentioned, the landing and discharging, lading or shipping of goods, wares, and merchandize, at the town, and within the harbour, of Boston, in the province of Massachuset's Bay, in North America.

"That it may be proper to repeal an act, made in the 14th year of the reign of his present majesty, intituled, An act for the impartial administration of justice, in cases of persons questioned for any acts done by them in the execution of the law, or for the suppression of riots and tumults, in the province of Massachuset's Bay, in New England.

"That it is proper to repeal an act, made in the 14th year of the reign of his present majesty, intituled, An act for the better regulating the government of the province of Massachuset's Bay, in New England.

"That it is proper to explain and amend an act, made in the 35th year of the reign of King Henry VIII, intituled, An act for the trial of treasons committed out of the King's dominions.

"That, from the time when the general assembly, or general court, of any colony or plantation, in North America, shall have appointed, by act of assembly duly confirmed, a settled salary to the offices of the chief justice and judges of the superiour courts, it may be proper that the said chief justice and other judges of the superiour courts of such colony shall hold his and their office and offices during their good behaviour; and shall not be removed therefrom, but when the said removal shall be adjudged by his majesty in council, upon a hearing on complaint from the general assembly, or on a complaint from the governour, or council,

or the house of representatives, severally, of the colony in which
the said chief justice and other judges have exercised the said
office.

"That it may be proper to regulate the courts of admiralty;
or vice-admiralty, authorized by the 15th chapter of the 4th of
George III. in such a manner, as to make the same more commodious to those who sue, or are sued, in the said courts; *and to
provide for the more decent maintenance of the judges of the same.*"

A Letter to the Sheriffs of Bristol on the Affairs of America (1777)

Burke once summed up the motives of his politics by saying that he hated violence and loved liberty. None of his writings better illustrates the depth of both feelings, and the necessity of their work in combination, than his *Letter to the Sheriffs of Bristol.*

This letter was written to answer objections by Burke's supporters to the Rockingham party's decision to secede from Parliament whenever American affairs were discussed. The tactic had been urged by Burke himself, with the aim of denying the king the implicit sanction that even a tacit participation conferred. The party was gambling against the popular fervor early victories might breed, but as it turned out, the first years of war were auspicious for George III. Meanwhile the secession had an unintended effect: it smoothed the way for the passage of legislation suppressing the rights of the colonists and contracting the scope of English liberty. The Habeas Corpus Act mentioned here by Burke threw out habeas corpus for persons accused or suspected of treason out of the realm or piracy on the high seas. The weak vote in opposition caught the attention of radicals in Bristol. As they judged it, Burke's mistaken decision to secede bore some of the blame.

Burke's own stance in 1776 and 1777 betrayed a radicalism he would be hard pressed to explain in later years, though the contents of the *Letter* are in fact a patient, literal, and impassioned explanation of his hatred for all forms of oppression and injustice. His emotions of the time may be judged by a letter to Richard Shackleton (a childhood friend to whom he sometimes wrote with unusual frankness), dated 11 August 1776, on the brink of the setbacks he hoped to address in the pamphlet: "We are deeply in blood. We expect now to hear of some sharp affair, every hour. God knows how it will be. I do not know how to wish success to those whose victory is to separate us from a large part of our empire. Still less do I wish success to injustice, oppression, and absurdity. Things are in a bad train and in more ways than one. No good can come of any event in this war to any virtuous interest. We have forgot or thrown away our ancient principles. This view sometimes sinks my spirits." Burke did not want England to win the war. A victory on these crooked terms, he believed, would corrupt the manners, harden the arrogance, and shrink the generosity of those who administered the empire. Morally and politically, it would be more destructive than any defeat.

The *Letter to the Sheriffs of Bristol* is especially strong in denouncing the consequences of the war at home. These are apparent, for Burke, in a decay of civil manners as much as a declining regard for liberty. When violent coercion becomes as common as driving a bargain, the ordinary life of society itself is cheapened. Burke thought that England in the spring of 1777 was approaching a state of constant domestic turmoil: the natural result of the war against the colonies, which was, in all but name, a civil war. So, in the aftermath of the failure of his policy of conciliation, he asserts again the "great principle of connection" between people who share an inheritance of manners and customs; deplores the patriotic calls for unanimity in a national effort that cannot benefit the public good; and refuses to ratify by usage the pejorative term *rebellion*: "*General* rebellions and revolts of an whole people never were *encouraged*, now or at any time. They are always *provoked*." In its discursive way, the *Letter to the Sheriffs of Bristol* offers a definition of true liberty, and in the process turns away from the language of natural law, or a preference of one kind of political foundation over another: "If any ask me what a free government is, I answer, that, for any practical purpose, it is what the people think so, — and that they, and not I, are the natural, lawful, and competent judges of this matter." This is an important aspect of Burke's endorsement of the maxim that one must never be the judge in one's own cause. The people themselves run that risk in a democracy, where they are the ultimate source of authority, but the colonial subjects in America held no such status. Burke in any case thinks the judgment of the people most reliable when they declare what liberty is *not;* in doing so, they exercise an instinctive veto against their own oppression. The greatest peril to the English nation may be its growing callousness on just this point: "Liberty is in danger of being made unpopular to Englishmen."

Sheriffs were officers of the city whose functions, such as the supervision of elections, made them a fitting ostensible audience for a pamphlet touching on matters of local as well as national concern. The *Letter* was written rapidly, in a mood of nervous excitement; and Burke commented to his Bristol friend and ally Richard Champion: "If it is likely to be at all useful, it is far better that it should be early in its appearance, than late, with such perfection as I am capable of giving it, which is undoubtedly such, as never could compensate for any delay." He added, in defense of the heat of some passages: "When we speak only of things, not persons, we have a right to express ourselves with all possible energy; and if any one is offended, he only shows how improper that conduct has been which he cannot bear to have represented in its true colours. Besides, this little piece, though addressed to my constituents, is written to the public."

A Letter from Mr. Burke,

to John Farr and John Harris, Esqrs.,
Sheriffs of the City of Bristol,

on the Affairs of America

GENTLEMEN,

I have the honour of sending you the two last acts which have
been passed with regard to the troubles in America.[1] These acts
are similar to all the rest which have been made on the same
subject. They operate by the same principle; and they are derived from the very same policy. I think they complete the number of that sort of statutes to nine. It affords no matter for very
pleasing reflection, to observe, that our subjects diminish, as our
laws increase.

If I have the misfortune of differing with some of my fellow-
citizens on this great and arduous subject, it is no small consolation to me, that I do not differ from you. With you, I am perfectly
united. We are heartily agreed in our detestation of a civil war.
We have ever expressed the most unqualified disapprobation of
all the steps which have led to it, and of all those which tend to
prolong it. And I have no doubt that we feel exactly the same
emotions of grief and shame on all its miserable consequences;
whether they appear, on the one side or the other, in the shape
of victories or defeats, of captures made from the English on the
continent, or from the English in these islands; of legislative
regulations which subvert the liberties of our brethren, or which
undermine our own.

Of the first of these statutes (that for the letter of marque) I
shall say little. Exceptionable as it may be, and as I think it is in
some particulars, it seems the natural, perhaps necessary result

---

1 The American Treason Act and Letters of Marque Act. A letter of marque
originally meant a license granted by the king to an individual, authorizing reprisals
against another nation for damage done by its army; by this time, it had come to
mean a license for a privateer to capture the enemy's merchant shipping.

of the measures we have taken, and the situation we are in. The other (for a partial suspension of the *Habeas Corpus*) appears to me of a much deeper malignity. During its progress through the house of commons, it has been amended, so as to express more distinctly than at first it did, the avowed sentiments of those who framed it: and the main ground of my exception to it is, because it does express, and does carry into execution, purposes which appear to me so contradictory to all the principles, not only of the constitutional policy of Great Britain, but even of that species of hostile justice, which no asperity of war wholly extinguishes in the minds of a civilized people.

It seems to have in view two capital objects; the first, to enable administration to confine, as long as it shall think proper, those, whom that act is pleased to qualify by the name of *pirates*. Those so qualified, I understand to be, the commanders and mariners of such privateers and ships of war belonging to the colonies, as in the course of this unhappy contest may fall into the hands of the crown. They are therefore to be detained in prison, under the criminal description of piracy, to a future trial and ignominious punishment, whenever circumstances shall make it convenient to execute vengeance on them, under the colour of that odious and infamous offence.

To this first purpose of the law, I have no small dislike; because the act does not, (as all laws, and all equitable transactions ought to do) fairly describe its object. The persons, who make a naval war upon us, in consequence of the present troubles, may be rebels; but to call and treat them as pirates, is confounding, not only the natural distinction of things, but the order of crimes; which, whether by putting them from a higher part of the scale to the lower, or from the lower to the higher, is never done without dangerously disordering the whole frame of jurisprudence. Though piracy may be, in the eye of the law, a *less* offence than treason; yet as both are, in effect, punished with the same death, the same forfeiture, and the same corruption of blood, I never would take from any fellow creature whatever, any sort of advantage which he may derive to his safety from the pity of mankind, or to his reputation from their general feelings, by degrading his offence, when I cannot soften his punishment. The general sense of mankind tells me, that those offences, which may possibly arise from mistaken virtue, are not in the class of infamous actions. Lord Coke, the oracle of the English law, conforms to that general sense where he says, that "those things which are of the highest criminality, may be of the least disgrace."[2] The act prepares a sort of masked proceeding, not honourable to the justice of the kingdom, and by no means necessary for its safety. I cannot enter into it. If Lord Balmerino, in the last rebellion, had driven off the cattle of twenty clans, I should have thought it would have been a scandalous and low juggle, utterly unworthy of the manliness of an English judicature, to have tried him for felony as a stealer of cows.[3]

Besides, I must honestly tell you, that I could not vote for, or countenance in any way, a statute, which stigmatizes with the crime of piracy, these men, whom an act of parliament had previously put out of the protection of the law. When the legislature of this kingdom had ordered all their ships and goods, for the mere new-created offence of exercising trade, to be divided as a spoil among the seamen of the navy, — to consider the necessary reprisal of an unhappy, proscribed, interdicted people, as the crime of piracy, would have appeared in any other legislature than ours, a strain of the most insulting and most unnatural cruelty and injustice. I assure you, I never remember to have heard of any thing like it in any time or country.

The second professed purpose of the act is to detain in England for trial, those who shall commit high treason in America.

That you may be enabled to enter into the true spirit of the present law, it is necessary, gentlemen, to apprize you, that there is an act, made so long ago as in the reign of Henry the Eighth,

---

2 Sir Edward Coke (1552–1634), judge and expositor of the English common law, who argued that the principles of English liberty derived from an "ancient" and "immemorial" constitution.

3 Arthur Elphinstone (1688–1746), sixth Baron Balmerinoch, was a Jacobite rebel in 1715; he returned from exile to fight for Prince Charles in 1745, and was executed in 1746.

before the existence or thought of any English colonies in America, for the trial in this kingdom of treasons committed out of the realm. In the year 1769, parliament thought proper to acquaint the crown with their construction of that act in a formal address, wherein they intreated his majesty, to cause persons, charged with high treason in America, to be brought into this kingdom for trial. By this act of Henry the Eighth, *so construed and so applied*, almost all that is substantial and beneficial in a trial by jury, is taken away from the subject in the colonies. This is however saying too little; for to try a man under that act is, in effect, to condemn him unheard. A person is brought hither in the dungeon of a ship's hold; thence he is vomited into a dungeon on land; loaded with irons, unfurnished with money, unsupported by friends, three thousand miles from all means of calling upon or confronting evidence, where no one local circumstance that tends to detect perjury, can possibly be judged of; — such a person may be executed according to form, but he can never be tried according to justice.

I therefore could never reconcile myself to the bill I send you; which is expressly provided to remove all inconveniencies from the establishment of a mode of trial, which has ever appeared to me most unjust and most unconstitutional. Far from removing the difficulties which impede the execution of so mischievous a project, I would heap new difficulties upon it, if it were in my power. All the ancient, honest juridical principles and institutions of England are so many clogs to check and retard the headlong course of violence and oppression. They were invented for this one good purpose; that what was not just should not be convenient. Convinced of this, I would leave things as I found them. The old, cool-headed, general law, is as good as any deviation dictated by present heat.

I could see no fair justifiable expedience pleaded to favour this new suspension of the liberty of the subject. If the English in the colonies can support the independency, to which they have been unfortunately driven, I suppose nobody has such a fanatical zeal for the criminal justice of Henry the Eighth, that he will contend for executions which must be retaliated tenfold on his own friends; or who has conceived so strange an idea of English dignity, as to think the defeats in America compensated by the triumphs at Tyburn.[4] If on the contrary, the colonies are reduced to the obedience of the crown, there must be under that authority, tribunals in the country itself, fully competent to administer justice on all offenders. But if there are not, and that we must suppose a thing so humiliating to our government, as that all this vast continent should unanimously concur in thinking, that no ill fortune can convert resistance to the royal authority into a criminal act, we may call the effect of our victory peace, or obedience, or what we will; but the war is not ended: the hostile mind continues in full vigour, and it continues under a worse form. If your peace be nothing more than a sullen pause from arms; if their quiet be nothing but the meditation of revenge, where smitten pride smarting from its wounds, festers into new rancour, neither the act of Henry the Eighth, nor its handmaid of this reign,[5] will answer any wise end of policy or justice. For if the bloody fields, which they saw and felt, are not sufficient to subdue the reason of America (to use the expressive phrase of a great lord in office) it is not the judicial slaughter, which is made in another hemisphere against their universal sense of justice, that will ever reconcile them to the British government.

I take it for granted, gentlemen, that we sympathize in a proper horrour of all punishment further than as it serves for an example. To whom then does the example of an execution in England for this American rebellion apply? Remember, you are told every day, that the present is a contest between the two countries; and that we in England are at war for *our own* dignity against our rebellious children. Is this true? If it be, it is surely among such rebellious children that examples for disobedience should be made, to be in any degree instructive: for who ever

4 Place of public execution for Middlesex; now the location of the Marble Arch in Hyde Park.

5 The Treason Act of Henry VIII was reinstated in 1777.

thought of teaching parents their duty by an example from the punishment of an undutiful son? As well might the execution of a fugitive negro in the plantations, be considered as a lesson to teach masters humanity to their slaves. Such executions may indeed satiate our revenge; they may harden our hearts, and puff us up with pride and arrogance. Alas! this is not instruction!

If any thing can be drawn from such examples by a parity of the case, it is to shew, how deep their crime and how heavy their punishment will be who shall at any time dare to resist a distant power actually disposing of their property, without their voice or consent to the disposition; and overturning their franchises without charge or hearing. God forbid that England should ever read this lesson written in the blood of *any* of her offspring!

War is at present carried on between the king's natural and foreign troops, on one side, and the English in America on the other, upon the usual footing of other wars; and accordingly an exchange of prisoners has been regularly made from the beginning. If notwithstanding this hitherto equal procedure, upon some project of ending the war with success (which however may be delusive) administration prepares to act against those as *traitors* who remain in their hands at the end of the troubles, in my opinion we shall exhibit to the world as indecent a piece of injustice as ever civil fury has produced. If the prisoners who have been exchanged, have not by that exchange been *virtually pardoned*, the cartel (whether avowed or understood) is a cruel fraud; for you have received the life of a man, and you ought to return a life for it, or there is no parity or fairness in the transaction.

If on the other hand, we admit, that they, who are actually exchanged are pardoned, but contend that you may justly reserve for vengeance, those who remain unexchanged; then this unpleasant and unhandsome consequence will follow; that you judge of the delinquency of men merely by the time of their guilt, and not by the heinousness of it; and you make fortune and accidents, and not the moral qualities of human action, the rule of your justice.

These strange incongruities must ever perplex those, who confound the unhappiness of civil dissention, with the crime of treason. Whenever a rebellion really and truly exists, which is as easily known in fact, as it is difficult to define in words, government has not entered into such military conventions; but has ever declined all intermediate treaty, which should put rebels in possession of the law of nations with regard to war. Commanders would receive no benefits at their hands, because they could make no return for them. Who has ever heard of capitulation, and parole of honour, and exchange of prisoners in the late rebellions in this kingdom? The answer to all demands of that sort was, "we can engage for nothing; you are at the king's pleasure." We ought to remember, that if our present enemies be, in reality and truth, rebels, the king's generals have no right to release them upon any conditions whatsoever; and they are themselves answerable to the law, and as much in want of a pardon for doing so, as the rebels whom they release.

Lawyers, I know, cannot make the distinction, for which I contend; because they have their strict rule to go by. But legislators ought to do what lawyers cannot; for they have no other rules to bind them, but the great principles of reason and equity, and the general sense of mankind. These they are bound to obey and follow; and rather to enlarge and enlighten law by the liberality of legislative reason, than to fetter and bind their higher capacity by the narrow constructions of subordinate artificial justice. If we had adverted to this, we never could consider the convulsions of a great empire, not disturbed by a little disseminated faction, but divided by whole communities and provinces, and entire legal representatives of a people, as fit matter of discussion under a commission of Oyer and Terminer.[6] It is as opposite to reason and prudence, as it is to humanity and justice.

This act, proceeding on these principles, that is, preparing to

6 Traveling justices were given a commission of Oyer and Terminer to "hear and determine" each case; here, magistrates were empowered by the Treason Act to commit people charged with treason in America to special prisons.

end the present troubles by a trial of one sort of hostility, under the name of piracy, and of another by the name of treason, and executing the act of Henry the Eighth according to a new and unconstitutional interpretation, I have thought evil and dangerous, even though the instruments of effecting such purposes had been merely of a neutral quality.

But it really appears to me, that the means which this act employs are, at least, as exceptionable as the end. Permit me to open myself a little upon this subject, because it is of importance to me, when I am obliged to submit to the power without acquiescing in the reason of an act of legislature, that I should justify my dissent, by such arguments as may be supposed to have weight with a sober man.

The main operative regulation of the act is to suspend the common law, and the statute *Habeas Corpus*, (the sole securities either for liberty or justice) with regard to all those who have been out of the realm, or on the high seas, within a given time. The rest of the people, as I understand, are to continue as they stood before.

I confess, gentlemen, that this appears to me, as bad in the principle, and far worse in its consequence, than an universal suspension of the *Habeas Corpus* act; and the limiting qualification, instead of taking out the sting, does in my humble opinion sharpen and envenom it to a greater degree. Liberty, if I understand it at all, is a *general* principle, and the clear right of all the subjects within the realm, or of none. Partial freedom seems to me a most invidious mode of slavery. But unfortunately, it is the kind of slavery the most easily admitted in times of civil discord; for parties are but too apt to forget their own future safety in their desire of sacrificing their enemies. People without much difficulty admit the entrance of that injustice of which they are not to be the immediate victims. In times of high proceeding it is never the faction of the predominant power that is in danger; for no tyranny chastises its own instruments. It is the obnoxious and the suspected who want the protection of law; and there is nothing to bridle the partial violence of state factions, but this; "that whenever an act is made for a cessation of law and justice, the whole people should be universally subjected to the same suspension of their franchises." The alarm of such a proceeding would then be universal. It would operate as a sort of *Call of the nation*. It would become every man's immediate and instant concern to be made very sensible of *the absolute necessity* of this total eclipse of liberty. They would more carefully advert to every renewal, and more powerfully resist it. These great determined measures are not commonly so dangerous to freedom. They are marked with too strong lines to slide into use. No plea, nor pretence of *inconvenience or evil example* (which must in their nature be daily and ordinary incidents) can be admitted as a reason for such mighty operations. But the true danger is, when liberty is nibbled away, for expedients, and by parts. The *Habeas Corpus* act supposes, contrary to the genius of most other laws, that the lawful magistrate may see particular men with a malignant eye, and it provides for that identical case. But when men, in particular descriptions, marked out by the magistrate himself, are delivered over by parliament to this possible malignity, it is not the *Habeas Corpus* that is occasionally suspended, but its spirit, that is mistaken, and its principle that is subverted. Indeed nothing is security to any individual but the common interest of all.

This act therefore, has this distinguished evil in it, that it is the first *partial* suspension of the *Habeas Corpus* that has been made. The precedent, which is always of very great importance, is now established. For the first time a distinction is made among the people within this realm. Before this act, every man putting his foot on English ground, every stranger owing only a local and temporary allegiance, even negro slaves who had been sold in the colonies and under an act of parliament, became as free as every other man who breathed the same air with them.[7] Now a line is drawn, which may be advanced further and further at pleasure, on the same argument of mere expedience, on which it

7 Referring to the case of James Somerset, a former slave granted a writ of habeas corpus in 1772 by the lord chief-justice, Lord Mansfield.

was first described. There is no equality among us; we are not fellow citizens, if the mariner who lands on the quay, does not rest on as firm legal ground as the merchant who sits in his compting-house. Other laws may injure the community, this dissolves it. As things now stand, every man in the West Indies, every one inhabitant of three unoffending provinces on the continent, every person coming from the East Indies, every gentleman who has travelled for his health or education, every mariner who has navigated the seas, is, for no other offence, under a temporary proscription. Let any of these facts (now become presumptions of guilt) be proved against him, and the bare suspicion of the crown puts him out of the law. It is even by no means clear to me, whether the negative proof does not lie upon the person apprehended on suspicion, to the subversion of all justice.

I have not debated against this bill in its progress through the house; because it would have been vain to oppose, and impossible to correct it. It is some time since I have been clearly convinced, that in the present state of things all opposition to any measures proposed by ministers, where the name of America appears, is vain and frivolous. You may be sure that I do not speak of my opposition, which in all circumstances must be so; but that of men of the greatest wisdom and authority in the nation. Every thing proposed against America is supposed of course to be in favour of Great Britain. Good and ill success are equally admitted as reasons for persevering in the present methods. Several very prudent, and very well-intentioned persons were of opinion, that during the prevalence of such dispositions, all struggle rather inflamed than lessened the distemper of the publick counsels. Finding such resistance to be considered as factious by most within doors, and by very many without, I cannot conscientiously support what is against my opinion, nor prudently contend with what I know is irresistible. Preserving my principles unshaken, I reserve my activity for rational endeavours; and I hope that my past conduct has given sufficient evidence, that if I am a single day from my place, it is not owing to indolence or love of dissipation. The slightest hope of doing good is sufficient to recal me to what I quitted with regret. In declining for some time my usual strict attendance, I do not in the least condemn the spirit of those gentlemen, who with a just confidence in their abilities, (in which I claim a sort of share from my love and admiration of them) were of opinion that their exertions in this desperate case might be of some service. They thought, that by contracting the sphere of its application, they might lessen the malignity of an evil principle. Perhaps they were in the right. But when my opinion was so very clearly to the contrary, for the reasons I have just stated, I am sure *my* attendance would have been ridiculous.

I must add in further explanation of my conduct, that far from softening the features of such a principle, and thereby removing any part of the popular odium or natural terrours attending it, I should be sorry, that any thing framed in contradiction to the spirit of our constitution did not instantly produce in fact, the grossest of the evils, with which it was pregnant in its nature. It is by lying dormant a long time, or being at first very rarely exercised, that arbitrary power steals upon a people. On the next unconstitutional act, all the fashionable world will be ready to say — Your prophecies are ridiculous, your fears are vain, you see how little of the mischiefs which you formerly foreboded are come to pass. Thus, by degrees, that artful softening of all arbitrary power, the alleged infrequency or narrow extent of its operation, will be received as a sort of aphorism — and Mr. *Hume* will not be singular in telling us, that the felicity of mankind is no more disturbed by it, than by earthquakes or thunder, or the other more unusual accidents of nature.

The act of which I speak is among the fruits of the American war; a war in my humble opinion productive of many mischiefs, of a kind which distinguish it from all others. Not only our policy is deranged, and our empire distracted, but our laws and our legislative spirit appear to have been totally perverted by it. We have made war on our colonies, not by arms only, but by laws. As hostility and law are not very concordant ideas, every step we have taken in this business, has been made by trampling on some maxim of justice, or some capital principle of wise government. What precedents were established, and what principles overturned, (I will not say of English privilege, but of general justice) in the Boston Port, the Massachuset's Charter, the Military Bill, and all that long array of hostile acts of parliament, by which the war with America has been begun and supported! Had the principles of any of these acts been first exerted on English ground, they would probably have expired as soon as they touched it. But by being removed from our persons, they have rooted in our laws; and the latest posterity will taste the fruits of them.

Nor is it the worst effect of this unnatural contention, that our *laws* are corrupted. Whilst *manners* remain entire, they will correct the vices of law, and soften it at length to their own temper. But we have to lament, that in most of the late proceedings we see very few traces of that generosity, humanity, and dignity of mind which formerly characterized this nation. War suspends the rules of moral obligation, and what is long suspended is in danger of being totally abrogated. Civil wars strike deepest of all into the manners of the people. They vitiate their politicks; they corrupt their morals; they pervert even the natural taste and relish of equity and justice. By teaching us to consider our fellow citizens in a hostile light, the whole body of our nation becomes gradually less dear to us. The very names of affection and kindred, which were the bond of charity whilst we agreed, become new incentives to hatred and rage, when the communion of our country is dissolved. We may flatter ourselves that we shall not fall into this misfortune. But we have no charter of exemption, that I know of, from the ordinary frailties of our nature.

What but that blindness of heart which arises from the phrenzy of civil contention, could have made any persons conceive the present situation of the British affairs as an object of triumph to themselves, or of congratulation to their sovereign? Nothing surely could be more lamentable to those who remember the flourishing days of this kingdom, than to see the insane joy of several unhappy people, amidst the sad spectacle which our affairs and conduct exhibit to the scorn of Europe. We behold, (and it seems some people rejoice in beholding) our native land, which used to sit the envied arbiter of all her neighbours, reduced to a servile dependance on their mercy; acquiescing in assurances of friendship which she does not trust; complaining of hostilities which she dares not resent; deficient to her allies; lofty to her subjects, and submissive to her enemies; whilst the liberal government of this free nation is supported by the hireling sword of German boors and vassals; and three millions of the subjects of Great Britain are seeking for protection to English privileges in the arms of France!

These circumstances appear to me more like shocking prodigies, than natural changes in human affairs. Men of firmer minds may see them without staggering or astonishment. — Some may think them matters of congratulation and complimentary addresses; but I trust your candour will be so indulgent to my weakness, as not to have the worse opinion of me for my declining to participate in this joy; and my rejecting all share whatsoever in such a triumph. I am too old, too stiff in my inveterate partialities, to be ready at all the fashionable evolutions of opinion. I scarcely know how to adapt my mind to the feelings with which the court gazettes mean to impress the people. It is not instantly that I can be brought to rejoice, when I hear of the slaughter and captivity of long lists of those names which have been familiar to my ears from my infancy, and to rejoice that they have fallen under the sword of strangers, whose barbarous appellations I scarcely know how to pronounce. The glory acquired at the White Plains by Colonel Rahl, has no charms for me; and I fairly acknowledge, that I have not yet learned to delight in finding Fort Kniphausen in the heart of the British dominions.[8]

It might be some consolation for the loss of our old regards, if

---

8 A hireling of Britain, Colonel Johann Gottlieb Rahl (ca. 1720–76) participated in the Battle of White Plains (28 October 1776) and the capture of Fort Washington — itself subsequently named for Baron Wilhelm von Knyphausen (1716–1800), whose army of German auxiliaries occupied upper Manhattan for much of the war.

our reason were enlightened in proportion as our honest prejudices are removed. Wanting feelings for the honour of our country, we might then in cold blood be brought to think a little of our interests as individual citizens, and our private conscience as moral agents.

Indeed our affairs are in a bad condition. I do assure those gentlemen who have prayed for war, and obtained the blessing they have sought, that they are at this instant in very great straits. The abused wealth of this country continues a little longer to feed its distemper. As yet they, and their German allies of twenty hireling states, have contended only with the unprepared strength of our own infant colonies. But America is not subdued. Not one unattacked village which was originally adverse throughout that vast continent, has yet submitted from love or terrour. You have the ground you encamp on; and you have no more. The cantonments of your troops and your dominions are exactly of the same extent. You spread devastation, but you do not enlarge the sphere of authority.

The events of this war are of so much greater magnitude than those who either wished or feared it, ever looked for, that this alone ought to fill every considerate mind with anxiety and diffidence. Wise men often tremble at the very things which fill the thoughtless with security. For many reasons I do not choose to expose to publick view, all the particulars of the state in which you stood with regard to foreign powers, during the whole course of the last year. Whether you are yet wholly out of danger from them, is more than I know, or than your rulers can divine. But even if I were certain of my safety, I could not easily forgive those who had brought me into the most dreadful perils, because by accidents, unforeseen by them or me, I have escaped.

Believe me, gentlemen, the way still before you is intricate, dark, and full of perplexed and treacherous mazes. Those who think they have the clue, may lead us out of this labyrinth. We may trust them as amply as we think proper; but as they have most certainly a call for all the reason which their stock can furnish, why should we think it proper to disturb its operation by inflaming their passions? I may be unable to lend an helping hand to those who direct the state; but I should be ashamed to make myself one of a noisy multitude to hollow and hearten them into doubtful and dangerous courses. A conscientious man would be cautious how he dealt in blood. He would feel some apprehension at being called to a tremendous account for engaging in so deep a play, without any sort of knowledge of the game. It is no excuse for presumptuous ignorance, that it is directed by insolent passion. The poorest being that crawls on earth, contending to save itself from injustice and oppression, is an object respectable in the eyes of God and man. But I cannot conceive any existence under heaven, (which in the depths of its wisdom, tolerates all sorts of things) that is more truly odious and disgusting, than an impotent helpless creature, without civil wisdom or military skill, without a consciousness of any other qualification for power but his servility to it, bloated with pride and arrogance, calling for battles which he is not to fight, contending for a violent dominion which he can never exercise, and satisfied to be himself mean and miserable, in order to render others contemptible and wretched.

If you and I find our talents not of the great and ruling kind, our conduct at least, is conformable to our faculties. No man's life pays the forfeit of our rashness. No desolate widow weeps tears of blood over our ignorance. Scrupulous and sober in a well-grounded distrust of ourselves, we would keep in the port of peace and security; and perhaps in recommending to others something of the same diffidence, we should shew ourselves more charitable to their welfare, than injurious to their abilities.

There are many circumstances in the zeal shewn for civil war, which seem to discover but little of real magnanimity. The addressers offer their own persons, and they are satisfied with hiring Germans. They promise their private fortunes, and they mortgage their country. They have all the merit of volunteers, without risk of person or charge of contribution; and when the unfeeling arm of a foreign soldiery pours out their kindred blood like water, they exult and triumph as if they themselves had performed some notable exploit. I am really ashamed of the fashionable language which has been held for some time past; which to say the best of it, is full of levity. You know, that I allude to the general cry against the cowardice, of the Americans, as if we despised them for not making the king's soldiery purchase the advantage they have obtained, at a dearer rate. It is not, gentlemen, it is not, to respect the dispensations of Providence, nor to provide any decent retreat in the mutability of human affairs. It leaves no medium between insolent victory and infamous defeat. It tends to alienate our minds further and further from our natural regards, and to make an eternal rent and schism in the British nation. Those who do not wish for such a separation, would not dissolve that cement of reciprocal esteem and regard, which can alone bind together the parts of this great fabrick. It ought to be our wish, as it is our duty, not only to forbear this style of outrage ourselves, but to make every one as sensible as we can of the impropriety and unworthiness of the tempers which give rise to it, and which designing men are labouring with such malignant industry to diffuse amongst us. It is our business to counteract them, if possible; if possible to awake our natural regards; and to revive the old partiality to the English name. Without something of this kind I do not see how it is ever practicable really to reconcile with those, whose affection, after all, must be the surest hold of our government; and which is a thousand times more worth to us, than the mercenary zeal of all the circles of Germany.

I can well conceive a country completely overrun, and miserably wasted, without approaching in the least to settlement. In my apprehension, as long as English government is attempted to be supported over Englishmen by the sword alone, things will thus continue. I anticipate in my mind the moment of the final triumph of foreign military force. When that hour arrives, (for it may arrive) then it is, that all this mass of weakness and violence will appear in its full light. If we should be expelled from America, the delusion of the partisans of military government might still continue. They might still feed their imaginations with the possible good consequences which might have attended success. Nobody could prove the contrary by facts. But in case the sword should do all, that the sword can do, the success of their arms and the defeat of their policy, will be one and the same thing. You will never see any revenue from America. Some increase of the means of corruption, without ease of the publick burthens, is the very best that can happen. Is it for this that we are at war; and in such a war?

As to the difficulties of laying once more the foundations of that government, which, for the sake of conquering what was our own, has been voluntarily and wantonly pulled down by a court faction here, I tremble to look at them. Has any of these gentlemen, who are so eager to govern all mankind, shewn himself possessed of the first qualification towards government, some knowledge of the object, and of the difficulties which occur in the task they have undertaken?

I assure you, that on the most prosperous issue of your arms, you will not be where you stood, when you called in war to supply the defects of your political establishment. Nor would any disorder or disobedience to government which could arise from the most abject concession on our part, ever equal those which will be felt, after the most triumphant violence. You have got all the intermediate evils of war into the bargain.

I think I know America. If I do not, my ignorance is incurable, for I have spared no pains to understand it; and I do most solemnly assure those of my constituents who put any sort of confidence in my industry and integrity, that every thing that has been done there has arisen from a total misconception of the object: that our means of originally holding America, that our means of reconciling with it after quarrel, of recovering it after separation, of keeping it after victory, did depend, and must depend, in their several stages and periods, upon a total renunciation of that unconditional submission, which has taken such possession of the minds of violent men. The whole of those maxims, upon which we have made and continued this war, must be abandoned. Nothing indeed, (for I would not deceive you) can place us in our former situation. That hope must be laid aside. But there is a difference between bad and the worst of all. Terms relative to the cause of the war ought to be offered by the authority of parliament. An arrangement at home promising some security for them ought to be made. By doing this, without the least impairing of our strength, we add to the credit of our moderation, which in itself, is always strength more or less.

I know many have been taught to think, that moderation, in a case like this, is a sort of treason; and that all arguments for it are sufficiently answered by railing at rebels and rebellion, and by charging all the present or future miseries which we may suffer, on the resistance of our brethren. But I would wish them, in this grave matter, and if peace is not wholly removed from their hearts, to consider seriously, first, that to criminate and recriminate never yet was the road to reconciliation, in any difference amongst men. In the next place, it would be right to reflect, that the American English (whom they may abuse, if they think it honourable to revile the absent) can, as things now stand, neither be provoked at our railing, or bettered by our instruction. All communication is cut off between us, but this we know with certainty, that though we cannot reclaim them, we may reform ourselves. If measures of peace are necessary, they must begin somewhere; and a conciliatory temper must precede and prepare every plan of reconciliation. Nor do I conceive that we suffer any thing by thus regulating our own minds. We are not disarmed by being disencumbered of our passions. Declaiming on rebellion never added a bayonet, or a charge of powder to your military force; but I am afraid that it has been the means of taking up many muskets against you.

This outrageous language, which has been encouraged and kept alive by every art, has already done incredible mischief. For a long time, even amidst the desolations of war, and the insults of hostile laws daily accumulated on one another; the American leaders seem to have had the greatest difficulty in bringing up their people to a declaration of total independence. But the court gazette accomplished what the abettors of independence had attempted in vain. When that disingenuous compilation, and strange medley of railing and flattery, was adduced, as a proof of the united sentiments of the people of Great Britain, there was a great change throughout all America. The tide of popular affection, which had still set towards the parent country, begun immediately to turn; and to flow with great rapidity in a contrary course. Far from concealing these wild declarations of enmity, the author of the celebrated pamphlet which prepared the minds of the people for independence, insists largely on the multitude and the spirit of these addresses; and he draws an argument from them, which (if the fact were as he supposes) must be irresistible.[9] For I never knew a writer on the theory of government so partial to authority, as not to allow, that the hostile mind of the rulers to their people, did fully justify a change of government; nor can any reason whatever be given, why one people should voluntarily yield any degree of pre-eminence to another, but on a supposition of great affection and benevolence towards them. Unfortunately your rulers, trusting to other things, took no notice of this great principle of connection. From the beginning of this affair, they have done all they could to alienate your minds from your own kindred; and if they could excite hatred enough in one of the parties towards the other, they seemed to be of opinion that they had gone half the way towards reconciling the quarrel.

I know it is said, that your kindness is only alienated on account of their resistance; and therefore if the colonies surrender at discretion, all sort of regard, and even much indulgence is meant towards them in future. But can those who are partisans for continuing a war to enforce such a surrender, be responsible, (after all that has passed) for such a future use of a power, that is bound by no compacts, and restrained by no terror? Will they tell us what they call indulgencies? Do they not at this instant call the present war and all its horrours, a lenient and merciful proceeding?

9 Alluding to the argument and impact of *Common Sense*, by Thomas Paine.

No conqueror, that I ever heard of, has *professed* to make a cruel, harsh, and insolent use of his conquest. No! The man of the most declared pride, scarcely dares to trust his own heart, with this dreadful secret of ambition. But it will appear in its time; and no man who professes to reduce another to the insolent mercy of a foreign arm, ever had any sort of good-will towards him. The profession of kindness, with that sword in his hand, and that demand of surrender, is one of the most provoking acts of his hostility. I shall be told, that all this is lenient as against rebellious adversaries. But are the leaders of their faction more lenient to those who submit? Lord Howe and General Howe have powers under an act of parliament, to restore to the king's peace and to free trade any men, or district, which shall submit. Is this done? We have been over and over informed by the authorized gazette, that the city of New York, and the countries of Staten and Long Island have submitted voluntarily and cheerfully, and that many are very full of zeal to the cause of administration. Were they instantly restored to trade? Are they yet restored to it? Is not the benignity of two commissioners, naturally most humane and generous men, some way fettered by instructions, equally against their dispositions and the spirit of parliamentary faith; when Mr. Tryon, vaunting of the fidelity of the city in which he is governour,[10] is obliged to apply to ministry for leave to protect the king's loyal subjects, and to grant to them (not the disputed rights and privileges of freedom) but the common rights of men, by the name of *graces*? Why do not the commissioners restore them on the spot? Were they not named as commissioners for that express purpose? But we see well enough to what the whole leads. The trade of America is to be dealt out in *private indulgencies and graces*; that is in jobs to recompense the incendiaries of war. They will be informed of the proper time in which to send our their merchandise. From a national, the American trade is to be turned into a personal monopoly: and one set of merchants are to be rewarded for the pretended zeal,

---

10 William Tryon (1725–88), governor of New York from 1771 to 1778.

of which another set are the dupes; and thus between craft and credulity, the voice of reason is stifled; and all the misconduct, all the calamities of the war are covered and continued.

If I had not lived long enough to be little surprised at any thing, I should have been in some degree astonished at the continued rage of several gentlemen, who not satisfied with carrying fire and sword into America, are animated nearly with the same fury against those neighbours of theirs, whose only crime it is, that they have charitably and humanely wished them to entertain more reasonable sentiments, and not always to sacrifice their interest to their passion. All this rage against unresisting dissent, convinces me, that at bottom, they are far from satisfied they are in the right. For what is it they would have? A war? They certainly have at this moment the blessing of something that is very like one; and if the war they enjoy at present be not sufficiently hot and extensive, they may shortly have it as warm and as spreading as their hearts can desire. Is it the force of the kingdom they call for? They have it already; and if they choose to fight their battles in their own person, no body prevents their setting sail to America in the next transports. Do they think, that the service is stinted for want of liberal supplies? Indeed they complain without reason. The table of the house of commons will glut them, let their appetite for expence be never so keen. And I assure them further, that those who think with them in the house of commons are full as easy in the control, as they are liberal in the vote of these expences. If this be not supply or confidence sufficient, let them open their own private purse strings and give from what is left to them, as largely and with as little care as they think proper.

Tolerated in their passions, let them learn not to persecute the moderation of their fellow citizens. If all the world joined them in a full cry against rebellion, and were as hotly inflamed against the whole theory and enjoyment of freedom, as those who are the most factious for servitude, it could not in my opinion answer any one end whatsoever in this contest. The leaders of this war could not hire (to gratify their friends) one German more, than they do; or inspire him with less feeling for the persons, or less value for the privileges of their revolted brethren. If we all adopted their sentiments to a man, their allies the savage Indians, could not be more ferocious than they are: they could not murder one more helpless woman or child, or with more exquisite refinements of cruelty, torment to death one more of their English flesh and blood, than they do already. The publick money is given to purchase this alliance; — and they have their bargain.

They are continually boasting of unanimity, or calling for it. But before this unanimity can be matter either of wish or congratulation, we ought to be pretty sure, that we are engaged in a rational pursuit. Phrensy does not become a slighter distemper on account of the number of those who may be infected with it. Delusion and weakness produce not one mischief the less, because they are universal. I declare, that I cannot discern the least advantage which could accrue to us, if we were able to persuade our colonies that they had not a single friend in Great Britain. On the contrary, if the affections and opinions of mankind be not exploded as principles of connection, I conceive it would be happy for us, if they were taught to believe, that there was even a formed American party in England, to whom they could always look for support! Happy would it be for us, if in all tempers, they might turn their eyes to the parent state; so that their very turbulence and sedition should find vent in no other place than this. I believe there is not a man (except those who prefer the interest of some paltry faction to the very being of their country) who would not wish that the Americans should from time to time carry many points, and even some of them not quite reasonable, by the aid of any denomination of men here, rather than they should be driven to seek for protection against the fury of foreign mercenaries, and the waste of savages, in the arms of France.

When any community is subordinately connected with another, the great danger of the connection is the extreme pride and self-complacency of the superiour, which in all matters of controversy will probably decide in its own favour. It is a powerful corrective to such a very rational cause of fear, if the inferiour body can be made to believe, that the party inclination or political views of several in the principal state, will induce them in some degree to counteract this blind and tyrannical partiality. There is no danger that any one acquiring consideration or power in the presiding state should carry this leaning to the inferiour too far. The fault of human nature is not of that sort. Power in whatever hands is rarely guilty of too strict limitations on itself. But one great advantage to the support of authority attends such an amicable and protecting connection, that those who have conferred favours obtain influence; and from the foresight of future events can persuade men, who have received obligations, sometimes to return them. Thus by the mediation of those healing principles, (call them good or evil) troublesome discussions are brought to some sort of adjustment; and every hot controversy is not a civil war.

But, if the colonies (to bring the general matter home to us) could see, that in Great Britain the mass of the people is melted into its government, and that every dispute with the ministry, must of necessity be always a quarrel with the nation; they can stand no longer in the equal and friendly relation of fellow-citizens to the subjects of this kingdom. Humble as this relation may appear to some, when it is once broken, a strong tie is dissolved. Other sort of connections will be sought. For, there are very few in the world, who will not prefer an useful ally to an insolent master.

Such discord has been the effect of the unanimity into which so many have of late been seduced or bullied, or into the appearance of which they have sunk through mere despair. They have been told that their dissent from violent measures is an encouragement to rebellion. Men of great presumption and little knowledge will hold a language which is contradicted by the whole course of history. *General* rebellions and revolts of an whole people never were *encouraged*, now or at any time. They are always *provoked*. But if this unheard-of doctrine of the encouragement of rebellion were true, if it were true that an assurance of the friendship of numbers in this country towards the colonies, could become an encouragement to them to break off all connection with it, what is the inference? Does any body seriously maintain, that charged with my share of the publick councils, I am obliged not to resist projects which I think mischievous, lest men who suffer should be encouraged to resist? The very tendency of such projects to produce rebellion is one of the chief reasons against them. Shall that reason not be given? Is it then a rule, that no man in this nation shall open his mouth in favour of the colonies, shall defend their rights, or complain of their sufferings? Or when war finally breaks out, no man shall express his desires of peace? Has this been the law of our past, or is it to be the terms of our future connection? Even looking no further than ourselves, can it be true loyalty to any government, or true patriotism towards any country, to degrade their solemn councils into servile drawing-rooms, to flatter their pride and passions, rather than to enlighten their reason, and to prevent them from being cautioned against violence lest others should be encouraged to resistance? By such acquiescence great kings and mighty nations have been undone; and if any are at this day in a perilous situation from rejecting truth, and listening to flattery, it would rather become them to reform the errours under which they suffer, than to reproach those who forewarned them of their danger.

But the rebels looked for assistance from this country. They did so in the beginning of this controversy most certainly; and they sought it by earnest supplications to government, which dignity rejected, and by a suspension of commerce, which the wealth of this nation enabled you to despise. When they found that neither prayers nor menaces had any sort of weight, but that a firm resolution was taken to reduce them to unconditional obedience by a military force, they came to the last extremity. Despairing of us, they trusted in themselves. Not strong enough themselves, they sought succour in France. In proportion as all encouragement here lessened, their distance from this country increased. The encouragement is over; the alienation is complete.

In order to produce this favourite unanimity in delusion, and to prevent all possibility of a return to our ancient happy concord, arguments for our continuance in this course, are drawn from the wretched situation itself into which we have been betrayed. It is said, that being at war with the colonies, whatever our sentiments might have been before, all ties between us are now dissolved; and all the policy we have left is to strengthen the hands of government to reduce them. On the principle of this argument, the more mischiefs we suffer from any administration, the more our trust in it is to be confirmed. Let them but once get us into a war, and then their power is safe, and an act of oblivion past for all their misconduct.

But is it really true, that government is always to be strengthened with the instruments of war, but never furnished with the means of peace? In former times ministers, I allow, have been sometimes driven by the popular voice to assert by arms the national honour against foreign powers. But the wisdom of the nation has been far more clear, when those ministers have been compelled to consult its interests by treaty. We all know that the sense of the nation obliged the court of Charles the Second to abandon the *Dutch war*; a war next to the present the most impolitick which we ever carried on.[11] The good people of England considered Holland as a sort of dependency on this kingdom; they dreaded to drive it to the protection, or subject it to the power of France, by their own inconsiderate hostility. They paid but little respect to the court jargon of that day; nor were they inflamed by the pretended rivalship of the Dutch in trade; by the massacre at Amboyna, acted on the stage to provoke the publick vengeance; nor by declamations against the ingratitude of the United Provinces for the benefits England had conferred upon them in their infant state. They were not moved from their evident interest by all these arts; nor was it enough to tell them, they were at war; that they must go through with it; and that the cause of the dispute was lost in the consequences. The people of En-

11 The third Dutch war (1672–74) was expensive and inconclusive. The Duke of York had encouraged Charles II to continue it in order to strengthen royal power and maintain an alliance with France.

gland were then, as they are now, called upon to make government strong. They thought it a great deal better to make it wise and honest.

When I was amongst my constituents at the last summer assizes, I remember that men of all descriptions did then express a very strong desire for peace, and no slight hopes of attaining it from the commission sent out by my Lord Howe. And it is not a little remarkable, that in proportion as every person shewed a zeal for the court measures, he was then earnest in circulating an opinion of the extent of the supposed powers of that commission. When I told them that Lord Howe had no powers to treat, or to promise satisfaction on any point whatsoever of the controversy, I was hardly credited; so strong and general was the desire of terminating this war by the method of accommodation. As far as I could discover, this was the temper then prevalent through the kingdom. The king's forces, it must be observed, had at that time been obliged to evacuate Boston. The superiority of the former campaign rested wholly with the colonists. If such powers of treaty were to be wished, whilst success was very doubtful, how came they to be less so, since his majesty's arms have been crowned with many considerable advantages? Have these successes induced us to alter our mind, as thinking the season of victory not the time for treating with honour or advantage? Whatever changes have happened in the national character, it can scarcely be our wish, that terms of accommodation never should be proposed to our enemy, except when they must be attributed solely to our fears. It has happened, let me say unfortunately, that we read of his majesty's commission for making peace, and his troops evacuating his last town in the thirteen colonies at the same hour, and in the same gazette. It was still more unfortunate, that no commission went to America to settle the troubles there until several months after an act had been passed to put the colonies out of the protection of this government, and to divide their trading property without a possibility of restitution, as spoil among the seamen of the navy. The most abject submission on the part of the colonies could not redeem them. There was no man on that whole continent, or within three thousand miles of it, qualified by law to follow allegiance with protection, or submission with pardon. A proceeding of this kind has no example in history. Independency, and independency with an enmity (which putting ourselves out of the question would be called natural and much provoked) was the inevitable consequence. How this came to pass, the nation may be one day in an humour to inquire.

All the attempts made this session to give fuller powers of peace to the commanders in America, were stifled by the fatal confidence of victory, and the wild hopes of unconditional submission. There was a moment favourable to the king's arms, when if any powers of concession had existed, on the other side of the Atlantick, even after all our errours, peace in all probability might have been restored. But calamity is unhappily the usual season of reflection; and the pride of men will not often suffer reason to have any scope until it can be no longer of service.

I have always wished, that as the dispute had its apparent origin from things done in parliament, and as the acts passed there had provoked the war, that the foundations of peace should be laid in parliament also. I have been astonished to find, that those whose zeal for the dignity of our body was so hot, as to light up the flames of civil war, should even publickly declare, that these delicate points ought to be wholly left to the crown. Poorly as I may be thought affected to the authority of parliament, I shall never admit that our constitutional rights can ever become a matter of ministerial negotiation.

I am charged with being an American. If warm affection towards those over whom I claim any share of authority, be a crime, I am guilty of this charge. But I do assure you (and they who know me publickly and privately will bear witness to me) that if ever one man lived, more zealous than another, for the supremacy of parliament, and the rights of this imperial crown, it was myself. Many others indeed might be more knowing in the extent of the foundation of these rights. I do not pretend to be an antiquary, a lawyer, or qualified for the chair of professor in metaphysicks. I never ventured to put your solid interests upon speculative grounds. My having constantly declined to do so has been attributed to my incapacity for such disquisitions; and I am inclined to believe it is partly the cause. I never shall be ashamed to confess, that where I am ignorant I am diffident. I am indeed not very solicitous to clear myself of this imputed incapacity; because men, even less conversant than I am, in this kind of subtleties, and placed in stations, to which I ought not to aspire, have by the mere force of civil discretion, often conducted the affairs of great nations with distinguished felicity and glory.

When I first came into a publick trust, I found your parliament in possession of an unlimited legislative power over the colonies. I could not open the statute book, without seeing the actual exercise of it, more or less, in all cases whatsoever. This possession passed with me for a title. It does so in all human affairs. No man examines into the defects of his title to his paternal estate, or to his established government. Indeed common sense taught me, that a legislative authority, not actually limited by the express terms of its foundation, or by its own subsequent acts, cannot have its powers parcelled out by argumentative distinctions, so as to enable us to say, that here they can, and there they cannot bind. Nobody was so obliging as to produce to me any record of such distinctions, by compact or otherwise, either at the successive formation of the several colonies, or during the existence of any of them. If any gentlemen were able to see, how one power could be given up, (merely on abstract reasoning) without giving up the rest, I can only say, that they saw further than I could; nor did I ever presume to condemn any one for being clear-sighted, when I was blind. I praise their penetration and learning; and hope that their practice has been correspondent to their theory.

I had indeed very earnest wishes to keep the whole body of this authority perfect and entire as I found it, and to keep it so, not for our advantage solely; but principally for the sake of those, on whose account all just authority exists; I mean the people to be governed. For I thought I saw, that many cases might well happen, in which the exercise of every power comprehended in the broadest idea of legislature, might become in its time and circumstances, not a little expedient for the peace and union of the colonies amongst themselves, as well as for their perfect harmony with Great Britain. Thinking so, (perhaps erroneously) but being honestly of that opinion, I was at the same time very sure, that the authority of which I was so jealous, could not under the actual circumstances of our plantations be at all preserved in any of its members, but by the greatest reserve in its application; particularly in those delicate points, in which the feelings of mankind are the most irritable. They who thought otherwise, have found a few more difficulties in their work, than (I hope) they were thoroughly aware of, when they undertook the present business. I must beg leave to observe, that it is not only the invidious branch of taxation that will be resisted, but that no other given part of legislative rights can be exercised, without regard to the general opinion of those who are to be governed. That general opinion is the vehicle, and organ of legislative omnipotence. Without this, it may be a theory to entertain the mind, but it is nothing in the direction of affairs. The completeness of the legislative authority of parliament *over this kingdom* is not questioned; and yet many things indubitably included in the abstract idea of that power, and which carry no absolute injustice in themselves, yet being contrary to the opinions and feelings of the people, can as little be exercised, as if parliament in that case had been possessed of no right at all. I see no abstract reason, which can be given, why the same power which made and repealed the high commission court and the star-chamber, might not revive them again; and these courts, warned by their former fate, might possibly exercise their powers with some degree of justice.[12] But the madness would be as unquestionable, as the competence of that par-

12 The high commission court originated with the ecclesiastical commission, but became a notorious prosecutor of political offenses. The star chamber, an emanation of the king's council, prosecuted libel and sedition under Charles I. The Long Parliament abolished both courts in 1641.

liament, which should attempt such things. If any thing can be supposed out of the power of human legislature, it is religion; I admit, however, that the established religion of this country has been three or four times altered by act of parliament; and therefore that a statute binds even in that case. But we may very safely affirm, that notwithstanding this apparent omnipotence, it would be now found as impossible for king and parliament to alter the established religion of this country, as it was to King James alone, when he attempted to make such an alteration without a parliament.[13] In effect, to follow, not to force the publick inclination; to give a direction, a form, a technical dress, and a specifick sanction, to the general sense of the community, is the true end of legislature.

It is so with regard to the exercise of all the powers, which our constitution knows in any of its parts, and indeed to the substantial existence of any of the parts themselves. The king's negative to bills is one of the most indisputed of the royal prerogatives; and it extends to all cases whatsoever. I am far from certain, that if several laws, which I know, had fallen under the stroke of that sceptre, that the publick would have had a very heavy loss. But it is not the *propriety* of the exercise which is in question. The exercise itself is wisely foreborne.[14] Its repose may be the preservation of its existence; and its existence may be the means of saving the constitution itself, on an occasion worthy of bringing it forth. As the disputants, whose accurate and logical reasonings have brought us into our present condition, think it absurd, that powers or members of any constitution should exist, rarely or ever to be exercised, I hope I shall be excused in mentioning another instance, that is material. We know, that the convocation of the clergy had formerly been called, and sat with nearly as much regularity to business as parliament itself. It is now called for form only. It sits for the purpose of making some polite

---

13 James II issued by royal fiat a Declaration of Indulgence (1687) to lighten penalties against Catholics.

14 The royal prerogative to veto a bill had not been exercised since 1708.

ecclesiastical compliments to the king; and when that grace is said, retires and is heard of no more. It is however *a part of the constitution*, and may be called out into act and energy, whenever there is occasion; and whenever those, who conjure up that spirit, will choose to abide the consequences. It is wise to permit its legal existence; it is much wiser to continue it a legal existence only. So truly has prudence, (constituted as the god of this lower world) the entire dominion over every exercise of power, committed into its hands; and yet I have lived to see prudence and conformity to circumstances, wholly set at naught in our late controversies, and treated as if they were the most contemptible and irrational of all things. I have heard it a hundred times very gravely alleged, that in order to keep power in wind, it was necessary, by preference, to exert it in those very points in which it was most likely to be resisted, and the least likely to be productive of any advantage.

These were the considerations, gentlemen, which led me early to think, that, in the comprehensive dominion which the Divine Providence had put into our hands, instead of troubling our understandings with speculations concerning the unity of empire, and the identity or distinction of legislative powers, and inflaming our passions with the heat and pride of controversy, it was our duty, in all soberness, to conform our government to the character and circumstances of the several people who composed this mighty and strangely diversified mass. I never was wild enough to conceive, that one method would serve for the whole; that the natives of Hindostan and those of Virginia could be ordered in the same manner; or that the Cutchery court[15] and the grand jury of Salem could be regulated on a similar plan. I was persuaded that government was a practical thing, made for the happiness of mankind, and not to furnish out a spectacle of uniformity, to gratify the schemes of visionary politicians. Our business was to rule, not to wrangle; and it would have been a

15 From the Hindi *kacheri*, a chamber-of-audience or courthouse.

poor compensation that we had triumphed in a dispute, whilst we lost an empire.

If there be one fact in the world perfectly clear, it is this: "That the disposition of the people of America is wholly averse to any other than a free government;" and this is indication enough to any honest statesman, how he ought to adapt whatever power he finds in his hands to their case. If any ask me what a free government is, I answer that, for any practical purpose, it is what the people think so; and that they, and not I, are the natural, lawful, and competent judges of this matter. If they practically allow me a greater degree of authority over them than is consistent with any correct ideas of perfect freedom, I ought to thank them for so great a trust, and not to endeavour to prove from thence, that they have reasoned amiss, and that having gone so far, by analogy, they must hereafter have no enjoyment but by my pleasure.

If we had seen this done by any others, we should have concluded them far gone in madness. It is melancholy as well as ridiculous, to observe the kind of reasoning with which the publick has been amused, in order to divert our minds from the common sense of our American policy. There are people, who have split and anatomised the doctrine of free government, as if it were an abstract question concerning metaphysical liberty and necessity; and not a matter of moral prudence and natural feeling. They have disputed, whether liberty be a positive or a negative idea; whether it does not consist in being governed by laws; without considering what are the laws, or who are the makers; whether man has any rights by nature; and whether all the property he enjoys, be not the alms of his government, and his life itself their favour and indulgence. Others corrupting religion, as these have perverted philosophy, contend, that Christians are redeemed into captivity; and the blood of the Saviour of mankind has been shed to make them the slaves of a few proud and insolent sinners. These shocking extremes, provoking to extremes of another kind, speculations are let loose as destructive to all authority, as the former are to all freedom; and every government is called tyranny and usurpation which is not formed on their fancies. In this manner the stirrers-up of this contention, not satisfied with distracting our dependencies and filling them with blood and slaughter, are corrupting our understandings: they are endeavouring to tear up, along with practical liberty, all the foundations of human society, all equity and justice, religion and order.

Civil freedom, gentlemen, is not, as many have endeavoured to persuade you, a thing that lies hid in the depth of abstruse science. It is a blessing and a benefit, not an abstract speculation; and all the just reasoning that can be upon it, is of so coarse a texture, as perfectly to suit the ordinary capacities of those who are to enjoy, and of those who are to defend it. Far from any resemblance to those propositions in geometry and metaphysicks, which admit no medium, but must be true or false in all their latitude; social and civil freedom, like all other things in common life, are variously mixed and modified, enjoyed in very different degrees, and shaped into an infinite diversity of forms, according to the temper and circumstances of every community. The *extreme* of liberty (which is its abstract perfection, but its real fault) obtains no where, nor ought to obtain any where. Because extremes, as we all know, in every point which relates either to our duties or satisfactions in life, are destructive both to virtue and enjoyment. Liberty too must be limited in order to be possessed. The degree of restraint it is impossible in any case to settle precisely. But it ought to be the constant aim of every wise publick counsel, to find out by cautious experiments, and rational, cool endeavours, with how little, not how much of this restraint, the community can subsist. For liberty is a good to be improved, and not an evil to be lessened. It is not only a private blessing of the first order, but the vital spring and energy of the state itself, which has just so much life and vigour as there is liberty in it. But whether liberty be advantageous or not, (for I know it is a fashion to decry the very principle) none will dispute that peace is a blessing; and peace must in the course of human affairs be frequently bought by some indulgence and toleration at least to liberty. For as the sabbath, (though of divine institution) was made for man, not man for the sabbath, government, which can claim no higher origin or authority, in its exercise at least, ought to conform to the exigencies of the time, and the temper and character of the people, with whom it is concerned; and not always to attempt violently to bend the people to their theories of subjection. The bulk of mankind on their part are not excessively curious concerning any theories, whilst they are really happy; and one sure symptom of an ill-conducted state, is the propensity of the people to resort to them.

But when subjects, by a long course of such ill conduct, are once thoroughly inflamed, and the state itself violently distempered, the people must have some satisfaction to their feelings, more solid than a sophistical speculation on law and government. Such was our situation; and such a satisfaction was necessary to prevent recourse to arms; it was necessary towards laying them down; it will be necessary to prevent the taking them up again and again. Of what nature this satisfaction ought to be, I wish it had been the disposition of parliament seriously to consider. It was certainly a deliberation that called for the exertion of all their wisdom.

I am, and ever have been deeply sensible, of the difficulty of reconciling the strong presiding power, that is so useful towards the conservation of a vast, disconnected, infinitely diversified empire, with that liberty and safety of the provinces, which they must enjoy, (in opinion and practice at least) or they will not be provinces at all. I know, and have long felt the difficulty of reconciling the unwieldy haughtiness of a great ruling nation, habituated to command, pampered by enormous wealth, and confident from a long course of prosperity and victory, to the high spirit of free dependencies, animated with the first glow and activity of juvenile heat, and assuming to themselves as their birthright, some part of that very pride which oppresses them.

They who perceive no difficulty in reconciling these tempers, (which however to make peace must some way or other be reconciled) are much above my capacity, or much below the magnitude of the business. Of one thing I am perfectly clear, that it is not by deciding the suit, but by compromising the difference, that peace can be restored or kept. They who would put an end to such quarrels, by declaring roundly in favour of the whole demands of either party, have mistaken, in my humble opinion, the office of a mediator.

The war is now of full two years standing; the controversy of many more. In different periods of the dispute, different methods of reconciliation were to be pursued. I mean to trouble you with a short state of things at the most important of these periods, in order to give you a more distinct idea of our policy with regard to this most delicate of all objects. The colonies were from the beginning subject to the legislature of Great Britain, on principles which they never examined; and we permitted to them many local privileges, without asking how they agreed with that legislative authority. Modes of administration were formed in an insensible and very unsystematick manner. But they gradually adapted themselves to the varying condition of things. — What was first a single kingdom stretched into an empire; and an imperial superintendency of some kind or other became necessary. Parliament from a mere representative of the people, and a guardian of popular privileges for its own immediate constituents, grew into a mighty sovereign. Instead of being a control on the crown on its own behalf, it communicated a sort of strength to the royal authority; which was wanted for the conservation of a new object, but which could not be safely trusted to the crown alone. On the other hand, the colonies advancing by equal steps, and governed by the same necessity, had formed within themselves, either by royal instruction or royal charter, assemblies so exceedingly resembling a parliament, in all their forms, functions, and powers, that it was impossible they should not imbibe some opinion of a similar authority.

At the first designation of these assemblies, they were probably not intended for any thing more, (nor perhaps did they think themselves much higher) than the municipal corporations within this island, to which some at present love to compare them. But nothing in progression can rest on its original plan. We may as well think of rocking a grown man in the cradle of an infant. Therefore as the colonies prospered and increased to a numerous and mighty people, spreading over a very great tract of the globe; it was natural that they should attribute to assemblies, so respectable in their formal constitution, some part of the dignity of the great nations which they represented. No longer tied to by-laws, these assemblies made acts of all sorts and in all cases whatsoever. They levied money, not for parochial purposes, but upon regular grants to the crown, following all the rules and principles of a parliament to which they approached every day more and more nearly. Those who think themselves wiser than Providence and stronger than the course of nature, may complain of all this variation, on the one side or the other, as their several humours and prejudices may lead them. But things could not be otherwise; and English colonies must be had on these terms, or not had at all. In the mean time neither party felt any inconvenience from this double legislature, to which they had been formed by imperceptible habits, and old custom, the great support of all the governments in the world. Though these two legislatures were sometimes found perhaps performing the very same functions, they did not very grossly or systematically clash. In all likelihood this arose from mere neglect; possibly from the natural operation of things, which left to themselves, generally fall into their proper order. But whatever was the cause, it is certain that a regular revenue by the authority of parliament for the support of civil and military establishments, seems not to have been thought of until the colonies were too proud to submit, too strong to be forced, too enlightened not to see all the consequences which must arise from such a system.

If ever this scheme of taxation was to be pushed against the inclinations of the people, it was evident that discussions must arise, which would let loose all the elements that composed this double constitution; would shew how much each of their members had departed from its original principles; and would discover contradictions in each legislature, as well to its own first principles, as to its relation to the other, very difficult if not absolutely impossible to be reconciled.

Therefore at the first fatal opening of this contest, the wisest course seemed to be to put an end as soon as possible to the immediate causes of the dispute; and to quiet a discussion, not easily settled upon clear principles, and arising from claims, which pride would permit neither party to abandon, by resorting as nearly as possible to the old successful course. A mere repeal of the obnoxious tax, with a declaration of the legislative authority of this kingdom, was then fully sufficient to procure peace to *both sides*. Man is a creature of habit, and the first breach being of very short continuance, the colonies fell back exactly into their ancient state. The congress has used an expression with regard to this pacification, which appears to me truly significant. After the repeal of the Stamp Act, "the colonies fell," says this assembly, "into their ancient state of *unsuspecting confidence in the mother country*." This unsuspecting confidence is the true center of gravity amongst mankind, about which all the parts are at rest. It is this *unsuspecting confidence* that removes all difficulties, and reconciles all the contradictions which occur in the complexity of all ancient puzzled political establishments. Happy are the rulers which have the secret of preserving it!

The whole empire has reason to remember with eternal gratitude, the wisdom and temper of that man and his excellent associates, who, to recover this confidence, formed a plan of pacification in 1766.[16] That plan, being built upon the nature of man, and the circumstances and habits of the two countries, and not on any visionary speculations, perfectly answered its end, as long as it was thought proper to adhere to it. Without giving a rude shock to the dignity (well or ill understood) of this parlia-

16 Alluding to the Rockingham administration's repeal of the Stamp Act.

ment, they gave perfect content to our dependencies. Had it not been for the mediatorial spirit and talents of that great man, between such clashing pretensions and passions, we should then have rushed headlong (I know what I say) into the calamities of that civil war, in which, by departing from his system, we are at length involved; and we should have been precipitated into that war, at a time, when circumstances both at home and abroad were far, very far, more unfavourable unto us than they were at the breaking out of the present troubles.

I had the happiness of giving my first votes in parliament for that pacification. I was one of those almost unanimous members, who, in the necessary concessions of parliament, would as much as possible have preserved its authority, and respected its honour. I could not at once tear from my heart prejudices which were dear to me, and which bore a resemblance to virtue. I had then, and I have still my partialities. What parliament gave up I wished to be given as of grace, and favour, and affection, and not as a restitution of stolen goods. High dignity relented as it was soothed; and a benignity from old acknowledged greatness had its full effect on our dependencies. Our unlimited declaration of legislative authority produced not a single murmur. If this undefined power has become odious since that time, and full of horrour to the colonies, it it because the *unsuspicious confidence* is lost, and the parental affection, in the bosom of whose boundless authority they reposed their privileges, is become estranged and hostile.

It will be asked, if such was then my opinion of the mode of pacification, how I came to be the very person who moved, not only for a repeal of all the late coercive statutes, but for mutilating by a positive law, the entireness of the legislative power of parliament, and cutting off from it the whole right of taxation? I answer, because a different state of things requires a different conduct. When the dispute had gone to these last extremities (which no man laboured more to prevent than I did;) the concessions which had satisfied in the beginning, could satisfy no longer; because the violation of tacit faith required explicit security. The same cause which has introduced all formal compacts and convenants among men made it necessary. I mean habits of soreness, jealousy, and distrust. I parted with it, as with a limb; but as a limb to save the body; and I would have parted with more, if more had been necessary; any thing rather than a fruitless, hopeless, unnatural civil war. This mode of yielding, would, it is said, give way to independency, without a war. I am persuaded from the nature of things, and from every information, that it would have had a directly contrary effect. But if it had this effect, I confess that I should prefer independency without war, to independency with it; and I have so much trust in the inclinations and prejudices of mankind, and so little in any thing else, that I should expect ten times more benefit to this kingdom from the affection of America, though under a separate establishment, than from her perfect submission to the crown and parliament, accompanied with her terrour, disgust, and abhorrence. Bodies tied together by so unnatural a bond of union, as mutual hatred, are only connected to their ruin.

One hundred and ten respectable members of parliament voted for that conciliation. Many not present, when the motion was made, were of the sentiments of those who voted. I knew it would then have made peace. I am not without hopes that it would do so at present if it were adopted. No benefit, no revenue could be lost by it; something might possibly be gained by its consequences. For be fully assured, that, of all the phantoms that ever deluded the fond hopes of a credulous world, a parliamentary revenue in the colonies is the most perfectly chimerical. Your breaking them to any subjection, far from relieving your burthens, (the pretext for this war,) will never pay that military force which will be kept up to the destruction of their liberties and yours. I risk nothing in this prophecy.

Gentlemen, you have my opinions on the present state of publick affairs. Mean as they may be in themselves, your partiality has made them of some importance. Without troubling myself to inquire whether I am under a formal obligation to it, I have a pleasure in accounting for my conduct to my constituents. I feel warmly on this subject, and I express myself as I feel. If I presume to blame any publick proceeding, I cannot be supposed to be personal. Would to God I could be suspected of it. My fault might be greater, but the publick calamity would be less extensive. If my conduct has not been able to make any impression on the warm part of that ancient and powerful party, with whose support I was not honoured at my election; on my side, my respect, regard, and duty to them is not at all lessened. I owe the gentlemen who compose it my most humble service in every thing. I hope that whenever any of them were pleased to command me, that they found me perfectly equal in my obedience. But flattery and friendship are very different things; and to mislead is not to serve them. I cannot purchase the favour of any man by concealing from him what I think his ruin. By the favour of my fellow citizens, I am the representative of an honest, well-ordered, virtuous city; of a people, who preserve more of the original English simplicity, and purity of manners, than perhaps any other. You possess among you several men and magistrates of large and cultivated understandings; fit for any employment in any sphere. I do, to the best of my power, act so as to make myself worthy of so honourable a choice. If I were ready, on any call of my own vanity or interest, or to answer any election purpose, to forsake principles, (whatever they are) which I had formed at a mature age, on full reflection, and which had been confirmed by long experience, I should forfeit the only thing which makes you pardon so many errours and imperfections in me. Not that I think it fit for any one to rely too much on his own understanding; or to be filled with a presumption, not becoming a christian man, in his own personal stability and rectitude.

I hope I am far from that vain confidence, which almost always fails in trial. I know my weakness in all respects, as much at least as any enemy I have; and I attempt to take security against it. The only method which has ever been found effectual to preserve any man against the corruption of nature and example, is an habit of life and communication of councils with the most virtuous and publick-spirited men of the age you live in. Such a society cannot be kept without advantage or deserted without shame. For this rule of conduct I may be called in reproach a *party man*; but I am little affected with such aspersions. In the way which they call party, I worship the constitution of your fathers; and I shall never blush for my political company. All reverence to honour, all idea of what it is, will be lost out of the world, before it can be imputed as a fault to any man, that he has been closely connected with those incomparable persons, living and dead, with whom for eleven years I have constantly thought and acted. If I have wandered out of the paths of rectitude, into those of interested faction, it was in company with the Saviles, the Dowdeswells, the Wentworths, the Bentincks; with the Lenoxes, the Manchesters, the Keppels, the Saunders's; with the temperate, permanent, hereditary virtue of the whole house of Cavendish; names, among which, some have extended your fame and empire in arms, and all have fought the battle of your liberties in fields not less glorious. — These and many more like these, grafting publick principles on private honour, have redeemed the present age, and would have adorned the most splendid period in your history. Where could any man, conscious of his own inability to act alone, and willing to act as he ought to do, have arranged himself better? If any one thinks this kind of society to be taken up as the best method of gratifying low personal pride, or ambitious interest, he is mistaken; and knows nothing of the world.

Preferring this connection; I do not mean to detract in the slightest degree from others. There are some of those, whom I admire at something of a greater distance, with whom I have had the happiness also perfectly to agree, in almost all the particulars, in which I have differed from some successive administrations; and they are such, as it never can be reputable to any government to reckon among its enemies. I hope there are none of you, corrupted with the doctrine taught by wicked men for the worst purposes, and received by the malignant credulity of envy and ignorance, which is, that the men who act upon the publick stage are all alike; all equally corrupt; all influenced by no other views than the sordid lure of salary and pension. The thing, I know by experience to be false. Never expecting to find perfection in men, and not looking for divine attributes in created beings, in my commerce with my cotemporaries, I have found much human virtue. I have seen not a little publick spirit; a real subordination of interest to duty; and a decent and regulated sensibility to honest fame and reputation. The age unquestionably produces, (whether in a greater or less number than former times, I know not) daring profligates, and insidious hypocrites. What then? Am I not to avail myself of whatever good is to be found in the world, because of the mixture of evil that will always be in it? The smallness of the quantity in currency only heightens the value. They, who raise suspicions on the good on account of the behaviour of ill men, are of the party of the latter. The common cant is no justification for taking this party. I have been deceived, say they, by *Titius* and *Mævius*;[17] I have been the dupe of this pretender or of that mountebank; and I can trust appearances no longer. But my credulity and want of discernment cannot, as I conceive, amount to a fair presumption against any man's integrity. A conscientious person would rather doubt his own judgment, than condemn his species. He would say, I have observed without attention, or judged upon erroneous maxims; I trusted to profession, when I ought to have attended to conduct. Such a man will grow wise, not malignant, by his acquaintance with the world. But he that accuses all mankind of corruption ought to remember that he is sure to convict only one. In truth I should much rather admit those whom at any time I have disrelished the most, to be patterns of perfection, than seek a consolation to my own unworthiness, in a general communion of depravity with all about me.

That this ill-natured doctrine should be preached by the missionaries of a court I do not wonder. It answers their purpose. But that it should be heard among those who pretend to be

17 Standard names from examples in Roman law, translated elsewhere by Burke as John Doe and Richard Roe.

strong assertors of liberty, is not only surprising, but hardly natural. This moral levelling is a *servile principle*. It leads to practical passive obedience far better, than all the doctrines, which the pliant accommodation of theology to power has ever produced. It cuts up by the roots, not only all idea of forcible resistance, but even of civil opposition. It disposes men to an abject submission, not by opinion, which may be shaken by argument or altered by passion, but by the strong ties of publick and private interest. For if all men who act in a publick situation are equally selfish, corrupt, and venal, what reason can be given for desiring any sort of change, which besides the evils which must attend all changes, can be productive of no possible advantage? The active men in the state are true examples of the mass. If they are universally depraved, the commonwealth itself is not sound. We may amuse ourselves with talking as much as we please of the virtue of middle or humble life; that is, we may place our confidence in the virtue of those who have never been tried. But if the persons who are continually emerging out of that sphere, be no better than those whom birth has placed above it, what hopes are there in the remainder of the body, which is to furnish the perpetual succession of the state? All who have ever written on government, are unanimous, that among a people generally corrupt, liberty cannot long exist. And indeed how is it possible? when those who are to make the laws, to guard, to enforce, or to obey them, are by a tacit confederacy of manners, indisposed to the spirit of all generous and noble institutions.

I am aware that the age is not what we all wish. But I am sure, that the only means of checking its precipitate degeneracy, is heartily to concur with whatever is the best in our time; and to have some more correct standard of judging what that best is, than the transient and uncertain favour of a court. If once we are able to find, and can prevail on ourselves to strengthen an union of such men, whatever accidentally becomes indisposed to ill-exercised power, even by the ordinary operation of human passions, must join with that ferocity, and cannot long be joined, without in some degree assimilating to it. Virtue will catch as well as vice by contact; and the publick stock of honest manly principle will daily accumulate. We are not too nicely to scrutinize motives as long as action is irreproachable. It is enough, (and for a worthy man perhaps too much) to deal out its infamy to convicted guilt and declared apostacy.

This, gentlemen, has been from the beginning the rule of my conduct; and I mean to continue it, as long as such a body as I have described, can by any possibility be kept together; for I should think it the most dreadful of all offences, not only towards the present generation but to all the future, if I were to do any thing which could make the minutest breach in this great conservatory of free principles. Those who perhaps have the same intentions, but are separated by some little political animosities, will I hope discern at last, how little conducive it is to any rational purpose, to lower its reputation. For my part, gentlemen, from much experience, from no little thinking, and from comparing a great variety of things, I am thoroughly persuaded, that the last hopes of preserving the spirit of the English constitution, or of re-uniting the dissipated members of the English race upon a common plan of tranquillity and liberty, does entirely depend on their firm and lasting union; and above all on their keeping themselves from that despair, which is so very apt to fall on those, whom a violence of character and a mixture of ambitious views, do not support through a long, painful, and unsuccessful struggle.

There never, gentlemen, was a period in which the stedfastness of some men has been put to so sore a trial. It is not very difficult for well-formed minds to abandon their interest; but the separation of fame and virtue is an harsh divorce. Liberty is in danger of being made unpopular to Englishmen. Contending for an imaginary power, we begin to acquire the spirit of domination, and to lose the relish of honest equality. The principles of our forefathers become suspected to us, because we see them animating the present opposition of our children. The faults which grow out of the luxuriance of freedom, appear much more shocking to us, than the base vices which are generated from the rankness of servitude. Accordingly the least resistance to power appears more inexcusable in our eyes than the greatest abuses of authority. All dread of a standing military force is looked upon as a superstitious panick. All shame of calling in foreigners and savages in a civil contest is worn off. We grow indifferent to the consequences inevitable to ourselves from the plan of ruling half the empire by a mercenary sword. We are taught to believe that a desire of domineering over our countrymen is love to our country; that those who hate civil war abet rebellion, and that the amiable and conciliatory virtues of lenity, moderation, and tenderness to the privileges of those who depend on this kingdom are a sort of treason to the state.

It is impossible that we should remain long in a situation, which breeds such notions and dispositions, without some great alteration in the national character. Those ingenuous and feeling minds who are so fortified against all other things, and so unarmed to whatever approaches in the shape of disgrace, finding these principles, which they considered as sure means of honour, to be grown into disrepute, will retire disheartened and disgusted. Those of a more robust make, the bold, able, ambitious men, who pay some of their court to power through the people, and substitute the voice of transient opinion in the place of true glory, will give into the general mode; and those superiour understandings which ought to correct vulgar prejudice, will confirm and aggravate its errours. Many things have been long operating towards a gradual change in our principles. But this American war has done more in a very few years than all the other causes could have effected in a century. It is therefore not on its own separate account, but because of its attendant circumstances, that I consider its continuance, or its ending in any way but that of an honourable and liberal accommodation, as the greatest evils which can befal us. For that reason I have troubled you with this long letter. For that reason I intreat you again and again, neither to be persuaded, shamed, or frighted out of the principles that have hitherto led so many of you to abhor the war, its cause, and its consequences. Let us not be amongst the first who renounce the maxims of our forefathers.

> I have the honour to be,
> GENTLEMEN,
> Your most obedient,
> And faithful humble servant,
> EDMUND BURKE.

Beaconsfield,
April 3, 1777.

P.S. You may communicate this letter in any manner you think proper to my constituents.

Two Letters to Gentlemen in Bristol
on the Trade of Ireland (1778)

Here are two letters to constituents, done with a mastery, courtesy, and rhetorical vigor common in Burke and yet peculiar to him.

When he addressed the House of Commons in April and spoke for a Bill on Irish Trade that offered notable concessions to Ireland, Burke had emphasized Ireland's importance as the chief dependency of the crown now that America and its trade were lost. Samuel Span replied with a letter of protest on behalf of the Merchants Hall. Joseph Harford — a loyal supporter of Burke's — wrote for his firm to convey the apprehensions of merchants and manufacturers generally concerning the effects of the bill.

Burke points out to these merchants the consistency of his past opposition to restricting the trade of America and his present support for lifting restrictions on the trade of Ireland. He regarded Ireland as part of the empire, and believed its commercial interests should not be subordinated: "The world is large enough for us both. Let it be our care not to make ourselves too little for it." Behind his warning is a solid persuasion of the virtues of free trade: he observed in a note for a speech about this time that "a free trade is in truth the only source of wealth." The existence of trade implies a sense of partnership which its perpetuation tends to confirm. By adding to the variety of a nation, it softens manners and shows a way of harmonizing divergent interests; the economic good of a liberal trade, in this way, brings naturally with it moral as well as political benefits. Some such favorable result can be expected even from a trade between unequal partners. You will, says Burke, realize a greater advantage from the freedom of Ireland than from any imaginable restraint.

The two letters were published together as a pamphlet, having been published earlier in newspapers.

Two Letters from Mr. Burke, to Gentlemen in the City of Bristol, on the Bills Depending in Parliament relative to the Trade of Ireland 1778.

To Samuel Span, Esq.
Master of the Society of Merchants Adventurers of Bristol

Sir,

I am honoured with your letter of the 13th, in answer to mine, which accompanied the resolutions of the house relative to the trade of Ireland.

You will be so good as to present my best respects to the society, and to assure them, that it was altogether unnecessary to remind me of the interest of the constituents. I have never regarded any thing else, since I had a seat in parliament. Having frequently and maturely considered that interest, and stated it to myself in almost every point of view, I am persuaded, that, under the present circumstances, I cannot more effectually pursue it, than by giving all the support in my power to the propositions which I lately transmitted to the hall.

The fault I find in the scheme is, — that it falls extremely short of that liberality in the commercial system, which, I trust, will one day be adopted. If I had not considered the present resolutions, merely as preparatory to better things, and as a means of shewing experimentally, that justice to others is not always folly to ourselves, I should have contented myself with receiving them in a cold and silent acquiescence. Separately considered, they are matters of no very great importance. But they aim, however imperfectly, at a right principle. I submit to the restraint to appease prejudice: I accept the enlargement, so far as it goes, as the result of reason and of sound policy.

We cannot be insensible of the calamities which have been brought upon this nation by an obstinate adherence to narrow and restrictive plans of government. I confess, I cannot prevail on myself to take them up, precisely at a time, when the most decisive experience has taught the rest of the world to lay them down. The propositions in question did not originate from me, or from my particular friends. But when things are so right in themselves, I hold it my duty, not to inquire from what hands they come. I opposed the American measures upon the very same principle on which I support those that relate to Ireland. I was convinced, that the evils which have arisen from the adoption of the former, would be infinitely aggravated by the rejection of the latter.

Perhaps gentlemen are not yet fully aware of the situation of their country, and what its exigencies absolutely require. I find that we are still disposed to talk at our ease, and as if all things were to be regulated by our good pleasure. I should consider it as a fatal symptom, if, in our present distressed and adverse circumstances, we should persist in the errours which are natural only to prosperity. One cannot indeed sufficiently lament the continuance of that spirit of delusion, by which, for a long time past, we have thought fit to measure our necessities by our inclinations. Moderation, prudence, and equity, are far more suitable to our condition, than loftiness, and confidence, and rigour. We are threatened by enemies of no small magnitude, whom, if we think fit, we may despise, as we have despised others; but they are enemies who can only cease to be truly formidable, by our entertaining a due respect for their power. Our danger will not be lessened by our shutting our eyes to it; nor will our force abroad be increased by rendering ourselves feeble, and divided at home.

There is a dreadful schism in the British nation. Since we are not able to re-unite the empire, it is our business to give all possible vigour and soundness to those parts of it which are still content to be governed by our councils. Sir, it is proper to inform you, that our measures *must be healing*. Such a degree of strength must be communicated to all the members of the state, as may enable them to defend themselves, and to co-operate in the defence of the whole. Their temper too must be managed, and their good affections cultivated. They may then be disposed to bear the load with cheerfulness, as a contribution towards what may be called with truth and propriety, and not by an empty form of words, *a common cause*. Too little dependence cannot be had, at this time of day, on names and prejudices. The eyes of mankind are opened; and communities must be held together by an evident and solid interest. God forbid, that our conduct should demonstrate to the world, that Great Britain can, in no instance whatsoever, be brought to a sense of rational and equitable policy, but by coercion and force of arms!

I wish you to recollect, with what powers of concession, relatively to commerce, as well as to legislation, his majesty's commissioners to the united colonies have sailed from England within this week. Whether these powers are sufficient for their purposes, it is not now my business to examine. But we all know, that our resolutions in favour of Ireland are trifling and insignificant, when compared with the concessions to the Americans. At such a juncture, I would implore every man, who retains the least spark of regard to the yet remaining honour and security of this country, not to compel others to an imitation of their conduct; or by passion and violence, to force them to seek in the territories of the separation, that freedom, and those advantages, which they are not to look for whilst they remain under the wings of their ancient government.

After all, what are the matters we dispute with so much warmth? Do we in these resolutions *bestow* any thing upon Ireland? Not a shilling. We only consent to *leave* to them, in two or three instances, the use of the natural faculties which God has given to them, and to all mankind. Is Ireland united to the crown of Great Britain for no other purpose, than that we should counteract the bounty of Providence in her favour? And in proportion as that bounty has been liberal, that we are to regard it as an evil, which is to be met with in every sort of corrective? To say that Ireland interferes with us, and therefore must be checked, is, in my opinion, a very mistaken, and a very dangerous principle. I must beg leave to repeat, what I took the liberty of suggesting to you in my last letter, that Ireland is a country, in the same climate, and of the same natural qualities and productions, with this; and has consequently no other means of growing wealthy in herself, or, in other words, of being useful to us, but by doing the very same things which we do, for the same purposes. I hope that in Great Britain we shall always pursue, without exception, *every* means of prosperity; and of course, that Ireland *will* interfere with us in something or other; for either, in order to *limit* her, we *must restrain* ourselves, or we must fall into that shocking conclusion, that we are to keep our yet remaining dependency, upon a general and indiscriminate restraint, for the mere purpose of oppression. Indeed, Sir, England and Ireland may flourish together. The world is large enough for us both. Let it be our care not to make ourselves too little for it.

I know it is said, that the people of Ireland do not pay the same taxes, and therefore ought not in equity to enjoy the same benefits with this. I had hopes, that the unhappy phantom of a compulsory *equal taxation* had haunted us long enough. I do assure you, that until it is entirely banished from our imaginations, (where alone it has, or can have any existence) we shall never cease to do ourselves the most substantial injuries. To that argument of equal taxation, I can only say, — that Ireland pays as many taxes as those who are the best judges of her powers, are of opinion she can bear. To bear more, she must have more ability; and in the order of nature, the advantage must *precede* the charge. This disposition of things, being the law of God, neither you nor I *can* alter it. So that if you will have more help from Ireland, you must *previously* supply her with more means. I believe it will be found, that if men are suffered freely to cultivate their natural advantages, a virtual equality of contribution will come in its own time, and will flow by an easy descent through its own proper and natural channels. An attempt to disturb that course, and to force nature, will only bring on universal discontent, distress and confusion.

You tell me, Sir, that you prefer an union with Ireland to the little regulations which are proposed in parliament. This union is a great question of state, to which, when it comes properly before me in my parliamentary capacity, I shall give an honest and unprejudiced consideration. However, it is a settled rule with me, to make the most of my *actual situation*; and not to refuse to do a proper thing, because there is something else more proper, which I am not able to do. This union is a business of difficulty; and on the principles of your letter, a business impracticable. Until it can be matured into a feasible and desirable scheme, I wish to have as close an union of interest and affection with Ireland, as I can have; and that, I am sure, is a far better thing than any nominal union of government.

France, and indeed most extensive empires, which by various designs and fortunes have grown into one great mass, contain many provinces that are very different from each other in privileges and modes of government; and they raise their supplies in different ways; in different proportions; and under different authorities; yet none of them are for this reason curtailed of their natural rights; but they carry on trade and manufactures with perfect equality. In some way or other the true balance is found; and all of them are properly poised and harmonized. How much have you lost by the participation of Scotland in all your commerce? The external trade of England has more than doubled since that period; and I believe your internal (which is the most advantageous) has been augmented at least fourfold. Such virtue there is in liberality of sentiment, that you have grown richer even by the partnership of poverty.

If you think, that this participation was a loss, commercially considered, but that it has been compensated by the share which Scotland has taken in defraying the publick charge — I believe you have not very carefully looked at the publick accounts. Ireland, Sir, pays a great deal more than Scotland; and is perhaps as much, and as effectually united to England as Scotland is. But if Scotland, instead of paying little, had paid nothing at all, we should be gainers, not losers by acquiring the hearty cooperation of an active intelligent people, towards the increase of the common stock; instead of our being employed in watching and counteracting them, and their being employed in watching and counteracting us, with the peevish and churlish jealousy of rivals and enemies on both sides.

I am sure, Sir, that the commercial experience of the merchants of Bristol, will soon disabuse them of the prejudice, that they can trade no longer, if countries more lightly taxed are permitted to deal in the same commodities at the same markets. You know, that in fact, you trade very largely where you are met by the goods of all nations. You even pay high duties, on the import of your goods, and afterwards undersell nations less taxed, at their own markets; and where goods of the same kind are not charged at all. If it were otherwise, you could trade very little. You know, that the price of all sorts of manufacture is not a great deal inhanced (except to the domestick consumer) by any taxes paid in this country. This I might very easily prove.

The same consideration will relieve you from the apprehension you express, with relation to sugars, and the difference of the duties paid here and in Ireland. Those duties affect the interiour consumer only; and for obvious reasons, relative to the interest of revenue itself, they must be proportioned to his ability of payment; but in all cases in which sugar can be an *object of commerce*, and therefore (in this view) of rivalship, you are sensible, that you are at least on a par with Ireland. As to your apprehensions concerning the more advantageous situation of Ireland, for some branches of commerce, (for it is so but for some) I trust you will not find them more serious. Milford Haven, which is at your door, may serve to shew you, that the mere advantage of ports is not the thing which shifts the seat of commerce from one part of the world to the other. If I thought you inclined to take up this matter on local considerations, I should state to you, that I do not know any part of the kingdom so well situated for an advantageous commerce with Ireland as Bristol; and that none would be so likely to profit of its prosperity as our city. But your profit and theirs must concur. Beggary and bankruptcy are not the circumstances which invite to an intercourse with that or with any country; and I believe it will be found invariably true, that the superfluities of a rich nation furnish a better object of trade than the necessities of a poor one. It is the interest of the commercial world that wealth should be found every where.

The true ground of fear, in my opinion, is this; that Ireland, from the vitious system of its internal polity, will be a long time before it can derive any benefit from the liberty now granted, or from any thing else. But as I do not vote advantages, in hopes that they may not be enjoyed, I will not lay any stress upon this consideration. I rather wish, that the parliament of Ireland may, in its own wisdom, remove these impediments, and put their country in a condition to avail itself of its natural advantages. If they do not, the fault is with them, and not with us.

I have written this long letter, in order to give all possible satisfaction to my constituents with regard to the part I have taken in this affair. It gave me inexpressible concern to find, that my conduct had been a cause of uneasiness to any of them. Next to my honour and conscience, I have nothing so near and dear to me as their approbation. However, I had much rather run the risk of displeasing than of injuring them; — if I am driven to make such an option. You obligingly lament, that you are not to have me for your advocate; but if I had been capable of acting as an advocate in opposition to a plan so perfectly consonant to my known principles, and to the opinions I had publickly declared on an hundred occasions, I should only disgrace myself, without supporting with the smallest degree of credit or effect, the cause you wished me to undertake. I should have lost the only thing which can make such abilities as mine of any use to the world now or hereafter; I mean that authority which is derived from an opinion, that a member speaks the language of truth and sincerity; and that he is not ready to take up or lay down a great political system for the convenience of the hour; that he is in parliament to support his opinion of the publick good, and does not form his opinion in order to get into parliament, or to continue in it. It is in a great measure for your sake, that I wish to preserve this character. Without it, I am sure, I should be ill able to discharge, by any service, the smallest part of that debt of gratitude and affection which I owe you for the great and honourable trust you have reposed in me. I am, with the highest regard and esteem,

SIR,

You most obedient,

And humble servant,

E. B.

Beaconsfield,
23d April, 1778.

Copy of a Letter to Mess. ******* *******
and Co. Bristol

GENTLEMEN,

It gives me the most sensible concern to find, that my vote on the resolutions relative to the trade of Ireland, has not been fortunate enough to meet with your approbation. I have explained at large the grounds of my conduct on that occasion in my letters to the Merchants Hall: but my very sincere regard and esteem for you will not permit me to let the matter pass without an explanation, which is particular to yourselves, and which, I hope, will prove satisfactory to you.

You tell me, that the conduct of your late member is not much wondered at; but you seem to be at a loss to account for mine; and you lament, that I have taken so decided a part *against* my constituents.

This is rather an heavy imputation. Does it then really appear to you, that the propositions to which you refer, are, on the face of them, so manifestly wrong, and so certainly injurious to the trade and manufactures of Great Britain, and particularly to yours, that no man could think of proposing, or supporting them, except from resentment to you, or from some other oblique motive? If you suppose your late member, or if you suppose me, to act upon other reasons than we choose to avow, to what do you attribute the conduct of the *other* members, who in the beginning almost unanimously adopted those resolutions? To what do you attribute the strong part taken by the ministers, and along with the ministers, by several of their most declared opponents? This does not indicate a ministerial jobb; a party design; or a provincial or local purpose. It is therefore not so absolutely clear, that the measure is wrong, or likely to be injurious to the true interests of any place, or any person.

The reason, gentlemen, for taking this step, at this time, is but too obvious and too urgent. I cannot imagine, that you forget the great war, which has been carried on with so little success (and, as I thought, with so little policy) in America; or that you are not aware of the other great wars which are impending. Ireland has been called upon to repel the attacks of enemies of no small power, brought upon her by councils in which she has had no share. The very purpose and declared object of that original war, which has brought other wars, and other enemies on Ireland, was not very flattering to her dignity, her interest, or to the very principle of her liberty. Yet she submitted patiently to the evils she suffered from an attempt to subdue to *your* obedience, countries whose very commerce was not open to her. America was to be conquered, in order that Ireland should *not* trade thither; whilst the miserable trade which she is permitted to carry on to other places has been torn to pieces in the struggle. In this situation, are we neither to suffer her to have any real interest in our quarrel, or to be flattered with the hope of any future means of bearing the burdens which she is to incur in defending herself against enemies which we have brought upon her?

I cannot set my face against such arguments. Is it quite fair to suppose, that I have no other motive for yielding to them, but a desire of acting *against* my constituents? It is for *you*, and for *your* interest, as a dear, cherished, and respected part of a valuable whole, that I have taken my share in this question. You do not, you cannot suffer by it. If honesty be true policy with regard to the transient interest of individuals, it is much more certainly so with regard to the permanent interests of communities. I know, that it is but too natural for us to see our own *certain* ruin, in the *possible* prosperity of other people. It is hard to persuade us, that every thing which is *got* by another is not *taken* from ourselves. But it is fit, that we should get the better of these suggestions, which come from what is not the best and soundest part of our nature, and that we should form to ourselves a way of thinking, more rational, more just, and more religious. Trade is not a limited thing; as if the objects of mutual demand and consumption, could not stretch beyond the bounds of our jealousies. God has given the earth to the children of men, and he has undoubtedly, in giving it to them, given them what is abundantly sufficient for all their exigencies; not a scanty, but a most liberal provision for them all. The author of our nature has written it strongly in that nature, and has promulgated the same law in his written word, that man shall eat his bread by his labour; and I am persuaded, that no man, and no combination of men, for their own ideas of their particular profit, can, without great impiety, undertake to say, that he *shall not* do so; that they have no sort of right, either to prevent the labour, or to withhold the bread. Ireland having received no *compensation*, directly or indirectly, for any restraints on their trade; ought not, in justice or common honesty, to be made subject to such restraints. I do not mean to impeach the right of the parliament of Great Britain to make laws for the trade of Ireland. I only speak of what laws it is right for parliament to make.

It is nothing to an oppressed people, to say that in part they are protected at our charge. The military force which shall be kept up in order to cramp the natural faculties of a people, and to prevent their arrival to their utmost prosperity, is the instrument of their servitude not the means of their protection. To protect men, is to forward, and not to restrain their improvement. Else, what is it more, than to avow to them, and to the world, that you guard them from others, only to make them a prey to yourself? This fundamental nature of protection does not belong to free, but to all governments; and is as valid in Turkey as in Great Britain. No government ought to own that it exists for the purpose of checking the prosperity of its people, or that there is such a principle involved in its policy.

Under the impression of these sentiments, (and not as wanting every attention of my constituents, which affection and gratitude could inspire), I voted for these bills which you so much trouble. I voted for them, not as doing complete justice to Ireland, but as being something less unjust than the general prohibition which has hitherto prevailed. I hear some discourse, as if in one or two paltry duties on materials, Ireland had a preference; and that those who set themselves against this act of scanty justice, assert that they are only contending for an *equality*. What equality? Do they forget, that the whole woollen manufacture of Ireland, the most extensive and profitable of any, and the natural staple of that kingdom, has been in a manner so destroyed by restrictive laws of ours, and (at our persuasion, and on our promises) by restrictive laws of *their own*, that in a few years, it is probable, they will not be able to wear a coat of their own fabrick? Is this equality? Do gentlemen forget, that the understood faith upon which they were persuaded to such an unnatural act, has not been kept; but a linen-manufacture has been set up, and highly encouraged, against them? Is this equality? Do they forget the state of the trade of Ireland in beer, so great an article of consumption, and which now stands in so mischievous a position with regard to their revenue, their manufacture, and their agriculture? Do they find any equality in all this? Yet if the least step is taken towards doing them common justice in the slightest article for the most limited markets, a cry is raised, as if we were going to be ruined by partiality to Ireland.

Gentlemen, I know that the deficiency in these arguments is made up (not by you, but by others) by the usual resource on such occasions, the confidence in military force, and superiour power. But that ground of confidence, which at no time was perfectly just, or the avowal of it tolerably decent, is at this time very unseasonable. Late experience has shewn, that it cannot be altogether relied upon; and many, if not all of our present difficulties, have arisen from putting our trust in what may very possibly fail; and if it should fail, leaves those who are hurt by such a reliance, without pity. Whereas honesty and justice, reason and equity, go a very great way in securing prosperity to those who use them; and in case of failure, secure the best retreat, and the most honourable consolations.

It is very unfortunate that we should consider those as rivals, whom we ought to regard as fellow-labourers in a common cause. Ireland has never made a single step in its progress towards prosperity, by which you have not had a share, and perhaps the greatest share, in the benefit. That progress has been chiefly owing to her own natural advantages, and her own efforts, which, after a long time, and by slow degrees, have prevailed in some measure over the mischievous systems which have been adopted. Far enough she is still from having arrived even at an ordinary state of perfection; and if our jealousies were to be converted into politicks, as systematically as some would have them, the trade of Ireland would vanish out of the system of commerce. But believe me, if Ireland is beneficial to you, it is so not from the parts in which it is restrained, but from those in which it is left free, though not left unrivalled. The greater its freedom, the greater must be your advantage. If you should lose in one way, you will gain in twenty.

Whilst I remain under this unalterable and powerful conviction, you will not wonder at the *decided* part I take. It is my custom so to do, when I see my way clearly before me; and when I know, that I am not misled by any passion, or any personal interest; which in this case, I am very sure, I am not. I find that disagreeable things are circulated among my constituents; and I wish my sentiments, which form my justification, may be equally general with the circulation against me. I have the honour to be, with the greatest regard and esteem,

GENTLEMEN,
Your most obedient
and humble servant,
E. B.

Westminster,
May 2, 1778.

I send the bills.

Some Thoughts on the
Approaching Executions (1780)

The Gordon Riots shook London for seven days starting on 2 June 1780. Led by Lord George Gordon and the petitioners of his Protestant Association, the disturbance had begun in political agitation for repeal of the Catholic Relief Act of 1778. A meeting of about sixty thousand in St. George's Fields swelled to a general tumult with the burning of two Roman Catholic chapels, Newgate prison, and the house of Lord Mansfield (the lord chief-justice); with an attempt to storm the Bank of England; and with the mob's rough handling of members of both houses of Parliament. The order of the House of Commons was menaced, even as the petition was debated, by the periodic harangues of Lord George outside its doors.

Denounced in street and tavern as a known supporter of Catholic rights, Burke exhibited a courage and compassion that were remarked by many witnesses. He left a vivid testimony of his experience in a letter that tells of having spent part of the day on 6 June "in the street amidst this wild assembly into whose hands I delivered myself informing them who I was. Some of them were malignant and fanatical; but I think the far greater part of those, whom I saw, were rather dissolute and unruly, than very ill-disposed. I even found friends and well wishers amongst the blue cockades. My friends had come to persuade me to go out of town, representing, (from their kindness to me,) the danger to be much greater than it was. But I thought, that if my liberty was once gone, and that I could not walk the streets of this town with tranquillity, I was in no condition to perform the duties for which I ought alone to wish for life." He may deliberately understate the danger to himself; it is known that in other encounters his life was threatened. By the end of the riots, nearly a thousand persons were dead.

Burke's advice on punishments for the rioters follows from his belief that the way to calm a violent disorder is for the authorities to enforce a justice that is not revenge.

To Sir Grey Cooper, Bart[1]

DEAR SIR,

According to your desire, I send you a copy of the few reflections on the subject of the present executions, which occurred to me in the earliest period of the late disturbances, and which all my experience and observation since have most strongly confirmed. The executions, taking those, which have been made, which are now ordered, and which may be the natural consequence of the convictions in Surrey, will be undoubtedly too many to answer any good purpose. Great slaughter attended the suppression of the tumults; and this ought to be taken in discount from the execution of the law. For God's sake entreat of Lord North, to take a view of the sum total of the deaths before any are ordered for execution; for by not doing something of this kind, people are decoyed in detail into severities they never would have dreamed of, if they had the whole in their view at once. The scene in Surrey would have affected the hardest heart, that ever was in an human breast. Justice and Mercy have not such opposite interests as people are apt to imagine. I saw Lord Loughborough last night. He seemed strongly impressed with the sense of what necessity obliged him to go through, and I believe will enter into our ideas on the subject. On this matter you see that no time is to be lost. Before a final determination, the first thing I would recommend is, that if the very next execution cannot be delayed (by the way I do not see why it may not) it may be of but a single person; and that afterwards you should not exceed two or three; for it is enough for one riot, where the very Act of Parliament, on which you proceed, is rather a little hard in its sanctions and its construction: not that I mean to

1 Sir Grey Cooper (ca. 1726–1801) had been one of the secretaries of the treasury in the Rockingham administration of 1765–66.

complain of the latter, as either new or strained; but it was rigid from the first.

I am, Dear Sir,
Your most obedient
Tuesday,   Humble Servant,
18th July 1780.   EDMUND BURKE.

I really feel uneasy on this business, and should consider it as a sort of personal favour, if you do something to limit the extent and severity of the law on this point. — Present my best compliments to Lord North, and if he thinks, that I have had wishes to be serviceable to Government on the late occasion, I shall on my part think myself abundantly rewarded, if a few lives less than first intended should be saved; I should sincerely set it down as a personal obligation, though the thing stands upon general and strong reason of its own.

Some Thoughts on the
Approaching Executions,
Humbly Offered to Consideration

As the number of persons, convicted on account of the late un-happy tumults, will probably exceed what any one's idea of vengeance or example would deliver to capital punishment, it is to be wished, that the whole business, as well with regard to the number and description of those, who are to suffer death, as with regard to those, who shall be delivered over to lighter punishment, or wholly pardoned, should be entirely a work of reason.

It has happened frequently, in cases of this nature, that the fate of the convicts has depended more upon the accidental circumstance of their being brought earlier or later to trial, than to any steady principle of equity applied to their several cases. Without great care and sobriety, criminal justice generally begins with anger, and ends in negligence. The first, that are brought forward, suffer the extremity of the law, with circumstances of mitigation in their case; and, after a time, the most atrocious delinquents escape, merely by the satiety of punishment.

In the business now before His Majesty, the following thoughts are humbly submitted.

If I understand the temper of the publick at this moment, a very great part of the lower, and some of the middling people of this city, are in a very critical disposition, and such as ought to be managed with firmness and delicacy. In general, they rather approve than blame the principles of the rioters; though the better sort of them are afraid of the consequences of those very principles, which they approve. This keeps their minds in a suspended and anxious state, which may very easily be exasperated, by an injudicious severity, into desperate resolutions; or by weak measures, on the part of Government, it may be encouraged to the pursuit of courses, which may be of the most dangerous consequences to the publick.

There is no doubt, that the approaching executions will very much determine the future conduct of those people. They ought to be such as will humble, not irritate. Nothing will make Government more awful to them than to see, that it does not proceed by chance or under the influence of passion.

It is therefore proposed, that no execution should be made, until the number of persons, which Government thinks fit to try, is completed. When the whole is at once under the eye, an examination ought to be made into the circumstances of every particular convict; and *six*, at the very utmost, of the fittest examples may then be selected for execution, who ought to be brought out and put to death, on one and the same day, in six different places, and in the most solemn manner, that can be devised. Afterwards, great care should be taken, that their bodies may not be delivered to their friends, or to others, who may make them objects of compassion, or even veneration; some instances of the kind have happened, with regard to the bodies of those killed in the riots.

The rest of the malefactors ought to be either condemned, for larger or shorter terms, to the lighters;[2] houses of correction; service in the navy; and the like, according to the case.

This small number of executions, and all at one time, though in different places, is seriously recommended; because it is certain, that a great havock among criminals hardens, rather than subdues, the minds of people inclined to the same crimes; and therefore fails of answering its purpose as an example. Men who see their lives respected and thought of value by others, come to respect that gift of God themselves. To have compassion for oneself, or to care, more or less, for one's own life, is a lesson to be learned just as every other; and I believe it will be found, that conspiracies have been most common and most desperate, where their punishment has been most extensive and most severe.

---

2 Lighters were flat-bottomed barges often used to hold prisoners on the Thames.

Besides, the least excess in this way excites a tenderness in the milder sort of people, which makes them consider Government in an harsh and odious light. The sense of justice in men is overloaded and fatigued with a long series of executions, or with such a carnage at once, as rather resembles a massacre, than a sober execution of the laws. The laws thus lose their terrour in the minds of the wicked, and their reverence in the minds of the virtuous.

I have ever observed, that the execution of one man fixes the attention and excites awe; the execution of multitudes dissipates and weakens the effect: but men reason themselves into disapprobation and disgust; they compute more as they feel less; and every severe act, which does not appear to be necessary, is sure to be offensive.

In selecting the criminals, a very different line ought to be followed from that recommended by the champions of the Protestant Association. They recommend, that the offenders for plunder ought to be punished, and the offenders from principle spared. But the contrary rule ought to be followed. The ordinary executions, of which there are enough in conscience, are for the former species of delinquents; but such common plunderers would furnish no example in the present case, where the false or pretended principle of religion, which leads to crimes, is the very thing to be discouraged.

But the reason, which ought to make these people objects of selection for punishment, confines the selection to very few. For we must consider, that the whole nation has been, for a long time, guilty of their crime. Toleration is a new virtue in any country. It is a late ripe fruit in the best climates. We ought to recollect the poison, which, under the name of antidotes against Popery, and such like mountebank titles, has been circulated from our pulpits, and from our presses, from the heads of the Church of England, and the heads of the Dissenters. These publications, by degrees, have tended to drive all religion from our own minds, and to fill them with nothing but a violent hatred of the religion of other people, and, of course, with a hatred of their persons; and so, by a very natural progression, they have led men to the destruction of their goods and houses, and to attempts upon their lives.

This delusion furnishes no reason for suffering that abominable spirit to be kept alive by inflammatory libels, or seditious assemblies, or for Government's yielding to it, in the smallest degree, any point of justice, equity, or sound policy. The King certainly ought not to give up any part of his Subjects to the prejudices of another. So far from it, I am clearly of opinion, that on the late occasion, the Catholicks ought to have been taken, more avowedly than they were, under the protection of Government, as the Dissenters had been on a similar occasion.[3]

But, though we ought to protect against violence the bigotry of others, and to correct our own too, if we have any left, we ought to reflect, that an offence, which, in its cause, is national, ought not, in its effects, to be vindicated on individuals, but with a very well-tempered severity.

For my own part, I think the fire is not extinguished; on the contrary, it seems to require the attention of Government more than ever; but, as a part of any methodical plan for extinguishing this flame, it really seems necessary that the execution of justice should be as steady and as cool as possible.

3 Early in the reign of George I, when Jacobite rioters attacked dissenting meeting-houses, the government responded by ordering troops and passed the Riot Act of 1715 to allow prosecution of the offenders.

Some Additional Reflections
on the Executions

The great number of sufferers seems to arise from the misfortune incident to the variety of Judicatures, which have tried the crimes. It were well if the whole had been the business of one Commission; for now every trial seems as if it were a separate business, and in that light, each offence is not punished with greater severity than single offences of the kind are commonly marked: but, in reality and fact, this unfortunate affair, though diversified in the multitude of overt acts, has been one and the same riot; and therefore the executions, so far as regards the general effect on the minds of men, will have a reference to the unity of the offence, and will appear to be much more severe, than such a riot, atrocious as it was, can well justify in Government. I pray that it may be recollected, that the chief delinquents have hitherto escaped; and very many of those, who are fallen into the hands of Justice, are a poor, thoughtless set of creatures, very little aware of the nature of their offence. None of the list-makers, the assemblers of the mob, the directors and arrangers, have been convicted. The preachers of mischief remain safe, and are wicked enough not to feel for their deluded disciples; no, not at all.

I would not plead the ignorance of the Law in any, even the most ignorant, as a justification; but I am sure, that, when the question is of Mercy, it is a very great and powerful argument. I have all the reason in the world to believe that they did not know their offence was capital.

There is one argument, which I beg may not be considered as brought for any invidious purpose, or meant as imputing blame any where, but which, I think, with candid and considerate men, will have much weight. The unfortunate delinquents were perhaps much encouraged by some remissness on the part of Government itself. The absolute and entire impunity attending the same offence in Edinburgh, which was over and over again urged as an example and encouragement to these unfortunate people, might be a means of deluding them.[4] Perhaps, too, a languor in the beginning of the riots here (which suffered the leaders to proceed, until very many, as it were by the contagion of a sort of fashion, were carried to these excesses) might make these people think that there was something in the case, which induced Government to wink at the irregularity of the proceedings.

The conduct and condition of the Lord Mayor ought, in my opinion, to be considered. His answers to Lord Beauchamp, to Mr. Malo, and to Mr. Langdale, make him appear rather an accomplice in the crimes, than guilty of negligence as a Magistrate.[5] Such an example set to the mob by the first Magistrate of the City tends greatly to palliate their offence.

The license, and complete impunity too, of the publications, which, from the beginning, instigated the people to such actions, and, in the midst of trials and executions, still continues, does in a great degree render these creatures an object of compassion. In the Publick Advertiser of this morning, there are two or three paragraphs, strongly recommending such outrages; and stimulating the people to violence against the houses and persons of Roman Catholicks, and even against the chapels of the Foreign Ministers.

I would not go so far as to adopt the maxim, *quicquid multis peccatur, inultum*;[6] but, certainly, offences, committed by vast multitudes, are somewhat palliated in the *individuals*; who, when so many escape, are always looked upon rather as unlucky than criminal. All our loose ideas of justice, as it affects any individual, have in them something of comparison to the situation of oth-

4 The government by its immobility had appeared to countenance an Edinburgh riot protesting the extension into Scotland of the Catholic Relief Acts of 1778.

5 The lord mayor, Brackley Kennet, appeased the rioters and declined to protect buildings under attack, in the belief that "I must be cautious what I do lest I bring the mob to my house."

6 Lucan *Pharsalia* 5.260: "The sin of thousands always goes unpunished."

ers; and no systematick reasoning can wholly free us from such impressions.

Phil. de Comines says, our English civil wars were less destructive than others; because the cry of the conqueror always was, "Spare the common people." This principle of war should be at least as prevalent in the execution of justice. The appetite of Justice is easily satisfied, and it is best nourished, with the least possible blood. We may too recollect, that between capital punishment and total impunity there are many stages.

On the whole, every circumstance of Mercy, and of comparative Justice, does, in my opinion, plead in favour of such low, untaught, or ill-taught wretches. But, above all, the policy of Government is deeply interested, that the punishments should appear *one* solemn deliberate act, aimed not at random, and at particular offences, but done with a relation to the general spirit of the tumults; and they ought to be nothing more than what is sufficient to mark and discountenance that spirit.

CIRCUMSTANCES FOR MERCY

Not being principal.
Probable want of early and deliberate purposes.
Youth ⎫
Sex ⎭ where the highest malice does not appear.
Intoxication and levity, or mere wantonness of any kind.

Speech at Bristol Guildhall
Previous to the Election (1780)

Many things united Burke and his Bristol constituency. Among the most attentive and interested citizens were Quakers and Dissenters, and ever since 1773 Burke had stood out for religious toleration. Again, it was a mercantile city, and Burke helped negotiate local advantages and opportunities in trade. But here very gradually a division of judgment began to show. The Bristol merchants, partisans of free trade when it suited their interest, were eager for protection when threatened by national rivals. Burke, on the other hand, was a consistent free-trade advocate. The monopolistic abuse of trading privilege was a secondary reason for his attack on the East India Company, as it was a primary reason with Adam Smith, who pleased Burke once by telling him that on economic questions they had arrived independently at similar conclusions. But, however enlightened, his defense of the trading rights of Ireland in 1778 touched the nerves and pocketbooks of some who had been his warmest advocates.

Another cause of disagreement was Burke's advocacy of reform to lighten the penalties for debt, which still allowed creditors legally to subject debtors to indefinite confinement. A bill he supported in 1780 would have transferred from the plaintiff to the judge the authority to enforce such penalties. To the trading and banking interests of Bristol, however, this seemed to place in peril the system of property and credit. Finally, Burke had persisted in seeking reform of the penal laws against Catholics: a natural corollary to his defense of toleration for Dissenters, and made on much the same grounds; but as Burke's mother was Catholic and the extent of his

Catholic sympathies was regularly invoked and exaggerated in the press and caricatures, his motives were susceptible of a jaundiced reading. The Gordon Riots in the summer of 1780 heightened all these tensions. Burke had been unsparing in his condemnation of the Protestant Association, and many of his constituents objected on grounds of expedience: Bristol was a Protestant town, and that summer it had nearly endured a riot in sympathy with Gordon's cause. In the face of enormous pressure, Burke asserts an undeviating commitment to the reform of Catholic disabilities. He rightly portrays this as the largest issue in the election, and it receives his most sustained effort of exposition.

After a preliminary canvass, Burke judged that defeat was scarcely to be avoided. The speech at Guildhall is therefore a valediction as well as a retrospective defense of his conduct as representative. Though he confronts several obvious points of discord, Burke omits an irritant both sharper and less easily defined which cannot have been negligible. Democratic representation was then in its early stages, and constituents did not expect to be courted by representatives. But by the standards of the time, Bristol was eager to advise on decisions affecting its fate, and Burke was unusually stinting in his attentions. He had visited twice near the start of his service, and gave a sign of respect by the title and manner of his *Letter to the Sheriffs of Bristol*. Yet he appears to have made no visit during his last four years as member. The distinction he drew so carefully in 1774, between being a representative *of* Bristol and being a representative *in* Parliament, could seem to have proved itself in favor of the metropolis and against the place from which his authority emanated.

He had rejected, and continued to reject, the very idea of acting on instructions. But a historian of Burke in his Bristol years, Ernest Barker, has pointed out how nice a difference separates instructions from commissions: requests, that is, by individual constituents to advance their cause or to make a case on their behalf to the relevant government authority. Burke kept up the performance of routine commissions, with which he had long been familiar from pleading at the Board of Trade as agent for New York. Yet he could not help regarding these services with a disdain that sometimes crept into the language of his speeches. He recognized the legitimacy of political errand-running and at the same time deplored its tendency "to degrade the national representation into a confused and scuffling bustle of local agency." In short, Burke's perspective had grown cosmopolitan — more, perhaps, by the 1780s than it had been in the decades before, and more than it would be in the decade to follow. On the other hand, the center of Bristol's world remained Bristol.

He takes his stand on a lofty ground with the plainest of words: "I did not obey your instructions. No. I conformed to the instructions of truth and Nature, and maintained your interest, against your opinions, with a constancy that became me. A representative worthy of you ought to be a person of stability. I am to look, indeed, to your opinions, — but to such opinions as you and I *must* have five years hence. I was not to look to the flash of the day." This honest avowal would do nothing to allay the suspicion, already ventured in the hostile election pamphlets of six years before, that Burke's vaunted independence of local prejudices was lamentably consistent with the arrogance of the Rockingham party. Anyway Burke does not deny having other interests besides Bristol. He is concerned only to defend his reputation as a legislator who has acted as a good legislator ought to act.

This is not Burke's most soaring speech, but it is one of his most closely reasoned, and perhaps it is his noblest. He maintained his friendships in Bristol, and warm memories of the connection would be preserved on both sides. Yet Burke was passing from a distinguished phase of his political life, the phase that may have done most to earn him the title of statesman. He knew he would remain a leader of the Rockingham Whigs. Another seat would be found for him, though not one of the same eminence. He therefore had nothing to fear from patrons and nothing to gain from the electors, with whom his relation was now terminated, when he made this summary of his principles and his conduct without a trace of rebuke or recrimination. In the text of the speech itself, there is a touch (but only a touch) of the sentiment with which he saluted the audience at Guildhall: "Gentlemen . . . what shadows we are, and what shadows we pursue." The speech was delivered extemporaneously, and, in Burke's usual way, revised for emphasis before publication.

Mr. Burke's Speech at the Guildhall, in Bristol,

Previous to the Late Election in That City

MR. MAYOR, AND GENTLEMEN,

I am extremely pleased at the appearance of this large and respectable meeting. The steps I may be obliged to take will want the sanction of a considerable authority; and in explaining any thing which may appear doubtful in my publick conduct, I must naturally desire a very full audience.

I have been backward to begin my canvass. — The dissolution of the parliament was uncertain; and it did not become me, by an unseasonable importunity, to appear diffident of the fact of my six years endeavours to please you. I had served the city of Bristol honourably; and the city of Bristol had no reason to think, that the means of honourable service to the publick, were become indifferent to me.

I found on my arrival here, that three gentlemen had been long in eager pursuit of an object which but two of us can obtain. I found, that they had all met with encouragement. A contested election in such a city as this, is no light thing.[1] I paused on the brink of the precipice. These three gentlemen, by various merits, and on various titles, I made no doubt were worthy of your favour. I shall never attempt to raise myself by depreciating the merits of my competitors. In the complexity and confusion of these cross pursuits, I wished to take the authentick publick sense of my friends upon a business of so much delicacy. I wished to take your opinion along with me; that if I should give up the contest at the very beginning, my surrender of my post may not seem the effect of inconstancy, or timidity, or anger, or disgust, or indolence, or any other temper unbecoming a man who has engaged in the

---

1 Most parliamentary seats were filled by arrangement, the nobility of a given jurisdiction agreeing to divide up the seats among their respective candidates. A contested election was relatively uncommon.

publick service. If, on the contrary, I should undertake the election, and fail of success, I was full as anxious, that it should be manifest to the whole world, that the peace of the city had not been broken by my rashness, presumption, or fond conceit of my own merit.

I am not come, by a false and counterfeit shew of deference to your judgment, to seduce it in my favour. I ask it seriously and unaffectedly. If you wish that I should retire, I shall not consider that advice as a censure upon my conduct, or an alteration in your sentiments; but as a rational submission to the circumstances of affairs. If, on the contrary, you should think it proper for me to proceed on my canvass, if you will risk the trouble on your part, I will risk it on mine. My pretensions are such as you cannot be ashamed of, whether they succeed or fail.

If you call upon me, I shall solicit the favour of the city upon manly ground. I come before you with the plain confidence of an honest servant in the equity of a candid and discerning master. I come to claim your approbation, not to amuse you with vain apologies, or with professions still more vain and senseless. I have lived too long to be served by apologies, or to stand in need of them. The part I have acted has been in open day; and to hold out to a conduct, which stands in that clear and steady light for all its good and all its evil, to hold out to that conduct the paltry winking tapers of excuses and promises—I never will do it.— They may obscure it with their smoke; but they never can illumine sunshine by such a flame as theirs.

I am sensible that no endeavours have been left untried to injure me in your opinion. But the use of character is to be a shield against calumny. I could wish, undoubtedly (if idle wishes were not the most idle of all things) to make every part of my conduct agreeable to every one of my constituents. But in so great a city, and so greatly divided as this, it is weak to expect it.

In such a discordancy of sentiments, it is better to look to the nature of things than to the humours of men. The very attempt towards pleasing every body, discovers a temper always flashy, and often false and insincere. Therefore, as I have proceeded strait onward in my conduct, so I will proceed in my account of those parts of it which have been most excepted to. But I must first beg leave just to hint to you, that we may suffer very great detriment by being open to every talker. It is not to be imagined, how much of service is lost from spirits full of activity, and full of energy, who are pressing, who are rushing forward, to great and capital objects, when you oblige them to be continually looking back. Whilst they are defending one service, they defraud you of an hundred. Applaud us when we run; console us when we fall; cheer us when we recover; but let us pass on — for God's sake, let us pass on.

Do you think, gentlemen, that every publick act in the six years since I stood in this place before you — that all the arduous things which have been done in this eventful period, which has crowded into a few years space the revolutions of an age, can be opened to you on their fair grounds in half an hour's conversation?

But it is no reason, because there is a bad mode of inquiry, that there should be no examination at all. Most certainly it is our duty to examine; it is our interest too. — But it must be with discretion; with an attention to all the circumstances, and to all the motives; like sound judges, and not like cavilling pettyfoggers and quibbling pleaders, prying into flaws and hunting for exceptions. — Look, gentlemen, to the *whole tenour* of your member's conduct. Try whether his ambition or his avarice have justled him out of the strait line of duty; or whether that grand foe of the offices of active life, that master-vice in men of business, a degenerate and inglorious sloth, has made him flag and languish in his course? This is the object of our inquiry. If our member's conduct can bear this touch, mark it for sterling. He may have fallen into errours; he must have faults; but our errour is greater, and our fault is radically ruinous to ourselves, if we do not bear, if we do not even applaud, the whole compound and mixed mass of such a character. Not to act thus is folly; I had almost said it is impiety. He censures God, who quarrels with the imperfections of man.

Gentlemen, we must not be peevish with those who serve the

people. For none will serve us whilst there is a court to serve, but those who are of a nice and jealous honour. They who think every thing, in comparison of that honour, to be dust and ashes, will not bear to have it soiled and impaired by those, for whose sake they make a thousand sacrifices to preserve it immaculate and whole. We shall either drive such men from the publick stage, or we shall send them to the court for protection: where, if they must sacrifice their reputation, they will at least secure their interest. Depend upon it, that the lovers of freedom will be free. None will violate their conscience to please us, in order afterwards to discharge that conscience, which they have violated, by doing us faithful and affectionate service. If we degrade and deprave their minds by servility, it will be absurd to expect, that they who are creeping and abject towards us, will ever be bold and incorruptible assertors of our freedom, against the most seducing and the most formidable of all powers. No! human nature is not so formed; nor shall we improve the faculties or better the morals of publick men, by our possession of the most infallible receipt in the world for making cheats and hypocrites.

Let me say with plainness, I who am no longer in a publick character, that if by a fair, by an indulgent, by a gentlemanly behaviour to our representatives, we do not give confidence to their minds, and a liberal scope to their understandings; if we do not permit our members to act upon a *very* enlarged view of things; we shall at length infallibly degrade our national representation into a confused and scuffling bustle of local agency. When the popular member is narrowed in his ideas, and rendered timid in his proceedings, the service of the crown will be the sole nursery of statesmen. Among the frolicks of the court, it may at length take that of attending to its business. Then the monopoly of mental power will be added to the power of all other kinds it possesses. On the side of the people there will be nothing but impotence: for ignorance is impotence; narrowness of mind is impotence; timidity is itself impotence, and makes all other qualities that go along with it, impotent and useless.

At present it is the plan of the court to make its servants

insignificant. If the people should fall into the same humour, and should choose their servants on the same principles of mere obsequiousness, and flexibility, and total vacancy or indifference of opinion in all publick matters, then no part of the state will be sound; and it will be in vain to think of saving it.

I thought it very expedient at this time to give you this candid counsel; and with this counsel I would willingly close, if the matters which at various times have been objected to me in this city concerned only myself, and my own election. These charges, I think, are four in number; — my neglect of a due attention to my constituents, the not paying more frequent visits here; — my conduct on the affairs of the first Irish trade acts; — my opinion and mode of proceeding on lord Beauchamp's debtors bills; — and my votes on the late affairs of the Roman Catholicks. All of these (except perhaps the first) relate to matters of very considerable publick concern; and it is not lest you should censure me improperly, but lest you should form improper opinions on matters of some moment to you, that I trouble you at all upon the subject. My conduct is of small importance.

With regard to the first charge, my friends have spoken to me of it in the style of amicable expostulation; not so much blaming the thing, as lamenting the effects. — Others, less partial to me, were less kind in assigning the motives. I admit, there is a decorum and propriety in a member of parliament's paying a respectful court to his constituents. If I were conscious to myself that pleasure or dissipation, or low unworthy occupations, had detained me from personal attendance on you, I would readily admit my fault, and quietly submit to the penalty. But, gentlemen, I live at an hundred miles distance from Bristol; and at the end of a session I come to my own house, fatigued in body and in mind, to a little repose, and to a very little attention to my family and my private concerns. A visit to Bristol is always a sort of canvass; else it will do more harm than good. To pass from the toils of a session to the toils of a canvass, is the furthest thing in the world from repose. I could hardly serve you *as I have done*, and court you too. Most of you have heard, that I do not very remarkably spare myself in *publick* business; and in the *private* business of my constituents I have done very near as much as those who have nothing else to do. My canvass of you was not on the change, nor in the county meetings, nor in the clubs of this city: It was in the house of commons; it was at the custom-house; it was at the council; it was at the treasury; it was at the admiralty. I canvassed you through your affairs, and not your persons. I was not only your representative as a body; I was the agent, the solicitor of individuals; I ran about wherever your affairs could call me; and in acting for you I often appeared rather as a ship-broker, than as a member of parliament. There was nothing too laborious, or too low for me to undertake. The meanness of the business was raised by the dignity of the object. If some lesser matters have slipped through my fingers, it was because I filled my hands too full; and in my eagerness to serve you, took in more than any hands could grasp. Several gentlemen stand round me who are my willing witnesses; and there are others who, if they were here, would be still better; because they would be unwilling witnesses to the same truth. It was in the middle of a summer residence in London, and in the middle of a negotiation at the admiralty for your trade, that I was called to Bristol; and this late visit, at this late day, has been possibly in prejudice to your affairs.

Since I have touched upon this matter, let me say, gentlemen, that if I had a disposition, or a right to complain, I have some cause of complaint on my side. With a petition of this city in my hand, passed through the corporation without a dissenting voice, a petition in unison with almost the whole voice of the kingdom, (with whose formal thanks I was covered over) while I laboured on no less than five bills for a publick reform, and fought against the opposition of great abilities, and of the greatest power, every clause, and every word of the largest of those bills, almost to the very last day of a very long session; all this time a canvass in Bristol was as calmly carried on as if I were dead. I was considered as a man wholly out of the question. Whilst I watched, and fasted, and sweated in the house of commons — by the most easy and ordinary acts of election, by dinners and visits, by "How do you do's," and "My worthy friends," I was to be quietly moved out of my seat — and promises were made, and engagements entered into, without any exception or reserve, as if my laborious zeal in my duty had been a regular abdication of my trust.

To open my whole heart to you on this subject, I do confess, however, that there were other times besides the two years in which I did visit you, when I was not wholly without leisure for repeating that mark of my respect. But I could not bring my mind to see you. You remember, that in the beginning of this American war (that æra of calamity, disgrace and downfall, an æra which no feeling mind will ever mention without a tear for England) you were greatly divided; and a very strong body, if not the strongest, opposed itself to the madness which every art and every power were employed to render popular, in order that the errours of the rulers might be lost in the general blindness of the nation. This opposition continued until after our great, but most unfortunate victory at Long Island.[2] Then all the mounds and banks of our constancy were borne down at once; and the phrensy of the American war broke in upon us like a deluge. This victory, which seemed to put an immediate end to all difficulties, perfected us in that spirit of domination, which our unparalleled prosperity had but too long nurtured. We had been so very powerful, and so very prosperous, that even the humblest of us were degraded into the vices and follies of kings. We lost all measure between means and ends; and our headlong desires became our politicks and our morals. All men who wished for peace, or retained any sentiments of moderation, were overborne or silenced; and this city was led by every artifice (and probably with the more management, because I was one of your members) to distinguish itself by its zeal for that fatal cause. In this temper of yours and of my mind, I should have sooner fled to the extremities of the earth, than have shewn myself here. I, who saw in every American victory (for you have a long series of these misfortunes) the germ and seed of the naval power of

2 The Battle of Long Island, August 1776.

France and Spain, which all our heat and warmth against America was only hatching into life, — I should not have been a welcome visitant with the brow and the language of such feelings.
When afterwards, the other face of your calamity was turned
upon you, and shewed itself in defeat and distress, I shunned
you full as much. I felt sorely this variety in our wretchedness;
and I did not wish to have the least appearance of insulting you
with that shew of superiority, which, though it may not be assumed, is generally suspected in a time of calamity, from those
whose previous warnings have been despised. I could not bear to
shew you a representative whose face did not reflect that of his
constituents; a face that could not joy in your joys, and sorrow in
your sorrows. But time at length has made us all of one opinion;
and we have all opened our eyes on the true nature of the American war, to the true nature of all its successes and all its failures.

In that publick storm too I had my private feelings. I had seen
blown down and prostrate on the ground several of those houses
to whom I was chiefly indebted for the honour this city has done
me. I confess, that whilst the wounds of those I loved were yet
green, I could not bear to shew myself in pride and triumph in
that place into which their partiality had brought me, and to
appear at feasts and rejoicings, in the midst of the grief and
calamity of my warm friends, my zealous supporters, my generous benefactors. This is a true, unvarnished, undisguised state
of the affair. You will judge of it.

This is the only one of the charges in which I am personally
concerned. As to the other matters objected against me, which
in their turn I shall mention to you, remember once more I do
not mean to extenuate or excuse. Why should I, when the things
charged are among those upon which I found all my reputation?
What would be left to me, if I myself was the man, who softened,
and blended, and diluted, and weakened, all the distinguishing
colours of my life, so as to leave nothing distinct and determi-
nate in my whole conduct?

It has been said, and it is the second charge, that in the
questions of the Irish trade, I did not consult the interest of my

constituents, or, to speak out strongly, that I rather acted as a native of Ireland, than as an English member of parliament.

I certainly have very warm good wishes for the place of my birth. But the sphere of my duties is my true country. It was, as a man attached to your interests, and zealous for the conservation of your power and dignity, that I acted on that occasion, and on all occasions. You were involved in the American war. A new world of policy was opened, to which it was necessary we should conform, whether we would or not; and my only thought was how to conform to our situation in such a manner as to unite to this kingdom, in prosperity and in affection, whatever remained of the empire. I was true to my old, standing, invariable principle, that all things, which came from Great Britain, should issue as a gift of her bounty and beneficence, rather than as claims recovered against a struggling litigant; or at least, that if your beneficence obtained no credit in your concessions, yet that they should appear the salutary provisions of your wisdom and foresight; not as things wrung from you with your blood, by the cruel gripe of a rigid necessity. The first concessions, by being (much against my will) mangled and stripped of the parts which were necessary to make out their just correspondence and connection in trade, were of no use. The next year a feeble attempt was made to bring the thing into better shape. This attempt (countenanced by the minister) on the very first appearance of some popular uneasiness, was, after a considerable progress through the house, thrown out by *him*.

What was the consequence? The whole kingdom of Ireland was instantly in a flame. Threatened by foreigners, and, as they thought, insulted by England, they resolved at once to resist the power of France, and to cast off yours. As for us, we were able neither to protect nor to restrain them. Forty thousand men were raised and disciplined without commission from the crown.[3] Two illegal armies were seen with banners displayed at the same time and in the same country. No executive magistrate, no judicature,

3 The Irish Volunteers.

in Ireland, would acknowledge the legality of the army which bore the king's commission; and no law, or appearance of law, authorized the army commissioned by itself. In this unexampled state of things, which the least errour, the least trespass on the right or left, would have hurried down the precipice into an abyss of blood and confusion, the people of Ireland demand a freedom of trade with arms in their hands. They interdict all commerce between the two nations. They deny all new supply in the house of commons, although in time of war. They stint the trust of the old revenue, given for two years to all the king's predecessors, to six months. The British parliament, in a former session, frightened into a limited concession by the menaces of Ireland, frightened out of it by the menaces of England, were now frightened back again, and made an universal surrender of all that had been thought the peculiar, reserved, uncommunicable rights of England; — the exclusive commerce of America, of Africa, of the West Indies — all the enumerations of the acts of navigation — all the manufactures — iron, glass, even the last pledge of jealousy and pride, the interest hid in the secret of our hearts, the inveterate prejudice moulded into the constitution of our frame, even the sacred fleece itself, all went together.[4] No reserve; no exception; no debate; no discussion. A sudden light broke in upon us all. It broke in, not through well-contrived and well-disposed windows, but through flaws and breaches; through the yawning chasms of our ruin. We were taught wisdom by humiliation. No town in England presumed to have a prejudice; or dared to mutter a petition. What was worse, the whole parliament of England, which retained authority for nothing but surrenders, was despoiled of every shadow of its superintendence. It was, without any qualification, denied in theory, as it had been trampled upon in practice. This scene of shame and disgrace has, in a manner

---

4 Parliament granted free trade to Ireland in November 1779. The phrase "sacred fleece" here stands for wool, Britain's most important export throughout the eighteenth century. The wool trade had a strong parliamentary lobby.

whilst I am speaking, ended by the perpetual establishment of a military power in the dominions of this crown, without consent of the British legislature,[5] contrary to the policy of the constitution, contrary to the declaration of right: and by this your liberties are swept away along with your supreme authority—and both, linked together from the beginning, have, I am afraid, both together perished, for ever.

What! gentlemen, was I not to foresee, or foreseeing, was I not to endeavour to save you from all these multiplied mischiefs and disgraces? Would the little, silly, canvass prattle of obeying instructions, and having no opinions but yours, and such idle senseless tales, which amuse the vacant ears of unthinking men, have saved you from "the pelting of that pitiless storm,"[6] to which the loose improvidence, the cowardly rashness of those who dare not look danger in the face, so as to provide against it in time, and therefore throw themselves headlong into the midst of it, have exposed this degraded nation, beat down and prostrate on the earth, unsheltered, unarmed, unresisting? Was I an Irishman on that day, that I boldly withstood our pride? or on the day that I hung down my head, and wept in shame and silence over the humiliation of Great Britain? I became unpopular in England for the one, and in Ireland for the other. What then? What obligation lay on me to be popular? I was bound to serve both kingdoms. To be pleased with my service, was their affair, not mine.

I was an Irishman in the Irish business, just as much as I was an American, when on the same principles, I wished you to concede to America, at a time when she prayed concession at our feet. Just as much as I was an American, when I wished parliament to offer terms in victory, and not to wait the well chosen hour of defeat, for making good by weakness, and by supplication, a claim of prerogative, pre-eminence, and authority.

5 Irish perpetual mutiny act [*Burke's note*].
6 *King Lear* 3.4.29.

Instead of requiring it from me, as a point of duty, to kindle with your passions, had you all been as cool as I was, you would have been saved disgraces and distresses that are unutterable. Do you remember our commission? We sent out a solemn embassy across the Atlantick ocean, to lay the crown, the peerage, the commons of Great Britain, at the feet of the American congress. That our disgrace might want no sort of brightening and burnishing; observe who they were that composed this famous embassy. My lord Carlisle is among the first ranks of our nobility. He is the identical man who but two years before had been put forward, at the opening of a session in the house of lords, as the mover of a haughty and rigorous address against America. He was put in the front of the embassy of submission. Mr. Eden was taken from the office of lord Suffolk, to whom he was then under secretary of state; from the office of that lord Suffolk, who but a few weeks before, in his place in parliament, did not deign to inquire where a congress of vagrants was to be found. This lord Suffolk sent Mr. Eden to find these vagrants, without knowing where this king's generals were to be found, who were joined in the same commission of supplicating those whom they were sent to subdue. They enter the capital of America only to abandon it; and these assertors and representatives of the dignity of England, at the tail of a flying army, let fly their Parthian shafts of memorials and remonstrances at random behind them. Their promises and their offers, their flatteries and their menaces, were all despised; and we were saved the disgrace of their formal reception, only because the congress scorned to receive them; whilst the state-house of independent Philadelphia opened her doors to the publick entry of the ambassador of France. From war and blood we went to submission; and from submission plunged back again to war and blood; to desolate and be desolated, without measure, hope, or end. I am a Royalist, I blushed for this degradation of the crown. I am a Whig, I blushed for the dishonour of parliament. I am a true Englishman, I felt to the quick for the disgrace of England. I am a man, I felt for the melancholy reverse of human affairs, in the fall of the first power in the world.

To read what was approaching in Ireland, in the black and bloody characters of the American war, was a painful, but it was a necessary part of my publick duty. For, gentlemen, it is not your fond desires or mine that can alter the nature of things; by contending against which what have we got, or shall ever get, but defeat and shame? I did not obey your instructions: No. I conformed to the instructions of truth and nature, and maintained your interest, against your opinions, with a constancy that became me. A representative worthy of you, ought to be a person of stability. I am to look, indeed, to your opinions; but to such opinions as you and I *must* have five years hence. I was not to look to the flash of the day. I knew that you chose me, in my place, along with others, to be a pillar of the state, and not a weathercock on the top of the edifice, exalted for my levity and versatility, and of no use but to indicate the shiftings of every fashionable gale. Would to God, the value of my sentiments on Ireland and on America had been at this day a subject of doubt and discussion! No matter what my sufferings had been, so that this kingdom had kept the authority I wished it to maintain, by a grave foresight, and by an equitable temperance in the use of its power.

The next article of charge on my publick conduct, and that which I find rather the most prevalent of all, is, lord Beauchamp's bill. I mean his bill of last session, for reforming the law-process concerning imprisonment. It is said, to aggravate the offence, that I treated the petition of this city with contempt even in presenting it to the house, and expressed myself in terms of marked disrespect. Had this latter part of the charge been true, no merits on the side of the question which I took, could possibly excuse me. But I am incapable of treating this city with disrespect. Very fortunately, at this minute (if my bad eyesight does not deceive me) the worthy gentleman deputed on this business stands directly before me.[7] To him I appeal, whether I did not, though it militated with my oldest and my most recent publick opinions, deliver the petition with a strong, and more than usual

7 Mr. Williams [*Burke's note*].

recommendation to the consideration of the house, on account of the character and consequence of those who signed it. I believe the worthy gentleman will tell you, that the very day I received it, I applied to the solicitor, now the attorney general, to give it an immediate consideration; and he most obligingly and instantly consented to employ a great deal of his very valuable time to write an explanation of the bill. I attended the committee with all possible care and diligence, in order that every objection of yours might meet with a solution; or produce an alteration. I intreated your learned recorder (always ready in business in which you take a concern) to attend. But what will you say to those who blame me for supporting lord Beauchamp's bill, as a disrespectful treatment of your petition, when you hear, that out of respect to you, I myself was the cause of the loss of that very bill? for the noble lord who brought it in, and who, I must say, has much merit for this and some other measures, at my request consented to put it off for a week, which the speaker's illness lengthened to a fortnight; and then the frantick tumult about popery drove that and every rational business from the house. So that if I chose to make a defence of myself, on the little principles of a culprit, pleading in his exculpation, I might not only secure my acquittal, but make merit with the opposers of the bill. But I shall do no such thing. The truth is, that I did occasion the loss of the bill, and by a delay caused by my respect to you. But such an event was never in my contemplation. And I am so far from taking credit for the defeat of that measure, that I cannot sufficiently lament my misfortune, if but one man, who ought to be at large, has passed a year in prison by my means. I am a debtor to the debtors. I confess judgment. I owe what, if ever it be in my power, I shall most certainly pay, — ample atonement and usurious amends to liberty and humanity for my unhappy lapse. For, gentlemen, lord Beauchamp's bill was a law of justice and policy, as far as it went; I say as far as it went, for its fault was its being, in the remedial part, miserably defective.

There are two capital faults in our law with relation to civil debts. One is, that every man is presumed solvent. A presumption, in innumerable cases, directly against truth. Therefore the debtor is ordered, on a supposition of ability and fraud, to be coerced his liberty until he makes payment. By this means, in all cases of civil insolvency, without a pardon from his creditor, he is to be imprisoned for life: — and thus a miserable mistaken invention of artificial science, operates to change a civil into a criminal judgment, and to scourge misfortune or indiscretion with a punishment which the law does not inflict on the greatest crimes.

The next fault is, that the inflicting of that punishment is not on the opinion of an equal and publick judge; but is referred to the arbitrary discretion of a private, nay interested, and irritated, individual. He, who formally is, and substantially ought to be, the judge, is in reality no more than ministerial, a mere executive instrument of a private man, who is at once judge and party. Every idea of a judicial order is subverted by this procedure. If the insolvency be no crime, why is it punished with arbitrary imprisonment? If it be a crime, why is it delivered into private hands to pardon without discretion, or to punish without mercy and without measure?

To these faults, gross and cruel faults in our law, the excellent principle of lord Beauchamp's bill applied some sort of remedy. I know that credit must be preserved; but equity must be preserved too; and it is impossible that any thing should be necessary to commerce, which is inconsistent with justice. The principle of credit was not weakened by that bill. God forbid! The enforcement of that credit was only put into the same publick judicial hands on which we depend for our lives, and all that makes life dear to us. But, indeed, this business was taken up too warmly both here and elsewhere. The bill was extremely mistaken. It was supposed to enact what it never enacted; and complaints were made of clauses in it as novelties, which existed before the noble lord that brought in the bill was born. There was a fallacy that ran through the whole of the objections. The gentlemen who opposed the bill, always argued, as if the option lay between that bill and the ancient law. — But this is a grand mistake. For practically, the option is between, not that bill and the old law, but between that bill and those occasional laws, called acts of grace. For the operation of the old law is so savage, and so inconvenient to society, that for a long time past, once in every parliament, and lately twice, the legislature has been obliged to make a general arbitrary jail-delivery, and at once to set open, by its sovereign authority, all the prisons in England.

Gentlemen, I never relished acts of grace; nor ever submitted to them but from despair of better. They are a dishonourable invention, by which, not from humanity, not from policy; but merely because we have not room enough to hold these victims of the absurdity of our laws, we turn loose upon the publick three or four thousand naked wretches, corrupted by the habits, debased by the ignominy, of a prison. If the creditor had a right to those carcasses as a natural security for his property, I am sure we have no right to deprive him of that security. But if the few pounds of flesh were not necessary to his security, we had not a right to detain the unfortunate debtor, without any benefit at all to the person who confined him. — Take it as you will, we commit injustice. Now lord Beauchamp's bill intended to do deliberately, and with great caution and circumspection, upon each several case, and with all attention to the just claimant, what acts of grace do in a much greater measure, and with very little care, caution, or deliberation.

I suspect that here too, if we contrive to oppose this bill, we shall be found in a struggle against the nature of things. For as we grow enlightened, the publick will not bear, for any length of time, to pay for the maintenance of whole armies of prisoners, nor, at their own expense, submit to keep jails as a sort of garrisons, merely to fortify the absurd principle of making men judges in their own cause. For credit has little or no concern in this cruelty. I speak in a commercial assembly. You know that credit is given, because capital *must* be employed; that men calculate the chances of insolvency; and they either withhold the credit, or make the debtor pay the risk in the price. The counting-house has no alliance with the jail. Holland understands trade as well as we, and she has done much more than this obnoxious bill intended to do. There was not, when Mr. Howard visited Holland, more than one prisoner for debt in the great city of Rotterdam.[8] Although lord Beauchamp's act (which was previous to this bill, and intended to feel the way for it) has already preserved liberty to thousands; and though it is not three years since the last act of grace passed, yet by Mr. Howard's last account, there were near three thousand again in jail. I cannot name this gentleman without remarking, that his labours and writings have done much to open the eyes and hearts of mankind. He has visited all Europe, — not to survey the sumptuousness of palaces, or the stateliness of temples; not to take accurate measurements of the remains of ancient grandeur, nor to form a scale of the curiosity of modern art; not to collect medals, or collate manuscripts: — but to dive into the depths of dungeons; to plunge into the infection of hospitals; to survey the mansions of sorrow and pain; to take the gage and dimensions of misery, depression, and contempt; to remember the forgotten, to attend to the neglected, to visit the forsaken, and to compare and collate the distresses of all men in all countries. His plan is original; and it is as full of genius as it is of humanity. It was a voyage of discovery; a circumnavigation of charity. Already the benefit of his labour is felt more or less in every country: I hope he will anticipate his final reward, by seeing all its effects fully realized in his own. He will receive, not by retail but in gross, the reward of those who visit the prisoner; and he has so forestalled and monopolized this branch of charity, that there will be, I trust, little room to merit by such acts of benevolence hereafter.

Nothing now remains to trouble you with, but the fourth charge against me — the business of the Roman Catholicks. It is a business closely connected with the rest. They are all on one and the same principle. My little scheme of conduct, such as it is, is all

8 The philanthropist John Howard (ca. 1726–90) became interested in prison reform after being captured by a French privateer and imprisoned in France.

arranged. I could do nothing but what I have done on this subject, without confounding the whole train of my ideas, and disturbing the whole order of my life. Gentlemen, I ought to apologize to you, for seeming to think any thing at all necessary to be
said upon this matter. The calumny is fitter to be scrawled with
the midnight chalk of incendiaries, with "No popery," on walls
and doors of devoted houses, than to be mentioned in any civilized company. I had heard, that the spirit of discontent on that
subject was very prevalent here. With pleasure I find that I have
been grossly misinformed. If it exists at all in this city, the laws
have crushed its exertions, and our morals have shamed its appearance in day-light. I have pursued this spirit wherever I could
trace it; but it still fled from me. It was a ghost which all had
heard of, but none had seen. None would acknowledge that he
thought the publick proceedings with regard to our Catholick
dissenters to be blameable; but several were sorry it had made an
ill impression upon others, and that my interest was hurt by my
share in the business. I find with satisfaction and pride, that not
above four or five in this city (and I dare say these misled by some
gross misrepresentation) have signed that symbol of delusion
and bond of sedition, that libel on the national religion and
English character, the Protestant Association. It is therefore,
gentlemen, not by way of cure but of prevention, and lest the arts
of wicked men may prevail over the integrity of any one amongst
us, that I think it necessary to open to you the merits of this
transaction pretty much at large; and I beg your patience upon
it: for, although the reasonings that have been used to depreciate the act are of little force, and though the authority of the
men concerned in this ill design is not very imposing; yet the
audaciousness of these conspirators against the national honour, and the extensive wickedness of their attempts, have raised
persons of little importance to a degree of evil eminence, and
imparted a sort of sinister dignity to proceedings that had their
origin in only the meanest and blindest malice.

    In explaining to you the proceedings of parliament which
have been complained of, I will state to you, — first, the thing

that was done; — next, the persons who did it; — and lastly, the grounds and reasons upon which the legislature proceeded in this deliberate act of publick justice and publick prudence.

Gentlemen, the condition of our nature is such, that we buy our blessings at a price. The Reformation, one of the greatest periods of human improvement, was a time of trouble and confusion. The vast structures of superstition and tyranny, which had been for ages in rearing, and which was combined with the interest of the great and of the many; which was moulded into the laws, the manners, and civil institutions of nations, and blended with the frame and policy of states; could not be brought to the ground without a fearful struggle; nor could it fall without a violent concussion of itself and all about it. When this great revolution was attempted in a more regular mode by government, it was opposed by plots and seditions of the people; when by popular efforts, it was repressed as rebellion by the hand of power; and bloody executions (often bloodily returned) marked the whole of its progress through all its stages. The affairs of religion, which are no longer heard of in the tumult of our present contentions, made a principal ingredient in the wars and politicks of that time; the enthusiasm of religion threw a gloom over politicks; and political interests poisoned and perverted the spirit of religion upon all sides. The Protestant religion in that violent struggle, infected, as the Popish had been before, by worldly interest and worldly passions, became a persecutor in its turn, sometimes of the new sects, which carried their own principles further than it was convenient to the original reformers; and always of the body from whom they parted; and this persecuting spirit arose, not only from the bitterness of retaliation, but from the merciless policy of fear.

It was long before the spirit of true piety and true wisdom, involved in the principles of the Reformation, could be depurated from the dregs and feculence of the contention with which it was carried through. However, until this be done, the Reformation is not complete; and those who think themselves good Protestants, from their animosity to others, are in that respect no

Protestants at all. It was at first thought necessary, perhaps, to oppose to Popery another Popery, to get the better of it. Whatever was the cause, laws were made in many countries, and in this kingdom in particular, against Papists, which are as bloody as any of those which had been enacted by the popish princes and states; and where those laws were not bloody, in my opinion, they were worse; as they were slow, cruel outrages on our nature, and kept men alive only to insult in their persons every one of the rights and feelings of humanity. I pass those statutes, because I would spare your pious ears the repetition of such shocking things; and I come to that particular law, the repeal of which has produced so many unnatural and unexpected consequences.

A statute was fabricated in the year 1699, by which the saying mass (a church-service in the Latin tongue, not exactly the same as our liturgy, but very near it, and containing no offence whatsoever against the laws, or against good morals) was forged into a crime punishable with perpetual imprisonment. The teaching school, an useful and virtuous occupation, even the teaching in a private family, was in every Catholick subjected to the same unproportioned punishment. Your industry, and the bread of your children, was taxed for a pecuniary reward to stimulate avarice to do what nature refused, to inform and prosecute on this law. Every Roman Catholick was under the same act, to forfeit his estate to his nearest Protestant relation, until, through a profession of what he did not believe, he redeemed by his hypocrisy, what the law had transferred to the kinsman as the recompence of his profligacy. When thus turned out of doors from his paternal estate, he was disabled from acquiring any other by any industry, donation or charity; but was rendered a foreigner in his native land, only because he retained the religion, along with the property, handed down to him from those who had been the old inhabitants of that land before him.

Does any one who hears me, approve this scheme of things, or think there is common jutice, common sense, or common honesty in any part of it? If any does, let him say it, and I am ready to discuss the point with temper and candour. But instead of approving, I perceive a virtuous indignation beginning to rise in your minds on the mere cold stating of the statute.

But what will you feel, when you know from history how this statute passed, and what were the motives, and what the mode of making it? A party in this nation, enemies to the system of the revolution, were in opposition to the government of king William.[9] They knew that our glorious deliverer was an enemy to all persecution. They knew that he came to free us from slavery and popery, out of a country, where a third of the people are contented Catholicks under a Protestant government. He came with a party of his army composed of those very Catholicks, to overset the power of a popish prince. Such is the effect of a tolerating spirit: and so much is liberty served in every way, and by all persons, by a manly adherence to its own principles. Whilst freedom is true to itself, every thing becomes subject to it; and its very adversaries are an instrument in its hands.

The party I speak of (like some amongst us who would disparage the best friends of their country) resolved to make the king either violate his principles of toleration, or incur the odium of protecting Papists. They therefore brought in this bill, and made it purposely wicked and absurd that it might be rejected. The then court-party, discovering their game, turned the tables on them, and returned their bill to them stuffed with still greater absurdities, that its loss might lie upon its original authors. They, finding their own ball thrown back to them, kicked it back again to their adversaries. And thus this act, loaded with the double injustice of two parties, neither of whom intended to pass, what they hoped the other would be persuaded to reject, went through the legislature, contrary to the real wish of all parts of it, and of all the parties that composed it. In this manner these insolent and profligate factions, as if they were playing with balls and counters, made a sport of the fortunes and the liberties of their fellow-creatures. Other acts of persecution have been acts of malice.

---

9 Extreme Tories had opposed the 1689 revolution settlement that brought in the Protestant William of Orange as king.

This was a subversion of justice from wantonness and petulence. Look into the history of bishop Burnet.[10] He is a witness without exception.

The effects of the act have been as mischievous, as its origin was ludicrous and shameful. From that time every person of that communion, lay and ecclesiastick, has been obliged to fly from the face of day. The clergy, concealed in garrets of private houses, or obliged to take a shelter (hardly safe to themselves, but infinitely dangerous to their country) under the privileges of foreign ministers, officiated as their servants, and under their protection. The whole body of the Catholicks, condemned to beggary and to ignorance in their native land, have been obliged to learn the principles of letters, at the hazard of all their other principles, from the charity of your enemies. They have been taxed to their ruin at the pleasure of necessitous and profligate relations, and according to the measure of their necessity and profligacy. Examples of this are many and affecting. Some of them are known by a friend who stands near me in this hall. It is but six or seven years since a clergyman by the name of Maloney, a man of morals, neither guilty nor accused of any thing noxious to the state, was condemned to perpetual imprisonment for exercising the functions of his religion; and after lying in jail two or three years, was relieved by the mercy of government from perpetual imprisonment, on condition of perpetual banishment. A brother of the earl of Shrewsbury, a Talbot, a name respectable in this country, whilst its glory is any part of its concern, was hauled to the bar of the Old Bailey, among common felons, and only escaped the same doom, either by some errour in the process, or that the wretch who brought him there could not correctly describe his person; I now forget which. — In short, the persecution would never have relented for a moment, if the judges superseding (though with an ambiguous example) the strict rule of their artificial duty by the higher obligation of their conscience, did not constantly throw every difficulty in the way of such informers.

10 Gilbert Burnet, *History of His Own Times* (1724–34).

But so ineffectual is the power of legal evasion against legal iniquity, that it was but the other day, that a lady of condition, beyond the middle of life, was on the point of being stripped of her whole fortune by a near relation, to whom she had been a friend and benefactor; and she must have been totally ruined, without a power of redress or mitigation from the courts of law, had not the legislature itself rushed in, and by a special act of parliament rescued her from the injustice of its own statutes. One of the acts authorizing such things was that which we in part repealed, knowing what our duty was; and doing that duty as men of honour and virtue, as good Protestants, and as good citizens. Let him stand forth that disapproves what we have done!

Gentlemen, bad laws are the worst sort of tyranny. In such a country as this they are of all bad things the worst, worse by far than any where else; and they derive a particular malignity even from the wisdom and soundness of the rest of our institutions. For very obvious reasons you cannot trust the crown with a dispensing power over any of your laws. However, a government, be it as bad as it may, will in the exercise of a discretionary power, discriminate times and persons; and will not ordinarily pursue any man, when its own safety is not concerned. A mercenary informer knows no distinction. Under such a system, the obnoxious people are slaves, not only to the government, but they live at the mercy of every individual; they are at once the slaves of the whole community, and of every part of it; and the worst and most unmerciful men are those on whose goodness they most depend.

In this situation men not only shrink from the frowns of a stern magistrate; but they are obliged to fly from their very species. The seeds of destruction are sown in civil intercourse, in social habitudes. The blood of wholesome kindred is infected. Their tables and beds are surrounded with snares. All the means given by Providence to make life safe and comfortable, are perverted into instruments of terrour and torment. This species of universal subserviency, that makes the very servant who waits behind your chair, the arbiter of your life and fortune, has such a tendency to degrade and abase mankind, and to deprive them of that assured and liberal state of mind, which alone can make us what we ought to be, that I vow to God I would sooner bring myself to put a man to immediate death for opinions I disliked, and so to get rid of the man and his opinions at once, than to fret him with a feverish being, tainted with the jail-distemper of a contagious servitude to keep him above ground, an animated mass of putrefaction, corrupted himself, and corrupting all about him.

The act repealed was of this direct tendency; and it was made in the manner which I have related to you. I will now tell you by whom the bill of repeal was brought into parliament. I find it has been industriously given out in this city (from kindness to me unquestionably) that I was the mover or the seconder. The fact is, I did not once open my lips on the subject during the whole progress of the bill. I do not say this as disclaiming my share in that measure. Very far from it. I inform you of this fact, lest I should seem to arrogate to myself the merits which belong to others. To have been the man chosen out to redeem our fellow-citizens from slavery; to purify our laws from absurdity and injustice; and to cleanse our religion from the blot and stain of persecution, would be an honour and happiness to which my wishes would undoubtedly aspire; but to which nothing but my wishes could have possibly entitled me. That great work was in hands in every respect far better qualified than mine. The mover of the bill was Sir George Savile.[11]

When an act of great and signal humanity was to be done, and done with all the weight and authority that belonged to it, the world could cast its eyes upon none but him. I hope that few things which have a tendency to bless or to adorn life, have wholly escaped my observation in my passage through it. I have sought the acquaintance of that gentleman, and have seen him

---

11 Sir George Savile (1726–84), one of the most respected members of the House of Commons, a supporter of repeal of the Stamp Act, and an advocate of religious toleration.

in all situations. He is a true genius; with an understanding vigorous, and acute, and refined, and distinguishing even to excess; and illuminated with a most unbounded, peculiar, and original cast of imagination. With these he possesses many external and instrumental advantages; and he makes use of them all. His fortune is among the largest; a fortune which, wholly unincumbered, as it is, with one single charge from luxury, vanity, or excess, sinks under the benevolence of its dispenser. This private benevolence, expanding itself into patriotism, renders his whole being the estate of the publick, in which he has not reserved a *peculium*[12] for himself of profit, diversion, or relaxation. During the session, the first in, and the last out of the house of commons; he passes from the senate to the camp; and seldom seeing the seat of his ancestors, he is always in the senate to serve his country, or in the field to defend it. But in all well-wrought compositions, some particulars stand out more eminently than the rest; and the things which will carry his name to posterity, are his two bills; I mean that for a limitation of the claims of the crown upon landed estates; and this for the relief of the Roman Catholicks. By the former, he has emancipated property; by the latter he has quieted conscience; and by both, he has taught that grand lesson to government and subject, — no longer to regard each other as adverse parties.

Such was the mover of the act that is complained of by men, who are not quite so good as he is; an act, most assuredly not brought in by him from any partiality to the sect which is the object of it. For, among his faults, I really cannot help reckoning a greater degree of prejudice against that people, than becomes so wise a man. I know that he inclines to a sort of disgust, mixed with a considerable degree of asperity, to the system; and he has few, or rather no habits with any of its professors. What he has done was on quite other motives. The motives were these, which he declared in his excellent speech on his motion for the bill; namely, his extreme zeal to the Protestant religion, which he

12 Private purse.

thought utterly disgraced by the act of 1699; and his rooted hatred of all kind of oppression, under any colour or upon any pretence whatsoever.

The seconder was worthy of the mover, and the motion. I was not the seconder; it was Mr. Dunning, Recorder of this city. I shall say the less of him, because his near relation to you makes you more particularly acquainted with his merits. But I should appear little acquainted with them, or little sensible of them, if I could utter his name on this occasion without expressing my esteem for his character. I am not afraid of offending a most learned body, and most jealous of its reputation for that learning, when I say he is the first of his profession. It is a point settled by those who settle every thing else; and I must add (what I am enabled to say from my own long and close observation) that there is not a man, of any profession, or in any situation, of a more erect and independent spirit; of a more proud honour; a more manly mind; a more firm and determined integrity. Assure yourselves, that the names of two such men will bear a great load of prejudice in the other scale, before they can be entirely outweighed.

With this mover, and this seconder, agreed the *whole* house of commons; the *whole* house of lords; the *whole* bench of bishops; the king; the ministry; the opposition; all the distinguished clergy of the establishment; all the eminent lights (for they were consulted) of the dissenting churches. This according voice of national wisdom ought to be listened to with reverence. To say that all these descriptions of Englishmen unanimously concurred in a scheme for introducing the Catholick religion, or that none of them understood the nature and effects of what they were doing, so well as a few obscure clubs of people, whose names you never heard of, is shamelessly absurd. Surely it is paying a miserable compliment to the religion we profess, to suggest, that every thing eminent in the kingdom is indifferent, or even adverse to that religion, and that its security is wholly abandoned to the zeal of those, who have nothing but their zeal to distinguish them. In weighing this unanimous concurrence of whatever the nation has to boast of, I hope you will recollect, that all these concurring parties do by no means love one another enough to agree in any point, which was not, both evidently, and importantly, right.

To prove this; to prove, that the measure was both clearly and materially proper, I will next lay before you (as I promised) the political grounds and reasons for the repeal of that penal statute; and the motives to its repeal at that particular time.

Gentlemen, America — When the English nation seemed to be dangerously, if not irrecoverably divided; when one, and that the most growing branch, was torn from the parent stock, and ingrafted on the power of France, a great terrour fell upon this kingdom. On a sudden we awakened from our dreams of conquest, and saw ourselves threatened with an immediate invasion; which we were at that time very ill prepared to resist. You remember the cloud that gloomed over us all. In that hour of our dismay, from the bottom of the hiding-places, into which the indiscriminate rigour of our statutes had driven them, came out the body of the Roman Catholicks. They appeared before the steps of a tottering throne, with one of the most sober, measured, steady, and dutiful addresses that was ever presented to the crown.[13] It was no holiday ceremony; no anniversary compliment of parade and show. It was signed by almost every gentleman of that persuasion, of note or property, in England. At such a crisis, nothing but a decided resolution to stand or fall with their country could have dictated such an address; the direct tendency of which was to cut off all retreat; and to render them peculiarly obnoxious to an invader of their own communion. The address shewed what I long languished to see, that all the subjects of England had cast off all foreign views and connections, and that every man looked for his relief from every grievance, at the hands only of his own natural government.

It was necessary, on our part, that the natural government should shew itself worthy of that name. It was necessary, at the crisis I speak of, that the supreme power of the state should meet

13 Drafted by Burke himself.

the conciliatory dispositions of the subject. To delay protection would be to reject allegiance. And why should it be rejected, or even coldly and suspiciously received? If any independent Catholick state should choose to take part with this kingdom in a war with France and Spain, that bigot (if such a bigot could be found) would be heard with little respect, who could dream of objecting his religion to an ally, whom the nation would not only receive with its freest thanks, but purchase with the last remains of its exhausted treasure. To such an ally we should not dare to whisper a single syllable of those base and invidious topicks, upon which, some unhappy men would persuade the state, to reject the duty and allegiance of its own members. Is it then because foreigners are in a condition to set our malice at defiance, that with *them*, we are willing to contract engagements of friendship, and to keep them with fidelity and honour; but that, because we conceive some descriptions of our countrymen are not powerful enough to punish our malignity, we will not permit them to support our common interest? Is it on that ground, that our anger is to be kindled by their offered kindness? Is it on that ground, that they are to be subjected to penalties, because they are willing, by actual merit, to purge themselves from imputed crimes? Lest by an adherence to the cause of their country they should acquire a title to fair and equitable treatment, are we resolved to furnish them with causes of eternal enmity; and rather supply them with just and founded motives of disaffection, than not to have that disaffection in existence to justify an oppression, which, not from policy but disposition, we have pre-determined to exercise?

What shadow of reason could be assigned, why, at a time, when the most Protestant part of this Protestant empire found it for its advantage to unite with the two principal Popish states, to unite itself in the closest bonds with France and Spain, for our destruction, that we should refuse to unite with our own Catholick countrymen for our own preservation? Ought we, like madmen, to tear off the plaisters, that the lenient hand of prudence had spread over the wounds and gashes, which in our delirium of ambition we had given to our own body? No person ever reprobated the American war more than I did, and do, and ever shall. But I never will consent that we should lay additional voluntary penalties on ourselves, for a fault which carries but too much of its own punishment in its own nature. For one, I was delighted with the proposal of internal peace. I accepted the blessing with thankfulness and transport; I was truly happy to find *one* good effect of our civil distractions, that they had put an end to all religious strife and heart-burning in our own bowels. What must be the sentiments of a man, who would wish to perpetuate domestick hostility, when the causes of dispute are at an end; and who, crying out for peace with one part of the nation on the most humiliating terms, should deny it to those, who offer friendship without any terms at all?

But if I was unable to reconcile such a denial to the contracted principles of local duty, what answer could I give to the broad claims of general humanity? I confess to you freely, that the sufferings and distresses of the people of America in this cruel war, have at times affected me more deeply than I can express. I felt every Gazette of triumph as a blow upon my heart, which has an hundred times sunk and fainted within me at all the mischiefs brought upon those who bear the whole brunt of war in the heart of their country. Yet the Americans are utter strangers to me; a nation among whom I am not sure that I have a single acquaintance. Was I to suffer my mind to be so unaccountably warped; was I to keep such iniquitous weights and measures of temper and of reason, as to sympathize with those who are in open rebellion against an authority which I respect, at war with a country which by every title ought to be, and is most dear to me; and yet to have no feeling at all for the hardships and indignities suffered by men, who by their very vicinity, are bound up in a nearer relation to us; who contribute their share, and more than their share, to the common prosperity; who perform the common offices of social life, and who obey the laws to the

full as well as I do? Gentlemen, the danger to the state being out
of the question (of which, let me tell you, statesmen themselves
are apt to have but too exquisite a sense) I could assign no one
reason of justice, policy, or feeling, for not concurring most cordially, as most cordially I did concur, in softening some part of
that shameful servitude under which several of my worthy fellow-
citizens were groaning.

Important effects followed this act of wisdom. They appeared
at home and abroad, to the great benefit of this kingdom; and, let
me hope, to the advantage of mankind at large. It betokened
union among ourselves. It shewed soundness, even on the part of
the persecuted, which generally is the weak side of every community. But its most essential operation was not in England. The act
was immediately, though very imperfectly, copied in Ireland, and
this imperfect transcript of an imperfect act, this first faint sketch
of toleration, which did little more than disclose a principle, and
mark out a disposition, completed in a most wonderful manner
the re-union of the state, of all the Catholicks of that country. It
made us, what we ought always to have been, one family, one
body, one heart and soul, against the family-combination, and all
other combinations of our enemies. We have indeed obligations
to that people, who received such small benefits with so much
gratitude; and for which gratitude and attachment to us, I am
afraid they have suffered not a little in other places.

I dare say, you have all heard of the privileges indulged to the
Irish Catholicks residing in Spain. You have likewise heard with
what circumstances of severity they have been lately expelled
from the sea-ports of that kingdom; driven into the inland cities;
and there detained as a sort of prisoners of state. I have good
reason to believe, that it was the zeal to our government and our
cause, (somewhat indiscreetly expressed in one of the addresses
of the Catholicks of Ireland) which has thus drawn down on
their heads the indignation of the court of Madrid; to the inexpressible loss of several individuals, and in future, perhaps, to
the great detriment of the whole of their body. Now that our

people should be persecuted in Spain for their attachment to this country, and persecuted in this country for their supposed enmity to us, is such a jarring reconciliation of contradictory distresses, is a thing at once so dreadful and ridiculous, that no malice short of diabolical, would wish to continue any human creatures in such a situation. But honest men will not forget either their merit or their sufferings. There are men, (and many, I trust, there are) who, out of love to their country and their kind, would torture their invention to find excuses for the mistakes of their brethren; and who, to stifle dissention, would construe, even doubtful appearances, with the utmost favour: such men will never persuade themselves to be ingenious and refined in discovering disaffection and treason in the manifest palpable signs of suffering loyalty. Persecution is so unnatural to them, that they gladly snatch the very first opportunity of laying aside all the tricks and devices of penal politicks; and of returning home, after all their irksome and vexatious wanderings, to our natural family mansion, to the grand social principle, that unites all men, in all descriptions, under the shadow of an equal and impartial justice.

Men of another sort, I mean the bigotted enemies to liberty, may, perhaps, in their politicks, make no account of the good or ill affection of the Catholicks of England, who are but an handful of people (enough to torment, but not enough to fear) perhaps not so many, of both sexes and of all ages, as fifty thousand. But, gentlemen, it is possible you may not know, that the people of that persuasion in Ireland amount at least to sixteen or seventeen hundred thousand souls. I do not at all exaggerate the number. A *nation* to be persecuted! Whilst we were masters of the sea, embodied with America, and in alliance with half the powers of the continent, we might perhaps, in that remote corner of Europe, afford to tyrannize with impunity. But there is a revolution in our affairs, which makes it prudent to be just. In our late awkward contest with Ireland about trade, had religion been thrown in, to ferment and embitter the mass of discontents, the consequences might have been truly dreadful. But very happily, that cause of quarrel was previously quieted by the wisdom of the acts I am commending.

Even in England, where I admit the danger from the discontent of that persuasion to be less than in Ireland; yet even here, had we listened to the counsels of fanaticism and folly, we might have wounded ourselves very deeply; and wounded ourselves in a very tender part. You are apprised, that the Catholicks of England consist mostly of our best manufacturers. Had the legislature chosen, instead of returning their declarations of duty with correspondent good-will, to drive them to despair, there is a country at their very door, to which they would be invited; a country in all respects as good as ours, and with the finest cities in the world ready built to receive them. And thus the bigotry of a free country, and in an enlightened age, would have re-peopled the cities of Flanders, which, in the darkness of two hundred years ago, had been desolated by the superstition of a cruel tyrant. Our manufactures were the growth of the persecutions in the Low Countries.[14] What a spectacle would it be to Europe, to see us at this time of day, balancing the account of tyranny with those very countries, and by our persecutions, driving back trade and manufacture, as a sort of vagabonds, to their original settlement! But I trust we shall be saved this last of disgraces.

So far as to the effect of the act on the interests of this nation. With regard to the interests of mankind at large, I am sure the benefit was very considerable. Long before this act, indeed, the spirit of toleration began to gain ground in Europe. In Holland, the third part of the people are Catholicks; they live at ease; and are a sound part of the state. In many parts of Germany, Protestants and Papists partake the same cities, the same councils, and even the same churches. The unbounded liberality of the king of Prussia's conduct on this occasion is known to all the world;

14 The silk trade at Spitalfields was carried out by Huguenots — Protestant refugees who had fled France and the Low Countries after earlier episodes of persecution, most notably the St. Bartholomew's Day Massacre of 1572 and the revocation of the Edict of Nantes in 1685.

and it is of a piece with the other grand maxims of his reign. The magnanimity of the imperial court, breaking through the narrow principles of its predecessors, has indulged its protestant subjects, not only with property, with worship, with liberal education; but with honours and trusts, both civil and military. A worthy protestant gentleman of this country now fills, and fills with credit, a high office in the Austrian Netherlands. Even the Lutheran obstinacy of Sweden has thawed at length, and opened a toleration to all religions. I know myself, that in France the Protestants begin to be at rest. The army, which in that country is every thing, is open to them; and some of the military rewards and decorations which the laws deny, are supplied by others, to make the service acceptable and honourable. The first minister of finance in that country, is a Protestant. Two years war without a tax, is among the first-fruits of their liberality. Tarnished as the glory of this nation is, and as far as it has waded into the shades of an eclipse, some beams of its former illumination still play upon its surface; and what is done in England is still looked to, as argument, and as example. It is certainly true, that no law of this country ever met with such universal applause abroad, or was so likely to produce the perfection of that tolerating spirit, which, as I observed, has been long gaining ground in Europe; for abroad, it was universally thought that we had done, what, I am sorry to say, we had not; they thought we had granted a full toleration. That opinion was however so far from hurting the Protestant cause, that I declare, with the most serious solemnity, my firm belief, that no one thing done for these fifty years past, was so likely to prove deeply beneficial to our religion at large as Sir George Savile's act. In its effects it was, "an act for tolerating and protecting Protestantism throughout Europe:" and I hope that those who were taking steps for the quiet and settlement of our Protestant brethren in other countries, will even yet, rather consider the steady equity of the greater and better part of the people of Great Britain, than the vanity and violence of a few.

I perceive, gentlemen, by the manner of all about me, that you look with horrour on the wicked clamour which has been raised on this subject; and that instead of an apology for what was done, you rather demand from me an account, why the execution of the scheme of toleration, was not made more answerable to the large and liberal grounds on which it was taken up. The question is natural and proper; and I remember that a great and learned magistrate,[15] distinguished for his strong and systematick understanding, and who at that time was a member of the house of commons, made the same objection to the proceeding. The statutes, as they now stand, are, without doubt, perfectly absurd. But I beg leave to explain the cause of this gross imperfection, in the tolerating plan, as well and as shortly as I am able. It was universally thought, that the session ought not to pass over without doing *something* in this business. To revise the whole body of the penal statutes was conceived to be an object too big for the time. The penal statute therefore which was chosen for repeal (chosen to shew our disposition to conciliate, not to perfect a toleration) was this act of ludicrous cruelty, of which I have just given you the history. It is an act, which, though not by a great deal so fierce and bloody as some of the rest, was infinitely more ready in the execution. It was the act which gave the greatest encouragement to those pests of society, mercenary informers, and interested disturbers of household peace; and it was observed with truth, that the prosecutions, either carried to conviction or compounded, for many years, had been all commenced upon that act. It was said, that whilst we were deliberating on a more perfect scheme, the spirit of the age would never come up to the execution of the statutes which remained; especially as more steps, and a co-operation of more minds and powers, were required towards a mischievous use of them, than for the execution of the act to be repealed: that it was better to unravel this texture from below than from above, beginning with the latest, which, in general practice, is the severest evil. It was alleged, that this slow proceeding would be attended with the advantage of a

15 The Chancellor [*Burke's note*].

progressive experience; and that the people would grow reconciled to toleration, when they should find by the effects, that justice was not so irreconcileable an enemy to convenience as they had imagined.

These, gentlemen, were the reasons why we left this good work in the rude unfinished state, in which good works are commonly left, through the same circumspection with which a timid prudence so frequently enervates beneficence. In doing good, we are generally cold, and languid, and sluggish; and of all things afraid of being too much in the right. But the works of malice and injustice are quite in another style. They are finished with a bold masterly hand; touched as they are with the spirit of those vehement passions that call forth our energies whenever we oppress and persecute.

Thus this matter was left for the time, with a full determination in parliament, not to suffer other and worse statutes to remain for the purpose of counteracting the benefits proposed by the repeal of one penal law; for nobody then dreamed of defending what was done as a benefit on the ground of its being no benefit at all. We were not then ripe for so mean a subterfuge.

I do not wish to go over the horrid scene that was afterwards acted. Would to God it could be expunged for ever from the annals of this country! But since it must submit for our shame, let it submit for our instruction. In the year 1780, there were found in this nation men deluded enough (for I give the whole to their delusion) on pretences of zeal and piety, without any sort of provocation whatsoever, real or pretended, to make a desperate attempt, which would have consumed all the glory and power of this country, in the flames of London; and buried all law, order, and religion, under the ruins of the metropolis of the Protestant world. Whether all this mischief done, or in the direct train of doing, was in their original scheme, I cannot say; I hope it was not; but this would have been the unavoidable consequence of their proceedings, had not the flames they had lighted up in their fury been extinguished in their blood.

All the time that this horrid scene was acting, or avenging, as well as for some time before, and ever since, the wicked instigators of this unhappy multitude, guilty, with every aggravation, of all their crimes, and screened in a cowardly darkness from their punishment, continued, without interruption, pity or remorse, to blow up the blind rage of the populace, with a continued blast of pestilential libels, which infected and poisoned the very air we breathed in.

The main drift of all the libels, and all the riots, was, to force parliament (to persuade us was hopeless) into an act of national perfidy, which has no example. For, gentlemen, it is proper you should all know what infamy we escaped by refusing that repeal, for a refusal of which, it seems, I, among others, stand somewhere or other accused. When we took away, on the motives which I had the honour of stating to you, a few of the innumerable penalties upon an oppressed and injured people, the relief was not absolute, but given on a stipulation and compact between them and us; for we bound down the Roman Catholicks with the most solemn oaths, to bear true allegiance to this government; to abjure all sort of temporal power in any other; and to renounce, under the same solemn obligations, the doctrines of systematick perfidy, with which they stood (I conceive very unjustly) charged. Now our modest petitioners came up to us, most humbly praying nothing more, than that we should break our faith, without any one cause whatsoever of forfeiture assigned; and when the subjects of this kingdom had, on their part, fully performed their engagement, we should refuse on our part, the benefit we had stipulated on the performance of those very conditions that were prescribed by our own authority, and taken on the sanction of our publick faith — That is to say, when we had inveigled them with fair promises within our door, we were to shut it on them; and, adding mockery to outrage — to tell them, "Now we have got you fast — your consciences are bound to a power resolved on your destruction. We have made you swear, that your religion obliges you to keep your faith: fools as you are! we will now let you see, that our religion enjoins us to

keep no faith with you." — They who would advisedly call upon
us to do such things, must certainly have thought us not only a
convention of treacherous tyrants, but a gang of the lowest and
dirtiest wretches that ever disgraced humanity. Had we done
this, we should have indeed proved, that there were *some* in the
world whom no faith could bind; and we should have *convicted*
ourselves of that odious principle of which Papists stood *accused*
by those very savages, who wished us, on that accusation, to deliver them over to their fury.

In this audacious tumult, when our very name and character
as gentlemen, was to be cancelled for ever along with the faith
and honour of the nation, I, who had exerted myself very little
on the quiet passing of the bill, thought it necessary then to
come forward. I was not alone; but though some distinguished
members on all sides, and particularly on ours, added much to
their high reputation by the part they took on that day, (a part
which will be remembered as long as honour, spirit, and eloquence have estimation in the world) I may and will value myself
so far, that yielding in abilities to many, I yielded in zeal to none.
With warmth and vigour, and animated with a just and natural
indignation, I called forth every faculty that I possessed, and I
directed it in every way in which I could possibly employ it. I
laboured night and day. I laboured in parliament: I laboured out
of parliament. If therefore the resolution of the house of commons, refusing to commit this act of unmatched turpitude, be a
crime, I am guilty among the foremost. But indeed, whatever the
faults of that house may have been, no one member was found
hardy enough to propose so infamous a thing; and on full debate we passed the resolution against the petitions with as much
unanimity, as we had formerly passed the law of which these
petitions demanded the repeal.

There was a circumstance (justice will not suffer me to pass it
over) which, if any thing could enforce the reasons I have given,
would fully justify the act of relief, and render a repeal, or any
thing like a repeal, unnatural, impossible. It was the behaviour of
the persecuted Roman Catholicks under the acts of violence and

brutal insolence, which they suffered. I suppose there are not in London less than four or five thousand of that persuasion from my country, who do a great deal of the most laborious works in the metropolis; and they chiefly inhabit those quarters, which were the principal theatre of the fury of the bigotted multitude. They are known to be men of strong arms, and quick feelings, and more remarkable for a determined resolution, than clear ideas, or much foresight. But though provoked by every thing that can stir the blood of men, their houses and chapels in flames, and with the most atrocious profanations of every thing which they hold sacred before their eyes, not a hand was moved to retaliate, or even to defend. Had a conflict once begun, the rage of their persecutors would have redoubled. Thus fury increasing by the reverberation of outrages, house being fired for house, and church for chapel, I am convinced, that no power under heaven could have prevented a general conflagration; and at this day London would have been a tale. But I am well informed, and the thing speaks it, that their clergy exerted their whole influence to keep their people in such a state of forbearance and quiet, as, when I look back, fills me with astonishment; but not with astonishment only. Their merits on that occasion ought not to be forgotten; nor will they, when Englishmen come to recollect themselves. I am sure it were far more proper to have called them forth, and given them the thanks of both houses of parliament, than to have suffered those worthy clergymen, and excellent citizens, to be hunted into holes and corners, whilst we are making low-minded inquisitions into the number of their people; as if a tolerating principle was never to prevail, unless we were very sure that only a few could possibly take advantage of it. But indeed we are not yet well recovered of our fright. Our reason, I trust, will return with our security; and this unfortunate temper will pass over like a cloud.

Gentlemen, I have now laid before you a few of the reasons for taking away the penalties of the act of 1699, and for refusing to establish them on the riotous requisition of 1780. Because I would not suffer any thing which may be for your satisfaction to escape, permit me just to touch on the objections urged against our act and our resolves, and intended as a justification of the violence offered to both houses. "Parliament," they assert, "was too hasty, and they ought, in so essential and alarming a change, to have proceeded with a far greater degree of deliberation." The direct contrary. Parliament was too slow. They took four-score years to deliberate on the repeal of an act which ought not to have survived a second session. When at length, after a pro-crastination of near a century, the business was taken up, it pro-ceeded in the most publick manner, by the ordinary stages, and as slowly as a law so evidently right as to be resisted by none, would naturally advance. Had it been read three times in one day, we should have shewn only a becoming readiness to recog-nize by protection the undoubted dutiful behaviour of those whom we had but too long punished for offences of presumption or conjecture. But for what end was that bill to linger beyond the usual period of an unopposed measure? Was it to be delayed until a rabble in Edinburgh should dictate to the church of En-gland what measure of persecution was fitting for her safety?[16] Was it to be adjourned until a fanatical force could be collected in London, sufficient to frighten us out of all our ideas of policy and justice? Were we to wait for the profound lectures on the reason of state, ecclesiastical and political, which the Protestant association have since condescended to read to us? Or were we, seven hundred peers and commoners, the only persons ignorant of the ribbald invectives which occupy the place of argument in those remonstrances, which every man of common observation had heard a thousand times over, and a thousand times over had despised? All men had before heard what they have to say; and all men at this day know what they dare to do; and I trust, all honest men are equally influenced by the one, and by the other.

But they tell us, that those our fellow-citizens, whose chains we have a little relaxed, are enemies to liberty and our free

16 On the "rabble in Edinburgh" who tried to prevent the passage of the Catho-lic Relief Act, see "Some Thoughts on the Approaching Executions."

constitution. — Not enemies, I presume, to their *own* liberty. And as to the constitution, until we give them some share in it, I do not know on what pretence we can examine into their opinions about a business in which they have no interest or concern. But after all, are we equally sure, that they are adverse to our constitution, as that our statutes are hostile and destructive to them? For my part, I have reason to believe, their opinions and inclinations in that respect are various, exactly like those of other men: and if they lean more to the crown than I, and than many of you think *we* ought, we must remember, that he who aims at another's life, is not to be surprised if he flies into any sanctuary that will receive him. The tenderness of the executive power is the natural asylum of those upon whom the laws have declared war; and to complain that men are inclined to favour the means of their own safety, is so absurd, that one forgets the injustice in the ridicule.

I must fairly tell you, that so far as my principles are concerned, (principles, that I hope will only depart with my last breath) that I have no idea of a liberty unconnected with honesty and justice. Nor do I believe, that any good constitutions of government or of freedom, can find it necessary for their security to doom any part of the people to a permanent slavery. Such a constitution of freedom, if such can be, is in effect no more than another name for the tyranny of the strongest faction; and factions in republicks have been, and are, full as capable as monarchs, of the most cruel oppression and injustice. It is but too true, that the love, and even the very idea, of genuine liberty, is extremely rare. It is but too true, that there are many, whose whole scheme of freedom is made up of pride, perverseness, and insolence. They feel themselves in a state of thraldom, they imagine that their souls are cooped and cabbined in, unless they have some man, or some body of men, dependent on their mercy. This desire of having some one below them, descends to those who are the very lowest of all, — and a Protestant cobler, debased by his poverty, but exalted by his share of the ruling church, feels a pride in knowing it is by his generosity alone, that the peer, whose footman's instep he measures, is able to keep his chaplain from a jail. This disposition is the true source of the passion, which many men, in very humble life, have taken to the American war. *Our* subjects in America; *our* colonies; *our* dependants. This lust of party-power, is the liberty they hunger and thirst for; and this Syren song of ambition, has charmed ears, that one would have thought were never organized to that sort of musick.

This way of *proscribing the citizens by denominations and general descriptions*, dignified by the name of reason of state, and security for constitutions and commonwealths, is nothing better at bottom, than the miserable invention of an ungenerous ambition, which would fain hold the sacred trust of power, without any of the virtues or any of the energies, that give a title to it; a receipt of policy, made up of a detestable compound of malice, cowardice, and sloth. They would govern men against their will; but in that government they would be discharged from the exercise of vigilance, providence, and fortitude; and therefore, that they may sleep on their watch, they consent to take some one division of the society into partnership of the tyranny over the rest. But let government, in what form it may be, comprehend the whole in its justice, and restrain the suspicious by its vigilance; let it keep watch and ward; let it discover by its sagacity, and punish by its firmness, all delinquency against its power, whenever delinquency exists in the overt acts; and then it will be as safe as ever God and nature intended it should be. Crimes are the acts of individuals, and not of denominations; and therefore arbitrarily to class men under general descriptions, in order to proscribe and punish them in the lump for a presumed delinquency, of which perhaps but a part, perhaps none at all, are guilty, is indeed a compendious method, and saves a world of trouble about proof; but such a method instead of being law, is an act of unnatural rebellion against the legal dominion of reason and justice; and this vice, in any constitution that entertains it, at one time or other will certainly bring on its ruin.

We are told that this is not a religious persecution, and its abettors are loud in disclaiming all severities on account of conscience. Very fine indeed! then let it be so; they are not persecutors; they are only tyrants. With all my heart. I am perfectly indifferent concerning the pretexts upon which we torment one another; or whether it be for the constitution of the church of England, or for the constitution of the state of England, that people choose to make their fellow-creatures wretched. When we were sent into a place of authority, you that sent us had yourselves but one commission to give. You could give us none to wrong or oppress, or even to suffer any kind of oppression or wrong, on any grounds whatsoever; not on political, as in the affairs of America; not on commercial, as in those of Ireland; not in civil, as in the laws for debt; not in religious, as in the statutes against Protestant or Catholick dissenters. The diversified but connected fabrick of universal justice, is well cramped and bolted together in all its parts; and depend upon it, I never have employed, and I never shall employ, any engine of power which may come into my hands, to wrench it asunder. All shall stand, if I can help it, and all shall stand connected. After all, to complete this work, much remains to be done; much in the East, much in the West. But great as the work is, if our will be ready, our powers are not deficient.

Since you have suffered me to trouble you so much on this subject, permit me, gentlemen, to detain you a little longer. I am indeed most solicitous to give you perfect satisfaction. I find there are some of a better and softer nature than the persons with whom I have supposed myself in debate, who neither think ill of the act of relief, nor by any means desire the repeal, yet who, not accusing but lamenting what was done, on account of the consequences, have frequently expressed their wish, that the late act had never been made. Some of this description, and persons of worth, I have met with in this city. They conceive, that the prejudices, whatever they might be, of a large part of the people, ought not to have been shocked; that their opinions ought to have been previously taken, and much attended to; and that thereby the late horrid scenes might have been prevented.

I confess, my notions are widely different; and I never was less sorry for any action of my life. I like the bill the better, on account of the events of all kinds that followed it. It relieved the real sufferers; it strengthened the state; and, by the disorders that ensued, we had clear evidence that there lurked a temper somewhere, which ought not to be fostered by the laws. No ill consequences whatever could be attributed to the act itself. We knew beforehand, or we were poorly instructed, that toleration is odious to the intolerant; freedom to oppressors; property to robbers; and all kinds and degrees of prosperity to the envious. We knew, that all these kinds of men would gladly gratify their evil dispositions under the sanction of law and religion, if they could; if they could not, yet, to make way to their objects, they would do their utmost to subvert all religion and all law. This we certainly knew. But knowing this, is there any reason, because thieves break in and steal, and thus bring detriment to you, and draw ruin on themselves, that I am to be sorry that you are in possession of shops, and of warehouses, and of wholesome laws to protect them? Are you to build no houses, because desperate men may pull them down upon their own heads? Or, if a malignant wretch will cut his own throat because he sees you give alms to the necessitous and deserving; shall his destruction be attributed to your charity, and not to his own deplorable madness? If we repent of our good actions, what, I pray you, is left for our faults and follies? It is not the beneficence of the laws, it is the unnatural temper which beneficence can fret and sour, that is to be lamented. It is this temper which, by all rational means, ought to be sweetened and corrected. If froward men should refuse this cure, can they vitiate any thing but themselves? Does evil so react upon good, as not only to retard its motion, but to change its nature? If it can so operate, then good men will always be in the power of the bad; and virtue, by a dreadful reverse of order, must lie under perpetual subjection and bondage to vice.

As to the opinion of the people, which some think, in such cases, is to be implicitly obeyed; near two years tranquillity, which followed the act, and its instant imitation in Ireland, proved abundantly, that the late horrible spirit was, in a great measure, the effect of insidious art, and perverse industry, and gross mis-representation. But suppose that the dislike had been much more deliberate, and much more general than I am persuaded it was — When we know, that the opinions of even the greatest mul-titudes, are the standard of rectitude, I shall think myself obliged to make those opinions the matters of my conscience. But if it may be doubted whether Omnipotence itself is competent to alter the essential constitution of right and wrong, sure I am, that such *things*, as they and I, are possessed of no such power. No man carries further than I do the policy of making government pleasing to the people. But the widest range of this politick com-plaisance is confined within the limits of justice. I would not only consult the interest of the people, but I would cheerfully gratify their humours. We are all a sort of children that must be soothed and managed. I think I am not austere or formal in my nature. I would bear, I would even myself play my part in, any innocent buffooneries, to divert them. But I never will act the tyrant for their amusement. If they will mix malice in their sports, I shall never consent to throw them any living, sentient, creature what-soever, no not so much as a kitling, to torment.

"But if I profess all this impolitick stubbornness, I may chance never to be elected into Parliament." It is certainly not pleasing to be put out of the publick service. But I wish to be a member of Parliament, to have my share of doing good and resisting evil. It would therefore be absurd to renounce my objects, in order to obtain my seat. I deceive myself indeed most grossly, if I had not much rather pass the remainder of my life hidden in the recesses of the deepest obscurity, feeding my mind even with the visions and imaginations of such things, than to be placed on the most splendid throne of the universe, tantalized with a denial of the practice of all which can make the greatest situation any other than the greatest curse. Gentlemen, I have had my day. I can never sufficiently express my gratitude to you for having set me in a place, wherein I could lend the slightest help to great and laudable designs. If I have had my share, in any measure giving quiet to private property, and private conscience; if by my vote I have aided in securing to families the best possession, peace; if I have joined in reconciling kings to their subjects, and subjects to their prince; if I have assisted to loosen the foreign holdings of the citizen, and taught him to look for his protection to the laws of his country, and for his comfort to the goodwill of his countrymen; — if I have thus taken my part with the best of men in the best of their actions, I can shut the book; — I might wish to read a page or two more — but this is enough for my measure. — I have not lived in vain.

And now, Gentlemen, on this serious day, when I come, as it were, to make up my account with you, let me take to myself some degree of honest pride on the nature of the charges that are against me. I do not here stand before you accused of venality, or of neglect of duty. It is not said, that, in the long period of my service, I have, in a single instance, sacrificed the slightest of your interests to my ambition, or to my fortune. It is not alleged, that to gratify any anger, or revenge of my own, or of my party, I have had a share in wronging or oppressing any description of men, or any one man in any description. No! the charges against me, are all of one kind, that I have pushed the principles of general justice and benevolence too far; further than a cautious policy would warrant; and further than the opinions of many would go along with me. — In every accident which may happen through life, in pain, in sorrow, in depression, and distress — I will call to mind this accusation; and be comforted.

Gentlemen, I submit the whole to your judgment. Mr. Mayor, I thank you for the trouble you have taken on this occasion. In your state of health, it is particularly obliging. If this company should think it adviseable for me to withdraw, I shall respectfully retire; if you think otherwise, I shall go directly to the Council-house and to the Change, and, without a moment's delay, begin my canvass.

To the Earl of Hillsborough
and Lord Viscount Stormont
(3 October 1780)

Early in his parliamentary career, Burke had opposed in principle a design for government regulation of the East India Company. He changed his mind gradually as evidence mounted of the company's violent meddling in disputes over native jurisdiction, the largest single example being its support of the claims of Muhammad Ali, the Nabob of Arcot (hereafter Nawab), over the deposed Raja of the Hindu state of Tanjore. His growing distrust of East India policy may be gauged from his notes for a speech of 22 May 1777 on the importance of restoring Lord Pigot, the governor of Madras, a reformer who had been seized and held prisoner by the company's troops: "Some people great Lovers of uniformity—They are not satisfied with a rebellion in the West. They must have one in the East: They are not satisfied with losing one Empire—they must lose another. Lord N[orth] will weep that he has not more worlds to lose." That portent of heightened suspicion was followed two years later by an anonymous pamphlet, the *Policy of Making Conquests for the Mohometans,* whose authorship, P. J. Marshall has concluded, properly belongs to Burke himself in several sections, while the rest emerged from a collaboration with his friend William Burke.

The Earl of Hillsborough was in charge of East India affairs. Lord Viscount Stormont was secretary of state for the Northern District, and on 2 October had requested a postponement of orders affecting Madras until the return to London of Lord North, who was known to have objected strongly to the company's proceedings. Burke probably consulted with Stormont before writing this letter, which is, in effect, a memorandum to persons in government vested with authority on India.

To the Earl of Hillsborough
and Viscount Stormont

(3 October 1780)

MY LORDS,

I think it the right and the duty of every subject of this kingdom to communicate to his Majesty's ministers intelligence of every matter by which the King's interest and honour and that of the nation is likely to be affected.

The Chairman and Deputy Chairman of the East India Company have come to a resolution of seizing upon, and delivering over to the discretion of their servants at Madras, the revenues of the king of Tanjore, — an ally of the Company, and therefore of the Crown and nation of Great Britain, — in direct violation of a solemn treaty, by which the Company has engaged that none of their servants shall intermeddle in the internal government of that Prince.

This very extraordinary and dangerous design, leading to a general waste and robbery of the only now remaining native government, and the only flourishing country within the reach of our power in India, was carried through a very thin Court of Directors.

It was carried through in the absence of those directors who had formerly strenuously opposed, and by their opposition defeated, this very measure. The whole was also done without any notice whatsoever to those directors.

It was carried through the very day after the sitting of a General Court of the East India Company, without the least communication to the body they act for; and although that very General Court had come to a resolution to take the whole of their affairs into consideration on so early a day as the sixth of November next.

It was carried through in the absence of Lord North, and of

both Secretaries of the Treasury; though upon representations to his Lordship, this business has been formerly stopped; and at a time when he is at so great a distance from town, as to make his interposition, or even an immediate application to him utterly impracticable.

It was carried through immediately after Mr William Burke, one of the King of Tanjore's agents, had set off on a journey over land with a letter from Lord North, written by order of his Majesty, to whom the King of Tanjore had subjected his kingdom, and to whose decisions the said King had submitted his cause and all his grievances; and in the absence also of the Honourable William Waldegrave, joined in agency with Mr Burke, who had before protested to the directors against that very same predatory resolution, and desired to be heard against it; the King of Tanjore himself having then a regular complaint of grievances, and of extorting money in particular, before the Company.

It was carried through in the recess of Parliament, to which the said agents in the last session had prepared a petition; which petition was consented to be withheld solely on the directors putting a stop to this unjustifiable design.

It was carried through at a time when the very servants of the Company, to whom the kingdom of Tanjore is to be delivered, are under an inquiry of the Court of the very directors who deliver it to them, on but too just a suspicion of peculation and other evil practices.

And in order that no time should be allowed for the dissenting directors, proprietors, or agents, or even for the King's ministers to interfere, they resolved not to wait for the ships which are to depart, but have a prepared person suddenly to go off over land; so that if this design had not been providentially discovered, it was very possible, that on the evening of the very day the King of Tanjore was rejoicing on the receipt of a gracious letter from the King's minister, written by his Majesty's order, he might find his revenues forcibly seized on, in violation of the treaty, by an order of the directors, to the infinite scandal of the honour, justice, and policy of the British nation.

It is necessary to lay a matter of this high and criminal nature, pursued in this extraordinary manner, before his Majesty's servants; the Crown claiming on the part of the public a right in the possessions and territorial revenues of the Company, and the time for the renewal of the charter now approaching. I humbly venture to suggest that it is incumbent on his majesty's ministers, that so material a revolution involving the public faith and the obligation of treaties, together with the welfare of so great a part of the strength of Great Britain, should not be made, but on the fullest and most impartial consideration; or that kings and kingdoms, and the lives and properties of millions of innocent people should not be passed away, by obscure and collusive practices (with much less ceremony than the family settlement of a cottage is made or altered) between any confederacies of men, for their private and unjust emolument.

I make no apology for troubling your Lordships with the notification of so dangerous a proceeding; knowing your desire of obtaining information from every quarter in any matter which relates to his Majesty's service. On this well grounded assurance, I am ready to wait on your Lordships at any time you may be pleased to appoint, to lay before you, on the most authentic grounds, the futility and fraud of the pretences on which a violence of this extent is attempted by the Company's servants in India, and thus privately, without hearing or notice, consented to by their servants here.

I have the honor to be with the greatest respect, my Lords,

Your Lordships most obedient and most humble servant,

EDM BURKE

To Sir Thomas Rumbold
23 March 1781

At the time of this letter Sir Thomas Rumbold was MP for Shaftesbury. He had entered the service of the East India Company in 1752, risen to be a member of the council, and returned to England in 1769. He was sent back in 1777 as governor of Madras, where his disastrous policies were challenged by the company itself and by Parliament, and he was eventually dismissed.

Burke's refusal, defended at the letter's close, to flatter by private confidences any person he might be obliged to attack in public, was part of a code of honor to which he consistently adhered.

To Sir Thomas Rumbold

(23 March 1781)

S<small>IR</small>,

I am honoured with your letter and the inclosures which I received on my return very late on Wednesday night. My attendance on the Bengal committee and at the House has not left me sufficient leisure to thank you for your communication until this instant. Even now, I doubt I shall not have time to explain myself so clearly and fully as I could wish to do on the important matter you have done me the honour to lay before me.

The high opinion which, in common with the rest of the world, I entertain of Sir Hector Monro, gives in my mind very great weight to his testimony in your favour. The regard too, which I have long since felt for yourself, would naturally incline me to wish that every thing in your conduct during your government may be found perfectly honourable to you. I am sensible that the state into which the country where you presided, has been brought by a long train of ill policy, has made all your proceedings there very delicate and critical; and I am as much disposed as any man can be to allow for several errors that are almost unavoidable in that very difficult and embarrassed situation.

Not to engage rashly in wars with the powers of the country, is, in my eyes, an eminent degree of merit in an East India governor; and I am sincerely persuaded that your keeping out of them was an act purely voluntary. I feel, as a member of *this* community, and as a member of the community of mankind at large, your merit in discountenancing, as I understood you have done, the present ruinous Maratta war; and I shall ever acknowledge it as a publick service. In condemning the perverse policy which led to that war, and which had before given rise to the still less justifiable war against the Rohillas, I do not speak from the smallest degree of prejudice or personal animosity against the respectable person, (for such in many particulars he undoubtedly is) who was so unhappy as to be the author of both these measures.[1] I rather gave him my little voice as long as I thought it justifiable to afford him the smallest degree of support. I was always an admirer of his talents; and the farthest in the world from being engaged in a faction against him. I assure you, Sir, with great truth, that I am also very far from a connexion with any personal enemies of yours, if such you have; and that, in general, I am one of the latest and most reluctant in imputing blame to gentlemen who serve their country in distant and arduous situations.

But since your letter not only permits, but in a manner calls upon me, to deliver my opinion to you upon affairs of no trivial consequence, you will naturally excuse the liberty I shall take of laying open to you with plainness and sincerity, my thoughts on some late proceedings at Madras.

I have invariably considered the plan of amassing a great body of power in the hands of *one* of the potentates of the country of India by the destruction of all the original governments about him, as very ill conceived in the design, very pernicious during the execution, and perfectly ruinous in the consequences. This from the beginning appeared to me very clear in the theory, and every step towards the practice has more and more confirmed me in that persuasion.

I consider it also as very ill policy to set up a power of our own creating, and intrinsically dependent, in a state of fictitious independency, and not only of independency, but superiority, that wars might be carried on, and great depredations committed in his name, which in the real acting parties could scarcely escape the strictest animadversion.

Looking, as I did, upon every *new pretension*, and every *new subject of discussion*, as a means of new abuse of all kinds, I could not help viewing all encouragement to an attempt for unsettling the succession of the ruling families in India in their lawful

---

1 Warren Hastings, at this time governor-general of Bengal.

heirs—a succession recognized and settled by treaties and solemn acts—as a measure of a very pernicious tendency: first, to the people, who would be infinitely exhausted by the support of a party and a force to support this subversion of the regular order of succession; and, next, to the family itself, which sooner or later must be extinguished by its dissensions.

Having these and other motives all originating from the same principle, deeply and firmly rooted in my mind, you will easily see that it cannot arise from the smallest desire of finding fault with any acts in which you have had a share, that I have hesitated about the propriety of a great variety of things lately done or permitted at Madras, as continuing and enforcing the plan of mistaken policy so long predominant there, and aggravating all the unhappy effects of it.

I am unable to regard the acquisition of territory to the Company as matter of merit, until I find that in some one instance, the condition of the inhabitants has been improved by the revolution, or that the affairs of this kingdom have derived some benefit from it. For unfortunately in proportion to our acquisitions, both in Bengal and in the Deccan, we find the country infinitely injured, and the treasures and revenues both of the Company and the subordinate powers wasted and decayed.

The acquisition therefore of the Gentour Cicar seemed to me exactly like the rest of our late acquisitions. I thought neither better nor worse of it than of our acquisition of the country of the Rohillas, or the revenues of Oudh. But when I found, that this territory was no sooner acquired than it was delivered over to the barbarians; and that the whole of that unfortunate people were (as so many others have been) farmed out as cattle to the second son of the Nabob of Arcot, it seemed to me very evident, that as long as such an arrangement was tolerated, the natives were put out of the reach of the protection of this kingdom. In that light, I could not consider the whole of that transaction, without great doubt concering the propriety of it in every point of view.

The farming the Jaghire lands to the Nabob, or rather, in

substance and effect, to the same second son, a person (to speak the best of him) of very doubtful fidelity to this nation, appeared to me a measure of the same tendency. The original short tenure was undoubtedly too much; and the resumption and not the enlarging it would be the plain dictate of humanity and good policy. By these measures and by others of the same nature and operation we have not a foot of land through an immense region, which we can properly call our own, or in which we possess the ordinary means of protecting the people, or redressing their grievances, if ever we should become wise enough to intend it.

Whatever other measures have been pursued in the spirit of these, or which tend, by the oppression of the native princes or people, to aggravate that evil of usury, natural to the country, but which is infinitely extended and increased by uncertain demands and unsettled claims, all these appear to me equally exceptionable. My proceedings in the India House relative to Mr. Benfield will explain to you in what manner I think myself obliged to consider them.[2] How far gentlemen acting in India are excusable on account of the false systems, or variable systems which have been prevalent at home, for the mistakes of those employed abroad, I am unable to determine. No man will be more inclined to allow for them than I shall; and I never will readily hear of laying on one man that blame which ought to lie on many; if really there should be found any matter of blame at all.

I am more engaged than I can well describe to you, with various kinds of business. But whenever we have both a moment's leisure I shall be happy to converse with you on this

2 Paul Benfield (1741–1810), a speculator who brought home a stupendous fortune from East India, supplied loans to the Nawab of Arcot until recalled by the directors of the company. He petitioned for reinstatement, to which the Court of Directors agreed in early December 1780. But a group led by Burke — who acquired a thousand-pound holding of East India stock to gain a vote at the Court of Proprietors, which could override the Court of Directors — petitioned for an inquiry into his conduct. The main questions were whether such loans to a single native potentate were politically wise or financially prudent, and whether, given his rank and position, Benfield could have acquired by lawful means the money that he disbursed. He was restored to the service of the company on 24 January.

business or any other; though to speak after my manner, I do not choose privately to discuss matters with gentlemen with whom I may find myself obliged afterwards to differ in publick. It might give me advantages, which it would be *impossible* not to profit of, in some way or other, to their prejudice, and that, whether I would or not. To know any man's story that you cannot agree with is not pleasant.

I have the honour to be,
Sir your most obedient and humble servant,
E.B.

Speech on Reform of Representation (1782)

Burke had played an equivocal part in the agitations for Wilkes and Liberty in the late 1760s, denouncing the government for the stratagems by which it kept Wilkes out of the House of Commons, disclaiming association with the popular sentiment that backed him, and running interference between the Rockingham party and Wilkes himself. His position was delicate: the popular enthusiasm that massed with Wilkes was an undesirable force in representative government, yet the ministry's efforts to nullify his election, to prosecute and to unseat him, were plainly an even greater danger to constitutional balance. The Rockingham party manifesto of 1770, *Thoughts on the Cause of the Present Discontents,* asserted the good of party as such and its utility in opposing the excessive influence of the crown. Burke may thus have helped direct republican opinion in a way that neither he nor his party was ultimately prepared to follow. In 1780, his proposals for economic reform once more gave his politics a superficial resemblance to the politics of radical reformers. They had at least some of the same enemies.

The best known movement for parliamentary reform, Christopher Wyvill's Yorkshire Association, had sprung up in Rockingham's own neighborhood. Rockingham was able to talk them down from annual to triennial parliaments, but his party was divided and confused by the demand for increased representation. The Duke of Richmond and Sir George Savile favored such reforms, as Burke himself did not. Yet Burke's first response to a county meeting of Buckinghamshire had been cautiously sympathetic. "The people," he wrote in a letter to their chairman on 12 April 1780, "may be deceived in their choice of an object. But I can scarcely conceive any choice they can make to be so very mischievous as the existence of any human force capable of resisting it." In the years to come, he would grow markedly cooler toward all such petitioners, and this fragment of a major speech shows why.

Here Burke exhibits more clearly than in any of his speeches or writings on domestic politics the stringency of his reservations about democracy. He has no use for popular sovereignty. The active power of government resides in the House of Commons; the king, properly regarded, acts as a check against the errors of Parliament or the tendency of a successful administration to engross privilege and power; while the people (a term Burke defines variously, but always with a narrower reference than the republican pamphlet writers of his day) operate as a further check against the abuses of government. They can influence their own fate and fortune, at the rare times when to do so is necessary, either through their representatives or by the expression of grievance, in an orderly or less orderly fashion. Burke opposed any move toward the assertion of greater democratic control over government; his vehemence against an "inquiry into the state of representation" was extravagant even in 1782. Why did he go so far?

He bases his argument on two principles: what he calls prescription (the ancient authority of an established practice) and presumption (the human propensity to approve and perpetuate a familiar state of things). "It is a presumption in favour of any settled scheme of government against any untried project, that a nation has long existed and flourished under it." Any inquiry preliminary to a radical change, he believed, would tamper with the political system the English people had inherited and approved for generations, a system founded on aristocratic manners and the connection between representation and property. The people accept this system, in the long run, though they may be roused against it temporarily. All wise reform is gradual by definition — a fact of political life as it is of human nature — and the people act most wisely when not driven to gratify sudden demands. Thus a deliberative politics is consistent with stable representation in the House of Commons, and not with shorter terms for representatives or an expanded plan of representation. The confidence Burke rests on — "the species is wise, and when time is given to it, as a species it almost always acts right" — is a striking formulation of the evolutionary doctrine that would pervade his writings on France. Government is an accommodation of society to human nature, and it can only succeed over time. The egalitarian idea of natural right ought therefore to carry no authority beside the settled and habitual method of the English constitution. In *An Appeal from the New to the Old Whigs* (1791), responding to a new urgency in the demand for popular control of assemblies, Burke would recur to the same argument with still greater explicitness. "The people are the natural control on authority; but to exercise and control together is contradictory and impossible."

The dating of the speech adopted here is conjectural.

Speech

On a Motion made in the House of Commons,
the 7th of May 1782, for a Committee to inquire
into the state of the Representation
of the Commons in Parliament.

MR. SPEAKER,

We have now discovered, at the close of the eighteenth century,
that the Constitution of England, which for a series of ages had
been the proud distinction of this Country, always the admiration, and sometimes the envy of the wise and learned in every
other Nation, we have discovered that this boasted Constitution,
in the most boasted part of it, is a gross imposition upon the
understanding of mankind, an insult to their feelings, and acting
by contrivances destructive to the best and most valuable interests of the people. Our political architects have taken a survey of
the fabrick of the British Constitution. It is singular, that they
report nothing against the Crown, nothing against the Lords;
but in the House of Commons every thing is unsound; it is ruinous in every part. It is infested by the dry rot, and ready to tumble
about our ears without their immediate help. You know by the
faults they find, what are their ideas of the alteration. As all
government stands upon opinion, they know that the way utterly
to destroy it is to remove that opinion, to take away all reverence,
all confidence from it; and then, at the first blast of publick
discontent and popular tumult, it tumbles to the ground.

In considering this question, they, who oppose it, oppose it
on different grounds; one is, in the nature of a previous question; that some alterations may be expedient, but that this is not
the time for making them. The other is, that no essential alterations are at all wanting: and that neither *now*, nor at *any* time, is
it prudent or safe to be meddling with the fundamental principles, and ancient tried usages of our Constitution–that our Representation is as nearly perfect as the necessary imperfection of

human affairs and of human creatures will suffer it to be; and that it is a subject of prudent and honest use and thankful enjoyment, and not of captious criticism and rash experiment.

On the other side, there are two parties, who proceed on two grounds, in my opinion, as they state them, utterly irreconcileable. The one is juridical, the other political. The one is in the nature of a claim of right, on the supposed rights of man as man; this party desire the decision of a suit. The other ground, as far as I can divine what it directly means, is, that the Representation is not so politically framed as to answer the theory of its institution. As to the claim of *right*, the meanest petitioner, the most gross and ignorant, is as good as the best; in some respects his claim is more favourable on account of his ignorance; his weakness, his poverty and distress, only add to his titles; he sues in *forma pauperis*;[1] he ought to be a favourite of the Court. But when the *other* ground is taken, when the question is political, when a new Constitution is to be made on a sound theory of government, then the presumptuous pride of didactick ignorance is to be excluded from the counsel in this high and arduous matter, which often bids defiance to the experience of the wisest. The first claims a personal representation, the latter rejects it with scorn and fervour. The language of the first party is plain and intelligible; they, who plead an absolute right, cannot be satisfied with any thing short of personal representation, because all *natural* rights must be the rights of individuals; as by *nature* there is no such thing as politick or corporate personality; all these ideas are mere fictions of Law, they are creatures of voluntary institution; men as men are individuals, and nothing else. They therefore, who reject the principle of natural and personal representation, are essentially and eternally at variance with those, who claim it. As to the first set of Reformers, it is ridiculous to talk to them of the British Constitution upon any or upon all of its bases; for they lay it down, that every man ought to govern himself, and that where he cannot go himself he must send his Representative; that

---

1 The state of a pauper.

all other government is usurpation, and is so far from having a
claim to our obedience, it is not only our right, but our duty, to
resist it. Nine tenths of the Reformers argue thus, that is on the
natural right. It is impossible not to make some reflection on the
nature of this claim, or avoid a comparison between the extent of
the principle and the present object of the demand. If this claim
be founded, it is clear to what it goes. The House of Commons, in
that light, undoubtedly is no representative of the people as a
collection of individuals. Nobody pretends it, nobody can justify
such an assertion. When you come to examine into this claim of
right, founded on the right of self-government in each individual, you find the thing demanded infinitely short of the principle
of the demand. What! one *third* only of the Legislature, and of the
Government no share at all? What sort of treaty of partition is this
for those, who have an inherent right to the whole? Give them all
they ask, and your grant is still a cheat; for how comes only a third
to be their younger children's fortune in this settlement? How
came they neither to have the choice of Kings, or Lords, or
Judges, or Generals, or Admirals, or Bishops, or Priests, or Ministers, or Justices of Peace? Why, what have you to answer in favour
of the prior rights of the Crown and Peerage but this — our Constitution is a prescriptive Constitution; it is a Constitution, whose
sole authority is, that it has existed time out of mind. It is settled
in these *two* portions against one, legislatively; and in the whole
of the judicature, the whole of the federal capacity, of the executive, the prudential and the financial administration, in one
alone. Nor was your House of Lords and the prerogatives of the
Crown settled on any adjudication in favour of natural rights, for
they could never be so partitioned. Your King, your Lords, your
Judges, your Juries, grand and little, all are prescriptive; and what
proves it, is, the disputes not yet concluded, and never near
becoming so, when any of them first originated. Prescription is
the most solid of all titles, not only to property, but, which is to
secure that property, to Government. They harmonize with each
other, and give mutual aid to one another. It is accompanied with
another ground of authority in the constitution of the human

mind, presumption. It is a presumption in favour of any settled scheme of government against any untried project, that a nation has long existed and flourished under it. It is a better presumption even of the *choice* of a nation, far better than any sudden and temporary arrangement by actual election. Because a nation is not an idea only of local extent, and individual momentary aggegation, but it is an idea of continuity, which extends in time as well as in numbers, and in space. And this is a choice not of one day, or one set of people, not a tumultuary and giddy choice; it is a deliberate election of ages and of generations; it is a Constitution made by what is ten thousand times better than choice, it is made by the peculiar circumstances, occasions, tempers, dispositions, and moral, civil, and social habitudes of the people, which disclose themselves only in a long space of time. It is a vestment, which accommodates itself to the body. Nor is prescription of government formed upon blind unmeaning prejudices—for man is a most unwise, and a most wise, being. The individual is foolish. The multitude, for the moment, is foolish, when they act without deliberation; but the species is wise, and when time is given to it as a species it almost always acts right.

The reason for the Crown as it is, for the Lords as they are, is my reason for the Commons as they are, the Electors as they are. Now, if the Crown and the Lords, and the Judicatures, are all prescriptive, so is the House of Commons of the very same origin, and of no other. We and our Electors have their powers and privileges both made and circumscribed by prescription, as much to the full as the other parts; and as such we have always claimed them, and on no other title. The House of Commons is a legislative body corporate by prescription, not made upon any given theory, but existing prescriptively—just like the rest. This prescription has made it essentially what it is, an aggregate collection of three parts, Knights, Citizens, Burgesses. The question is, whether this has been always so, since the House of Commons has taken its present shape and circumstances, and has been an essential operative part of the Constitution; which, I take it, it has been for at least five hundred years.

This I resolve to myself in the affirmative: and then another question arises, whether this House stands firm upon its ancient foundations, and is not, by time and accidents, so declined from its perpendicular as to want the hand of the wise and experienced architects of the day to set it upright again, and to prop and buttress it up for duration; — whether it continues true to the principles, upon which it has hitherto stood; — whether this be *de facto* the Constitution of the House of Commons, as it has been since the time, that the House of Commons has, without dispute, become a necessary and an efficient part of the British Constitution? To ask whether a thing, which has always been the same, stands to its usual principle, seems to me to be perfectly absurd; for how do you know the principles but from the construction? and if that remains the same, the principles remain the same. It is true, that to say your Constitution is what it has been, is no sufficient defence for those, who say it is a bad Constitution. It is an answer to those, who say that it is a degenerate Constitution. To those, who say it is a bad one, I answer, look to its effects. In all moral machinery the moral results are its test.

On what grounds do we go, to restore our Constitution to what it has been at some given period, or to reform and reconstruct it upon principles more conformable to a sound theory of government? A prescriptive Government, such as ours, never was the work of any Legislator, never was made upon any foregone theory. It seems to me a preposterous way of reasoning, and a perfect confusion of ideas, to take the theories, which learned and speculative men have made from that Government, and then supposing it made on those theories, which were made from it, to accuse the Government as not corresponding with them. I do not vilify theory and speculation — no, because that would be to vilify reason itself. *Neque decipitur ratio, neque decipit unquam.*[2] No; whenever I speak against theory, I mean always a weak, erroneous, fallacious, unfounded, or imperfect theory; and one of the ways of discovering, that it is a false theory, is by

2 Manlius *Astronomica* 2.132: "Reason is not deceived, nor does it ever deceive."

comparing it with practice. This is the true touchstone of all theories, which regard man and the affairs of men — does it suit his nature in general; — does it suit his nature as modified by his habits?

The more frequently this affair is discussed, the stronger the case appears to the sense and the feelings of mankind. I have no more doubt than I entertain of my existence, that this very thing, which is stated as an horrible thing, is the means of the preservation of our Constitution, whilst it lasts; of curing it of many of the disorders, which, attending every species of institution, would attend the principle of an exact local representation, or a representation on the principle of numbers. If you reject personal representation, you are pushed upon expedience; and then what they wish us to do is, to prefer their speculations on that subject to the happy experience of this Country of a growing liberty and a growing prosperity for five hundred years. Whatever respect I have for their talents, this, for one, I will not do. Then what is the standard of expedience? Expedience is that, which is good for the community, and good for every individual in it. Now this expedience is the *desideratum*, to be sought either without the experience of means, or with that experience. If without, as in case of the fabrication of a new Commonwealth, I will hear the learned arguing what promises to be expedient: but if we are to judge of a Commonwealth actually existing, the first thing I inquire is, what has been *found* expedient or inexpedient? And I will not take their *promise* rather than the *performance* of the Constitution.

*   *   *   *   *

But no, this was not the cause of the discontents. I went through most of the Northern parts, — the Yorkshire Election was then raging; the year before, through most of the Western Counties — Bath, Bristol, Gloucester, — not one word, either in the towns or country, on the subject of representation; much on the Receipt Tax, something on Mr. Fox's ambition; much greater apprehension of danger from thence than from want of representation. One would think that the ballast of the ship was

shifted with us, and that our Constitution had the gunnel under
water. But can you fairly and distinctly point out what one evil or
grievance has happened, which you can refer to the Representative not following the opinion of his Constituents? What one
symptom do we find of this inequality? But it is not an arithmeti-
cal inequality, with which we ought to trouble ourselves. If there
be a moral, a political equality, this is the *desideratum* in our
Constitution, and in every Constitution in the world. Moral inequality is as between places and between classes. Now I ask,
what advantage do you find, that the places, which abound in
representation, possess over others, in which it is more scanty, in
security for freedom, in security for justice, or in any one of those
means of procuring temporal prosperity and eternal happiness,
the ends, for which society was formed? Are the local interests of
Cornwall and Wiltshire, for instance, their roads, canals, their
prisons, their police, better than Yorkshire, Warwickshire, or
Staffordshire? Warwick has Members; is Warwick, or Stafford,
more opulent, happy, or free, than Newcastle, or than Birming-
ham? Is Wiltshire the pampered favourite, whilst Yorkshire, like
the child of the bond-woman, is turned out to the desert? This is
like the unhappy persons, who live, if they can be said to live, in
the Statical Chair;[3] who are ever feeling their pulse, and who do
not judge of health by the aptitude of the body to perform its
functions, but by their ideas of what ought to be the true balance
between the several secretions. Is a Committee of Cornwall, &c
thronged, and the others deserted? No. You have an equal representation, because you have men equally interested in the prosperity of the whole, who are involved in the general interest
and the general sympathy; and, perhaps, those places, furnish-
ing a superfluity of publick agents and administrators, (whether
in strictness they are Representatives or not, I do not mean
to inquire, but they are agents and administrators,) will stand
clearer of local interests, passions, prejudices and cabals, than

---

3 The statical chair was invented by the Venetian physician Santorio (1561–
1636) to weigh the "insensible perspiration" of the human body.

the others, and therefore preserve the balance of the parts, and with a more general view, and a more steady hand, than the rest.

*   *   *   *   *

In every political proposal we must not leave out of the question the political views and object of the proposer; and these we discover, not by what he says, but by the principles he lays down. I mean, says he, a moderate and temperate reform; that is, I mean to do as little good as possible. If the Constitution be what you represent it, and there be no danger in the change, you do wrong not to make the reform commensurate to the abuse. Fine reformer indeed! generous donor! What is the cause of this parsimony of the liberty, which you dole out to the people? Why all this limitation in giving blessings and benefits to mankind? You admit that there is an extreme in liberty, which may be infinitely noxious to those, who are to receive it, and which in the end will leave them no liberty at all. I think so too; they know it, and they feel it. The question is then, what is the standard of that extreme? What that gentleman, and the Associations, or some parts of their phalanxes, think proper? Then our liberties are in their pleasure; it depends on their arbitrary will how far I shall be free. I will have none of that freedom. If, therefore, the standard of moderation be sought for, I will seek for it. Where? Not in their fancies, nor in my own; I will seek for it where I know it is to be found, in the Constitution I actually enjoy. Here it says to an encroaching prerogative, — Your sceptre has its length, you cannot add an hair to your head, or a gem to your Crown, but what an eternal Law has given to it. Here it says to an overween-ing peerage, — Your pride finds banks, that it cannot overflow: here to a tumultuous and giddy people, There is a bound to the raging of the Sea. Our Constitution is like our Island, which uses and restrains its subject Sea; in vain the waves roar. In that Con-stitution I know, and exultingly I feel, both that I am free, and that I am not free dangerously to myself or to others. I know that no power on earth, acting as I ought to do, can touch my life, my liberty, or my property. I have that inward and dignified con-

sciousness of my own security and independence, which constitutes, and is the only thing, which does constitute, the proud
and comfortable sentiment of freedom in the human breast. I
know too, and I bless God for my safe mediocrity; I know that, if I
possessed all the talents of the gentlemen on the side of the
House I sit, and on the other, I cannot by Royal favour, or by
popular delusion, or by oligarchical cabal, elevate myself above a
certain very limited point, so as to endanger my own fall, or the
ruin of my Country. I know there is an order, that keeps things
fast in their place; it is made to us, and we are made to it. Why not
ask another wife, other children, another body, another mind?

The great object of most of these Reformers is to prepare the
destruction of the Constitution, by disgracing and discrediting
the House of Commons. For they think, prudently, in my opinion, that if they can persuade the nation, that the House of
Commons is so constituted as not to secure the publick liberty;
not to have a proper connexion with the publick interests, so
constituted, as not either actually or virtually to be the Representative of the people, it will be easy to prove, that a Government,
composed of a Monarchy, an Oligarchy chosen by the Crown,
and such a House of Commons, whatever good can be in such a
system, can by no means be a system of free government.

The Constitution of England is never to have a quietus; it is to
be continually vilified, attacked, reproached, resisted; instead of
being the hope and sure anchor in all storms, instead of being
the means of redress to all grievances, itself is the grand grievance of the nation, our shame instead of our glory. If the only
specifick plan proposed, individual personal representation, is
directly rejected by the person, who is looked on as the great
support of this business, then the only way of considering it is a
question of convenience. An honourable gentleman,prefers the
individual to the present. He therefore himself sees no middle
term whatsoever, and therefore prefers of what he sees the individual; this is the only thing distinct and sensible, that has been
advocated. He has then a scheme, which is the individual representation; he is not at a loss, not inconsistent — which scheme

the other right honourable Gentleman reprobates. Now what does this go to, but to lead directly to anarchy? For to discredit the only Government, which he either possesses or can project, what is this but to destroy all government; and this is anarchy. My right honourable friend, in supporting this motion, disgraces his friends and justifies his enemies, in order to blacken the Constitution of his Country, even of that House of Commons, which supported him. There is a difference between a moral or political exposure of a publick evil, relative to the administration of government, whether in men or systems, and a declaration of defects, real or supposed, in the fundamental Constitution of your Country. The first may be cured in the individual by the motives of religion, virtue, honour, fear, shame, or interest. Men may be made to abandon also false systems, by exposing their absurdity or mischievous tendency to their own better thoughts, or to the contempt or indignation of the publick; and after all, if they should exist, and exist uncorrected, they only disgrace individuals as fugitive opinions. But it is quite otherwise with the frame and Constitution of the State; if that is disgraced, patriotism is destroyed in its very source. No man has ever willingly obeyed, much less was desirous of defending with his blood, a mischievous and absurd scheme of government. Our first, our dearest, most comprehensive relation, our Country, is gone.

It suggests melancholy reflections, in consequence of the strange course we have long held, that we are now no longer quarrelling about the character, or about the conduct of men, or the tenour of measures; but we are grown out of humour with the English Constitution itself; this is become the object of animosity of Englishmen. This Constitution in former days used to be the admiration and the envy of the world; it was the pattern for politicians; the theme of the eloquent; the meditation of the philosopher in every part of the world. As to Englishmen, it was their pride, their consolation. By it they lived, for it they were ready to die. Its defects, if it had any, were partly covered by partiality, and partly born by prudence. Now all its excellencies are forgot, its faults are now forcibly dragged into day, exagger-

ated by every artifice of representation. It is despised and rejected of men; and every device and invention of ingenuity, or
idleness, set up in opposition or in preference to it. It is to this
humour, and it is to the measures growing out of it, that I set
myself (I hope not alone) in the most determined opposition.
Never before did we at any time in this Country meet upon the
theory of our frame of Government, to sit in judgment on the
Constitution of our Country, to call it as a delinquent before us,
and to accuse it of every defect and every vice; to see whether it,
an object of our veneration, even our adoration, did or did not
accord with a pre-conceived scheme in the minds of certain
gentlemen. Cast your eyes on the journals of Parliament. It is for
fear of losing the inestimable treasure we have, that I do not
venture to game it out of my hands for the vain hope of improving it. I look with filial reverence on the Constitution of my
Country, and never will cut it in pieces, and put it into the kettle
of any magician, in order to boil it, with the puddle of their
compounds, into youth and vigour.[4] On the contrary, I will drive
away such pretenders; I will nurse its venerable age, and with
lenient arts extend a parent's breath.

4 When Jason's father, Aeson, was slain by his half brother, King Pelias of Iolcos,
Medea tricked the daughters of Pelias into avenging the death. She demonstrated a
recipe for rejuvenation — chopping up the body of an old ram, boiling it in a kettle,
and drawing a lamb out of the pot. The credulous daughters hacked their father to
pieces and boiled him.

Speech on Fox's East India Bill (1783)

By 1781, Burke's expertise and persuasiveness on Indian affairs were sufficient to carry a vote in the House of Commons for the Bengal Judicature Bill, which corrected some abuses in the application of English laws in India. He had come to believe, he said in a speech for the bill, that "we must now be guided, as we ought to have been with respect to America, by studying the genius, the temper, and the manners of the people, and adapting to them the laws that we establish." He was concerned above all to remove the climate of savage expediency that allowed a corrupt judge like Sir Elijah Impey to act as a tool of the governor-general, Warren Hastings.

The Rockingham party got a new lease on power in April 1783 by the anomaly of the Fox-North coalition, headed by two statesmen who had been public antagonists throughout the preceding decade. Fox's East India Bill (actually Burke's in all but name) was drafted as the party's leading instrument for the reform of imperial policy. The bill aimed to make the East India Company answerable to Parliament, by replacing the authority of shareholders over a Court of Directors with the more regular oversight of two commissions. The first, composed of seven members, would oversee the administration of India and be vested with the power to correct abuses, while the second would manage the commerce of the company. Both sets of commissioners would be appointed for terms of four years. The judgment behind this radical proposal Burke defended as a matter of prudential logic: "The very charter, which is held out to exclude Parliament from correcting malversation with regard to the high trust vested in the Company, is the very thing which at once gives a title and imposes a duty on us to interfere with effect, wherever power and authority originating from ourselves are perverted from their purposes, and become an instrument of wrong and violence." As for the provocation required to warrant so substantial a measure, it met all the necessary conditions: the object in view, an entire subcontinent, was great; the abuse was likewise great; the abuse had become habitual; and the state of affairs was incurable as relations then stood between the company and Parliament.

The peculiarity of the company's situation which seemed to render it invulnerable to criticism — the fact that it was a private and mercantile establishment entrusted with the governance of a large portion of the empire — Burke treated as an incitement to reforms he thought morally imperative. He applied to its case the old maxim that *imperium in imperio* (an empire within the empire) is a solecism in government. British India had seen the displacement of the political rights of the people by the commercial interests of a company. The servants and directors of the company were, said Burke, short-sighted even by the calculus of narrow self-interest; for by plundering a subject country, instead of enriching it by generous policy, they robbed England of all the benefits of a vigorous partner in trade and war. But a question of principle was also involved. The public good of a nation is prior to, and ought to override, the private good of a corporation. A nation's duty to assure impartial justice supersedes any claim by a corporation. The corporation is answerable to none but its investors whereas the nation is answerable to the public good and the human rights of the people it governs. It follows that a nation held hostage to the interests of a company is liable to be wrecked by private greed.

Here, as in the *Letter to the Sheriffs of Bristol,* Burke shows how the eruption of a crisis abroad affects the manners and morality of civic life at home. The unscrupulous traits the company picks out to reward in its servants are now debasing the quality of English life itself. Commercial and imperial arrogance, working together, have infused a spirit of cynicism into the ambitious young. They are sent out to govern in India and are brought back still hungry as the possessors of sudden fortunes. Burke reckoned that Paul Benfield, a member of Parliament formerly of the company, by 1784 controlled eight votes in Parliament, and that this faction was largely responsible for the settlement, without investigation, of the Nawab of Arcot's debts in 1785. In his speech on the sixth article of impeachment, he would say of the peril dramatically: "Today the Commons of Great Britain prosecute the delinquents of India: tomorrow the delinquents of India may be the Commons of Great Britain."

As early as 1783, Burke was still more troubled by the kind of fame and the kind of example such representatives left behind in India itself:

> The Tartar invasion was mischievous; but it is our protection that destroys India. It was their enmity, but it is our friendship. Our conquest there, after twenty years, is as crude as it was the first day. The natives scarcely know what it is to see the gray head of an Englishman. Young men (boys almost) govern there, without society, and without sympathy with the natives. They have no more social habits with the people, than if they still resided in England; nor indeed any species of intercourse but that which is necessary to making a sudden fortune, with a view to a remote settlement. Animated with all the avarice of age, and all the impetuosity of youth, they roll in one after another; wave after wave; and there is nothing before the eyes of the natives but an endless, hopeless prospect of new flights of birds of prey and passage, with appetites continually renewing for a food that is continually wasting.

This loss of the ability to sympathize with the people of another country brings with it a loss of self-respect—a moral feeling indispensable for restraint in everyday affairs. The shameless facility with which the East India men deploy their fortunes in English politics shows that for them the idea of honor has become unreal.

Much of the argument is a historical sketch of the British presence in India, against the background of its predecessors. Burke exhibits here a grandeur in keeping with his other qualities and affords a sublimity like Gibbon's without the archness of his irony. The speech closes with a eulogy to Charles James Fox—a sincerely felt gesture, but also an artifice well understood as such by all in attendance. Fox's name was on the bill, and he was the parliamentary leader of the Rockingham party; yet Burke had been his mentor in politics, and the India legislation owed to Burke its guiding impulse and every touch of its execution, down to the minutest detail of language. In speaking of Fox, Burke is thus speaking also of himself, and he presents the self-imagining by his choice of terms of praise. He concludes that for a statesman true fame can only come from a benevolent use of power.

The speech served its immediate purpose: the Commons passed the bill by 217 votes to 103. Meanwhile, an opposition campaign routinely slandered it as a scheme for patronage dressed up as high-toned policy, and it was doomed in the House of Lords once the king gave the lords to understand that he would look on its supporters as his enemies. The bill's eventual defeat in December 1783, and with it the sacking of Fox and North, signaled the end of the coalition and the rise of a new leader in the House of Commons, the young William Pitt.

Mr. Burke's Speech on Mr. Fox's East-India Bill

MR. SPEAKER,

I thank you for pointing to me. I really wished much to engage your attention in an early stage of the debate. I have been long very deeply, though perhaps ineffectually, engaged in the preliminary inquiries, which have continued without intermission for some years. Though I have felt, with some degree of sensibility, the natural and inevitable impressions of the several matters of fact, as they have been successively disclosed, I have not at any time attempted to trouble you on the merits of the subject; and very little on any of the points which incidentally arose in the course of our proceedings. But I should be sorry to be found totally silent upon this day. Our inquiries are now come to their final issue: — It is now to be determined whether the three years of laborious parliamentary research, whether the twenty years of patient Indian suffering, are to produce a substantial reform in our eastern administration; or whether our knowledge of the grievances has abated our zeal for the correction of them, and our very enquiry into the evil was only a pretext to elude the remedy which is demanded from us by humanity, by justice, and by every principle of true policy. Depend upon it, this business cannot be indifferent to our fame. It will turn out a matter of great disgrace or great glory to the whole British nation. We are on a conspicuous stage, and the world marks our demeanour.

I am therefore a little concerned to perceive the spirit and temper in which the debate has been all along pursued upon one side of the house. The declamation of the gentlemen who oppose the bill has been abundant and vehement; but they have been reserved and even silent about the fitness or unfitness of the plan to attain the direct object it has in view. By some gentlemen it is taken up (by way of exercise I presume) as a point of law on a question of private property, and corporate franchise; by others it is regarded as the petty intrigue of a faction at court, and argued merely as it tends to set this man a little higher, or that a little lower in situation and power. All the void has been filled up with invectives against coalition; with allusions to the loss of America; with the activity and inactivity of ministers. The total silence of these gentlemen concerning the interest and well-being of the people of India, and concerning the interest which this nation has in the commerce and revenues of that country, is a strong indication of the value which they set upon these objects.

It has been a little painful to me to observe the intrusion into this important debate of such company as *quo warranto*, and *mandamus*, and *certiorari*;[1] as if we were on a trial about mayors and aldermen, and capital burgesses; or engaged in a suit concerning the borough of Penryn, or Saltash, or St. Ives, or St. Mawes. Gentlemen have argued with as much heat and passion, as if the first things in the world were at stake; and their topics are such, as belong only to matter of the lowest and meanest litigation. It is not right, it is not worthy of us, in this manner to depreciate the value, to degrade the majesty, of this grave deliberation of policy and empire.

For my part, I have thought myself bound, when a matter of this extraordinary weight came before me, not to consider (as some gentlemen are so fond of doing) whether the bill originated from a secretary of state for the home department, or from a secretary for the foreign, from a minister of influence or a minister of the people; from Jacob or from Esau.[2] I asked myself, and I asked myself nothing else, what part it was fit for a member of parliament, who has supplied a mediocrity of talents by the extreme of diligence, and who has thought himself obliged, by the research of years, to wind himself into the inmost recesses and labyrinths of the Indian detail, what part, I say, it became

---

1 Writs issued to investigate the workings of chartered bodies.
2 An allusion made by Mr. Powis [*Burke's note*].

such a member of parliament to take, when a minister of state, in conformity to a recommendation from the throne, has brought before us a system for the better government of the territory and commerce of the east. In this light, and in this only, I will trouble you with my sentiments.

It is not only agreed but demanded, by the right honourable gentleman,[3] and by those who act with him, that a *whole* system ought to be produced; that it ought not to be an *half measure*; that it ought to be no *palliative*; but a legislative provision, vigorous, substantial, and effective. — I believe that no man who understands the subject can doubt for a moment, that those must be the conditions of any thing deserving the name of a reform in the Indian government; that any thing short of them would not only be delusive, but, in this matter which admits no medium, noxious in the extreme.

To all the conditions proposed by his adversaries the mover of the bill perfectly agrees; and on his performance of them he rests his cause. On the other hand, not the least objection has been taken, with regard to the efficiency, the vigour, or the completeness of the scheme. I am therefore warranted to assume, as a thing admitted, that the bills accomplish what both sides of the house demand as essential. The end is completely answered, so far as the direct and immediate object is concerned.

But though there are no direct, yet there are various collateral objections made; objections from the effects which this plan of reform for Indian administration may have on the privileges of great publick bodies in England; from its probable influence on the constitutional rights, or on the freedom and integrity of the several branches of the legislature.

Before I answer these objections, I must beg leave to observe, that if we are not able to contrive some method of governing India *well*, which will not of necessity become the means of governing Great Britain *ill*, a ground is laid for their eternal separa-

3 Mr. Pitt [*Burke's note*].

tion; but none for sacrificing the people of that country to our constitution. I am however far from being persuaded that any such incompatibility of interest does at all exist. On the contrary I am certain that every means, effectual to preserve India from oppresion, is a guard to preserve the British constitution from its worst corruption. To shew this, I will consider the objections, which I think are four.

1st. That the bill is an attack on the chartered rights of men.

2dly. That it increases the influence of the crown.

3dly. That it does *not* increase, but diminishes, the influence of the crown, in order to promote the interests of certain ministers and their party.

4thly. That it deeply affects the national credit.

As to the first of these objections; I must observe that the phrase of "the chartered rights *of men*," is full of affectation; and very unusual in the discussion of privileges conferred by charters of the present description. But it is not difficult to discover what end that ambiguous mode of expression, so often reiterated, is meant to answer.

The rights of *men*, that is to say, the natural rights of mankind, are indeed sacred things; and if any publick measure is proved mischievously to affect them, the objection ought to be fatal to that measure, even if no charter at all could be set up against it. If these natural rights are further affirmed and declared by express covenants, if they are clearly defined and secured against chicane, against power, and authority, by written instruments and positive engagements, they are in a still better condition: they partake not only of the sanctity of the object so secured, but of that solemn publick faith itself, which secures an object of such importance. Indeed this formal recognition, by the sovereign power, of an original right in the subject, can never be subverted, but by rooting up the holding radical principles of government, and even of society itself. The charters, which we call by distinction *great*, are publick instruments of this nature; I mean the charters of king John and king Henry the third.[4] The things secured by these instruments may, without any deceitful ambiguity, be very fitly called the *chartered rights of men.*

These charters have made the very name of a charter dear to the heart of every Englishman. — But, Sir, there may be, and there are charters, not only different in nature, but formed on principles the *very reverse* of those of the great charter. Of this kind is the charter of the East-India company. *Magna charta* is a charter to restrain power, and to destroy monopoly. The East-India charter is a charter to establish monopoly, and to create power. Political power and commercial monopoly are *not* the rights of men; and the rights of them derived from charters, it is fallacious and sophistical to call "the chartered rights of men." These chartered rights, (to speak of such charters and of their effects in terms of the greatest possible moderation) do at least suspend the natural rights of mankind at large; and in their very frame and constitution are liable to fall into a direct violation of them.

It is a charter of this latter description (that is to say a charter of power and monopoly) which is affected by the bill before you. The bill, Sir, does, without question, affect it; it does affect it essentially and substantially. But having stated to you of what description the chartered rights are which this bill touches, I feel no difficulty at all in acknowledging the existence of those chartered rights, in their fullest extent. They belong to the company in the surest manner; and they are secured to that body by every sort of publick sanction. They are stamped by the faith of the king; they are stamped by the faith of parliament; they have been bought for money, for money honestly and fairly paid; they have been bought for valuable consideration, over and over again.

I therefore freely admit to the East-India company their claim to exclude their fellow-subjects from the commerce of half the globe. I admit their claim to administer an annual territorial

---

4 King John signed the Great Charter in 1215; the second reference may be to the confirmation of charters by Henry III in 1265.

revenue of seven millions sterling; to command an army of sixty thousand men; and to dispose, (under the controul of a sovereign imperial discretion, and with the due observance of the natural and local law) of the lives and fortunes of thirty millions of their fellow-creatures. All this they possess by charter and by acts of parliament, (in my opinion) without a shadow of controversy.

Those who carry the rights and claims of the company the furthest do not contend for more than this; and all this I freely grant. But granting all this, they must grant to me in my turn, that all political power which is set over men, and that all privilege claimed or exercised in exclusion of them, being wholly artificial, and for so much a derogation from the natural equality of mankind at large, ought to be some way or other exercised ultimately for their benefit.

If this is true with regard to every species of political dominion, and every description of commercial privilege, none of which can be original self-derived rights, or grants for the mere private benefit of the holders, then such rights, or privileges, or whatever else you choose to call them, are all in the strictest sense a *trust*; and it is of the very essence of every trust to be rendered *accountable*; and even totally to *cease*, when it substantially varies from the purposes for which alone it could have a lawful existence.

This I conceive, Sir, to be true of trusts of power vested in the highest hands, and of such as seem to hold of no human creature. But about the application of this principle to subordinate *derivative* trusts, I do not see how a controversy can be maintained. To whom then would I make the East-India company accountable? Why, to parliament, to be sure; to parliament, from whom their trust was derived; to parliament, which alone is capable of comprehending the magnitude of its object, and its abuse; and alone capable of an effectual legislative remedy. The very charter, which is held out to exclude parliament from correcting malversation with regard to the high trust vested in the company, is the very thing which at once gives a title and imposes a duty on us to interfere with effect, wherever power and authority originating from ourselves are perverted from their purposes, and become instruments of wrong and violence.

If parliament, Sir, had nothing to do with this charter, we might have some sort of Epicurean excuse to stand aloof, indifferent spectators of what passes in the company's name in India and in London. But if we are the very cause of the evil, we are in a special manner engaged to the redress; and for us passively to bear with oppressions committed under the sanction of our own authority, is in truth and reason for this house to be an active accomplice in the abuse.

That the power notoriously, grossly abused has been bought from us is very certain. But this circumstance, which is urged against the bill, becomes an additional motive for our interference; lest we should be thought to have sold the blood of millions of men, for the safe consideration of money. We sold, I admit, all that we had to sell; that is, our authority, not our controul. We had not a right to make a market of our duties.

I ground myself therefore on this principle — that if the abuse is proved, the contract is broken; and we re-enter into all our rights; that is, into the exercise of all our duties: Our own authority is indeed as much a trust originally, as the company's authority is a trust derivatively; and it is the use we make of the resumed power that must justify or condemn us in the resumption of it. When we have perfected the plan laid before us by the right honourable mover, the world will then see what it is we destroy, and what it is we create. By that test we stand or fall; and by that test I trust that it will be found in the issue, that we are going to supersede a charter abused to the full extent of all the powers which it could abuse, and exercised in the plenitude of despotism, tyranny and corruption; and that in one and the same plan, we provide a real chartered security for the *rights of men* cruelly violated under that charter.

This bill, and those connected with it, are intended to form the *magna charta* of Hindostan. Whatever the treaty of Westphalia is to the liberty of princes and free cities of the empire, and to the three religions there professed[5] — Whatever the great charter, the statute of tallage, the petition of right, and the declaration of right, are to Great Britain, these bills are to the people of India. Of this benefit, I am certain, their condition is capable; and when I know that they are capable of more, my vote shall most assuredly be for our giving to the full extent of their capacity of receiving; and no charter of dominion shall stand as a bar in my way to their charter of safety and protection.

The strong admission I have made of the company's rights (I am conscious of it) binds me to do a great deal. I do not presume to condemn those who argue *a priori*, against the propriety of leaving such extensive political powers in the hands of a company of merchants. I know much is, and much more may be, said against such a system. But, with my particular ideas and sentiments, I cannot go that way to work. I feel an insuperable reluctance in giving my hand to destroy any established institution of government, upon a theory, however plausible it may be. My experience in life teaches me nothing clear upon the subject. I have known merchants with the sentiments and the abilities of great statesmen; and I have seen persons in the rank of statesmen, with the conceptions and character of pedlars. Indeed, my observation has furnished me with nothing that is to be found in any habits of life or education, which tends wholly to disqualify men for the functions of government, but that, by which the power of exercising those functions is very frequently obtained, I mean a spirit and habits of low cabal and intrigue; which I have never, in one instance, seen united with a capacity for sound and manly policy.

To justify us in taking the administration of their affairs out of the hands of the East-India company, on my principles, I must see several conditions. 1st. The object affected by the abuse should

---

5 The Treaty of Westphalia (1648) secured religious toleration for the three main religious groups of the Holy Roman Empire: Catholics, Lutherans, and Calvinists.

be great and important. 2d. The abuse affecting this great object ought to be a great abuse. 3d. It ought to be habitual, and not accidental. 4th. It ought to be utterly incurable in the body as it now stands constituted. All this ought to be made as visible to me as the light of the sun, before I should strike off an atom of their charter. A right honourable gentleman[6] has said, and said I think but once, and that very slightly (whatever his original demand for a plan might seem to require) that "there are abuses in the company's government." If that were all, the scheme of the mover of this bill, the scheme of his learned friend, and his own scheme of reformation (if he has any) are all equally needless. There are, and must be, abuses in all governments. It amounts to no more than a nugatory proposition. But before I consider of what nature these abuses are, of which the gentleman speaks so very lightly, permit me to recall to your recollection the map of the country which this abused chartered right affects. This I shall do, that you may judge whether in that map I can discover any thing like the first of my conditions; that is, Whether the object affected by the abuse of the East-India company's power be of importance sufficiently to justify the measure and means of reform applied to it in this bill.

With very few, and those inconsiderable intervals, the British dominion, either in the company's name, or in the names of princes absolutely dependent upon the company, extends from the mountains that separate India from Tartary, to cape Comorin, that is, one-and-twenty degrees of latitude!

In the northern parts it is a solid mass of land, about eight hundred miles in length, and four or five hundred broad. As you go southward, it becomes narrower for a space. It afterwards dilates; but narrower or broader, you possess the whole eastern and north-eastern coast of that vast country, quite from the borders of Pegu. — Bengal, Bahar, and Orissa, with Benares, (now unfortunately in our immediate possession) measure 161,978 square English miles; a territory considerably larger

6 Mr. Pitt [*Burke's note*].

than the whole kingdom of France. Oude, with its dependent provinces, is 53,286 square miles, not a great deal less than England. The Carnatick, with Tanjour and the Circars, is 65,948 square miles, very considerably larger than England; and the whole of the company's dominions, comprehending Bombay and Salsette, amounts to 281,412 square miles; which forms a territory larger than any European dominion, Russia and Turkey excepted. Through all that vast extent of country there is not a man who eats a mouthful of rice but by permission of the East-India company.

So far with regard to the extent. The population of this great empire is not easy to be calculated. When the countries, of which it is composed, came into our possession, they were all eminently peopled, and eminently productive; though at that time considerably declined from their ancient prosperity. But since they are come into our hands! ——! However, if we make the period of our estimate immediately before the utter desolation of the Carnatick, and if we allow for the havock which our government had even then made in these regions, we cannot, in my opinion, rate the population at much less than thirty millions of souls; more than four times the number of persons in the island of Great Britain.

My next inquiry to that of the number, is the quality and description of the inhabitants. This multitude of men does not consist of an abject and barbarous populace; much less of gangs of savages, like the Guaranies and Chiquitos, who wander on the waste borders of the river of Amazons, or the Plate; but a people for ages civilized and cultivated; cultivated by all the arts of polished life, whilst we were yet in the woods. There, have been (and still the skeletons remain) princes once of great dignity, authority, and opulence. There, are to be found the chiefs of tribes and nations. There, is to be found an ancient and venerable priesthood, the depository of their laws, learning, and history, the guides of the people whilst living, and their consolation in death; a nobility of great antiquity and renown; a multitude of cities, not exceeded in population and trade by those of the first class in Europe; merchants and bankers, individual houses of whom have once vied in capital with the bank of England; whose credit had often supported a tottering state, and preserved their governments in the midst of war and desolation; millions of ingenious manufacturers and mechanicks; millions of the most diligent, and not the least intelligent, tillers of the earth. Here are to be found almost all the religions professed by men, the Braminical, the Mussulman, the Eastern and the Western Christian.

If I were to take the whole aggregate of our possessions there, I should compare it, as the nearest parallel I can find, with the empire of Germany. Our immediate possessions I should compare with the Austrian dominions, and they would not suffer in the comparison. The nabob of Oude might stand for the king of Prussia; the nabob of Arcot I would compare, as superiour in territory, and equal in revenue, to the elector of Saxony. Cheyt Sing, the rajah of Benares, might well rank with the prince of Hesse, at least; and the rajah of Tanjore (though hardly equal in extent of dominion, superiour in revenue) to the elector of Bavaria. The Polygars and the northern Zemindars,[7] and other great chiefs, might well class with the rest of the princes, dukes, counts, marquisses, and bishops in the empire; all of whom I mention to honour, and surely without disparagement to any or all of those most respectable princes and grandees.

All this vast mass, composed of so many orders and classes of men, is again infinitely diversified by manners, by religion, by hereditary employment, through all their possible combinations. This renders the handling of India a matter in a high degree critical and delicate. But oh! it has been handled rudely indeed. Ever some of the reformers seem to have forgot that they had any thing to do but to regulate the tenants of a manor, or the shopkeepers of the next county town.

It is an empire of this extent, of this complicated nature, of this dignity and importance, that I have compared to Germany, and the German government; not for an exact resemblance, but

7 Landholders.

as a sort of a middle term, by which India might be approximated to our understandings, and if possible to our feelings; in order to awaken something of sympathy for the unfortunate natives, of which I am afraid we are not perfectly susceptible, whilst we look at this very remote object through a false and cloudy medium.

My second condition, necessary to justify me in touching the charter, is, Whether the company's abuse of their trust, with regard to this great object, be an abuse of great atrocity. I shall beg your permission to consider their conduct in two lights; first the political, and then the commercial. Their political conduct (for distinctness) I divide again into two heads; the external, in which I mean to comprehend their conduct in their federal capacity, as it relates to powers and states independent, or that not long since were such; the other internal, namely their conduct to the countries either immediately subject to the company, or to those who, under the apparent government of native sovereigns, are in a state much lower, and much more miserable, than common subjection.

The attention, Sir, which I wish to preserve to method will not be considered as unnecessary or affected. Nothing else can help me to selection out of the infinite mass of materials which have passed under my eye; or can keep my mind steady to the great leading points I have in view.

With regard therefore to the abuse of the external federal trust, I engage myself to you to make good these three positions: — First, I say, that from mount Imaus, (or whatever else you call that large range of mountains that walls the northern frontier of India) where it touches us in the latitude of twenty-nine, to Cape Comorin, in the latitude of eight, that there is not a *single* prince, state, or potentate, great or small, in India, with whom they have come into contact, whom they have not sold. I say *sold*, though sometimes they have not been able to deliver according to their bargain. — Secondly, I say, that there is not a *single treaty* they have ever made, which they have not broken. — Thirdly, I say, that there is not a single prince or state, who ever put any trust in the company, who is not utterly ruined; and that none are in any degree secure or flourishing, but in the exact proportion to their settled distrust and irreconcileable enmity to this nation.

These assertions are universal. I say in the full sense *universal.* They regard the external and political trust only; but I shall produce others fully equivalent in the internal. For the present, I shall content myself with explaining my meaning; and if I am called on for proof whilst these bills are depending (which I believe I shall not) I will put my finger on the appendixes to the reports, or on papers of record in the house, or the committees, which I have distinctly present to my memory, and which I think I can lay before you at half an hour's warning.

The first potentate sold by the company for money, was the Great Mogul — the descendant of Tamerlane.[8] This high personage, as high as human veneration can look at, is by every account amiable in his manners, respectable for his piety according to his mode, and accomplished in all the Oriental literature. All this, and the title derived under his *charter,* to all that we hold in India, could not save him from the general *sale.* Money is coined in his name; in his name justice is administered; he is prayed for in every temple through the countries we possess — But he was sold.

It is impossible, Mr. Speaker, not to pause here for a moment, to reflect on the inconstancy of human greatness, and the stupendous revolutions that have happened in our age of wonders. Could it be believed when I entered into existence, or when you, a younger man, were born, that on this day, in this house, we should be employed in discussing the conduct of those British subjects who had disposed of the power and person of the Grand

8 Shah Alam II (1728–1806), descendant of Tamburlaine (1336–1405), who conquered large parts of India. By the terms of the Treaty of Allahabad in 1765, he gave the company the *diwani,* or right to collect revenues over Bengal and other territories, in return for an annual revenue of twenty-six lakhs of rupees (a lakh at this time was worth about ten thousand pounds). Later, in view of his implication with the Marathas, the company broke the treaty and stopped payment of his revenue.

Mogul? This is no idle speculation. Awful lessons are taught by it, and by other events, of which it is not yet too late to profit.

This is hardly a digression; but I return to the sale of the Mogul. Two districts, Corah, and Allahabad, out of his immense grants, were reserved as a royal demesne to the donor of a kingdom, and the rightful sovereign of so many nations. — After withholding the tribute of 260,000*l.* a year, which the company was, by the *charter* they had received from this prince, under the most solemn obligation to pay, these districts were sold to his chief minister Sujah ul Dowlah; and, what may appear to some the worst part of the transaction, these two districts were sold for scarcely two years purchase. The descendant of Tamerlane now stands in need almost of the common necessaries of life; and in this situation we do not even allow him, as bounty, the smallest portion of what we owe him in justice.

The next sale was that of the whole nation of the Rohillas, which the grand salesman, without a pretence of quarrel, and contrary to his own declared sense of duty and rectitude, sold to the same Sujah ul Dowlah. He sold the people to utter *extirpation*, for the sum of four hundred thousand pounds. Faithfully was the bargain performed on our side. Hafiz Rhamet, the most eminent of their chiefs, one of the bravest men of his time, and as famous throughout the East for the elegance of his literature, and the spirit of his poetical compositions (by which he supported the name of Hafiz) as for his courage, was invaded with an army of an hundred thousand men, and an English brigade. This man, at the head of inferiour forces was slain valiantly fighting for his country. His head was cut off, and delivered for money to a barbarian. His wife and children, persons of that rank, were seen begging an handful of rice through the English camp. The whole nation, with inconsiderable exceptions, was slaughtered or banished. The country was laid waste with fire and sword; and that land, distinguished above most others by the cheerful face of paternal government and protected labour, the chosen seat of cultivation and plenty, is now almost throughout a dreary desert, covered with rushes and briers, and jungles full of wild beasts.

The British officer who commanded in the delivery of the people thus sold, felt some compunction at his employment. He represented these enormous excesses to the president of Bengal, for which he received a severe reprimand from the civil governor; and I much doubt whether the breach caused by the conflict, between the compassion of the military and the firmness of the civil governor, be closed at this hour.

In Bengal, Seraja Dowla was sold to Mir Jaffier; Mir Jaffier was sold to Mir Coffim; and Mir Coffim was sold to Mir Jaffier again. The sucession to Mir Jaffier was sold to his eldest son; — another son of Mir Jaffier, Mobarech ul Dowla, was sold to his step-mother — The Maratta empire was sold to Ragoba; and Ragoba was sold and delivered to the Peishwa of the Marattas. Both Ragoba and the Peishwa of the Marattas were offered to sale to the rajah of Berar. Scindia, the chief of Malva, was offered to sale to the same rajah; and the Subah of the Decan was sold to the great trader Mahomet Ali, nabob of Arcot. To the same nabob of Arcot they sold Hyder Ali and the kingdom of Mysore. To Mahomet Ali they twice sold the kingdom of Tanjore. To the same Mahomet Ali they sold at least twelve sovereign princes, called the Polygars. But to keep things even, the territory of Tinnivelly, belonging to their nabob, they would have sold to the Dutch; and to conclude the account of sales, their great customer, the nabob of Arcot himself, and his lawful succession, has been sold to his second son, Amir ul Omrah, whose character, views, and conduct, are in the accounts upon your table. It remains with you whether they shall finally perfect this last bargain.

All these bargains and sales were regularly attended with the waste and havock of the country, always by the buyer, and sometimes by the object of the sale. This was explained to you by the honourable mover, when he stated the mode of paying debts due from the country powers to the company. An honourable gentleman, who is not now in his place, objected to his jumping near two thousand miles for an example. But the southern example is perfectly applicable to the northern claim, as the northern is to the southern; for, throughout the whole space of these two thousand miles, take your stand where you will, the proceeding is perfectly uniform, and what is done in one part will apply exactly to the other.

My second assertion is, that the company never has made a treaty which they have not broken. This position is so connected with that of the sales of provinces and kingdoms, with the negotiation of universal distraction in every part of India, that a very minute detail may well be spared on this point. It has not yet been contended, by any enemy to the reform, that they have observed any publick agreement. When I hear that they have done so in any one instance (which hitherto, I confess, I never heard alleged) I shall speak to the particular treaty. The governour general has even amused himself and the court of directors in a very singular letter to that board, in which he admits he has not been very delicate with regard to publick faith; and he goes so far as to state a regular estimate of the sums which the company would have lost, or never acquired, if the rigid ideas of publick faith entertained by his colleagues had been observed. The learned gentleman over against me has indeed saved me much trouble.[9] On a former occasion he obtained no small credit, for the clear and forcible manner in which he stated what we have not forgot, and I hope he has not forgot, that universal systematick breach of treaties which had made the British faith proverbial in the East.

It only remains, Sir, for me just to recapitulate some heads. — The treaty with the mogul, by which we stipulated to pay him 260,000l. annually, was broken. This treaty they have broken, and not paid him a shilling. They broke their treaty with him, in which they stipulated to pay 400,000l. a year to the soubah of Bengal. They agreed with the mogul, for services admitted to have been performed, to pay Nudjif Cawn a pension. They broke

9 Mr. Dundas, lord Advocate of Scotland [*Burke's note*]. Henry Dundas (1741–1811), formerly lord advocate in the Fox-North Coalition, was now serving Pitt as an adviser on Indian affairs. He had been an influential member of the Secret Committee entrusted with scrutinizing the management of Indian affairs during North's administration, and earlier in the year had proposed an alternative reorganization of the government's relations to the company and its charter.

this article with the rest, and stopped also this small pension. They broke their treaties with the nizam, and with Hyder Ali. As to the Marattas, they had so many cross treaties with the states general of that nation, and with each of the chiefs, that it was notorious that no one of these agreements could be kept without grossly violating the rest. It was observed, that if the terms of these several treaties had been kept, two British armies would at one and the same time have met in the field to cut each other's throats. The wars which desolate India, originated from a most atrocious violation of publick faith on our part. In the midst of profound peace, the company's troops invaded the Maratta territories, and surprised the island and fortress of Salsette. The Marattas nevertheless yielded to a treaty of peace, by which solid advantages were procured to the company. But this treaty, like every other treaty, was soon violated by the company. Again the company invaded the Maratta dominions. The disaster that ensued gave occasion to a new treaty. The whole army of the company was obliged, in effect, to surrender to this injured, betrayed, and insulted people. Justly irritated, however, as they were, the terms which they prescribed were reasonable and moderate; and their treatment of their captive invaders of the most distinguished humanity. But the humanity of the Marattas was of no power whatsoever to prevail on the company to attend to the observance of the terms dictated by their moderation. The war was renewed with greater vigour than ever; and such was their insatiable lust of plunder, that they never would have given ear to any terms of peace, if Hyder Ali had not broke through the Gauts, and rushing like a torrent into the Carnatick, swept away every thing in his career. This was in consequence of that confederacy, which by a sort of miracle united the most discordant powers for our destruction, as a nation in which no other could put any trust, and who were the declared enemies of the human species.[10]

10 In 1779, Mysore, under the leadership of Haider Ali Khan (here called Hyder Ali), joined in confederacy with the Nizam and Marathas in a war against the British.

It is very remarkable, that the late controversy between the several presidencies, and between them and the court of directors, with relation to these wars and treaties, has not been, which of the parties might be defended for his share in them; but on which of the parties the guilt of all this load of perfidy should be fixed. But I am content to admit all these proceedings to be perfectly regular, to be full of honour and good faith; and wish to fix your attention solely to that single transaction which the advocates of this system select for so transcendent a merit as to cancel the guilt of all the rest of their proceedings; I mean the late treaties with the Marattas.[11]

I make no observation on the total cession of territory, by which they surrendered all they had obtained by their unhappy successes in war, and almost all they had obtained under the treaty of Poorunder. The restitution was proper, if it had been voluntary and seasonable. I attach on the spirit of the treaty, the dispositions it shewed, the provisions it made for a general peace, and the faith kept with allies and confederates; in order that the house may form a judgment, from this chosen piece, of the use which has been made (and is likely to be made, if things continue in the same hands) of the trust of the federal powers of this country.

It was the wish of almost every Englishman, that the Maratta peace might lead to a general one; because the Maratta war was only a part of a general confederacy formed against us on account of the universal abhorrence of our conduct which prevailed in every state and almost in every house in India. Mr. Hastings was obliged to pretend some sort of acquiescence in this general and rational desire. He therefore consented, in order to satisfy the point of honour of the Marattas, that an article should be inserted to admit Hyder Ali to accede to the pacification. But

11 By the Treaty of Salbai of March 1782, and subsequent agreements of 1783, the company negotiated a peace with the Maratha leader Sindhia (d. 1794). This marked the end of the First Maratha War, which had begun in 1775, and enabled the British to concentrate their forces against Tipu Sultan, the son and successor of Hyder Ali. Tipu ascended the throne in 1783 and continued the war.

observe, Sir, the spirit of this man (which if it were not made manifest by a thousand things, and particularly by his proceedings with regard to lord Macartney) would be sufficiently manifest by this — What sort of article think you does he require this essential head of a solemn treaty of general pacification to be? In his instruction to Mr. Anderson, he desires him to admit "a *vague* article" in favour of Hyder. Evasion and fraud were the declared basis of the treaty. These *vague* articles, intended for a more vague performance, are the things which have damned our reputation in India.

Hardly was this vague article inserted, than, without waiting for any act on the part of Hyder, Mr. Hastings enters into a negotiation with the Maratta chief, Scindia, for a partition of the territories of the prince who was one of the objects to be secured by the treaty. He was to be parcelled out in three parts — one to Scindia; one to the peishwa of the Marattas; and the third to the East India company, or to (the old dealer and chapman) Mahomet Ali.

During the formation of this project, Hyder dies; and before his son could take any one step, either to conform to the tenour of the article, or to contravene it, the treaty of partition is renewed on the old footing, and an instruction is sent to Mr. Anderson to conclude it in form.

A circumstance intervened, during the pendency of this negotiation, to set off the good faith of the company with an additional brilliancy, and to make it sparkle and glow with a variety of splendid faces. General Matthews had reduced that most valuable part of Hyder's dominions called the County of Biddenore. When the news reached Mr. Hastings he instructed Mr. Anderson to contend for an alteration in the treaty of partition, and to take the Biddenore country out of the common stock, which was to be divided, and to keep it for the company.

The first ground for this variation was its being a separate conquest made before the treaty had actually taken place. Here was a new proof given of the fairness, equity, and moderation of the company. But the second of Mr. Hastings's reasons for retaining the Biddenore as a separate portion, and his conduct on that second ground, is still more remarkable. He asserted that that country could not be put into the partition stock, because general Matthews had received it on the terms of some convention, which might be incompatible with the partition proposed. This was a reason in itself both honourable and solid; and it shewed a regard to faith somewhere, and with some persons. But in order to demonstrate his utter contempt of the plighted faith which was alleged on one part as a reason for departing from it on another, and to prove his impetuous desire for sowing a new war, even in the prepared soil of a general pacification, he directs Mr. Anderson, if he should find strong difficulties impeding the partition, on the score of the subtraction of Biddenore, wholly to abandon that claim, and to conclude the treaty on the original terms. General Matthews's convention was just brought forward sufficiently to demonstrate to the Marattas the slippery hold which they had on their new confederate; on the other hand that convention being instantly abandoned, the people of India were taught, that no terms on which they can surrender to the company are to be regarded when farther conquests are in view.

Next, Sir, let me bring before you the pious care that was taken of our allies under that treaty which is the subject of the company's applauses. These allies were Ragonaut Row, for whom we had engaged to find a throne; the Guickwar, (one of the Guzerat princes) who was to be emancipated from the Maratta authority, and to grow great by several accessions of dominion; and lastly, the rana of Gohud, with whom we had entered into a treaty of partition for eleven sixteenths of our joint conquests. Some of these inestimable securities, called *vague* articles, were inserted in favour of them all.

As to the first, the unhappy abdicated peishwa, and pretender to the Maratta throne, Ragonaut Row was delivered up to his people, with an article for safety, and some provision. This man, knowing how little vague the hatred of his countrymen was towards him, and well apprised of what black crimes he stood accused (among which our invasion of his country would not appear the least) took a mortal alarm at the security we had provided for him. He was thunderstruck at the article in his favour, by which he was surrendered to his enemies. He never had the least notice of the treaty; and it was apprehended that he would fly to the protection of Hyder Ali, or some other, disposed or able to protect him. He was therefore not left without comfort; for Mr. Anderson did him the favour to send a special messenger, desiring him to be of good cheer and to fear nothing. And his old enemy, Scindia, at our request, sent him a message equally well calculated to quiet his apprehensions.[12]

By the same treaty the Guickwar was to come again, with no better security, under the dominion of the Maratta state. As to the rana of Gohud, a long negotiation depended for giving him up. At first this was refused by Mr. Hastings with great indignation; at another stage it was admitted as proper, because he had shewn himself a most perfidious person. But at length a method of reconciling these extremes was found out, by contriving one of the usual articles in his favour. What I believe will appear beyond all belief, Mr. Anderson exchanged the final ratifications of that treaty by which the rana was nominally secured in his possessions, in the camp of the Maratta chief, Scindia, whilst he was (really, and not nominally) battering the castle of Gualior, which we had given, agreeably to treaty, to this deluded ally. Scindia had already reduced the town; and was at the very time, by various detachments, reducing, one after another, the fortresses of our protected ally, as well as in the act of chastising all the rajahs who had assisted colonel Carnac in his invasion.[13] I have seen a letter from Calcutta, that the rana of Gohud's agent would have represented these hostilities (which went hand in

12 Under the Treaty of Salbai (1782), Raghunath Rao, now removed from British protection, was to receive an allowance from the Maratha leader Sindhia, on the condition that he agree to reside with him.

13 Camac had led troops against Sindhia and captured the fortress of Gwalior, which the company then gave into the keeping of the Rana of Gohad. When Sindhia came over to the British side, Warren Hastings allowed him to recover his property from the same Rana of Gohad — "this deluded ally" as Burke calls him.

hand with the protecting treaty) to Mr. Hastings; but he was not admitted to his presence.

In this manner the company has acted with their allies in the Maratta war. But they did not rest here: the Marattas were fearful lest the persons delivered to them by that treaty should attempt to escape into the British territories, and thus might elude the punishment intended for them, and by reclaiming the treaty, might stir up new disturbances. To prevent this, they desired an article to be inserted in the supplemental treaty, to which they had the ready consent of Mr. Hastings, and the rest of the company's representatives in Bengal. It was this, "That the English and Maratta governments mutually agree not to afford refuge to any *chiefs, merchants, or other persons,* flying for protection to the territories of the other." This was readily assented to, and assented to without any exception whatever, in favour of our surrendered allies. On their part a reciprocity was stipulated which was not unnatural for a government like the company's to ask; a government conscious that many subjects had been, and would in future be, driven to fly from its jurisdiction.

To complete the system of pacifick intention and publick faith, which predominate in these treaties, Mr. Hastings fairly resolved to put all peace, except on the terms of absolute conquest, wholly out of his own power. For, by an article in this second treaty with Scindia, he binds the company not to make any peace with Tippoo Saheb, without the consent of the peishwa of the Marattas; and binds Scindia to him by a reciprocal agreement. The treaty between France and England obliges us mutually to withdraw our forces, if our allies in India do not accede to the peace within four months; Mr. Hastings's treaty obliges us to continue the war as long as the peishwa thinks fit. We are now in that happy situation, that the breach of the treaty with France, or the violation of that with the Marattas, is inevitable; and we have only to take our choice.

My third assertion, relative to the abuse made of the right of war and peace is, that there are none who have ever confided in us who have not been utterly ruined. The examples I have given of Ragonaut Row, of Guickwar, of the rana of Gohud, are recent. There is proof more than enough in the condition of the mogul; in the slavery and indigence of the nabob of Oude; the exile of the rajah of Benares; the beggary of the nabob of Bengal; the undone and captive condition of the rajah and kingdom of Tanjour; the destruction of the polygars; and lastly, in the destruction of the nabob of Arcot himself, who, when his dominions were invaded, was found entirely destitute of troops, provisions, stores, and (as he asserts) of money, being a million in debt to the company, and four millions to others: the many millions which he had extorted from so many extirpated princes and their desolated countries having (as he has frequently hinted) been expended for the ground rent of his mansion-house in an alley in the suburbs of Madras. Compare the condition of all these princes with the power and authority of all the Maratta states; with the independence and dignity of the Soubah of the Decan; and the mighty strength, the resources, and the manly struggle of Hyder Ali; and then the house will discover the effects on every power in India, of an easy confidence, or of a rooted distrust in the faith of the company.

These are some of my reasons, grounded on the abuse of the external political trust of that body, for thinking myself not only justified, but bound, to declare against those chartered rights which produce so many wrongs. I should deem myself the wickedest of men, if any vote of mine could contribute to the continuance of so great an evil.

Now, Sir, according to the plan I proposed, I shall take notice of the company's internal government, as it is exercised first on the dependent provinces, and then as it affects those under the direct and immediate authority of that body. And here, Sir, before I enter into the spirit of their interiour government, permit me to observe to you, upon a few of the many lines of difference which are to be found between the vices of the company's government, and those of the conquerors who preceded us in India; that we may be enabled a little the better to see our way in an attempt to the necessary reformation.

The several irruptions of Arabs, Tartars, and Persians, into India were, for the greater part, ferocious, bloody, and wasteful in the extreme: our entrance into the dominion of that country, was, as generally, with small comparative effusion of blood; being introduced by various frauds and delusions, and by taking advantage of the incurable, blind, and senseless animosity, which the several country powers bear towards each other, rather than by open force. But the difference in favour of the first conquerors is this; the Asiatick conquerors very soon abated of their ferocity, because they made the conquered country their own. They rose or fell with the rise or fall of the territory they lived in. Fathers there deposited the hopes of their posterity; and children there beheld the monuments of their fathers. Here their lot was finally cast; and it is the natural wish of all, that their lot should not be cast in a bad land. Poverty, sterility, and desolation, are not a recreating prospect to the eye of man; and there are very few who can bear to grow old among the curses of a whole people. If their passion or their avarice drove the Tartar lords to acts of rapacity or tyranny, there was time enough, even in the short life of man, to bring round the ill effects of an abuse of power upon the power itself. If hoards were made by violence and tyranny, they were still domestick hoards; and domestick profusion, or the rapine of a more powerful and prodigal hand, restored them to the people. With many disorders, and with few political checks upon power, nature had still fair play; the sources of acquisition were not dried up; and therefore the trade, the manufactures, and the commerce of the country flourished. Even avarice and usury itself operated, both for the preservation and the employment of national wealth. The husbandman and manufacturer paid heavy interest, but then they augmented the fund from whence they were again to borrow. Their resources were dearly bought, but they were sure; and the general stock of the community grew by the general effort.

But under the English government all this order is reversed. The Tartar invasion was mischievous; but it is our protection that destroys India. It was their enmity, but it is our friendship. Our conquest there, after twenty years, is as crude as it was the first day. The natives scarcely know what it is to see the grey head of an Englishman. Young men (boys almost) govern there, without society, and without sympathy with the natives. They have no more social habits with the people, than if they still resided in England; nor indeed any species of intercourse but that which is necessary to making a sudden fortune, with a view to a remote settlement. Animated with all the avarice of age, and all the impetuosity of youth, they roll in one after another; wave after wave; and there is nothing before the eyes of the natives but an endless, hopeless prospect of new flights of birds of prey and passage, with appetites continually renewing for a food that is continually wasting. Every rupee of profit made by an Englishman is lost for ever to India. With us are no retributory superstitions, by which a foundation of charity compensates, through ages, to the poor, for the rapine and injustice of a day. With us no pride erects stately monuments which repair the mischiefs which pride had produced, and which adorn a country out of its own spoils. England has erected no churches, no hospitals,[14] no palaces, no schools; England has built no bridges, made no high roads, cut no navigations, dug out no reservoirs. Every other conqueror of every other description has left some monument, either of state or beneficence, behind him. Were we to be driven out of India this day, nothing would remain, to tell that it had been possessed, during the inglorious period of our dominion, by any thing better than the ouran-outang or the tiger.

There is nothing in the boys we send to India worse, than in the boys whom we are whipping at school, or that we see trailing a pike, or bending over a desk at home. But as English youth in India drink the intoxicating draught of authority and dominion before their heads are able to bear it, and as they are full grown in fortune long before they are ripe in principle, neither nature nor reason have any opportunity to exert themselves for remedy of

14 The paltry foundation at Calcutta is scarcely worth naming as an exception [*Burke's note*].

the excesses of their premature power. The consequences of their conduct, which in good minds, (and many of theirs are probably such) might produce penitence or amendment, are unable to pursue the rapidity of their flight. Their prey is lodged in England; and the cries of India are given to seas and winds, to be blown about, in every breaking up of the monsoon, over a remote and unhearing ocean. In India all the vices operate by which sudden fortune is acquired; in England are often displayed by the same persons, the virtues which dispense hereditary wealth. Arrived in England, the destroyers of the nobility and gentry of a whole kingdom will find the best company in this nation, at a board of elegance and hospitality. Here the manufacturer and husbandman will bless the just and punctual hand that in India has torn the cloth from the loom, or wrested the scanty portion of rice and salt from the peasant of Bengal, or wrung from him the very opium in which he forgot his oppressions and his oppressor. They marry into your families; they enter into your senate; they ease your estates by loans; they raise their value by demand; they cherish and protect your relations which lie heavy on your patronage; and there is scarcely an house in the kingdom that does not feel some concern and interest that makes all reform of our eastern government appear officious and disgusting; and on the whole, a most discouraging attempt. In such an attempt you hurt those who are able to return kindness, or to resent injury. If you succeed, you save those who cannot so much as give you thanks. All these things shew the difficulty of the work we have on hand: but they shew its necessity too. Our Indian government is in its best state a grievance. It is necessary that the correctives should be uncommonly vigorous; and the work of men, sanguine, warm, and even impassioned in the cause. But it is an arduous thing to plead against abuses of a power which originates from your own country, and affects those whom we are used to consider as strangers.

I shall certainly endeavour to modulate myself to this temper; though I am sensible that a cold style of describing actions which appear to me in a very affecting light, is equally contrary to the justice due to the people, and to all genuine human feelings about them. I ask pardon of truth and nature for this compliance. But I shall be very sparing of epithets either to persons or things. It has been said (and, with regard to one of them, with truth) that Tacitus and Machiavel, by their cold way of relating enormous crimes, have in some sort appeared not to disapprove them; that they seem a sort of professors of the art of tyranny, and that they corrupt the minds of their readers, by not expressing the detestation and horrour that naturally belong to horrible and detestable proceedings. But we are in general, Sir, so little acquainted with Indian details; the instruments of oppression under which the people suffer are so hard to be understood; and even the very names of the sufferers are so uncouth and strange to our ears, that it is very difficult for our sympathy to fix upon these objects. I am sure that some of us have come down stairs from the committee-room with impressions on our minds, which to us were the inevitable results of our discoveries, yet if we should venture to express ourselves, in the proper language of our sentiments, to other gentlemen, not at all prepared to enter into the cause of them, nothing could appear more harsh and dissonant, more violent and unaccountable, than our language and behaviour. All these circumstances are not, I confess, very favourable to the idea of our attempting to govern India at all. But there we are; there we are placed by the Sovereign Disposer; and we must do the best we can in our situation. The situation of man is the preceptor of his duty.

Upon the plan which I laid down, and to which I beg leave to return, I was considering the conduct of the company to those nations which are indirectly subject to their authority. The most considerable of the dependent princes is the nabob of Oude.[15]

15 The Wazir of Oudh, Asaf al-Daula (d. 1797). Under the Treaty of Faizibad, he agreed to pay an annual subsidy of seventy-four lakhs of rupees in exchange for the company's maintaining of two regiments in Oudh to uphold his rule. Even as the Wazir fell into arrears, Hastings required ever larger sums to pay for the company's wars with Mysore, the Marathas, and Chait Singh. The Wazir sent Hastings to the Begams of Oudh for the necessary money; see note 24, below.

My right honourable friend, to whom we owe the remedial bills on your table, has already pointed out to you,[16] in one of the reports, the condition of that prince, and as it stood in the time he alluded to. I shall only add a few circumstances that may tend to awaken some sense of the manner in which the condition of the people is affected by that of the prince, and involved in it; and to shew you, that when we talk of the sufferings of princes, we do not lament the oppression of individuals; and that in these cases the high and the low suffer together.

In the year 1779, the nabob of Oude represented, through the British resident at his court, that the number of company's troops stationed in his dominions was a main cause of his distress; and that all those which he was not bound by treaty to maintain should be withdrawn, as they had greatly diminished his revenue, and impoverished his country. I will read you, if you please, a few extracts from these representations.

He states, "that the country and cultivation are abandoned; and this year in particular, from the excessive drought of the season, deductions of many lacks[17] having been allowed to the farmers, who are still left unsatisfied;" and then he proceeds with a long detail of his own distress, and that of his family, and all his dependants; and adds, "that the new-raised brigade is not only quite useless to my government, but is moreover the cause of much loss, both in revenues and customs. The detached body of troops under European officers bring nothing *but confusion to the affairs of my government, and are entirely their own masters.*" Mr. Middleton, Mr. Hastings's confidential resident, vouches for the truth of this representation in its fullest extent. "I am concerned to confess, that there is too good ground for this plea. *The misfortune has been general throughout the whole of the vizier's* [the nabob of Oude] *dominions,* obvious to everybody; and so *fatal* have been its consequences, that no person of either credit or character, would enter into engagements with government for farming the

---

16 Mr. Fox [*Burke's note*].
17 About ten thousand pounds; see note 8.

country." He then proceeds to give strong instances of the general calamity, and its effects.

It was now to be seen what steps the governor-general and council took for the relief of this distressed country, long labouring under the vexations of men, and now stricken by the hand of God. The case of a general famine is known to relax the severity even of the most rigorous government. — Mr. Hastings does not deny, or shew the least doubt of the fact. The representation is humble, and almost abject. On this representation from a great prince to the distress of his subjects, Mr. Hastings falls into a violent passion; such (as it seems) would be unjustifiable in any one who speaks of any part of *his* conduct. He declares, "that the *demands*, the *tone* in which they were asserted, and the *season* in which they were made, are all equally alarming, and appear to him to require an adequate degree of firmness in this board, in *opposition* to them." He proceeds to deal out very unreserved language, on the person and character of the nabob and his ministers. He declares, that in a division between him and the nabob, "*the strongest must decide.*" With regard to the urgent and instant necessity, from the failure of the crops, he says, "that *perhaps* expedients *may be found* for affording a *gradual* relief from the burthen of which he so heavily complains, and it shall be my endeavour to seek them out:" and lest he should be suspected of too much haste to alleviate sufferings, and to remove violence, he says, "that these must be *gradually* applied, and their complete *effect* may be *distant*; and this I conceive *is all* he can claim of right."

This complete effect of his lenity is distant indeed. Rejecting this demand, (as he calls the nabob's abject supplication) he attributes it, as he usually does all things of the kind, to the division in their government; and says, "this is a powerful motive with *me* (however inclined I might be, *upon any other occasion*, to yield to some *part* of his demand) to give them an *absolute and unconditional refusal* upon the present; and even *to bring to punishment, if my influence can produce that effect, those incendiaries who have endeavoured to make themselves the instruments of division between us.*"

Here, Sir, is much heat and passion; but no more consideration of the distress of the country, from a failure of the means of subsistence, and (if possible) the worse evil of an useless and licentious soldiery, than if they were the most contemptible of all trifles. A letter is written in consequence, in such a style of lofty despotism, as I believe has hitherto been unexampled and unheard-of in the records of the East. The troops were continued. The *gradual* relief, whose effect was to be so *distant*, has *never* been substantially and beneficially applied — and the country is ruined.

Mr. Hastings, two years after, when it was too late, saw the absolute necessity of a removal of the intolerable grievance of this licentious soldiery, which, under pretence of defending it, held the country under military execution. A new treaty and arrangement, according to the pleasure of Mr. Hastings, took place; and this new treaty was broken in the old manner, in every essential article.[18] The soldiery were again sent, and again set loose. The effect of all his manœuvres, from which it seems he was sanguine enough to entertain hopes, upon the state of the country, he himself informs us, "the event has proved the *reverse* of his hopes, and *accumulation of distress, debasement, and dissatisfaction* to the nabob, and *disappointment and disgrace to me.* — Every measure [which he had himself proposed] has been *so conducted* as to give him cause of displeasure; there are no officers established by which his affairs could be regularly conducted; mean, incapable, and indigent men have been appointed. A number of the districts without authority, and without the means of personal protection; some of them have been murdered by the zemindars, and those zemindars, instead of punishment, have been permitted to retain their zemindaries, with independent authority; *all* the other zemindars suffered to rise up in rebellion, and to insult the authority of the sircar,[19] without any attempt made to

18 By the Treaty of Chunar (1781), the company agreed to reduce the number of its troops in Oudh, which served as a buffer between the British and the Marathas.
19 Head administrator of a province.

suppress them; and the company's debt, instead of being discharged by the assignments and extraordinary sources of money provided for that *purpose, is likely to exceed even the amount at which it stood at the time in which the arrangement with his excellency was concluded."* The house will smile at the resource on which the directors take credit as such a certainty in this curious account.

This is Mr. Hastings's own narrative of the effects of his own settlement. This is the state of the country which we have been told is in perfect peace and order; and, what is curious, he informs us, that *every part of this was foretold to him in the order and manner in which it happened,* at the very time he made his arrangement of men and measures.

The invariable course of the company's policy is this: Either they set up some prince too odious to maintain himself without the necessity of their assistance; or they soon render him odious, by making him the instrument of their government. In that case troops are bountifully sent to him to maintain his authority. That he should have no want of assistance, a civil gentleman, called a resident, is kept at his court, who, under pretence of providing duly for the pay of these troops, gets assignments on the revenue into his hands. Under his provident management, debts soon accumulate; new assignments are made for these debts; until, step by step, the whole revenue, and with it the whole power of the country, is delivered into his hands. The military do not behold without a virtuous emulation the moderate gains of the civil department. They feel that, in a country driven to habitual rebellion by the civil government, the military is necessary; and they will not permit their services to go unrewarded. Tracts of country are delivered over to their discretion. Then it is found proper to convert their commanding officers into farmers of revenue. Thus between the well paid civil, and well-rewarded military establishment, the situation of the natives may be easily conjectured. The authority of the regular and lawful government is every where and in every point extinguished. Disorders and violences arise; they are repressed by other disorders and other violences. Wherever the collectors of the revenue, and the farming colonels and majors move, ruin is about them, rebellion before and behind them. The people in crowds fly out of the country; and the frontier is guarded by lines of troops, not to exclude an enemy, but to prevent the escape of the inhabitants.

By these means, in the course of not more than four or five years, this once opulent and flourishing country, which, by the accounts given in the Bengal consultations, yielded more than three crore of Sicca rupees, that is, above three millions sterling annually, is reduced, as far as I can discover, in a matter purposely involved in the utmost perplexity, to less than one million three hundred thousand pounds, and that exacted by every mode of rigour that can be devised. To complete the business, most of the wretched remnants of this revenue are mortgaged, and delivered into the hands of the usurers at Benares (for there alone are to be found some lingering remains of the ancient wealth of these regions) at an interest of near *thirty percent. per annum.*

The revenues in this manner failing, they seized upon the estates of every person of eminence in the country, and under the name of *resumption,* confiscated their property. I wish, Sir, to be understood universally and literally, when I assert, that there is not left one man of property and substance for his rank, in the whole of these provinces, in provinces which are nearly the extent of England and Wales taken together. Not one landholder, not one banker, not one merchant, not one even of those who usually perish last, the *ultimum moriens*[20] in a ruined state, not one farmer of revenue.

One country for a while remained, which stood as an island in the midst of the grand waste of the company's dominion. My right honourable friend, in his admirable speech on moving the bill, just touched the situation, the offences, and the punishment of a native prince, called Fizulla Khân.[21] This man, by

20 Last to die.
21 Faizullah Khan (d. 1794), a Rohilla chief who was permitted to retain his territories at Rampur under supervision of the East India Company.

policy and force, had protected himself from the general extirpation of the Rohilla chiefs. He was secured (if that were any
security) by a treaty. It was stated to you, as it was stated by the
enemies of that unfortunate man — "that the whole of his country *is* what the whole country of the Rohillas *was*, cultivated like a
garden, without one neglected spot in it." — Another accuser
says, "Fyzoolah Khan, though a bad soldier, [that is the true
source of his misfortune] has approved himself a good aumil;[22]
having, it is supposed, in the course of a few years, at least *doubled*
the population and revenue of his country." — In another part
of the correspondence he is charged with making his country an
asylum for the oppressed peasants, who fly from the territories of
Oude. The improvement of his revenue, arising from this single
crime, (which Mr. Hastings considers as tantamount to treason)
is stated at an hundred and fifty thousand pounds a year.

Dr. Swift somewhere says, that he who could make two blades
of grass grow where but one grew before, was a greater benefactor
to the human race than all the politicians that ever existed.[23] This
prince, who would have been deified by antiquity, who would
have been ranked with Osiris, and Bacchus, and Ceres, and the
divinities most propitious to men, was, for those very merits, by
name attacked by the company's government, as a cheat, a robber, a traitor. In the same breath in which he was accused as a
rebel, he was ordered at once to furnish 5,000 horse. On delay, or
(according to the technical phrase, when any remonstrance is
made to them) "*on evasion*," he was declared a violator of treaties,
and every thing he had was to be taken from him. — Not one
word, however, of horse in this treaty.

The territory of this Fizulla Khân, Mr. Speaker, is less than the
county of Norfolk. It is an island country, full seven hundred
miles from any seaport, and not distinguished for any one considerable branch of manufacture whatsoever. From this territory
several very considerable sums had at several times been paid to

22 Revenue administrator.
23 *Gulliver's Travels*, bk. 2, ch. 7.

the British resident. The demand of cavalry, without a shadow or decent pretext of right, amounted to three hundred thousand a year more, at the lowest computation; and it is stated, by the last person sent to negotiate, as a demand of little use, if it could be complied with; but that the compliance was impossible, as it amounted to more than his territories could supply, if there had been no other demand upon him—three hundred thousand pounds a year from an inland country not so large as Norfolk!

The thing most extraordinary was to hear the culprit defend himself from the imputation of his virtues, as if they had been the blackest offences. He extenuated the superiour cultivation of his country. He denied its population. He endeavoured to prove that he had often sent back the poor peasant that sought shelter with him.—I can make no observation on this.

After a variety of extortions and vexations, too fatiguing to you, too disgusting to me, to go through with, they found "that they ought to be in a better state to warrant forcible means;" they therefore contented themselves with a gross sum of 150,000 pounds for their present demand. They offered him indeed an indemnity from their exactions in future for three hundred thousand pounds more. But he refused to buy their securities; pleading (probably with truth) his poverty: but if the plea were not founded, in my opinion very wisely; not choosing to deal any more in that dangerous commodity of the company's faith; and thinking it better to oppose distress and unarmed obstinacy to uncoloured exaction, than to subject himself to be considered as a cheat, if he should make a treaty in the least beneficial to himself.

Thus they executed an exemplary punishment on Fizulla Khân for the culture of his country. But, conscious that the prevention of evils is the great object of all good regulation, they deprived him of the means of increasing that criminal cultivation in future, by exhausting his coffers; and, that the population of his country should no more be a standing reproach and libel on the company's government, they bound him, by a positive engagement, not to afford any shelter whatsoever to the farmers and labourers who should seek refuge in his territories, from the exactions of the British residents in Oude. When they had done all this effectually, they gave him a full and complete acquittance from all charges of rebellion, or of any intention to rebel, or of his having originally had any interest in, or any means of rebellion.

These intended rebellions are one of the company's standing resources. When money has been thought to be heaped up any where, its owners are universally accused of rebellion, until they are acquitted of their money and their treasons at once. The money once taken, all accusation, trial, and punishment ends. It is so settled a resource, that I rather wonder how it comes to be omitted in the directors account; but I take it for granted this omission will be supplied in their next edition.

The company stretched this resource to the full extent, when they accused two old women, in the remotest corner of India (who could have no possible view or motive to raise disturbances) of being engaged in rebellion, with an intent to drive out the English nation, in whose protection, purchased by money and secured by treaty, rested the sole hope of their existence. But the company wanted money, and the old women *must* be guilty of a plot.[24] They were accused of rebellion, and they were convicted of wealth. Twice had great sums been extorted from them, and as often had the British faith guaranteed the remainder. A body of British troops, with one of the military farmers general at their head, was sent to seize upon the castle in which these helpless women resided. Their chief eunuchs, who were their agents, their guardians, protectors, persons of high rank according to the Eastern manners, and of great trust, were thrown into dun-

24 Referring to the Begams of Oudh, the mother and grandmother of Asaf al-Daula, Wazir of Oudh. They had control of a substantial income from land grants (*jagirs*) and were guardians of the late ruler's treasure. The company gathered many affidavits, with a slender body of evidence, to argue that the Begams were in rebellion; when the Wazir could not meet demands for new payments in 1781, Hastings ordered the money extracted from the Begams. It amounted to fifty-five lakhs of rupees and was taken by force.

geons, to make them discover their hidden treasures; and there they lie at present. The lands assigned for the maintenance of the women were seized and confiscated. Their jewels and effects were taken, and set up to a pretended auction in an obscure place, and bought at such a price as the gentlemen thought proper to give. No account has ever been transmitted of the articles or produce of this sale. What money was obtained is unknown, or what terms were stipulated for the maintenance of these despoiled and forlorn creatures; for by some particulars it appears as if an engagement of the kind was made.

Let me here remark, once for all, that though the act of 1773 requires that an account of all proceedings should be diligently transmitted, that this like all the other injunctions of the law, is totally despised; and that half at least of the most important papers are intentionally withheld.

I wish you, Sir, to advert particularly, in this transaction, to the quality and the numbers of the persons spoiled, and the instrument by whom that spoil was made. These ancient matrons called the Begums, or Princesses, were of the first birth and quality in India, the one mother, the other wife, of the late nabob of Oude, Sujah Dowlah, a prince possessed of extensive and flourishing dominions, and the second man in the Mogul empire.[25] This prince (suspicious, and not unjustly suspicious, of his son and successor) at his death committed his treasures and his family to the British faith. That family and household, consisted of *two thousand women*; to which were added two other seraglios of near kindred, and said to be extremely numerous, and (as I am well informed) of about fourscore of the nabob's children, with all the eunuchs, the ancient servants, and a multitude of the dependants of his splendid court. These were all to be provided, for present maintenance and future establishment, from the lands assigned as dower, and from the treasures which he left to these matrons, in trust for the whole family.

25 The mother of the late Nawab (Sujah Dowlah) was Sadr al-Nissa (d. 1796); his wife was Bahu Begam (ca. 1728–1818).

So far as to the objects of the spoil. The *instrument* chosen by Mr. Hastings to despoil the relict of Sujah Dowlah was *her own son*, the reigning nabob of Oude. It was the pious hand of a son that was selected to tear from his mother and grandmother the provision of their age, the maintenance of his brethren, and of all the ancient household of his father. [Here a laugh from some young members] — The laugh is *seasonable*, and the occasion decent and proper.

By the last advices something of the sum extorted remained unpaid. The women in despair refused to deliver more, unless their lands are restored, and their ministers released from prison: but Mr. Hastings and his council, steady to their point, and consistent to the last in their conduct, write to the resident to stimulate the son to accomplish the filial acts he had brought so near to their perfection. "We desire," say they in their letter to the resident, (written so late as March last) "that you will inform us if any, and what means, have been taken for recovering the balance due from the Begum [Princess] at Fizabad; and that, if necessary, you *recommend* it to the vizier to enforce *the most effectual means* for that purpose."

What their effectual means of enforcing demands on women of high rank and condition are, I shall shew you, Sir, in a few minutes; when I represent to you another of these plots and rebellions, which *always*, in India, though so *rarely* any where else, are the offspring of an easy condition, and hoarded riches.

Benares is the capital city of the Indian religion. It is regarded as holy by a particular and distinguished sanctity; and the Gentoos in general think themselves as much obliged to visit it once in their lives as the Mahometans to perform their pilgrimage to Mecca. By this means that city grew great in commerce and opulence; and so effectually was it secured by the pious veneration of that people, that in all wars and in all violences of power, there was so sure an asylum, both for poverty and wealth, (as it were under a divine protection) that the wisest laws and best assured free constitution could not better provide for the relief of the one, or the safety of the other; and this tranquillity influenced to the greatest degree the prosperity of all the country, and the territory of which it was the capital. The interest of money there was not more than half the usual rate in which it stood in all other places. The reports have fully informed you of the means and of the terms in which this city and the territory called Gazipour, of which it was the head, came under the sovereignty of the East India company.

If ever there was a subordinate dominion pleasantly circumstanced to the superiour power, it was this; a large rent or tribute, to the amount of two hundred and sixty thousand pounds a year, was paid in monthly instalments with the punctuality of a dividend at the bank. If ever there was a prince who could not have an interest in disturbances, it was its sovereign, the rajah Cheit Sing.[26] He was in possession of the capital of his religion, and a willing revenue was paid by the devout people who resorted to him from all parts. His sovereignty and his independence, except his tribute, was secured by every tie. His territory was not much less than half of Ireland, and displayed in all parts a degree of cultivation, ease, and plenty, under his frugal and paternal management, which left him nothing to desire, either for honour or satisfaction.

This was the light in which this country appeared to almost every eye. But Mr. Hastings beheld it askance. Mr. Hastings tells us that it was *reported* of this Cheit Sing, that his father left him a million sterling, and that he made annual accessions to the hoard. Nothing could be so obnoxious to indigent power. So much wealth could not be innocent. The house is fully acquainted with the unfounded and unjust requisitions which

26 Chait Singh was Raja of Benares from 1770 to 1781. A *zamindar,* he retained also something of the status of a ruling prince and had engaged with the company to submit the annual tribute listed above. In 1778 and 1779, Hastings broke the agreement by demanding an additional five lakhs of rupees. When the demand was repeated the following year, Chait Singh sent a gift of two lakhs of rupees, but Hastings now demanded an additional tribute of two thousand horsemen. For refusal of this last request, Chait Singh was fined and placed under house arrest, and had his kingdom taken from him. Troops loyal to him massacred Hastings's small force, but Hastings later recaptured Benares. Chait Singh escaped to Gwalior.

were made upon this prince.[27] The question has been most ably and conclusively cleared up in one of the reports of the select committee, and in an answer of the court of directors to an extraordinary publication against them by their servant, Mr. Hastings. But I mean to pass by these exactions, as if they were perfectly just and regular; and, having admitted to them, I take what I shall now trouble you with, only as it serves to shew the spirit of the company's government, the mode in which it is carried on, and the maxims on which it proceeds.

Mr. Hastings, from whom I take the doctrine, endeavours to prove that Cheit Sing was no sovereign prince; but a mere zemindar or common subject, holding land by rent. If this be granted to him, it is next to be seen under what terms he is of opinion such a landholder, that is a British subject, holds his life and property under the company's government. It is proper to understand well the doctrines of the person whose administration has lately received such distinguished approbation from the company. His doctrine is — "that the company, or the *person delegated by it*, holds *an absolute* authority over such zemindars; — that he [such a subject] owes *an implicit* and *unreserved* obedience to its authority, at the *forfeiture* even of his *life* and *property*, at the DISCRETION of those who held *or fully represented* the sovereign authority; — and that *these* rights are *fully* delegated *to him* Mr. Hastings."

Such is a British governour's idea of the condition of a great zemindar holding under a British authority; and this kind of authority he supposes fully delegated to *him*; though no such delegation appears in any commission, instruction, or act of parliament. At his *discretion* he may demand, of the substance of any zemindar over and above his rent or tribute, even what he pleases, with a sovereign authority; and if he does not yield an *implicit unreserved* obedience to all his commands, he forfeits his lands, his life, and his property, at Mr. Hastings's *discretion*. But, extravagant, and even frantick as these positions appear, they are

27 Referring to the additional payment required of Chait Singh starting in 1778.

less so than what I shall now read to you; for he asserts, that if any one should urge an exemption from more than a stated payment, or should consider the deeds, which passed between him and the board, "as bearing *the quality and force* of a treaty between equal states," he says, "that such an opinion is itself criminal to the state of which he is a subject; and that he was himself amenable to its justice, if he gave *countenance* to such a *belief.*" Here is a new species of crime invented, that of countenancing a belief— but a belief of what? A belief of that which the court of directors, Hastings's masters, and a committee of this house, have decided as this prince's indisputable right.

But supposing the rajah of Benares to be a mere subject, and that subject a criminal of the highest form; let us see what course was taken by an upright English magistrate. Did he cite this culprit before his tribunal? Did he make a charge? Did he produce witnesses? These are not forms; they are parts of substantial and eternal justice. No, not a word of all this, Mr. Hastings concludes him, *in his own mind*, to be guilty; he makes this conclusion on reports, on hearsays, on appearances, on rumours, on conjectures, on presumptions; and even these never once hinted to the party, nor publickly to any human being, till the whole business was done.

But the governour tells you his motive for this extraordinary proceeding, so contrary to every mode of justice towards either a prince or a subject, fairly and without disguise; and he puts into your hands the key of his whole conduct: — "I will suppose, for a moment, that I have acted with unwarrantable rigour towards Cheit Sing, and even with injustice. — Let my MOTIVE be consulted. I left Calcutta, impressed with a belief that *extraordinary means* were necessary, and those exerted with a *steady hand*, to preserve the company's *interests from sinking under the accumulated weight which oppressed them.* I saw a *political necessity* for curbing the *overgrown* power of a great member of their dominion, and *for making it contribute to the relief of their pressing exigencies.*" This is plain speaking; after this, it is no wonder that the rajah's wealth and his offence, the necessities of the judge, and the opulence of the delinquent, are never separated, through the whole of Mr. Hastings's apology. "The justice and *policy* of exacting *a large pecuniary mulct.*" The resolution "*to draw from his guilt* the means *of relief to the company's distresses.*" His determination "to make him *pay largely* for his pardon, or to execute a severe vengeance for past delinquency." That "as his *wealth was great,* and the *company's exigencies* pressing, he thought it a measure of justice and policy to exact from him a large pecuniary mulct for *their relief.*" — "The sum (says Mr. Wheler,[28] bearing evidence, at his desire, to his intentions) to which the governour declared his resolution to extend his fine, was forty or fifty lacks, *that is four or five hundred thousand pounds*; and that if he refused, he was to be removed from his zemindary entirely; or by taking possession of his forts, to obtain, *out of the treasure deposited in them,* the above sum for the company."

Crimes so convenient, crimes so politick, crimes so necessary, crimes so alleviating of distress, can never be wanting to those who use no process, and who produce no proofs.

But there is another serious part (what is not so?) in this affair. Let us suppose that the power, for which Mr. Hastings contends, a power which no sovereign ever did, or ever can vest in any of his subjects, namely, his own sovereign authority, to be conveyed by the act of parliament to any man or body of men whatsoever; it certainly was never given to Mr. Hastings. The powers given by the act of 1773 were formal and official; they were given not to the governour general, but to the major vote of the board, as a board, on discussion amongst themselves, in their publick character and capacity; and their acts in that characer and capacity were to be ascertained by records and minutes of council. The despotick acts exercised by Mr. Hastings were done merely in his *private* character; and, if they had been moderate and just, would still be the acts of an usurped authority, and without any one of

28 Edward Wheler (1733–84), a member of the Supreme Council of the East India Company from 1777, began as an opponent of Hastings but became his staunch supporter.

the legal modes of proceeding which could give him competence for the most trivial exertion of power. There was no proposition or deliberation whatsoever in council, no minute on record, by circulation or otherwise, to authorize his proceedings.
No delegation of power to impose a fine, or to take any step to
deprive the rajah of Benares of his government, his property, or
his liberty. The minutes of consultation assign to his journey a
totally different object, duty, and destination. Mr. Wheler, at his
desire, tells us long after, that he had a confidential conversation
with him on various subjects, of which this was the principal, in
which Mr. Hastings notified to him his secret intentions; "and
that he *bespoke* his support of the measures which he intended to
pursue towards him (the rajah)." This confidential discourse,
and *bespeaking* of support, could give him no power, in opposition to an express act of parliament, and the whole tenour of the
orders of the court of directors.

In what manner the powers thus usurped were employed, is
known to the whole world. All the house knows, that the design
on the rajah proved as unfruitful as it was violent. The unhappy
prince was expelled, and his more unhappy country was en-
slaved and ruined; but not a rupee was acquired. Instead of
treasure to recruit the company's finances, wasted by their wanton wars and corrupt jobs, they were plunged into a new war
which shook their power in India to its foundation; and, to use
the governor's own happy simile, might have dissolved it like a
magick structure, if the talisman had been broken.

But the success is no part of my consideration, who should
think just the same of this business, if the spoil of one rajah had
been fully acquired, and faithfully applied to the destruction of
twenty other rajahs. Not only the arrest of the rajah in his palace
was unnecessary and unwarrantable, and calculated to stir up any
manly blood which remained in his subjects; but the despotick
style, and the extreme insolence of language and demeanour,
used to a person of great condition among the politest people in
the world, was intolerable. Nothing aggravates tyranny so much
as contumely. *Quicquid superbia in contumeliis* was charged by a

great man of antiquity, as a principal head of offence against the
governour general of that day.[29] The unhappy people were still
more insulted. A relation, but an *enemy* to the family, a notorious
robber and villain, called Ussaun Sing,[30] kept as a hawk in a mew,
to fly upon this nation, was set up to govern there, instead of a
prince honoured and beloved. But when the business of insult
was accomplished, the revenue was too serious a concern to be
entrusted to such hands. Another was set up in his place, as
guardian to an infant.[31]

But here, Sir, mark the effect of all these *extraordinary* means,
of all this policy and justice. The revenues which had been hitherto paid with such astonishing punctuality, fell into arrear. The
new prince guardian was deposed without ceremony; and with as
little, cast into prison. The government of that once happy country has been in the utmost confusion ever since such good order
was taken about it. But, to complete the contumely offered to
this undone people, and to make them feel their servitude in all
its degradation, and all its bitterness, the government of their
sacred city, the government of that Benares which had been so
respected by Persian and Tartar conquerors, though of the Mussulman persuasion, that, even in the plenitude of their pride,
power and bigotry, no magistrate of that sect entered the place,
was now delivered over by English hands to a Mahometan; and
an Ali Ibrahim Khân was introduced, under the company's authority, with the power of life and death, into the sanctuary of
the Gentoo religion.[32]

After this, the taking off a slight payment, cheerfully made by
pilgrims to a chief of their own rites, was represented as a mighty
benefit. It remains only to shew, through the conduct in this

29 Cicero *Verrine Orations:* "Every possible insolence of abuse."

30 Ausan Singh (d. 1800), an enemy of Chait Singh.

31 Chait Singh was succeeded by his nephew Mahipnarayan Singh (d. 1795), a
minor, whose father, Drigbijai Singh, served as regent.

32 Ali Ibrahim Khan (d. 1793), president of the tribunal at Benares under
Warren Hastings.

business, the spirit of the company's government, and the respect they pay towards other prejudices not less regarded in the east than those of religion; I mean the reverence paid to the female sex in general, and particularly to women of high rank and condition. During the general confusion of the country of Gazypore, Panna, the mother of Cheit Sing, was lodged with her train in a castle called Bidgé Gur, in which were likewise deposited a large portion of the treasures of her son, or more probably her own. To whomsoever they belonged was indifferent; for though no charge of rebellion was made on this woman (which was rather singular, as it would have cost nothing) they were resolved to secure her with her fortune. The castle was besieged by major Popham.[33]

There was no great reason to apprehend that soldiers ill paid, that soldiers who thought they had been defrauded of their plunder on former services of the same kind, would not have been sufficiently attentive to the spoil they were expressly come for; but the gallantry and generosity of the profession was justly expected, as being likely to set bounds to military rapaciousness. The company's first civil magistrate discovered the greatest uneasiness lest the women should have any thing preserved to them. Terms, tending to put some restraint on military violence, were granted. He writes a letter to Mr. Popham, referring to some letter written before to the same effect, which I do not remember to have seen; but it shews his anxiety on this subject. Hear himself: — "I think *every* demand she has made on you, except that of safety and respect to her person, is unreasonable. If the reports brought to me are true, your rejecting her offers, or *any negotiation*, would soon obtain you the fort upon your own terms. I apprehend she will attempt to *defraud the captors of a considerable part of their booty, by being suffered to retire without examination.* But this is your concern, not mine. I should *be very sorry* that your officers and soldiers lost *any* part of the reward to which they are

33 William Popham (1740–1821).

so well entitled; but you must be the best judge of the *promised* indulgence to the ranny:[34] what you have engaged for I will certainly ratify; but as to suffering the ranny to hold the purgunna of Hurlich, or any other zemindary, without being subject to the authority of the zemindar, *or any lands whatsoever*, or indeed making *any* condition with her for a *provision*, I will *never consent.*"

Here your governour stimulates a rapacious and licentious soldiery to the personal search of women, lest these unhappy creatures should avail themselves of the protection of their sex to secure any supply for their necessities; and he positively orders that no stipulation should be made for any provision for them. The widow and mother of a prince, well informed of her miserable situation, and the cause of it, a woman of this rank became a suppliant to the domestick servant of Mr. Hastings (they are his own words that I read;) "imploring his intercession, that she may be relieved *from the hardships and dangers of her present situation*; and offering to surrender the fort, and the *treasure and valuable effects contained* in it, provided she can be assured *of safety and protection to her person and honour*, and to that of her family and attendants." He is so good as to consent to this, provided she surrenders every thing of value, with the reserve *only* of such articles as *you* shall think *necessary* to her condition, or as you *yourself* shall be disposed to indulge her with. — But should she refuse to execute the promise she has made, or delay it beyond the term of twenty-four hours, it is *my positive* injunction, that you immediately put a stop to any further intercourse or negotiation with her, and on no pretext renew it. If she disappoints or *trifles* with me, after I have subjected *my duan*[35] to the disgrace of returning ineffectually, and of course myself to discredit, I shall consider it as a *wanton* affront and indignity *which I can never forgive*; nor will I grant her *any* conditions whatever, but leave her exposed *to those* dangers which she has chosen to risk, rather

34 The queen.
35 Hastings's servant Krishna Kant Nandy (ca. 1720–94); a *duan* is a steward or controller of revenues.

than trust to the clemency and generosity of our government. I think she cannot be ignorant of these consequences, and will not venture to incur them; and it is for this reason I place a dependence on her offers, and have consented to send my duan to her." The dreadful secret hinted at by the merciful governour in the latter part of the letter, is well understood in India; where those who suffer corporeal indignities, generally expiate the offences of others with their own blood. However, in spite of all these, the temper of the military did, some way or other, operate. They came to terms which have never been transmitted. It appears that a fifteenth *per cent.* of the plunder was reserved to the captives, of which the unhappy mother of the prince of Benares was to have a share. This ancient matron, born to better things [a laugh from certain young gentlemen] — I see no cause for this mirth. A good author of antiquity reckons among the calamities of his time, *Nobilissimarum sœminarum exilia et fugas.*[36] I say, Sir, this ancient lady was compelled to quit her house with three hundred helpless women, and a multitude of children in her train; but the lower fort in the camp it seems could not be restrained. They did not forget the good lessons of the governour general. They were unwilling "to be defrauded of a considerable part of their booty, by suffering them to pass without examination." — They examined them, Sir, with a vengeance, and the sacred protection of that awful character, Mr. Hastings's maitre d'hotel, could not secure them from insult, and plunder. Here is Popham's narrative of the affair: — "The ranny came out of the fort, with her family and dependants, the 10th at night, owing to which such attention was not paid to her as I wished; and I am exceedingly sorry to inform you, that the *licentiousness of our followers was beyond the bounds of control; for, notwithstanding all I could do, her people were plundered on the road of most of the things which they brought out of the fort, by which means one of the articles of surrender has been much infringed.* The distress I have felt upon this occasion cannot be expressed, and can only be allayed by a firm

36 Tacitus *Agricola* 45: "the flight and exile of the most noble women."

performance of the other articles of the treaty, which I shall make it my business to enforce.

"The suspicions which the officers had of treachery, and the delay made to our getting possession, had enraged them, as well as the troops, so much, that the treaty was at first regarded as void, but this determination was soon succeeded by pity and compassion for the unfortunate besieged."—After this comes, in his due order, Mr. Hastings; who is full of sorrow and indignation, &c. &c. &c. according to the best and most authentick precedents established upon such occasions.

The women being thus disposed of, that is, completely despoiled, and pathetically lamented, Mr. Hastings at length recollected the great object of his enterprise, which, during his zeal lest the officers and soldiers should lose any part of their reward, he seems to have forgot; that is to say, "to draw from the rajah's guilt the means of relief to the company's distresses." This was to be the strong hold of his defence. This compassion to the company, he knew by experience would sanctify a great deal of rigour towards the natives. But the military had distresses of their own, which they considered first. Neither Mr. Hastings's authority, nor his supplications, could prevail on them to assign a shilling to the claim he made on the part of the company. They divided the booty amongst themselves. Driven from his claim, he was reduced to petition for the spoil as a loan. But the soldiers were too wise to venture as a loan, what the borrower claimed as a right. In defiance of all authority, they shared among themselves about two hundred thousand pounds sterling, besides what had been taken from the women.

In all this there is nothing wonderful. We may rest assured, that when the maxims of any government establish among its resources extraordinary means, and those exerted with a strong hand, that strong hand will provide those extraordinary means for *itself.* Whether the soldiers had reason or not (perhaps much might be said for them) certain it is, the military discipline of India was ruined from that moment; and the same rage for plunder, the same contempt of subordination, which blasted all the hopes of extraordinary means from your strong hand at Benares, have very lately lost you an army in Mysore.[37] This is visible enough from the accounts in the last Gazette.

There is no doubt but that the country and city of Benares, now brought into the same order, will very soon exhibit, if it does not already display, the same appearance with those countries and cities which are under better subjection. A great master, Mr. Hastings, has himself been at the pains of drawing a picture of one of these countries, I mean the province and city of Farruckabad. There is no reason to question his knowledge of the facts; and his authority (on this point at least) is above all exception, as well for the state of the country as for the cause. In his minute of consultation, Mr. Hastings describes forcibly the consequences which arise from the degradation into which we have sunk the native government. "The total want (says he) of all order, regularity, or authority, in his (the nabob of Farruckabad's) government, and to which, among other obvious causes, it may no doubt be owing that the country of Farruckabad is become *almost an entire waste, without cultivation or inhabitants*; that the capital, which, but a very short time ago, was distinguished as one of the most populous and opulent commercial cities in Hindostan, at present exhibits nothing but *scenes of the most wretched poverty, desolation and misery*; and that the *nabob himself*, though in the possession of a tract of country which, with only common care, is notoriously capable of yielding an annual revenue of between thirty and forty lacks, (three or four hundred thousand pounds) with *no military establishment* to maintain, scarcely commands *the means of a bare subsistence.*"

This is a true and unexaggerated picture, not only of Farruckabad, but of at least three fourths of the country which we possess, or rather lay waste, in India. Now, Sir, the house will be desirous to know for what purpose this picture was drawn. It was

37 The troops of Brigadier Richard Mathews (d. 1783), when they captured Bednur in the war against Tipu Sultan, were reported to have fought over the spoils. They soon after fell into Tipu's hands.

for a purpose, I will not say laudable, but necessary, that of taking the unfortunate prince and his country out of the hands of a sequestrator sent thither by the nabob of Oude, the mortal enemy of the prince thus ruined, and to protect him by means of a British resident, who might carry his complaints to the superiour resident at Oude, or transmit them to Calcutta. But mark how the reformer persisted in his reformation. The effect of the measure was better than was probably expected. The prince began to be at ease; the country began to recover; and the revenue began to be collected. These were alarming circumstances. Mr. Hastings not only recalled the resident, but he entered into a formal stipulation with the nabob of Oude, never to send an English subject again to Farruckabad; and thus the country, described as you have heard by Mr. Hastings, is given up for ever to the very persons to whom he had attributed its ruin, that is, to the Sezawals or sequestrators of the nabob of Oude.

Such was the issue of the first attempt to relieve the distresses of the dependent provinces. I shall close what I have to say on the condition of the northern dependencies, with the effect of the last of these attempts. You will recollect, Sir, the account I have not long ago stated to you as given by Mr. Hastings, of the ruined condition of the destroyer of others, the nabob of Oude, and of the recal, in consequence, of Hannay, Middleton, and Johnson.[38] When the first little sudden gust of passion against these gentlemen was spent, the sentiments of old friendship began to revive. Some healing conferences were held between them and the superiour government. Mr. Hannay was permitted to return to Oude; but death prevented the further advantages intended for him, and the future benefits proposed for the country by the provident care of the council general.

One of these gentlemen was accused of the grossest peculations. Two of them by Mr. Hastings himself, of what he con-

38 Colonel Alexander Hannay (ca. 1742–82), chief military collector in Oudh from 1778; Nathaniel Middleton (d. 1807), British resident at the court of the Nawab of Oudh; Richard Johnson (d. 1807), deputy resident at Oudh. All three were recalled when Middleton failed to convince the Wazir to plunder the Begams.

sidered as very gross offences. The court of directors were informed, by the governour general and council, that a severe inquiry would be instituted against the two survivors; and they requested that court to suspend its judgment, and to wait the event of their proceedings. A mock inquiry has been instituted, by which the parties could not be said to be either acquitted or condemned.[39] By means of the bland and conciliatory dispositions of the charter governours, and proper private explanations, the publick inquiry has in effect died away; the supposed peculators and destroyers of Oude repose in all security in the bosoms of their accusers; whilst others succeed to them to be instructed by their example.

It is only to complete the view I proposed of the conduct of the company, with regard to the dependent provinces, that I shall say *any* thing at all of the Carnatick, which is the scene, if possible, of greater disorder than the northern provinces. Perhaps it were better to say of this center and metropolis of abuse, whence all the rest in India and in England diverge; from whence they are fed and methodized, what was said of Carthage — *de Carthagine satius est silere quam parum dicere.*[40] This country, in all its denominations, is about 46,000 square miles. It may be affirmed universally, that not one person of substance or property, landed, commercial or monied, excepting two or three bankers, who are necessary deposits and distributors of the general spoil, is left in all that region. In that country the moisture, the bounty of Heaven, is given but at a certain season. Before the æra of our influence, the industry of man carefully husbanded that gift of God. The Gentoos preserved, with a provident and religious care, the precious deposit of the periodical rain in reservoirs, many of them works of royal grandeur; and from these, as occasion demanded, they fructified the whole country. To maintain these reservoirs, and to keep up an annual advance to the

39 The inquiry by the Bengal Council lasted from June to October 1783.

40 Sallust *Jugurthine War* 19.2: "About Carthage, it is better to be silent than to say too little."

cultivators, for feed and cattle, formed a principal object of the piety and policy of the priests and rulers of the Gentoo religion.

This object required a command of money; and there was no pollam, or castle, which in the happy days of the Carnatick was without some hoard of treasure, by which the governours were enabled to combat with the irregularity of the seasons, and to resist or to buy off the invasion of an enemy. In all the cities were multitudes of merchants and bankers, for all occasions of monied assistance; and on the other hand, the native princes were in condition to obtain credit from them. The manufacturer was paid by the return of commodities, or by imported money, and not, as at present, in the taxes that had been originally exacted from his industry. In aid of casual distress, the country was full of choultries, which were inns and hospitals, where the traveller and the poor were relieved. All ranks of people had their place in the publick concern, and their share in the common stock and common prosperity; but *the chartered rights of men*, and the right which it was thought proper to set up in the nabob of Arcot, introduced a new system. It was their policy to consider hoards of money as crimes; to regard moderate rents as frauds on the sovereign; and to view, in the lesser princes, any claim of exemption from more than settled tribute, as an act of rebellion. Accordingly all the castles were, one after the other, plundered and destroyed. The native princes were expelled; the hospitals fell to ruin; the reservoirs of water went to decay; the merchants, bankers, and manufacturers disappeared; and sterility, indigence, and depopulation, overspread the face of these once flourishing provinces.

The company was very early sensible of these mischiefs, and of their true cause. They gave precise orders "that the native princes, called polygars, should *not be extirpated.*" — "The rebellion [so they choose to call it] of the polygars, may (they fear) *with too much justice*, be attributed to the mal-administration of the nabob's collectors:" — They observe with concern, that their "troops have been put to *disagreeable* services." They might have used a stronger expression without impropriety. But they make amends in another place. Speaking of the polygars, the directors say, that "it was repugnant to humanity to *force* them to such dreadful extremities *as they underwent.*" That some examples of severity *might* be necessary, "when they fell into the nabob's hands," *and not by the destruction of the country*: "That *they fear* his government is *none of the mildest*; and that there is *great oppression* in collecting his revenues." They state, that the wars in which he has involved the Carnatick, had been a cause of its distress: "that these distresses have been certainly great; but those by *the nabob's oppressions* they believe *to be greater than all.*" Pray, Sir, attend to the reason for their opinion that the government of this their instrument is more calamitous to the country than the ravages of war. — Because, say they, his oppressions are "*without intermission.* — The others are temporary; by all which *oppressions* we believe the nabob has great wealth in store." From this store neither he nor they could derive any advantage whatsoever upon the invasion of Hyder Ali in the hour of their greatest calamity and dismay.[41]

It is now proper to compare these declarations with the company's conduct. The principal reason which they assigned against the *extirpation* of the polygars was, that the *weavers* were protected in their fortresses. They might have added, that the company itself, which stung them to death, had been warmed in the bosom of these unfortunate princes: for, on the taking of Madras by the French, it was in their hospitable pollams, that most of the inhabitants found refuge and protection. But, notwithstanding all these orders, reasons, and declarations, they at length gave an indirect sanction, and permitted the use of a very direct and irresistible force, to measures which they had, over and over again, declared to be false policy, cruel, inhuman, and oppressive. Having, however, forgot all attention to the princes and the people, they remembered that they had some sort of interest in the trade of the country; and it is matter of curiosity to observe the protection which they afforded to this their natural object.

41 Haider Ali joined the Nizam and the Marathas in the war against the British, and invaded the Carnatic in 1780.

Full of anxious cares on this head, they direct, "that in reducing the polygars they (their servants) were to be *cautious*, not to deprive the *weavers and manufacturers* of the protection they often met with in the strong holds of the polygar countries;" — and they write to their instrument, the nabob of Arcot, concerning these poor people in a most pathetick strain. "We *entreat* your excellency (say they) in particular, to make the manufacturers the object of your *tenderest care*; particularly when you *root out* the polygars, you do not deprive the *weavers of the protection they enjoyed under them.*" When they root out the protectors in favour of the oppressor, they shew themselves religiously cautious of the rights of the protected. When they extirpate the shepherd and the shepherd's dog, they piously recommend the helpless flock to the mercy, and even to the *tenderest care*, of the wolf. This is the uniform strain of their policy, strictly forbidding, and at the same time strenuously encouraging and enforcing, every measure that can ruin and desolate the country committed to their charge. After giving the company's idea of the government of this their instrument, it may appear singular, but it is perfectly consistent with their system, that, besides wasting for him, at two different times, the most exquisite spot upon the earth, Tanjour, and all the adjacent countries, they have even voluntarily put their own territory, that is, a large and fine country adjacent to Madras, called their jaghire, wholly out of their protection; and have continued to farm their subjects, and their duties towards these subjects, to that very nabob, whom they themselves constantly represent as an habitual oppressor, and a relentless tyrant. This they have done without any pretence of ignorance of the objects of oppression for which this prince has thought fit to become their renter; for he has again and again told them, that it is for the sole purpose of exercising authority he holds the jaghire lands; and he affirms (and I believe with truth) that he pays more for that territory than the revenues yield. This deficiency he must make up from his other territories; and thus, in order to furnish the means of oppressing one part of the Carnatick, he is led to oppress all the rest.

The house perceives that the livery of the company's government is uniform. I have described the condition of the countries indirectly, but most substantially, under the company's authority. And now I ask, whether, with this map of misgovernment before me, I can suppose myself bound by my vote to continue, upon any principles of pretended publick faith, the management of these countries in those hands? If I kept such a faith, (which in reality is no better than a *fides latronum*) [42] with what is called the company, I must break the faith, the covenant, the solemn, original, indispensable oath, in which I am bound, by the eternal frame and constitution of things, to the whole human race.

As I have dwelt so long on these who are indirectly under the company's administration, I will endeavour to be a little shorter upon the countries immediately under this charter government. — These are the Bengal provinces. The condition of these provinces is pretty fully detailed in the sixth and ninth reports, and in their appendixes. I will select only such principles and instances as are broad and general. To your own thoughts I shall leave it, to furnish the detail of oppressions involved in them. I shall state to you, as shortly as I am able, the conduct of the company; — 1st, towards the landed interests; — next, the commercial interests; — 3dly, the native government; — and lastly, to their own government.

Bengal, and the provinces that are united to it, are larger than the kingdom of France; and once contained, as France does contain, a great and independent landed interest, composed of princes, of great lords, of a numerous nobility and gentry, of freeholders, of lower tenants, of religious communities, and publick foundations. So early as 1769, the company's servants perceived the decay into which these provinces had fallen under English administration, and they made a strong representation upon this decay, and what they apprehended to be the causes of it. Soon after this representation, Mr. Hastings became president of Bengal. Instead of administering a remedy to this melancholy

---

42 The fidelity of a bandit.

disorder, upon the heels of a dreadful famine, in the year 1772, the succour which the new president and the council lent to this afflicted nation was — shall I be believed in relating it? — the landed interest of a whole kingdom, of a kingdom to be compared to France, was set up to publick auction! They set up (Mr. Hastings set up) the whole nobility, gentry, and freeholders, to the highest bidder. No preference was given to the ancient proprietors. They must bid against every usurer, every temporary adventurer, every jobber and schemer, every servant of every European, or they were obliged to content themselves, in lieu of their extensive domains, with their house, and such a pension as the state auctioneers thought fit to assign. In this general calamity, several of the first nobility thought (and in all appearance justly) that they had better submit to the necessity of this pension, than continue, under the name of zemindars, the objects and instruments of a system, by which they ruined their tenants, and were ruined themselves. Another reform has since come upon the back of the first; and a pension having been assigned to these unhappy persons, in lieu of their hereditary lands, a new scheme of œconomy has taken place, and deprived them of that pension.

The menial servants of Englishmen, persons (to use the emphatical phrase of a ruined and patient eastern chief) "*whose fathers they would not have set with the dogs of their flock,*"[43] entered into their patrimonial lands. Mr. Hastings's banian[44] was, after this auction, found possessed of territories yielding a rent of one hundred and forty thousand pounds a year.

Such an universal proscription, upon any pretence, has few examples. Such a proscription, without even a pretence of delinquency, has none. It stands by itself. It stands as a monument to astonish the imagination, to confound the reason of mankind. I confess to you, when I first came to know this business in its true nature and extent, my surprise did a little suspend my indigna-

43 Job 30:1.
44 A banian is a broker, in this case Hastings's steward.

tion. I was in a manner stupified by the desperate boldness of a few obscure young men, who having obtained, by ways which they could not comprehend, a power of which they saw neither the purposes nor the limits, tossed about, subverted, and tore to pieces, as if it were in the gambols of a boyish unluckiness and malice, the most established rights, and the most ancient and most revered institutions, of ages and nations. Sir, I will not now trouble you with any detail with regard to what they have since done with these same lands and land-holders; only to inform you, that nothing has been suffered to settle for two seasons together upon any basis; and that the levity and inconstancy of these mock legislators were not the least afflicting parts of the oppressions suffered under their usurpation; nor will any thing give stability to the property of the natives, but an administration in England at once protecting and stable. The country sustains, almost every year, the miseries of a revolution. At present, all is uncertainty, misery, and confusion. There is to be found through these vast regions no longer one landed man, who is a resource for voluntary aid, or an object for particular rapine. Some of them were, not long since, great princes; they possessed treasures, they levied armies. There was a zemindar in Bengal (I forget his name) that, on the threat of an invasion, supplied the soubah of these provinces with the loan of a million sterling. The family at this day wants credit for a breakfast at the bazar.

I shall now say a word or two on the company's care of the commercial interest of those kingdoms. As it appears in the reports, that persons in the highest stations in Bengal have adopted, as a fixed plan of policy, the destruction of all intermediate dealers between the company and the manufacturer, native merchants have disappeared of course. The spoil of the revenues is the sole capital which purchases the produce and manufactures; and through three or four foreign companies transmits the official gains of individuals to Europe. No other commerce has an existence in Bengal. The transport of its plunder is the only traffick of the country. I wish to refer you to the appendix to the ninth report for a full account of the manner in which the company have protected the commercial interests of their dominions in the east.

As to the native government and the administration of justice, it subsisted in a poor tottering manner for some years. In the year 1781, a total revolution took place in that establishment. In one of the usual freaks of legislation of the council of Bengal, the whole criminal jurisdiction of these courts, called the Phoujdary Judicature, exercised till then by the principal Mussulmen, was in one day, without notice, without consultation with the magistrates or the people there, and without communication with the directors or ministers here, totally subverted.[45] A new institution took place, by which this jurisdiction was divided between certain English servants of the company and the Gentoo zemindars of the country, the latter of whom never petitioned for it, nor, for ought that appears, ever desired this boon. But its natural use was made of it; it was made a pretence for new extortions of money.

The natives had however one consolation in the ruin of their judicature; they soon saw that it fared no better with the English government itself. That too, after destroying every other, came to its period. This revolution may well be rated for a most daring act, even among the extraordinary things that have been doing in Bengal since our unhappy acquisition of the means of so much mischief.

An establishment of English government for civil justice, and for the collection of revenue, was planned and executed by the president and council of Bengal, subject to the pleasure of the directors, in the year 1772. According to this plan, the country was divided into six districts, or provinces. In each of these was established a provincial council, which administered the revenue; and of that council one member by monthly rotation, presided in the courts of civil resort; with an appeal to the council of

45 On 6 April 1781, British judges took over the supervision of criminal (*faujdari*) justice.

the province, and thence to Calcutta. In this system (whether, in other respects, good or evil) there were some capital advantages. There was in the very number of persons in each provincial council, authority, communication, mutual check, and control. They were obliged, on their minutes of consultation, to enter their reasons and dissents; so that a man of diligence, of research, and tolerable sagacity, sitting in London, might, from these materials, be enabled to form some judgment of the spirit of what was going on on the furthest banks of the Ganges and Burrampooter.

The court of directors so far ratified this establishment, (which was consonant enough to their general plan of government) that they gave precise orders, that no alteration should be made in it, without their consent. So far from being apprized of any design against this constitution, they had reason to conceive that on trial it had been more and more approved by their council general, at least by the governour general, who had planned it. At the time of the revolution, the council general was nominally in two persons, virtually in one. At that time measures of an arduous and critical nature ought to have been forborne, even if, to the fullest council, this specifick measure had not been prohibited by the superiour authority. It was in this very situation, that one man had the hardiness to conceive, and the temerity to execute, a total revolution in the form and the persons composing the government of a great kingdom. Without any previous step, at one stroke, the whole constitution of Bengal, civil and criminal, was swept away. The counsellors were recalled from their provinces. Upwards of fifty of the principal officers of government were turned out of employ, and rendered dependent on Mr. Hastings for their immediate subsistence, and for all hope of future provision. The chief of each council, and one European collector of revenue, was left in each province.

But here, Sir, you may imagine a new government, of some permanent description, was established in the place of that which had been thus suddenly overturned. No such thing. Lest these chiefs without councils should be conceived to form the ground plan of some future government, it was publickly declared, that their continuance was only temporary and permissive. The whole subordinate British administration of revenue was then vested in a committee in Calcutta, all creatures of the governour general; and the provincial management, under the permissive chief, was delivered over to native officers.

But, that the revolution, and the purposes of the revolution might be complete, to this committee were delegated, not only the functions of all the inferiour, but, what will surprise the house, those of the supreme administration of revenue also. Hitherto the governour general and council had, in their revenue department, administered the finances of those kingdoms. By the new scheme they are delegated to this committee, who are only to report their proceedings for approbation.

The key to the whole transaction is given in one of the instructions to the committee, "that it is not necessary that they should enter dissents." By this means the ancient plan of the company's administration was destroyed; but the plan of concealment was perfected. To that moment the accounts of the revenues were tolerably clear; or at least means were furnished for inquiries, by which they might be rendered satisfactory. In the obscure and silent gulph of this committee every thing is now buried. The thickest shades of night surround all their transactions. No effectual means of detecting fraud, mismanagement or misrepresentation, exist. The directors, who have dared to talk with such confidence on their revenues, know nothing about them. What used to fill volumes is now comprised under a few dry heads on a sheet of paper. The natives, a people habitually made to concealment, are the chief managers of the revenue throughout the provinces. I mean by natives, such wretches as your rulers select out of them as most fitted for their purposes. As a proper key-stone to bind the arch, a native, one Gunga Govind Sing, a man turned out of his employment by Sir John Clavering, for malversation in office, is made the corresponding secretary; and indeed the great moving principle of their new board.

As the whole revenue and civil administration was thus subverted, and a clandestine government substituted in the place of it, the judicial institution underwent a like revolution. In 1772 there had been six courts formed out of the six provincial councils. Eighteen new ones are appointed in their place, with each a judge, taken from the *junior* servants of the company. To maintain these eighteen courts, a tax is levied on the sums in litigation, of 2½ *per cent.* on the great, and of 5 *per cent.* on the less. This money is all drawn from the provinces of Calcutta. The chief justice (the same who stays in defiance of a vote of this house, and of his majesty's recal)[46] is appointed at once the treasurer and disposer of these taxes, levied, without any sort of authority, from the company, from the crown, or from parliament.

In effect, Sir, every legal regular authority in matters of revenue, of political administration, of criminal law, of civil law, in many of the most essential parts of military discipline, is laid level with the ground; and an oppressive, irregular, capricious, unsteady, rapacious, and peculating despotism, with a direct disavowal of obedience to any authority at home, and without any fixed maxim, principle, or rule of proceeding, to guide them in India, is at present the state of your charter-government over great kingdoms.

As the company has made this use of their trust, I should ill discharge mine, if I refused to give my most chearful vote for the redress of these abuses, by putting the affairs of so large and valuable a part of the interests of this nation, and of mankind, into some steady hands, possessing the confidence, and assured of the support of this house, until they can be restored to regularity, order, and consistency.

I have touched the heads of some of the grievances of the people, and the abuses of government. But I hope and trust, you will give me credit, when I faithfully assure you, that I have not mentioned one-fourth part of what has come to my knowledge

---

46 Sir Elijah Impey (1732–1809) was recalled to England by Parliament in 1782, but delayed his return until the next year. His impeachment was the precursor of Hastings's.

in your committee; and further, I have full reason to believe, that not one-fourth part of the abuses are come to my knowledge, by that or by any other means. Pray consider what I have said only as an index to direct you in your inquiries.

If this then, Sir, has been the use made of the trust of political powers internal and external, given by you in the charter, the next thing to be seen is the conduct of the company with regard to the commercial trust. And here I will make a fair offer: — If it can be proved that they have acted wisely, prudently, and frugally, as merchants, I shall pass by the whole mass of their enormities as statesmen. That they have not done this their present condition is proof sufficient. Their distresses are said to be owing to their wars. This is not wholly true. But if it were, is not that readiness to engage in wars which distinguishes them, and for which the committee of secrecy has so branded their politicks, founded on the falsest principles of mercantile speculation?

The principle of buying cheap and selling dear is the first, the great foundation of mercantile dealing. Have they ever attended to this principle? Nay, for years have they not actually authorized in their servants a total indifference as to the prices they were to pay?

A great deal of strictness in driving bargains for whatever we contract, is another of the principles of mercantile policy. Try the company by that test! Look at the contracts that are made for them. Is the company so much as a good commissary to their own armies? I engage to select for you, out of the innumerable mass of their dealings, all conducted very nearly alike, one contract only, the excessive profits on which during a short term would pay the whole of their year's dividend. I shall undertake to shew, that upon two others, the inordinate profits given, with the losses incurred in order to secure those profits, would pay a year's dividend more.

It is a third property of trading men to see that their clerks do not divert the dealings of the master to their own benefit. It was the other day only, when their governour and council taxed the company's investment with a sum of fifty thousand pounds, as an inducement to persuade only seven members of their board of trade to give their *honour* that they would abstain from such profits upon that investment as they must have violated their *oaths* if they had made at all.

It is a fourth quality of a merchant to be exact in his accounts. What will be thought, when you have fully before you the mode of accounting made use of in the treasury of Bengal? — I hope you will have it soon. With regard to one of their agencies, when it came to the material part, the prime cost of the goods on which a commission of fifteen *per cent.* was allowed, to the astonishment of the factory to whom the commodities were sent, the accountant general reports that he did not think himself authorized to call for *vouchers* relative to this and other particulars, — because the agent was upon his *honour* with regard to them. A new principle of account upon honour seems to be regularly established in their dealings and their treasury, which in reality amounts to an entire annihilation of the principle of all accounts.

It is a fifth property of a merchant, who does not meditate a fraudulent bankruptcy, to calculate his probable profits upon the money he takes up to vest in business. Did the company, when they bought goods on bonds bearing 8 *per cent.* interest, at ten and even twenty *per cent.* discount, even ask themselves a question concerning the possibility of advantage from dealing on these terms?

The last quality of a merchant I shall advert to, is the taking care to be properly prepared, in cash or goods, in the ordinary course of sale, for the bills which are drawn on them. Now I ask, whether they have ever calculated the clear produce of any given sales, to make them tally with the four million of bills which are come and coming upon them, so as at the proper periods to enable the one to liquidate the other? No, they have not. They are now obliged to borrow money of their own servants to purchase their investment. The servants stipulate five *per cent.* on the capital they advance, if their bills should not be paid at the time when they become due; and the value of the rupee on which they charge this interest is taken at two shillings and a penny. Has the company ever troubled themselves to inquire whether their sales can bear the payment of that interest, and at that rate of exchange? Have they once considered the dilemma in which they are placed—the ruin of their credit in the East Indies, if they refuse the bills—the ruin of their credit and existence in England, if they accept them? Indeed no trace of equitable government is found in their politicks; not one trace of commercial principle in their mercantile dealing; and hence is the deepest and maturest wisdom of parliament demanded, and the best resources of this kingdom must be strained, to restore them; that is, to restore the countries destroyed by the misconduct of the company, and to restore the company itself, ruined by the consequences of their plans for destroying what they were bound to preserve.

I required, if you remember, at my outset, a proof that these abuses were habitual. But surely this is not necessary for me to consider as a separate head; because I trust I have made it evident beyond a doubt, in considering the abuses themselves, that they are regular, permanent, and systematical.

I am now come to my last condition, without which, for one, I will never readily lend my hand to the destruction of any established government; which is, That in its present state, the government of the East India company is absolutely incorrigible.

Of this great truth I think there can be little doubt, after all that has appeared in this house. It is so very clear, that I must consider the leaving any power in their hands, and the determined resolution to continue and countenance every mode and every degree of peculation, oppression, and tyranny, to be one and the same thing. I look upon that body incorrigible, from the fullest consideration both of their uniform conduct, and their present real and virtual constitution.

If they had not constantly been apprized of all the enormities committed in India under their authority; if this state of things had been as much a discovery to them as it was to many of us; we might flatter ourselves that the detection of the abuses would lead to their reformation. I will go further: If the court of directors had not uniformly condemned every act which this house or any of its committees had condemned; if the language in which they expressed their disapprobation against enormities and their authors had not been much more vehement and indignant than any ever used in this house, I should entertain some hopes. If they had not on the other hand, as uniformly commended all their servants who had done their duty and obeyed their orders, as they had heavily censured those who rebelled; I might say, These people have been in an errour, and when they are sensible of it they will mend. But when I reflect on the uniformity of their support to the objects of their uniform censure; and the state of insignificance and disgrace to which all of those have been reduced whom they approved; and that even utter ruin and premature death have been among the fruits of their favour; I must be convinced, that in this case, as in all others, hypocrisy is the only vice that never can be cured.

Attend, I pray you, to the situation and prosperity of Benfield, Hastings, and others of that sort. The last of these has been treated by the company with an asperity of reprehension that has no parallel. They lament "that the power of disposing of their property for perpetuity, should fall into such hands." Yet for fourteen years, with little interruption, he has governed all their affairs, of every description, with an absolute sway. He has had himself the means of heaping up immense wealth; and, during that whole period, the fortunes of hundreds have depended on his smiles and frowns. He himself tells you he is incumbered with two hundred and fifty young gentlemen, some of them of the best families in England, all of whom aim at returning with vast fortunes to Europe in the prime of life. He has then two hundred and fifty of your children as his hostages for your good behaviour; and loaded for years, as he has been, with the execrations of the natives, with the censures of the court of directors, and struck and blasted with the resolutions of this house, he still maintains the most despotick power ever known in India. He domineers with an overbearing sway in the assemblies of his pretended masters; and it is thought in a degree rash to venture to name his offences in this house, even as grounds of a legislative remedy.

On the other hand, consider the fate of those who have met with the applauses of the directors. Colonel Monson, one of the best of men, had his days shortened by the applauses, destitute of the support, of the company. General Clavering, whose panegyrick was made in every dispatch from England, whose hearse was bedewed with the tears, and hung round with the eulogies of the court of directors, burst an honest and indignant heart at the treachery of those who ruined him by their praises. Uncommon patience and temper, supported Mr. Francis a while longer under the baneful influence of the commendation of the court of directors.[47] His health however gave way at length; and, in utter despair, he returned to Europe. At his return the doors of the India House were shut to this man, who had been the object of their constant admiration. He has indeed escaped with life, but he has forfeited all expectation of credit, consequence, party, and following. He may well say, *Me nemo ministro fur erit, atque ideo nulli comes exeo.*[48] This man, whose deep reach of thought, whose large legislative conceptions, and whose grand plans of policy make the most shining part of our reports, from whence we have all learned our lessons, if we have learned any good ones; this man, from whose materials those gentlemen who have least acknowledged it have yet spoken as from a brief; this man, driven from his employment, discountenanced by the directors, has had no other reward, and no other distinction, but that inward "sunshine of the soul"[49] which a good conscience can always bestow upon itself. He has not yet had so much as a good word,

47 The Honorable George Monson (1730–76) and Sir John Clavering (1722–77), together with Philip Francis (1740–1818), for a time made up the majority against Hastings on the Supreme Council. Both men died in India. Francis had been wounded in a duel with Hastings in 1780.

48 Juvenal *Satires* 3.46–47: "No man will get my help in robbery, and so no governor will put me on his staff."

49 Pope *Essay on Man* 4.168–69.

but from a person too insignificant to make any other return, for the means with which he has been furnished for performing his share of a duty which is equally urgent on us all.

Add to this, that from the highest in place to the lowest, every British subject, who, in obedience to the company's orders, has been active in the discovery of peculations, has been ruined. They have been driven from India. When they made their appeal at home they were not heard; when they attempted to return they were stopped. No artifice of fraud, no violence of power, has been omitted to destroy them in character as well as in fortune.

Worse, far worse, has been the fate of the poor creatures, the natives of India, whom the hypocrisy of the company has betrayed into complaint of oppression, and discovery of peculation. The first women in Bengal, the ranny of Rajeshahi, the ranny of Burdwan, the ranny of Amboa, by their weak and thoughtless trust in the company's honour and protection, are utterly ruined: the first of these women, a person of princely rank, and once of correspondent fortune, who paid above two hundred thousand a year quit-rent to the state, is, according to very credible information, so completely beggared as to stand in need of the relief of alms. Mahomed Reza Khân, the second Mussulman in Bengal, for having been distinguished by the ill-omened honour of the countenance and protection of the court of directors, was, without the pretence of any inquiry whatsoever into his conduct, stripped of all his employments, and reduced to the lowest condition. His ancient rival for power, the rajah Nundcomar, was, by an insult on every thing which India holds respectable and sacred, hanged in the face of all his nation, by the judges you sent to protect that people; hanged for a pretended crime, upon an *ex post facto* British act of parliament, in the midst of his evidence against Mr. Hastings. The accuser they saw hanged. The culprit, without acquittal or inquiry, triumphs on the ground of that murder: a murder not of Nundcomar only, but of all living testimony, and even of evidence yet unborn. From that time not a complaint has been heard from the natives against their governours. All the grievances of India have found a complete remedy.

Men will not look to acts of parliament, to regulations, to declarations, to votes, and resolutions. No, they are not such fools. They will ask, what is the road to power, credit, wealth, and honours? They will ask, what conduct ends in neglect, disgrace, poverty, exile, prison and gibbet? These will teach them the course which they are to follow. It is your distribution of these that will give the character and tone of your government. All the rest is miserable grimace.

When I accuse the court of directors of this habitual treachery, in the use of reward and punishment, I do not mean to include all the individuals in that court. There have been, Sir, very frequently, men of the greatest integrity and virtue amongst them; and the contrariety in the declarations and conduct of that court has arisen, I take it, from this: — That the honest directors have, by the force of matter of fact on the records, carried the reprobation of the evil measures of the servants in India. This could not be prevented, whilst these records stared them in the face; nor were the delinquents, either here or there, very solicitous about their reputation, as long as they were able to secure their power. The agreement of their partisans to censure them, blunted for a while the edge of a severe proceeding. It obtained for them a character of impartiality, which enabled them to recommend, with some sort of grace, what will always carry a plausible appearance, those treacherous expedients, called moderate measures. Whilst these were under discussion, new matter of complaint came over, which seemed to antiquate the first. The same circle was here trod round once more; and thus through years they proceeded in a compromise of censure for punishment; until, by shame and despair, one after another, almost every man, who preferred his duty to the company to the interest of their servants, has been driven from that court.

This, Sir, has been their conduct; and it has been the result of the alteration which was insensibly made in their constitution. The change was made insensibly; but it is now strong and adult, and as publick and declared, as it is fixed beyond all power of reformation. So that there is none who hears me, that is not as certain as I am, that the company, in the sense in which it was formerly understood, has no existence. The question is not, what injury you may do to the proprietors of India stock; for there are no such men to be injured. If the active ruling part of the company who form the general court, who fill the offices, and direct the measures (the rest tell for nothing) were persons who held their stock as a means of their subsistence, who in the part they took were only concerned in the government of India, for the rise or fall of their dividend, it would be indeed a defective plan of policy. The interest of the people who are governed by them would not be their primary object; perhaps a very small part of their consideration at all. But then they might well be depended on, and perhaps more than persons in other respects preferable, for preventing the peculation of their servants to their own prejudice. Such a body would not easily have left their trade as a spoil to the avarice of those who received their wages. But now things are totally reversed. The stock is of no value, whether it be the qualification of a director or proprietor; and it is impossible that it should. A director's qualification may be worth about two thousand five hundred pounds—and the interest, at eight *per cent.* is about one hundred and sixty pounds a year. Of what value is that, whether it rise to ten, or fall to six, or to nothing, to him whose son, before he is in Bengal two months, and before he descends the steps of the council chamber, sells the grant of a single contract for forty thousand pounds? Accordingly, the stock is bought up in qualifications. The vote is not to protect the stock, but the stock is bought to acquire the vote; and the end of the vote is to cover and support, against justice, some man of power who has made an obnoxious fortune in India; or to maintain in power those who are actually employing it in the acquisition of such a fortune; and to avail themselves in return of his patronage, that he may shower the spoils of the east, "barbarick pearl and gold,"[50] on them, their families, and dependents. So that all the relations of the company are not only changed, but inverted. The

50 *Paradise Lost* 2.4; describing the throne of Satan.

servants in India are not appointed by the directors, but the directors are chosen by them. The trade is carried on with their capitals. To them the revenues of the country are mortgaged. The seat of the supreme power is in Calcutta. The house in Leadenhall Street[51] is nothing more than a change for their agents, factors, and deputies to meet in, to take care of their affairs, and support their interests; and this so avowedly, that we see the known agents of the delinquent servants marshalling and disciplining their forces, and the prime spokesmen in all their assemblies.

Every thing has followed in this order, and according to the natural train of events. I will close what I have to say on the incorrigible condition of the company, by stating to you a few facts that will leave no doubt of the obstinacy of that corporation, and of their strength too, in resisting the reformation of their servants. By these facts you will be enabled to discover the sole grounds upon which they are tenacious of their charter. It is now more than two years that, upon account of the gross abuses and ruinous situation of the company's affairs, (which occasioned the cry of the whole world long before it was taken up here) that we instituted two committees to inquire into the mismanagements by which the company's affairs had been brought to the brink of ruin. These inquiries had been pursued with unremitting diligence; and a great body of facts was collected and printed for general information. In the result of those inquiries, although the committees consisted of very different descriptions, they were unanimous. They joined in censuring the conduct of the Indian administration, and enforcing the responsibility upon two men, whom this house, in consequence of these reports, declared it to be the duty of the directors to remove from their stations, and recal to Great Britain, "*because they had acted in a manner repugnant to the honour and policy of this nation, and thereby brought great calamities on India, and enormous expences on the East-India company.*"

Here was no attempt on the charter. Here was no question of

---

51 Residence of the East India Company in London.

their privileges. To vindicate their own honour, to support their own interests, to enforce obedience to their own orders; these were the sole object of the monitory resolution of this house. But as soon as the general court could assemble, they assembled to demonstrate who they really were. Regardless of the proceedings of this house, they ordered the directors not to carry into effect any resolution they might come to for the removal of Mr. Hastings and Mr. Hornby.[52] The directors, still retaining some shadow of respect to this house, instituted an inquiry themselves, which continued from June to October; and after an attentive perusal and full consideration of papers, resolved to take steps for removing the persons who had been the objects of our resolution; but not without a violent struggle against evidence. Seven directors went so far as to enter a protest against the vote of their court. Upon this the general court takes the alarm; it re-assembles; it orders the directors to rescind their resolution, that is, not to recall Mr. Hastings and Mr. Hornby, and to despise the resolution of the house of commons. Without so much as the pretence of looking into a single paper, without the formality of instituting any committee of inquiry, they superseded all the labours of their own directors, and of this house.

It will naturally occur to ask, how it was possible that they should not attempt some sort of examination into facts, as a colour for their resistance to a publick authority, proceeding so very deliberately; and exerted, apparently at least, in favour of their own? The answer, and the only answer which can be given, is, that they were afraid that their true relation should be mistaken. They were afraid that their patrons and masters in India should attribute their support of them to an opinion of their cause, and not to an attachment to their power. They were afraid it should be suspected, that they did not mean blindly to support them in the use they made of that power. They determined to shew that they at least were set against reformation; that they

52 William Hornby (ca. 1722–1803) was governor of Bombay; parliamentary resolutions against Hastings and Hornby passed on 30 May 1782.

were firmly resolved to bring the territories, the trade, and the stock of the company, to ruin, rather than be wanting in fidelity to their nominal servants and real masters, in the ways they took to their private fortunes.

Even since the beginning of this session, the same act of audacity was repeated, with the same circumstances of contempt of all the decorum of inquiry on their part, and of all the proceedings of this house. They again made it a request to their favourite, and your culprit, to keep his post; and thanked and applauded him, without calling for a paper which could afford light into the merit or demerit of the transaction, and without giving themselves a moment's time to consider, or even to understand the articles of the Maratta peace. The fact is, that for a long time there was a struggle, a faint one indeed, between the company and their servants. But it is a struggle no longer. For some time the superiority has been decided. The interests abroad are become the settled preponderating weight both in the court of proprietors, and the court of directors. Even the attempt you have made to inquire into their practices and to reform abuses, has raised and piqued them to a far more regular and steady support. The company has made a common cause, and identified themselves, with the destroyers of India. They have taken on themselves all that mass of enormity; they are supporting what you have reprobated; those you condemn they applaud; those you order home to answer for their conduct, they request to stay, and thereby encourage to proceed in their practices. Thus the servants of the East-India company triumph, and the representatives of the people of Great Britain are defeated.

I therefore conclude, what you all conclude, that this body, being totally perverted from the purposes of its institution, is utterly incorrigible; and because they are incorrigible, both in conduct and constitution, power ought to be taken out of their hands; just on the same principles on which have been made all the just changes and revolutions of government that have taken place since the beginning of the world.

I will now say a few words to the general principle of the plan which is set up against that of my right honourable friend. It is to re-commit the government of India to the court of directors. Those who would commit the reformation of India to the destroyers of it, are the enemies to that reformation. They would make a distinction between directors and proprietors, which, in the present state of things, does not, cannot exist. But a right honourable gentleman says, he would keep the present government of India in the court of directors; and would, to curb them, provide salutary regulations; — wonderful! That is, he would appoint the old offenders to correct the old offences; and he would render the vicious and the foolish wise and virtuous, by salutary regulations. He would appoint the wolf as guardian of the sheep; but he has invented a curious muzzle, by which this protecting wolf shall not be able to open his jaws above an inch or two at the utmost. Thus his work is finished. But I tell the right honourable gentleman, that controuled depravity is not innocence; and that it is not the labour of delinquency in chains, that will correct abuses. Will these gentlemen of the direction animadvert on the partners of their own guilt? Never did a serious plan of amending of any old tyrannical establishment propose the authors and abettors of the abuses as the reformers of them. If the undone people of India see their old oppressors in confirmed power, even by the reformation, they will expect nothing but what they will certainly feel, a continuance, or rather an aggravation, of all their former sufferings. They look to the seat of power, and to the persons who fill it; and they despise those gentlemen's regulations as much as the gentlemen do who talk of them.

But there is a cure for every thing. Take away, say they, the court of proprietors, and the court of directors will do their duty. Yes; as they have done it hitherto. That the evils in India have solely arisen from the court of proprietors, is grossly false. In many of them, the directors were heartily concurring; in most of them, they were encouraging, and sometimes commanding; in all, they were conniving.

But who are to choose this well-regulated and reforming court of directors? — Why, the very proprietors who are excluded from all management, for the abuse of their power. They will choose, undoubtedly, out of themselves, men like themselves; and those who are most forward in resisting your authority, those who are most engaged in faction or interest with the delinquents abroad, will be the objects of their selection. But gentlemen say, that when this choice is made, the proprietors are not to interfere in the measures of the directors, whilst those directors are busy in the control of their common patrons and masters in India. No, indeed, I believe they will not desire to interfere. They will choose those whom they know may be trusted, safely trusted, to act in strict conformity to their common principles, manners, measures, interests, and connections. They will want neither monitor nor control. It is not easy to choose men to act in conformity to a publick interest against their private: but a sure dependance may be had on those who are chosen to forward their private interest, at the expense of the publick. But if the directors should slip, and deviate into rectitude, the punishment is in the hands of the general court, and it will surely be remembered to them at their next election.

If the government of India wants no reformation; but gentlemen are amusing themselves with a theory, conceiving a more democratick or aristocratick mode of government for these dependancies, or if they are in a dispute only about patronage; the dispute is with me of so little concern, that I should not take the pains to utter an affirmative or negative to any proposition in it. If it be only for a theoretical amusement that they are to propose a bill; the thing is at best frivolous and unnecessary. But if the company's government is not only full of abuse, but is one of the most corrupt and destructive tyrannies, that probably ever existed in the world, (as I am sure it is) what a cruel mockery would it be in me, and in those who think like me, to propose this kind of remedy for this kind of evil!

I now come to the third objection, That this bill will increase the influence of the crown. An honourable gentleman has demanded of me, whether I was in earnest when I proposed to this house a plan for the reduction of that influence. Indeed, Sir, I was much, very much, in earnest. My heart was deeply concerned in it; and I hope the publick has not lost the effect of it. How far my judgment was right, for what concerned personal favour and consequence to myself, I shall not presume to determine; nor is its effect upon *me* of any moment. But as to this bill, whether it increases the influence of the crown, or not, is a question I should be ashamed to ask. If I am not able to correct a system of oppression and tyranny, that goes to the utter ruin of thirty millions of my fellow-creatures and fellow-subjects, but by some increase to the influence of the crown, I am ready here to declare, that I, who have been active to reduce it, shall be at least as active and strenuous to restore it again. I am no lover of names; I contend for the substance of good and protecting government, let it come from what quarter it will.

But I am not obliged to have recourse to this expedient. Much, very much the contrary. I am sure that the influence of the crown will by no means aid a reformation of this kind; which can neither be originated nor supported, but by the uncorrupt publick virtue of the representatives of the people of England. Let it once get into the ordinary course of administration, and to me all hopes of reformation are gone. I am far from knowing or believing, that this bill will increase the influence of the crown. We all know, that the crown has ever had some influence in the court of directors; and that it has been extremely increased by the acts of 1773 and 1780. The gentlemen who, as part of their reformation, propose "a more active control on the part of the crown," which is to put the directors under a secretary of state, specially named for that purpose, must know, that their project will increase it further. But that old influence has had, and the new will have, incurable inconveniences which cannot happen under the parliamentary establishment proposed in this bill. An honourable gentleman,[53] not now in his place, but who is well acquainted with the India company, and by no means a friend to this bill, has told you, that a ministerial influence has always been

53 Governour Johnstone [*Burke's note*].

predominant in that body; and that to make the directors pliant
to their purposes, ministers generally caused persons meanly
qualified to be chosen directors. According to his idea, to secure
subserviency, they submitted the company's affairs to the direction of incapacity. This was to ruin the company, in order to
govern it. This was certainly influence in the very worst form in
which it could appear. At best it was clandestine and irresponsible. Whether this was done so much upon system as that gentleman supposes, I greatly doubt. But such in effect the operation of
government on that court unquestionably was; and such, under a
similar constitution, it will be for ever. Ministers must be wholly
removed from the management of the affairs of India, or they
will have an influence in its patronage. The thing is inevitable.
Their scheme of a new secretary of state, "with a more vigorous
control," is not much better than a repetition of the measure
which we know by experience will not do. Since the year 1773
and the year 1780, the company has been under the control of
the secretary of state's office, and we had then three secretaries
of state. If more than this is done, then they annihilate the direction which they pretend to support; and they augment the influence of the crown, of whose growth they affect so great an horrour. But in truth this scheme of reconciling a direction really
and truly deliberative, with an office really and substantially con-
trolling, is a sort of machinery that can be kept in order but a very
short time. Either the directors will dwindle into clerks, or the
secretary of state, as hitherto has been the course, will leave every
thing to them, often through design, often through neglect. If
both should affect activity, collision, procrastination, delay, and
in the end, utter confusion must ensue.

But, Sir, there is one kind of influence far greater than that of
the nomination to office. This gentlemen in opposition have
totally overlooked, although it now exists in its full vigour; and it
will do so, upon their scheme, in at least as much force as it does
now. That influence this bill cuts up by the roots: I mean the
influence of protection. I shall explain myself: — The office given to a
young man going to India is of trifling consequence. But he that

goes out an insignificant boy, in a few years returns a great nabob. Mr. Hastings says he has two hundred and fifty of that kind of raw materials, who expect to be speedily manufactured into the merchantable quality I mention. One of these gentlemen, suppose, returns hither, loaded with odium and with riches. When he comes to England, he comes as to a prison, or as to a sanctuary; and either is ready for him, according to his demeanour. What is the influence in the grant of any place in India, to that which is acquired by the protection or compromise with such guilt, and with the command of such riches, under the dominion of the hopes and fears which power is able to hold out to every man in that condition? That man's whole fortune, half a million perhaps, becomes an instrument of influence, without a shilling of charge to the civil list; and the influx of fortunes which stand in need of this protection is continual. It works both ways; it influences the delinquent, and it may corrupt the minister. Compare the influence acquired by appointing for instance even a governour general, and that obtained by protecting him. I shall push this no further. But I wish gentlemen to roll it a little in their own minds.

The bill before you cuts off this source of influence. Its design and main scope is to regulate the administration of India upon the principles of a court of judicature; and to exclude, as far as human prudence can exclude, all possibility of a corrupt partiality, in appointing to office, or supporting in office, or covering from inquiry and punishment, any person who has abused or shall abuse his authority. At the board, as appointed and regulated by this bill, reward and punishment cannot be shifted and reversed by a whisper. That commission becomes fatal to cabal, to intrigue, and to secret representation, those instruments of the ruin of India. He that cuts off the means of premature fortune, and the power of protecting it when acquired, strikes a deadly blow at the great fund, the bank, the capital stock of Indian influence, which cannot be vested any where, or in any hands, without most dangerous consequences to the publick.

The third and contradictory objection is, That this bill does not increase the influence of the crown. On the contrary, That the just power of the crown will be lessened, and transferred to the use of a party, by giving the patronage of India to a commission nominated by parliament, and independent of the crown. The contradiction is glaring, and it has been too well exposed to make it necessary for me to insist upon it. But passing the contradiction, and taking it without any relation, of all objections that is the most extraordinary. Do not gentlemen know, that the crown has not at present the grant of a single office under the company, civil or military, at home or abroad? So far as the crown is concerned, it is certainly rather a gainer; for the vacant offices in the new commission are to be filled up by the king.

It is argued as a part of the bill, derogatory to the prerogatives of the crown, that the commissioners named in the bill are to continue for a short term of years, too short in my opinion; and because, during that time, they are not at the mercy of every predominant faction of the court. Does not this objection lie against the present directors; none of whom are named by the crown, and a proportion of whom hold for this very term of four years? Did it not lie against the governour general and council named in the act of 1773 — who were invested by name, as the present commissioners are to be appointed in the body of the act of parliament, who were to hold their places for a term of terms, and were not removable at the discretion of the crown? Did it not lie against the re-appointment, in the year 1780, upon the very same terms? Yet at none of these times, whatever other objections the scheme might be liable to, was it supposed to be a derogation to the just prerogative of the crown, that a commission created by act of parliament should have its members named by the authority which called it into existence? This is not the disposal by parliament of any office derived from the authority of the crown, or now disposable by that authority. It is so far from being any thing new, violent, or alarming, that I do not recollect, in any parliamentary commission, down to the commissioners of the land tax, that it has ever been otherwise.

The objection of the tenure for four years is an objection to all places that are not held during pleasure; but in that objection I pronounce the gentlemen, from my knowledge of their complexion and of their principles, to be perfectly in earnest. The party (say these gentlemen) of the minister who proposes this scheme will be rendered powerful by it; for he will name his party friends to the commission. This objection against party is a party objection; and in this too these gentlemen are perfectly serious. They see that if, by any intrigue, they should succeed to office, they will lose the *clandestine* patronage, the true instrument of clandestine influence, enjoyed in the name of subservient directors, and of wealthy trembling Indian delinquents. But as often as they are beaten off this ground, they return to it again. The minister will name his friends, and persons of his own party. — Whom should he name? Should he name his adversaries? Should he name those whom he cannot trust? Should he name those to execute his plans, who are the declared enemies to the principles of his reform? His character is here at stake. If he proposes for his own ends (but he never will propose) such names as, from their want of rank, fortune, character, ability, or knowledge, are likely to betray or to fall short of their trust, he is in an independent house of commons; in a house of commons which has, by its own virtue, destroyed the instruments of parliamentary subservience. This house of commons would not endure the sound of such names. He would perish by the means which he is supposed to pursue for the security of his power. The first pledge he must give of his sincerity in this great reform, will be in the confidence which ought to be reposed in those names.

For my part, Sir, in this business I put all indirect considerations wholly out of my mind. My sole question, on each clause of the bill, amounts to this: — Is the measure proposed required by the necessities of India? I cannot consent totally to lose sight of the real wants of the people who are the objects of it, and to hunt after every matter of party squabble that may be started on the several provisions. On the question of the duration of the commission I am clear and decided. Can I, can any one who has taken the smallest trouble to be informed concerning the affairs of

India, amuse himself with so strange an imagination, as that the habitual despotism and oppression, that the monopolies, the peculations, the universal destruction of all the legal authority of this kingdom, which have been for twenty years maturing to their present enormity, combined with the distance of the scene, the boldness and artifice of delinquents, their combination, their excessive wealth, and the faction they have made in England, can be fully corrected in a shorter term than four years? None has hazarded such an assertion — None, who has a regard for his reputation, will hazard it.

Sir, the gentlemen, whoever they are, who shall be appointed to this commission, have an undertaking of magnitude on their hands, and their stability must not only be, but it must be thought, real; — and who is it will believe, that any thing short of an establishment made, supported, and fixed in its duration, with all the authority of parliament, can be thought secure of a reasonable stability? The plan of my honourable friend is the reverse of that of reforming by the authors of the abuse. The best we could expect from them is, that they should not continue their ancient pernicious activity. To those we could think of nothing but applying *control*; as we are sure, that even a regard to their reputation (if any such thing exists in them) would oblige them to cover, to conceal, to suppress, and consequently to prevent, all cure of the grievances of India. For what can be discovered, which is not to their disgrace? Every attempt to correct an abuse would be a satire on their former administration. Every man they should pretend to call to an account, would be found their instrument or their accomplice. They can never see a beneficial regulation, but with a view to defeat it. The shorter the tenure of such persons, the better would be the chance of some amendment.

But the system of the bill is different. It calls in persons in no wise concerned with any act censured by parliament; persons generated with, and for, the reform, of which they are themselves the most essential part. To these the chief regulations in the bill are helps, not fetters; they are authorities to support, not regulations to restrain them. From these we look for much more than innocence. From these we expect zeal, firmness, and unremitted activity. Their duty, their character, binds them to proceedings of vigour; and they ought to have a tenure in their office which precludes all fear, whilst they are acting up to the purposes of their trust; a tenure without which, none will undertake plans that require a series and system of acts. When they know that they cannot be whispered out of their duty, that their publick conduct cannot be censured without a publick discussion; that the schemes which they have begun will not be committed to those who will have an interest and credit in defeating and disgracing them; then we may entertain hopes. The tenure is for four years, or during their good behaviour. That good behaviour is as long as they are true to the principles of the bill; and the judgment is in either house of parliament. This is the tenure of your judges; and the valuable principle of the bill is to make a judicial administration for India. It is to give confidence in the execution of a duty, which requires as much perseverance and fortitude as can fall to the lot of any that is born of woman.

As to the gain by party, from the right honourable gentleman's bill, let it be shewn, that this supposed party advantage is pernicious to its object, and the objection is of weight; but until this is done, and this has not been attempted, I shall consider the sole objection, from its tendency to promote the interest of a party, as altogether contemptible. The kingdom is divided into parties, and it ever has been so divided, and it ever will be so divided; and if no system for relieving the subjects of this kingdom from oppression, and snatching its affairs from ruin, can be adopted until it is demonstrated that no party can derive an advantage from it, no good can ever be done in this country. If party is to derive an advantage from the reform of India, (which is more than I know, or believe) it ought to be that party which alone, in this kingdom, has its reputation, nay its very being, pledged to the protection and preservation of that part of the empire. Great fear is expressed, that the commissioners named in this bill will shew some regard to a minister out of place. To men made like the objectors, this must appear criminal. Let it however be remembered by others, that if the commissioners should be his friends, they cannot be his slaves. But dependants are not in a condition to adhere to friends, nor to principles, nor to any uniform line of conduct. They may begin censors, and be obliged to end accomplices. They may be even put under the direction of those whom they were appointed to punish.

The fourth and last objection is, That the bill will hurt publick credit. I do not know whether this requires an answer. But if it does, look to your foundations. The sinking fund is the pillar of credit in this country; and let it not be forgot, that the distresses, owing to the mismanagement of the East India company, have already taken a million from that fund by the non-payment of duties.[54] The bills drawn upon the company, which are about four millions, cannot be accepted without the consent of the treasury. The treasury, acting under a parliamentary trust and authority, pledges the publick for these millions. If they pledge the publick, the publick must have a security in its hands for the management of this interest, or the national credit is gone. For otherwise it is not only the East India company, which is a great interest, that is undone, but, clinging to the security of all your funds, it drags down the rest, and the whole fabrick perishes in one ruin. If this bill does not provide a direction of integrity and of ability competent to that trust, the objection is fatal. If it does, publick credit must depend on the support of the bill.

It has been said, if you violate this charter, what security has the charter of the bank, in which publick credit is so deeply concerned, and even the charter of London, in which the rights of so many subjects are involved? I answer, In the like case they have no security at all — No — no security at all. If the bank should, by every species of mismanagement, fall into a state similar to that

54 The East India Company had again petitioned Parliament for financial relief in March 1783.

of the East India company; if it should be oppressed with demands that it could not answer, engagements which it could not perform, and with bills for which it could not procure payment; no charter should protect the mismanagement from correction, and such publick grievances from redress. If the city of London had the means and will of destroying an empire, and of cruelly oppressing and tyrannizing over millions of men as good as themselves, the charter of the city of London should prove no sanction to such tyranny and such oppression. Charters are kept, when their purposes are maintained: they are violated, when the privilege is supported against its end and its object.

Now, Sir, I have finished all I proposed to say, as my reasons for giving my vote to this bill. If I am wrong, it is not for want of pains to know what is right. This pledge, at least, of my rectitude I have given to my country.

And now, having done my duty to the bill, let me say a word to the author.[55] I should leave him to his own noble sentiments, if the unworthy and illiberal language with which he has been treated, beyond all example of parliamentary liberty, did not make a few words necessary; not so much in justice to him, as to my own feelings. I must say then, that it will be a distinction honourable to the age, that the rescue of the greatest number of the human race that ever were so grievously oppressed, from the greatest tyranny that was ever exercised, has fallen to the lot of abilities and dispositions equal to the task; that it has fallen to one who has the enlargement to comprehend, the spirit to undertake, and the eloquence to support, so great a measure of hazardous benevolence. His spirit is not owing to his ignorance of the state of men and things; he well knows what snares are spread about his path, from personal animosity, from court intrigues, and possibly from popular delusion. But he has put to hazard his

55 Charles James Fox (1749–1806), a leader, with Burke, of parliamentary opposition to the American war, and greatly admired for his eloquence in debate and his skill at persuasion, had lately seen his reputation as a principled statesman tarnished by the apparent opportunism of his coalition with Lord North.

ease, his security, his interest, his power, even his darling popularity, for the benefit of a people whom he has never seen. This is
the road that all heroes have trod before him. He is traduced and
abused for his supposed motives. He will remember, that obloquy
is a necessary ingredient in the composition of all true glory: he
will remember, that it was not only in the Roman customs, but it is
in the nature and constitution of things, that calumny and abuse
are essential parts of triumph. These thoughts will support a
mind, which only exists for honour, under the burthen of temporary reproach. He is doing indeed a great good; such as rarely
falls to the lot, and almost as rarely coincides with the desires, of
any man. Let him use his time. Let him give the whole length of
the reins to his benevolence. He is now on a great eminence,
where the eyes of mankind are turned to him. He may live long,
he may do much. But here is the summit. He never can exceed
what he does this day.

He has faults; but they are faults that, though they may in
a small degree tarnish the lustre, and sometimes impede the
march of his abilities, have nothing in them to extinguish the fire
of great virtues. In those faults, there is no mixture of deceit, of
hypocrisy, of pride, of ferocity, of complexional despotism, or
want of feeling for the distresses of mankind. His are faults which
might exist in a descendant of Henry the Fourth of France, as
they did exist in that father of his country. Henry the Fourth
wished that he might live to see a fowl in the pot of every peasant in his kingdom. That sentiment of homely benevolence was
worth all the splendid sayings that are recorded of kings. But he
wished perhaps for more than could be obtained, and the goodness of the man exceeded the power of the king. But this gentleman, a subject, may this day say this at least, with truth, that he
secures the rice in his pot to every man in India. A poet of
antiquity thought it one of the first distinctions to a prince whom
he meant to celebrate, that through a long succession of generations, he had been the progenitor of an able and virtuous citizen,
who by force of the arts of peace, had corrected governments of
oppression, and suppressed wars of rapine.

> Indole proh quanta juvenis, quantumque daturus
> Ausoniæ populis, ventura in sæcula civem.
> Ille super Gangem, super exauditus et Indos;
> Implebit terras voce; et furialia bella
> Fulmine compescet linguæ. —[56]

This was what was said of the predecessor of the only person to whose eloquence it does not wrong that of the mover of this bill to be compared. But the Ganges and the Indus are the patrimony of the fame of my honourable friend, and not of Cicero. I confess, I anticipate with joy the reward of those, whose whole consequence, power, and authority, exist only for the benefit of mankind; and I carry my mind to all the people, and all the names and descriptions, that, relieved by this bill, will bless the labours of this parliament, and the confidence which the best house of commons has given to him who the best deserves it. The little cavils of party will not be heard, where freedom and happiness will be felt. There is not a tongue, a nation, or religion in India, which will not bless the presiding care and manly beneficence of this house, and of him who proposes to you this great work. Your names will never be separated before the throne of the Divine Goodness, in whatever language, or with whatever rites, pardon is asked for sin, and reward for those who imitate the Godhead in his universal bounty to his creatures. These honours you deserve, and they will surely be paid, when all the jargon of influence, and party, and patronage, are swept into oblivion.

I have spoken what I think, and what I feel, of the mover of this bill. An honourable friend of mine, speaking of his merits, was charged with having made a studied panegyrick. I don't know what his was. Mine, I am sure, is a studied panegyrick; the fruit of much meditation; the result of the observation of near

---

56 Silius Italicus *Punic Wars* 8.406–10: "How noble was his youthful promise, and how great the immortal descendant he was to give to Italy. That voice, beyond the Ganges and beyond the peoples of India, shall fill all the earth; and the lightning of his tongue shall calm the fury of war." Burke omits the last words of this passage about Cicero: "and shall leave behind him a renown that no orator of after-times can hope to equal."

twenty years. For my own part, I am happy that I have lived to see this day; I feel myself overpaid for the labours of eighteen years, when, at this late period, I am able to take my share, by one humble vote, in destroying a tyranny that exists to the disgrace of this nation, and the destruction of so large a part of the human species.

To Miss Mary Palmer
(19 January 1786)

Mary Palmer was the niece of Sir Joshua Reynolds, one of Burke's oldest and most trusted friends. Having lived with her uncle since 1773, she was on familiar terms with Burke; and, prompted by a letter from a friend, she had asked him a question then in many people's minds. Why did he seek to destroy the reputation of Warren Hastings? And why now press his charges so far as to threaten impeachment? It was widely assumed that a motive of personal revenge must be driving the prosecution, or an idea of party interest strangely misjudged.

To Miss Mary Palmer

(19 January 1786)

MY DEAR MISS PALMER,

How could you apologize, and apologize to me too, for an act of good nature and kindness? I hear enough of my faults from my enemies; shall I not bear to hear them from my friends? Shall I bear wounds in the field of battle, and quarrel with my surgeons, who open them only to heal them in my tent? Tell your worthy correspondent who is so good as to take an interest in me, that I am truly thankful to him or her (whoever it may be) for their obliging solicitude. I am an old acquaintance of your house; I believe of not much less than thirty years standing; though a much later personal acquaintance of *yours*; and you, according to your ages, are best judges whether I am that very intemperate man, that I am described to be in the cool and moderate climate of Bengal. I am far from the least title to *Great*; perhaps I am not much nearer to that of *good*, though I endeavour all I can at the latter — nothing at all, I assure you, at the former. However, I am not, at my years, a person of a childish credulity, nor apt to run away with every report. Having been employed for years in the business of arranging and stating, as well as collecting, *evidence*, it would not much become me of all men to be light and careless about matter of fact. It is indeed much the interest of those on whom facts bear hard, so to represent me; and I do not blame them for doing the only thing which can be done in their cause. It is not uncommon, nor blameable, to make use of a *report* — when a motion is made in the House of Commons for papers that may verify, contradict, or qualify the matter of the report, according to its nature. Almost all motions for papers are made upon that ground. However, I am, perhaps, the only active man in the House, that never did make a motion without a very good previous knowledge of the paper I moved for. I will tell you this business just as it is. I found, that they had received at the India House, a paper of instructions from Mr Hastings to Mr Bristow, one of which was to apprehend, and to put to death, a certain gentleman called Almas Ali Khan. I had a copy of that curious secret instruction in my pocket. I moved, that this instruction should be laid before the House; stating, as my ground, the precarious tenure on which people of distinction in that country held their honours, fortunes, and lives; — but never, either directly or indirectly, said one word of his wife, children, parents, or relations; not having reason to know that he had any wife, nor having received any report, made directly to me or through the intervention of any other person, that should lead me to such a conclusion. If I had mentioned any such thing it must have been a mere fiction of my own brain. My motion, which stands on the Journals, will verify this; in which there is not a word of his widow — nor of his death — but solely of the *order* to seize upon him, and to cause him to be put to death. The paper was given. It appeared just as I had represented. It was printed by order of the House. It excited a general indignation; and the newspapers fell to work on that ground, to frame petitions from his wife and children &ca &c — The only favour I have to beg of my friends, is, that they will form their judgments of me, by what the records of Parliament, and not the fictions of newspapers, relate concerning me. In those records, they will find eleven pretty large volumes; *some* of which are *entirely* mine; and the materials of *all* of which I have diligently perused, and compared — and if on collation with the authorities at home or abroad, they find that I have abused the trust placed in me by Parliament, by recording rumours instead of facts taken from official papers, or oral evidence judicially given at a committee table, I shall be very ready to excuse them in supposing me to be, what at my age, and with my very large experience, it is very unfit I should be, a man of a giddy credulous nature, apt to be run away with every idle rumour, and to commit myself rashly upon it. I certainly do not expect, (and I should be a fool if I did) that the reports of my conduct and character from the Bengal gentlemen in London, to the Bengal gentlemen at Calcutta, should be favourable to me. Mr Hastings has given their stations to several of them; and if they wish to imitate his conduct — it is certain that they can never have me for their friend. I have not fallen into any traps laid by their patron against my reputation. He was *very* near falling into a trap, laid, not by me, but by himself; and from which he escaped, if he has escaped, by greater trap mechanists than he has ever been, or can be.[1] I know him very well; though never having seen him, but in the dusk of one evening, in a walk with you and your uncle, and in the midst of a squadron. I am sure I could not distinguish his face; but I know him in his actions and his writings. I likewise am an old acquaintance of Almas Ali Khan, of whom there is a great deal in the papers before our Committee not yet reported — and on the whole, perhaps, there are not very many gentlemen at Calcutta so well informed of the state of the upper provinces as I am, at least to a certain period — and I am as little likely to fall into a gross error, as to persons or facts, as any of them. Your correspondent says, and does me only justice in saying, that "I do all the good in my power to the party I represent." But I must beg leave to inform you, that in India affairs, I have not acted at all with any party from the beginning to the end. I know of no party which goes in a body upon this subject; they are all so distracted with personal considerations; and that perhaps may be among the causes of the cry against myself in particular. I began this India business in the administration of Lord North, to which in all its periods I was in direct opposition; and acted in it with several of those who voted on his side of the House, and against some of my own description, who have been among the loudest against me on that account. I have no party in this business, my dear Miss Palmer, but among a set of people, who have none of your lilies and roses in their faces, but who are the images of the great Pattern as well as you or I. I know what I am doing; whether the white people like it or not. They hear, it

1 Alluding to the possibility that Pitt and his administration may have formed a tacit design not to punish Warren Hastings.

seems, at Calcutta, that "I am declined in popular favour." That cannot be; for I never had any to lose. I never conformed myself to the humours of the people. I cannot say that opinion is indifferent to me: but I will take it, if I can, as my companion; never as my guide. I see, that the same imputation of *intemperance* has been laid upon me by a gentleman, at the meeting to remonstrate against Mr Pitt's bill. It is natural, from his connexions, that he should do so; and should take an occasion (from a measure I abhor, and certainly had no share in, except in expressing my detestation of it, and hoping that no man who had a regard to his character would suffer himself to be balloted for the execution of it) to cast reflexions upon me, rather than upon those whose act he opposes.[2] I have always wished that no man should be prosecuted for offenses, but before tribunals known to the law; and that when inquisitions are made, they should be into the actions, and not the fortunes, of the persons under accusation. I never found men guilty in the mass; nor proceeded against their estates, without knowing whether I had any fault to find with their proceedings. I found the general tenor of the Company's internal and external system to be bad. The actors and advisers of that evil system, I knew; I pointed out; and would have punished if I could. But I never wished to make a previous enquiry into what they were worth, in order to drive them to a composition for the delinquencies I should presume from the degree of their power in ransoming themselves. There are those who like neither the methods of the present ministry nor mine — but some lately returned, I am sure, would greatly prefer that of persons now in power to mine. They, therefore, support the ministry and they persecute me, in the only way they can, by their calumnies. As to the gentlemen who serve in India, as a *body*, I have nothing to say to them; because I have nothing to say to men in *bodies*. I attach myself to the guilty, where alone guilt can lie, *individually*; and if the servants in general think, that my

2 Servants of the company resented the inventory of possessions upon their return from India required by the terms of Pitt's India Act.

charges against Sir Elijah Impey, Mr Hastings, and Mr Benfield, are ill founded, or frivolous, it would give me a worse opinion of them than I have yet entertained, who have a most sincere esteem for several of them. Is not this, my dear Miss Palmer, a strange account to you, who care not three straws for such things? But it is written *through* you, not *to* you; and I wish you to send it (blots and all, for I have written in a good deal of haste) to your Indian friend. It is as a friend to you I write it — from my real love to all of your connexions; who, (if I had taken ways to power which I never could prevail on myself to take) would have found some results from my good wishes to some of them, as well as to other persons in India; I, whom you know to be so far from a general enemy and persecutor of any description of men, that I would not hurt any creature on earth, till I found him intolerable to every other creature. My dearest Miss Palmer, God bless you; and send your friend home to you rich and innocent; and may you long enjoy your own sweet repose; and the love and esteem of all those who know how to value elegance, taste, abilities, and simplicity. I am ever

Your affectionate friend

EDM BURKE

Speech in Opening the Impeachment of Warren Hastings (1788)

Born in 1732, almost an exact contemporary of Burke's, Warren Hastings was admired early for his scholarly gifts at Westminster School, and in 1750 was appointed Writer for the East India Company. He learned the Persian and Hindostan languages, and caught the eye of Lord Clive, who named him the company's resident at the court of the Nawab of Bengal. Having made some initial efforts to introduce uniformity into the company's dealings with native authorities, Hastings came to rely on a Nawab, Mir Qasim, as enforcer; but he lost his bid for control, and saw the old system restored after the massacre of two hundred Europeans by Mir Qasim at Patna. He resigned in December 1764, and returned to England, where his reputation prospered. In 1769, he was sent back as second in council at Madras. The company promoted him to governor of Bengal in February 1772.

Vested with supreme authority, Hastings was now expected to repair the troubles of the commercial enterprise that acted in place of an English government in India. Until he took command, the company had suffered from ruinous mismanagement, both in India and at home, but Hastings's regime was a triumph of cynical policy over unorganized corruption. He showed a consistent readiness, where it served the company's interest, to employ bribery and coercion, to undertake wars of systematic plunder with native surrogates, and to resort to every plausible means of self-aggrandizement. The movers of the company in England regarded Hastings as an indispensable presence, and in 1776 a vote by the directors to unseat him was turned back by the Court of Proprietors. On 28 May 1782, the

House of Commons, at the instigation of Burke, voted that it was the duty of the directors to remove Hastings, but the defeat of Fox's East India Bill brought down the Fox-North coalition, and the order was rescinded by the Court of Proprietors.

In the traditions of the East India Company and the British empire, and still today in the writings of many historians, Warren Hastings is remembered as an ambitious and worthy statesman who brought a necessary realism to the enterprise of ruling an empire. And it needs to be said that the display of arbitrary power was never Hastings's preferred method; nor was he universally hated and feared by the natives, as Burke supposed that he was. Yet the vices of his policy sprang from two inseparable premises: first, that the people of India were accustomed to "Oriental despotism," so that Western principles of equity and justice did not apply to them; and second, that he himself as governor, while obliged to serve the people of India, could not but rank them least among his several responsibilities. Before the people of India came the interests of the empire, and before the interests of the empire came those of the East India Company.

Hastings accordingly gave himself the latitude for a warlike policy, wherever he deemed this necessary to protect the company's acquisitions against local or regional chiefs, against French imperial interests, or against the possibility of a coalition between the two. Such a strategy was justified by the moral conventions that Europe then observed in the treatment of colonies, and yet every element of that justification was rejected by Burke: the idea of a natural oriental submissiveness to despotism, which permitted a lower standard of conduct toward Asiatic peoples; the belief that reason-of-state could be employed to warrant preemptive wars by an ascendant power; and the supposition that the welfare of the people need not be uppermost in the conscience of an imperial officer who governed them. In this last respect, Hastings's conduct doubtless recalled to Burke the empire's policy of extracting the maximum of selfish profit from its American colonies. It likewise brought to mind the system of religious exclusion, and of commercial ascendancy and exploitation, which England had imposed on Ireland ever since the invasion of Cromwell. Two years after his "Speech in

Opening," he would mention Hastings and the East India men as a clue to all that was most depraved in the morale of the revolutionists in France. They thought of the entire country as a province they had to subdue.

When Hastings returned to England, in 1785, he was a controversial but a celebrated figure. He expected to be honored and to acquire the personal fortune he had largely refrained from amassing in India. By then, Burke's preparations for impeachment were already far advanced. Various private motives were alleged at the time, and the malicious rumor was circulated that Burke stood to gain financially from his proposed reform of the company. Tucked under this fiction was a grain of fact. Burke, along with his brother Richard and his friend William Burke, had suffered heavy financial losses in 1769 with the sudden depreciation of the company's stock. But the setback had done no more than rivet his attention to India, if it did that; his speeches through the early 1770s sided with the worldly wisdom that favored total autonomy for the company. What eventually turned Burke against the company seems to have been a growing knowledge of Hastings's actions in the Rohilla war (which Burke believed to have been a war of extermination); his forcing of exorbitant tribute from Chait Singh, the Raja of Benares, to pay for the company's war against the confederacy of Hindu chiefs known as the Marathas; and his confiscation of all the domains and treasures of the Begams (the Princesses) of Oudh. By consultation with Philip Francis, an opponent of the governor-general on the five-man Court of Directors in India, Burke was able to form an intimate idea of Hastings's modus operandi.

The tangible result of collaboration with Francis was the *Ninth Report of the Select Committee on India,* written by Burke — a massive inquiry that formed the basis of the impeachment — and there is no reason to doubt Burke's statement of his motives in February 1785, in the "Speech on the Nabob of Arcot's Debts": "Baffled, discountenanced, subdued, discredited, as the cause of justice and humanity is, it will be only the dearer to me. Whoever therefore shall at any time bring before you any thing towards the relief of our distressed fellow-citizens in India, and towards a subversion of the present most corrupt and oppressive system for its government, in me shall find, a weak I am afraid, but a steady, earnest, and faithful assistant." After Burke's four-day "Speech in Opening," in 1788 — of which the exordium and the peroration are given below — many observers felt that the prosecution would prevail. Its chances narrowed with the adoption of restrictive rules on the admission of evidence and the requirement that the managers of the impeachment present their entire case before Hastings was asked to reply. As the cause of Hastings became fashionable, some of the managers lost heart for the enterprise. Burke held on with unswerving tenacity. At the acquittal in 1795, even an anonymous contemporary historian sympathetic to Hastings felt obliged to confess that the ordeal had accomplished something: "It has served, in its commencement, progress, and termination, to define the political situation of this Country with respect to India; to give greater precision to her maxims both of policy and jurisprudence in that country; to ascertain the line of conduct that may be pursued, on various emergencies, by the Civil and Military Officers of the Company and the Crown."

More was at stake than the exposure of a leading officer and delinquent of the empire. The conception of a public "sacred drama" — recently expounded in connection with the United Nations by Conor Cruise O'Brien — helps to explain Burke's purpose here. He remarked in the *Reflections on the Revolution in France* that the theatre may be a better school of moral sentiments than churches; and, for him, the impeachment of Hastings did gradually take on a quality of sacred drama. Its seven years of enactment, after seven of preparation, would make a symbolic and practical testimony of the bond of human solidarity between the governors of the empire and the people over whom they ruled. The process would thus refute the very idea of a "geographical morality" changeable according to local custom and self-interest. In a ceremonial setting of the highest dignity, with the Lords Spiritual, the Temporal Lords, and the Prince of Wales all in attendance, and a seat reserved for the king if he should choose to attend, this trial by the House of Lords of an officer accused by the Commons ideally represented the conscience of Great Britain judging the policy of its servants before the tribunal of "human nature itself."

Speech in Opening the Impeachment
of Warren Hastings, Esq.
First Day, 15th February 1788.

My Lords,

The Gentlemen who have it in command to support the impeachment against Mr. Hastings, have directed me to open the Cause with a general view of the grounds, upon which the Commons have proceeded in their Charge against him. They have directed me to accompany this with another general view of the extent, the magnitude, the nature, the tendency, and the effect of the crimes, which they allege to have been by him committed. They have also directed me to give an explanation (with their aid I may be enabled to give it) of such circumstances, preceding the crimes charged on Mr. Hastings, or concomitant with them, as may tend to elucidate whatever may be found obscure in the Articles as they stand. To these they wished me to add a few illustrative remarks on the laws, customs, opinions, and manners of the People concerned, and who are the objects of the Crimes we charge on Mr. Hastings.

The several Articles, as they appear before you, will be opened by other Gentlemen with more particularity, with more distinctness, and, without doubt, with infinitely more ability, when they come to apply the Evidence, which naturally belongs to each Article of this accusation. This, my Lords, is the plan, which we mean to pursue on the great Charge, which is now to abide your judgment.

My Lords, I must look upon it as an auspicious circumstance to this cause, in which the honour of the kingdom and the fate of many nations are involved, that, from the first commencement of our Parliamentary process to this the hour of solemn Trial, not the smallest difference of opinion has arisen between the two Houses.

My Lords, there are persons, who, looking rather upon what was to be found in our records and histories, than what was to be expected from the publick justice, had formed hopes consolatory to themselves and dishonourable to us. They flattered themselves, that the corruptions of India would escape amidst the dissensions of Parliament. They are disappointed. They will be disappointed in all the rest of their expectations, which they have formed upon every thing, except the merits of their Cause. The Commons will not have the melancholy unsocial glory of having acted a solitary part in a noble, but imperfect, work. What the greatest Inquest of the Nation has begun, its highest Tribunal will accomplish. At length justice will be done in India. It is true, that your Lordships will have your full share in this great achievement; but the Commons have always considered, that whatever honour is divided with you is doubled on themselves.

My Lords, I must confess, that amidst these encouraging prospects the Commons do not approach your Bar without awe and anxiety. The magnitude of the interests, which we have in charge, will reconcile some degree of solicitude for the event with the undoubting confidence, with which we repose ourselves upon your Lordships justice. For we are men, my Lords; and men are so made, that it is not only the greatness of danger, but the value of the adventure, which measures the degree of our concern in every undertaking. I solemnly assure your Lordships, that no standard is sufficient to estimate the value, which the Commons set upon the event of the Cause they now bring before you. My Lords, the business of this day is not the business of this man — it is not solely, whether the Prisoner at the Bar be found innocent, or guilty; but whether millions of mankind shall be made miserable, or happy.

Your Lordships will see in the progress of this Cause, that there is not only a long connected, systematick series of misdemeanours, but an equally connected system of maxims and principles, invented to justify them. Upon both of these you must judge. According to the judgment, that you shall give upon the past transactions in India, inseparably connected as they are with the principles, which support them, the whole character of your future Government in that distant empire is to be unalterably decided. It will take its perpetual tenour, it will receive its final impression, from the stamp of this very hour.

It is not only the interest of India, now the most considerable part of the British Empire, which is concerned, but the credit and honour of the British Nation itself will be decided by this decision. We are to decide by this judgment, whether the crimes of individuals are to be turned into publick guilt and national ignominy; or whether this Nation will convert the very offences, which have thrown a transient shade upon its Government, into something that will reflect a permanent lustre upon the honour, justice, and humanity of this Kingdom.

My Lords, there is another consideration, which augments the solicitude of the Commons, equal to those other two great interests I have stated, those of our Empire and our national character; something, that, if possible, comes more home to the hearts and feelings of every Englishman: I mean, the interests of our Constitution itself, which is deeply involved in the event of this Cause. The future use, and the whole effect, if not the very existence, of the process of an Impeachment of High Crimes and Misdemeanours before the Peers of this Kingdom, upon the Charge of the Commons, will very much be decided by your judgment in this Cause. This Tribunal will be found (I hope it will always be found) too great for petty causes: if it should at the same time be found incompetent to one of the greatest; that is, if little offences, from their minuteness, escape you, and the greatest, from their magnitude, oppress you; it is impossible, that this form of trial should not, in the end, vanish out of the Constitution. For we must not deceive ourselves: whatever does not stand with credit cannot stand long. And if the Constitution should be deprived, I do not mean in form, but virtually, of this resource, it is virtually deprived of everything else, that is valuable in it. For this process is the cement, which binds the whole together; this is the individuating principle, that makes England what England is. In this Court it is, that no subject, in no part of the Empire, can fail of competent and proportionable justice: here it is, that we provide for that, which is the substantial excellence of our Constitution; I mean, the great circulation of responsibility, by which (excepting the supreme power) no man, in no circumstance, can escape the account, which he owes to the laws of his country. It is by this process, that magistracy, which tries and controls all other things, is itself tried and controled. Other constitutions are satisfied with making good subjects; this is a security for good governours. It is by this Tribunal, that statesmen, who abuse their power, are accused by statesmen, and tried by statesmen, not upon the niceties of a narrow jurisprudence, but upon the enlarged and solid principles of state morality. It is here, that those, who by the abuse of power have violated the spirit of law, can never hope for protection from any of its forms: — it is here, that those, who have refused to conform themselves to its perfections, can never hope to escape through any of its defects. It ought, therefore, my Lords, to become our common care to guard this your precious deposit, rare in its use, but powerful in its effect, with a religious vigilance, and never to suffer it to be either discredited or antiquated. For this great end your Lordships are invested with great and plenary powers: but you do not suspend, you do not supersede, you do not annihilate any subordinate jurisdiction; on the contrary, you are auxiliary and supplemental to them all.

Whether it is owing to the felicity of our times, less fertile in great offences, than those, which have gone before us; or whether it is from a sluggish apathy, which has dulled and enervated the publick justice, I am not called upon to determine: but, whatever may be the cause, it is now sixty-three years since any impeachment, grounded upon abuse of authority and misdemeanour in office, has come before this Tribunal. The last is that of Lord Macclesfield, which happened in the year 1725. So that the oldest process known to the Constitution of this Country has, upon its revival, some appearance of novelty. At this time, when all Europe is in a state of, perhaps, contagious fermentation; when antiquity has lost all its reverence and all its effect on the minds of men, at the same time that novelty is still attended with the suspicions, that always will be attached to whatever is new; we have been anxiously careful in a business, which seems to combine the objections both to what is antiquated and what is novel, so to conduct ourselves, that nothing in the revival of this great Parliamentary Process shall afford a pretext for its future disuse.

My Lords, strongly impressed as they are with these sentiments, the Commons have conducted themselves with singular care and caution. Without losing the spirit and zeal of a publick prosecution, they have comported themselves with such moderation, temper, and decorum, as would not have ill become the final judgment, if with them rested the final judgment, of this great Cause.

With very few intermissions, the affairs of India have constantly engaged the attention of the Commons for more than fourteen years. We may safely affirm, we have tried every mode of legislative provision, before we had recourse to any thing of penal process. It was in the year 1774 we framed an Act of Parliament for remedy to the then existing disorders in India, such as the then information before us enabled us to enact. Finding, that the Act of Parliament did not answer all the ends, that were expected from it, we had, in the year 1782, recourse to a body of monitory resolutions. Neither had we the expected fruit from them. When, therefore, we found, that our inquiries and our reports, our laws and our admonitions, were alike despised; that enormities increased in proportion as they were forbidden, detected, and exposed; when we found, that guilt stalked with an erect and upright front, and that legal authority seemed to skulk and hide its head like outlawed guilt; when we found, that some of those very persons, who were appointed by Parliament to assert the authority of the laws of this kingdom, were the most forward, the most bold, and the most active, in the conspiracy for their destruction; then it was time for the justice of the Nation to recollect itself. To have forborn longer would not have been patience, but collusion; it would have been participation with guilt; it would have been to make ourselves accomplices with the criminal.

We found it was impossible to evade painful duty, without betraying a sacred trust. Having, therefore, resolved upon the last and only resource, a penal prosecution, it was our next business to act in a manner worthy of our long deliberation. In all points we proceeded with selection. We have chosen (we trust, it will so appear to your Lordships) such a crime, and such a criminal, and such a body of evidence, and such a mode of process, as would have recommended this course of justice to posterity, even if it had not been supported by any example in the practice of our forefathers.

First, to speak of the process: we are to inform your Lordships, that, besides that long previous deliberation of fourteen years, we examined, as a preliminary to this proceeding, every circumstance, which could prove favourable to parties apparently delinquent, before we finally resolved to prosecute. There was no precedent to be found, in the Journals, favourable to persons in Mr. Hastings's circumstances, that was not applied to. Many measures utterly unknown to former Parliamentary proceedings, and which, indeed, seemed in some degree to enfeeble them, but which were all to the advantage of those, that were to be prosecuted, were adopted, for the first time, upon this occasion. — In an early stage of the proceeding, the Criminal desired to be heard. He was heard; and he produced before the Bar of the House that insolent and unbecoming paper, which lies upon our table. It was deliberately given in by his own hand, and signed with his own name. The Commons, however, passed by every thing offensive in that paper with a magnanimity, that became them. They considered nothing in it, but the facts, that the Defendant alleged, and the principles he maintained; and after a deliberation, not short of judicial, we proceeded with confidence to your Bar.

So far as to the process; which, though I mentioned last in the line and order, in which I stated the objects of our selection, I thought it best to dispatch first.

As to the crime, which we chose, we first considered well what it was in its nature, under all the circumstances, which attended it. We weighed it with all its extenuations, and with all its aggravations. On that review we are warranted to assert, that the crimes, with which we charge the Prisoner at the Bar, are substantial crimes; that they are no errours or mistakes, such as wise and good men might possibly fall into; which may even produce very pernicious effects, without being in fact great offences. The Commons are too liberal, not to allow for the difficulties of a great and arduous publick situation. They know too well the domineering necessities, which frequently occur in all great affairs. They know the exigency of a pressing occasion, which, in its precipitate career, bears every thing down before it, which does not give time to the mind to recollect its faculties, to reinforce its reason, and to have recourse to fixed principles, but, by compelling an instant and tumultuous decision, too often obliges men to decide in a manner, that calm judgment would certainly have rejected. We know, as we are to be served by men, that the persons, who serve us, must be tried as men, and with a very large allowance indeed to human infirmity and human errour. This, my Lords, we knew, and we weighed before we came before you. But the crimes, which we charge in these Articles, are not lapses, defects, errours, of common human frailty, which, as we know and feel, we can allow for. We charge this Offender with no crimes, that have not arisen from passions, which it is criminal to harbour; with no offences, that have not their root in avarice, rapacity, pride, insolence, ferocity, treachery, cruelty, malignity of temper; in short, in nothing, that does not argue a total extinction of all moral principle; that does not manifest an inveterate blackness of heart, died in grain with malice, vitiated, corrupted, gangrened to the very core. If we do not plant his crimes in those vices, which the breast of man is made to abhor, and the spirit of all laws, human and divine, to interdict, we desire no longer to be heard upon this occasion. Let every thing, that can be pleaded on the ground of surprise or errour, upon those grounds be pleaded with success: we give up the whole of those predicaments. We urge no crimes, that were not crimes of forethought. We charge him with nothing, that he did not commit upon deliberation; that he did not commit against advice, supplication, and remonstrance; that he did not commit against the direct command of lawful authority; that he did not commit after reproof and reprimand, the reproof and reprimand of those, who are authorized by the laws to reprove and reprimand him. The crimes of Mr. Hastings are crimes not only in themselves, but aggravated by being crimes of contumacy. They were crimes, not against forms, but against those eternal laws of justice, which are our rule and our birthright. His offences are not, in formal, technical language, but in reality, in substance and effect, *High* Crimes and High Misdemeanours.

So far as to the Crimes. As to the Criminal, we have chosen him on the same principle, on which we selected the crimes. We have not chosen to bring before you a poor, puny, trembling delinquent, misled, perhaps, by those, who ought to have taught him better, but who have afterwards oppressed him by their power, as they had first corrupted him by their example. Instances there have been many, wherein the punishment of minor offences, in inferiour persons, has been made the means of screening crimes of an high order, and in men of high description. Our course is different. We have not brought before you an obscure offender, who, when his insignificance and weakness are weighed against the power of the prosecution, gives even to publick justice something of the appearance of oppression; no, my Lords, we have brought before you the first Man of India in rank, authority, and station. We have brought before you the Chief of the tribe, the Head of the whole body of Eastern offenders; a Captain-general of iniquity, under whom all the fraud, all the peculation, all the tyranny, in India, are embodied, disciplined, arrayed, and paid. This is the person, my Lords, that we bring before you. We have brought before you such a person, that, if you strike at him with the firm and decided arm of justice, you will not have need of a great many more examples. You strike at the whole corps, if you strike at the head.

So far as to the Crime: so far as to the Criminal. Now, my Lords, I shall say a few words relative to the Evidence, which we have brought to support such a Charge, and which ought to be equal in weight to the Charge itself. It is chiefly evidence of record, officially signed by the Criminal himself in many instances. We have brought before you his own letters, authenticated by his own hand. On these we chiefly rely. But we shall likewise bring before you living witnesses, competent to speak to the points, to which they are brought.

When you consider the late enormous power of the Prisoner; when you consider his criminal, indefatigable assiduity in the destruction of all recorded evidence; when you consider the influence he has over almost all living testimony; when you consider the distance of the scene of action; I believe your Lordships, and I believe the world, will be astonished, that so much, so clear, so solid, and so conclusive evidence of all kinds has been obtained against him. I have no doubt, that in nine instances in ten the evidence is such as would satisfy the narrow precision supposed to prevail, and to a degree rightly to prevail, in all subordinate power and delegated jurisdiction. But your Lordships will maintain, what we assert and claim as the right of the subjects of Great Britain — that you are not bound by any rules of evidence, or any other rules whatever, except those of natural, immutable, and substantial justice.

God forbid the Commons should desire, that any thing should be received as proof from them, which is not by nature adapted to prove the thing in question. If they should make such a request, they would aim at overturning the very principles of that justice, to which they resort. They would give the Nation an evil example, that would rebound back on themselves, and bring destruction upon their own heads, and on those of all their posterity.

On the other hand, I have too much confidence in the learning, with which you will be advised, and the liberality and nobleness of the sentiments, with which you are born, to suspect, that you would, by any abuse of the forms, and a technical course of proceeding, deny justice to so great a part of the world, that claims it at your hands. Your Lordships always had an ample power, and almost unlimited jurisdiction; you have now a boundless object. It is not from this district, or from that parish, not from this city, or the other province, that relief is now applied for: exiled and undone princes, extensive tribes, suffering nations, infinite descriptions of men, different in language, in manners, and in rites — men, separated by every barrier of nature from you, by the providence of God are blended in one common cause, and are now become suppliants at your Bar. For the honour of this Nation, in vindication of this mysterious providence, let it be known, that no rule formed upon municipal maxims (if any such rule exists) will prevent the course of that imperial justice, which you owe to the people, that call to you from all parts of a great disjointed world. For, situated as this kingdom is, an object, thank God, of envy to the rest of the nations; its conduct in that high and elevated situation will undoubtedly be scrutinized with a severity as great as its power is invidious.

It is well known, that enormous wealth has poured into this country from India through a thousand channels, publick and concealed; and it is no particular derogation from our honour to suppose a possibility of being corrupted by that, by which other empires have been corrupted, and assemblies, almost as respectable and venerable as your Lordships, have been directly or indirectly vitiated. Forty millions of money, at least, have within our memory been brought from India into England. In this case the most sacred judicature ought to look to its reputation. Without offence we may venture to suggest, that the best way to secure reputation is, not by a proud defiance of publick opinion, but by guiding our actions in such a manner, as that publick opinion may in the end be securely defied, by having been previously respected and dreaded. No direct false judgment is apprehended from the Tribunals of this country. But it is feared, that partiality may lurk and nestle in the abuse of our forms of proceeding. It is necessary, therefore, that nothing in that proceeding should appear to mark the slightest trace, should betray the faintest odour, of chicane. God forbid, that, when you try the most serious of all causes, that when you try the cause of Asia in the presence of Europe, there should be the least suspicion, that a narrow partiality, utterly destructive of justice, should so guide us, that a British Subject in power should appear in substance to possess rights, which are denied to the humble allies, to the attached dependents of this kingdom, who by their distance have a double demand upon your protection, and who, by an implicit (I hope not a weak and useless) trust in you, have stripped themselves of every other resource under heaven.

I do not say this from any fear, doubt, or hesitation, concerning what your Lordships will finally do, none in the world; but I cannot shut my ears to the rumours, which you all know to be disseminated abroad. The abusers of power may have a chance to cover themselves by those fences and intrenchments, which were made to secure the liberties of the people against men of that very description. But God forbid it should be bruited from Pekin to Paris, that the Laws of England are for the rich and the powerful; but to the poor, the miserable, and defenceless, they afford no resource at all. God forbid it should be said, no nation is equal to the English in *substantial* violence and in *formal* justice — that in this kingdom we feel ourselves competent to confer the most extravagant and inordinate powers upon publick ministers, but that we are deficient, poor, helpless, lame, and impotent in the means of calling them to account for their use of them. An opinion has been insidiously circulated through this kingdom, and through foreign nations, too, that, in order to cover our participation in guilt, and our common interest in the plunder of the East, we have invented a set of scholastick distinctions, abhorrent to the common sense, and unpropitious to the common necessities, of mankind; by which we are to deny ourselves the knowledge of what the rest of the world knows, and what so great a part of the world both knows and feels. I do not deprecate any appearance, which may give countenance to this aspersion, from suspicion, that any corrupt motive can influence this Court; I deprecate it from knowing, that hitherto we have moved within the narrow circle of municipal justice. I am afraid, that, from the habits acquired by moving within a circumscribed sphere, we may be induced rather to endeavour at forcing nature into that municipal circle, than to enlarge the circle of national justice to the necessities of the Empire we have obtained.

This is the only thing, which does create any doubt or difficulty in the minds of sober people. But there are those, who will not judge so equitably. Where two motives, neither of them perfectly justifiable, may be assigned, the worst has the chance of being preferred. If, from any appearance of chicane in the Court, justice should fail, all men will say, better there were no tribunals at all. In my humble opinion, it would be better a thousand times to give all complainants the short answer the Dey of Algiers gave a British Ambassadour, representing certain grievances suffered by the British merchants, — "My friend," (as the story is related by Dr. Shawe) "do not you know, that my subjects are a band of robbers, and that I am their captain?"[1] — better it would be a thousand times, and a thousand thousand times more manly, than an hypocritical process, which, under a pretended reverence to punctilious ceremonies and observances of law, abandons mankind, without help and resource, to all the desolating consequences of arbitrary power. The conduct and event of this Cause will put an end to such doubts, wherever they may be entertained. Your Lordships will exercise the great plenary powers, with which you are invested, in a manner, that will do honour to the protecting justice of this kingdom, that will completely avenge the great people, who are subjected to it. You will not suffer your proceedings to be squared by any rules, but by

1 Thomas Shaw (1694–1751), *Travels or Observations relating to Several Parts of Barbary and the Levant.*

their necessities, and by that law of a common nature, which cements them to us, and us to them. The reports to the contrary have been spread abroad with uncommon industry; but they will be speedily refuted by the humanity, simplicity, dignity, and nobleness of your Lordships justice.

*   *   *   *   *

FOURTH DAY, 18TH FEBRUARY 1788

My Lords, I do not mean now to go further, than just to remind your Lordships of this, that Mr. Hastings's government was one whole system of oppression, of robbery of individuals, of destruction of the publick, and of supersession of the whole system of the English government, in order to vest in the worst of the natives all the powers, that could possibly exist in any government; in order to defeat the ends, which all governments ought in common to have in view. Thus, my Lords, I show you, at one point of view, what you are to expect from him in all the rest. I have, I think, made out as clear as can be to your Lordships, so far as it was necessary to go, that his bribery and peculation was not occasional, but habitual; that it was not urged upon him at the moment, but was regular and systematick. I have shown to your Lordships the operation of such a system on the revenues.

My Lords, Mr. Hastings pleads one constant merit to justify those acts; namely, that they produce an increase of the publick revenue; and accordingly he never sells to any of those wicked agents any trusts whatever in the country, that you do not hear, that it will considerably tend to the increase of the revenue. — Your Lordships will see, when he sold to wicked men the province of Bahar in the same way, in which Debi Sing had this province of Dinagepore, that consequences of a horrid and atrocious nature (though not to so great an extent) followed from it. I will just beg leave to state to your Lordships, that the kingdom of Bahar is annexed to the kingdom of Bengal; that this kingdom was governed by another provincial council; that he turned out that provincial council, and sold that government to two wicked men, — one of no fortune at all, and the other of a very suspicious fortune; one a total bankrupt, the other justly excommunicated for his wickedness in his country, and then in prison for misdemeanors in a subordinate situation of government.

Mr. Hastings destroyed the council, that imprisoned him; and, instead of putting one of the best and most reputable of the natives to govern it, he takes out of prison this excommunicated wretch, hated by God and man, — this bankrupt, this man of evil and desperate character, this mismanager of the publick revenue in an inferiour station: and, as he had given Bengal to Gunga Govin Sing, he gave this province to Rajahs Kelleram, and Cullian Sing.

It was done upon this principle, that they would increase, and very much better, the revenue. These men seemed to be as strange instruments for improving a revenue as ever were chosen, I suppose, since the world began. Perhaps their merit was giving a bribe of 40,000*l.* to Mr. Hastings. How he disposed of it, I don't know. He says, I disposed of it to the publick, and it was in a case of emergency. You will see in the course of this business the falsehood of that pretence; for you will see, though the obligation is given for it as a round sum of money, that the payment was not accomplished till a year after; that therefore it could not answer any immediate exigence of the Company. Did it answer to an increase of the revenue? — The very reverse. Those persons, who had given this bribe of 40,000*l.* at the end of that year were found 80,000*l.* in debt to the Company. The Company always loses, when Mr. Hastings takes a bribe; and, when he proposes an increase of the revenue, the Company loses often double. But I hope, and trust, your Lordships will consider this idea of a monstrous rise of rent, given by men of desperate fortunes and characters, to be one of the grievances instead of one of the advantages of this system.

It has been necessary to lay these facts before you (and I have stated them to your Lordships far short of their reality, partly through my infirmity, and partly on account of the odiousness of the task of going through things, that disgrace human nature) that you may be enabled fully to enter into the dreadful consequences, which attend a system of bribery and corruption in a Governour General. On a transient view, bribery is rather a subject of disgust than horrour; the sordid practice of a venal, mean and abject mind; and the effect of the crime seems to end with the act. It looks to be no more than the corrupt transfer of property from one person to another; at worst a theft. But it will appear in a very different light, when you regard the consideration, for which the bribe is given; namely, that a Governour General, claiming an arbitrary power in himself, for that consideration delivers up the properties, the liberties, and the lives of an whole people to the arbitrary discretion of any wicked and rapacious person, who will be sure to make good from their blood the purchase he has paid for his power over them. It is possible, that a man may pay a bribe merely to redeem himself from some evil. It is bad however to live under a power, whose violence has no restraint except in its avarice. But no man ever paid a bribe for a power to charge and tax others, but with a view to oppress them. No man ever paid a bribe for the handling of the publick money, but to peculate from it. When once such offices become thus privately and corruptly venal, the very worst men will be chosen (as Mr. Hastings has in fact constantly chosen the very worst,) because none but these, who do not scruple the use of any means, are capable, consistently with profit, to discharge at once the rigid demands of a severe publick revenue, and the private bribes of a rapacious chief magistrate. Not only the worst men will be thus chosen, but they will be restrained by no dread whatsoever in the execution of their worst oppressions. Their protection is sure. The authority, that is to restrain, to control, to punish them, is previously engaged; he has his retaining fee for the support of their crimes. Mr. Hastings never dared, because he could not, arrest oppression in its course, without drying up the source of his own corrupt emolument. Mr. Hastings never dared, after the fact, to punish extortion in others, because he could not, without risking the discovery of bribery in himself. The same corruption, the same oppression, and the same impunity will reign through all the subordinate gradations.

A fair revenue may be collected without the aid of wicked, violent, and unjust instruments. But, when once the line of just and legal demand is transgressed, such instruments are of absolute necessity; and they comport themselves accordingly. When we know, that men must be well paid (and they ought to be well paid) for the performance of honourable duty, can we think, that men will be found to commit wicked, rapacious, and oppressive acts with fidelity and disinterestedness, for the sole emolument of dishonest employers? No; they must have their full share of the prey, and the greater share as they are the nearer and more necessary instruments of the general extortion. We must not therefore flatter ourselves, when Mr. Hastings takes 40,000*l.* in bribes for Dinagepore and its annexed provinces, that from the people nothing more than 40,000*l.* is extorted. I speak within compass, four times forty must be levied on the people; and these violent sales, fraudulent purchases, confiscations, inhuman and unutterable tortures, imprisonment, irons, whips, fines, general despair, general insurrection, the massacre of the officers of revenue by the people, the massacre of the people by the soldiery, and the total waste and destruction of the finest provinces in India, are things of course; and all a necessary consequence involved in the very substance of Mr. Hastings's bribery.

I, therefore, charge Mr. Hastings with having destroyed, for private purposes, the whole system of government by the six provincial councils, which he had no right to destroy.

I charge him with having delegated to others that power, which the act of parliament had directed him to preserve unalienably in himself.

I charge him with having formed a committee to be mere instruments and tools, at the enormous expense of 62,000*l.* per annum.

I charge him with having appointed a person their Dewan, to whom these Englishmen were to be subservient tools; whose name, to his own knowledge, was by the general voice of India, by the general recorded voice of the Company, by recorded official transactions, by every thing, that can make a man known, abhorred, and detested, stamped with infamy; and with giving him the whole power, which he had thus separated from the Council General, and from the provincial councils.

I charge him with taking bribes of Gunga Govin Sing.

I charge him with not having done that bribe-service, which fidelity even in iniquity requires at the hands of the worst of men.

I charge him with having robbed those people, of whom he took the bribes.

I charge him with having fraudulently alienated the fortunes of widows.

I charge him with having, without right, title, or purchase, taken the lands of orphans, and given them to wicked persons under him.

I charge him with having removed the natural guardians of a minor Rajah, and with having given that trust to a stranger, Debi Sing, whose wickedness was known to himself and all the world; and by whom the Rajah, his family, and dependents were cruelly oppressed.

I charge him with having committed to the management of Debi Sing three great provinces; and thereby, with having wasted the country, ruined the landed interest, cruelly harassed the peasants, burnt their houses, seized their crops, tortured and degraded their persons, and destroyed the honour of the whole female race of that country.

In the name of the Commons of England, I charge all this villany upon Warren Hastings, in this last moment of my application to you.

My Lords, what is it, that we want here to a great act of national justice? Do we want a cause, my Lords? You have the cause of oppressed princes, of undone women of the first rank, of desolated provinces, and of wasted kingdoms.

Do you want a criminal, my Lords? When was there so much iniquity ever laid to the charge of any one? — No, my Lords, you must not look to punish any other such delinquent from India. —

Warren Hastings has not left substance enough in India to nour-
ish such another delinquent.

My Lords, is it a prosecutor you want? — You have before you
the Commons of Great Britain as prosecutors; and, I believe, my
Lords, that the sun, in his beneficent progress round the world,
does not behold a more glorious sight than that of men, separated from a remote people by the material bounds and barriers
of nature, united by the bond of a social and moral community; — all the Commons of England resenting, as their own, the
indignities and cruelties, that are offered to all the people of
India.

Do we want a tribunal? My Lords, no example of antiquity,
nothing in the modern world, nothing in the range of human
imagination, can supply us with a tribunal like this. My Lords,
here we see virtually in the mind's eye that sacred majesty of the
crown, under whose authority you sit, and whose power you
exercise. We see in that invisible authority, what we all feel in
reality and life, the beneficent powers and protecting justice of
His Majesty. We have here the heir apparent to the crown, such
as the fond wishes of the people of England wish an heir apparent of the crown to be. We have here all the branches of the royal
family in a situation between majesty and subjection, between
the sovereign and the subject, — offering a pledge in that situation for the support of the rights of the crown, and the liberties
of the people, both which extremities they touch. My Lords, we
have a great hereditary Peerage here; those, who have their own
honour, the honour of their ancestors, and of their posterity, to
guard; and who will justify, as they have always justified, that
provision in the Constitution, by which justice is made an hereditary office. My Lords, we have here a new nobility, who have
risen, and exalted themselves by various merits, by great military
services, which have extended the fame of this country from the
rising to the setting sun: we have those, who by various civil
merits and various civil talents have been exalted to a situation,
which they well deserve, and in which they will justify the favour

of their sovereign, and the good opinion of their fellow subjects; and make them rejoice to see those virtuous characters, that were the other day upon a level with them, now exalted above them in rank, but feeling with them in sympathy what they felt in common with them before. We have persons exalted from the practice of the law, from the place, in which they administered high, though subordinate, justice, to a seat here, to enlighten with their knowledge, and to strengthen with their votes those principles, which have distinguished the courts, in which they have presided.

My Lords, you have here also the lights of our religion; you have the Bishops of England. My Lords, you have that true image of the primitive Church in its ancient form, in its ancient ordinances, purified from the superstitions and the vices, which a long succession of ages will bring upon the best institutions. You have the representatives of that religion, which says, that their God is love, that the very vital spirit of their institution is charity; a religion, which so much hates oppression, that, when the God, whom we adore, appeared in human form, he did not appear in a form of greatness and majesty, but in sympathy with the lowest of the people, — and thereby made it a firm and ruling principle, that their welfare was the object of all government; since the person, who was the Master of Nature, chose to appear himself in a subordinate position. These are the considerations, which influence them, which animate them, and will animate them, against all oppression; knowing, that He, who is called first among them, and first among us all, both of the flock, that is fed, and of those, who feed it, made Himself "the servant of all."

My Lords, these are the securities, which we have in all the constituent parts of the body of this House. We know them, we reckon, we rest upon them, and commit safely the interests of India and of humanity into your hands. Therefore, it is with confidence, that, ordered by the Commons,

I impeach Warren Hastings, Esquire, of High Crimes and Misdemeanors.

I impeach him in the name of the Commons of Great Britain in Parliament assembled, whose parliamentary trust he has betrayed.

I impeach him in the name of all the Commons of Great Britain, whose national character he has dishonoured.

I impeach him in the name of the people of India, whose laws, rights, and liberties he has subverted; whose properties he has destroyed, whose country he has laid waste and desolate.

I impeach him in the name, and by virtue, of those eternal laws of justice, which he has violated.

I impeach him in the name of human nature itself, which he has cruelly outraged, injured, and oppressed in both sexes, in every age, rank, situation, and condition of life.

To Charles-Jean-François Depont
(November 1789)

Because *Reflections on the Revolution in France* is already a long title, people sometimes forget the rest of it: *and on the proceedings in certain societies in London relative to that event: in a letter intended to have been sent to a gentleman in Paris.* Charles-Jean-François Depont was the gentleman and this letter the germ of the *Reflections.* Depont had visited Burke in 1785 and had come away with warm admiration of his powers as a champion of liberty. Elected in September 1789 to the *comité patriotique* of Metz, he wrote to Burke in early November to ask for his thoughts on the prospects of liberty in France.

The date is important. By the time he received Depont's letter, more than one crisis had sharpened Burke's suspicion about the changes this revolution might bring: the declaration by the Third Estate that it alone was the nation, which ruled out a mixed constitution balanced by the nobility and the clergy; the destruction of the Bastille, and the exhilarated putting-to-death of several officials, which showed the power of the Paris crowd in the streets to overwhelm the king's soldiers and its disposition to enforce its will by violence; and the forcible removal of the king and queen from Versailles to Paris, which exposed the hollowness of the understanding that the monarch was an autonomous partner in the new regime. An innovation that would prove decisive in hardening Burke's opposition was still to come: the appropriation of church lands by the revolutionary state and the subjection of the clergy to a civil oath.

This letter, with greater compression than the book it became and an eloquence less heated by rhapsody, explains Burke's conviction that liberty is a habit. Like other habits it becomes customary only over time. It is not an abstract principle that can be grafted onto a foreign people by the cunning and resolution of a few paramount minds. The liberty Burke cares for is rather a social good "secured by equality of restraint," a "constitution of things" in which no person or group is permitted to trespass on the liberty of another. The will of no person or group, not even the "general will," can ever be permitted to set itself above reason and justice. As an advocate of a mixed constitutional system, Burke relies on the deliberative freedom of assemblies for protection against the fury of the people and the threat of irregular justice. He here restates his belief, familiar from the "Speech on Conciliation," that the benefits and harms of any system ought to be judged circumstantially: "Nothing is good, but in proportion and with reference." This does not mean that compromise and piecemeal adjustment will always suffice to correct an oppressive social order. "One form of government may be better than another," and "a positively vicious and abusive government ought to be changed." But a statesman needs to be aware of the mixture of "checks" — safeguards whose utility is unforeseeable — which operate in the most apparently trivial practices. The anachronisms, the imperfections, the self-contradictions of a system, by impeding a unified social design may stand effectively in the way of despotism. By contrast, the striving to perfect a social contract may lead to "tearing to pieces the whole contexture of the commonwealth": the ends in prospect are so perfectly desirable that they may be used to justify any means. Burke urges his friend to act with a view of the immediate means, and their immediate good and evil, as an unsurpassable guide to the character of political ends. Courage, in some settings, is "to dare to be fearful, when all about you are full of presumption and confidence." Burke closes on this warning, without any detailed suggestion of policy; practical wisdom in any event belongs to people on the scene who are part of the daily discussions and maneuvering.

He evidently held the letter for several weeks before sending it.

To Charles-Jean-François Depont

(November 1789)

DEAR SIR,

We are extremely happy in your giving us leave to promise ourselves a renewal of the pleasure we formerly had in your company at Beconsfield and in London. It was too lively to be speedily forgotten on our part; and we are highly flattered to find that you keep so exactly in your memory all the particulars of the few attentions which you were so good to accept from us during your stay in England. We indulge ourselves in the hope that you will be able to execute what you intend in our favour; and that we shall be more fortunate in the coming spring, than we were in the last.

You have reason to imagine that I have not been as early as I ought, in acquainting you with my thankful acceptance of the correspondence you have been pleased to offer. Do not think me insensible to the honour you have done me. I confess I did hesitate for a time, on a doubt, whether it would be prudent to yield to my earnest desire of such a correspondence.

Your frank and ingenuous manner of writing would be ill answered by a cold, dry, and guarded reserve on my part. It would, indeed, be adverse to my habits and my nature, to make use of that sort of caution in my intercourse with any friend. Besides, as you are pleased to think that your splendid flame of liberty was first lighted up at my faint and glimmering taper, I thought you had a right to call upon me for my undisguised sentiments on whatever related to that subject. On the other hand, I was not without apprehension, that in this free mode of intercourse I might say something, not only disagreeable to your formed opinions upon points on which, of all others, we are most impatient of contradiction, but not pleasing to the power which should happen to be prevalent at the time of your receiving my letter. I was well aware that, in seasons of jealousy, suspicion is vigilant and active; that it is not extremely scrupulous in its means of inquiry; not perfectly equitable in its judgments; and not altogether deliberate in its resolutions. In the ill-connected and inconclusive logic of the passions, whatever may appear blameable is easily transferred from the guilty writer to the innocent receiver. It is an awkward as well as unpleasant accident; but it is one that has sometimes happened. A man may be made a martyr to tenets the most opposite to his own. At length a friend of mine, lately come from Paris, informed me that heats are beginning to abate, and that intercourse is thought to be more safe. This has given me some courage; and the reflection that the sentiments of a person of no more consideration than I am, either abroad or at home, could be of little consequence to the success of any cause or any party, has at length decided me to accept of the honour you are willing to confer upon me.

You may easily believe, that I have had my eyes turned, with great curiosity, to the astonishing scene now displayed in France. It has certainly given rise in my mind to many reflections, and to some emotions. These are natural and unavoidable; but it would ill become me to be too ready in forming a positive opinion upon matters transacted in a country, with the correct political map of which I must be very imperfectly acquainted. Things, indeed, have already happened so much beyond the scope of all speculation, that persons of infinitely more sagacity than I am, ought to be ashamed of any thing like confidence in their reasoning upon the operation of any principle, or the effect of any measure. It would become me, least of all, to be so confident, who ought, at my time of life, to have well learned the important lesson of self-distrust, — a lesson of no small value in company with the best information, but which alone can make any sort of amends for our not having learned other lessons so well as it was our business to learn them. I beg you, once for all, to apply this corrective of the diffidence I have, on my own judgment, to whatever I may happen to say with more positiveness than suits my knowledge and situation. If I should seem any where to express myself in the language of disapprobation, be so good as to consider it as no more than the expression of doubt.

You hope, sir, that I think the French deserving of liberty. I certainly do. I certainly think that all men who desire it, deserve it. It is not the reward of our merit, or the acquisition of our industry. It is our inheritance. It is the birthright of our species. We cannot forfeit our right to it, but by what forfeits our title to the privileges of our kind. I mean the abuse, or oblivion, of our rational faculties, and a ferocious indocility which makes us prompt to wrong and violence, destroys our social nature, and transforms us into something little better than the description of wild beasts. To men so degraded, a state of strong constraint is a sort of necessary substitute for freedom; since, bad as it is, it may deliver them in some measure from the worst of all slavery, — that is, the despotism of their own blind and brutal passions.

You have kindly said, that you began to love freedom from your intercourse with me. Permit me then to continue our conversation, and to tell you what the freedom is that I love, and that to which I think all men entitled. This is the more necessary, because, of all the loose terms in the world, liberty is the most indefinite. It is not solitary, unconnected, individual, selfish liberty, as if every man was to regulate the whole of his conduct by his own will. The liberty I mean is *social* freedom. It is that state of things in which liberty is secured by the equality of restraint. A constitution of things in which the liberty of no one man, and no body of men, and no number of men, can find means to trespass on the liberty of any person, or any description of persons, in the society. This kind of liberty is, indeed, but another name for justice; ascertained by wise laws, and secured by well-constructed institutions. I am sure that liberty, so incorporated, and in a manner identified with justice, must be infinitely dear to every one who is capable of conceiving what it is. But whenever a separation is made between liberty and justice, neither is, in my opinion, safe. I do not believe that men ever did submit, certain I am that they never ought to have submitted, to the arbitrary pleasure of one man; but, under circumstances in which the arbitrary pleasure of many persons in the community pressed with an intolerable hardship upon the just and equal rights of their fellows, such a choice might be made, as among evils. The moment *will* is set above reason and justice, in any community, a great question may arise in sober minds, in what part or portion of the community that dangerous dominion of *will* may be the least mischievously placed.

If I think all men who cultivate justice, entitled to liberty, and, when joined in states, entitled to a constitution framed to perpetuate and secure it, you may be assured, sir, that I think your countrymen eminently worthy of a blessing which is peculiarly adapted to noble, generous, and humane natures. Such I found the French, when, more than fifteen years ago, I had the happiness, though but for too short a time, of visiting your country; and I trust their character is not altered since that period.

I have nothing to check my wishes towards the establishment of a solid and rational scheme of liberty in France. On the subject of the relative power of nations, I may have my prejudices; but I envy internal freedom, security, and good order, to none. When, therefore, I shall learn that, in France, the citizen, by whatever description he is qualified, is in a perfect state of legal security, with regard to his life, — to his property, — to the uncontrolled disposal of his person, — to the free use of his industry and his faculties; — When I hear that he is protected in the beneficial enjoyment of the estates to which, by the course of settled law, he was born, or is provided with a fair compensation for them; — that he is maintained in the full fruition of the advantages belonging to the state and condition of life in which he had lawfully engaged himself, or is supplied with a substantial, equitable equivalent; — When I am assured that a simple citizen may decently express his sentiments upon public affairs, without hazard to his life, or safety, even though against a predominant and fashionable opinion; — When I know all this of France, I shall be as well pleased as every one must be, who has not forgot the general communion of mankind, nor lost his natural sympathy in local and accidental connexions.

If a constitution is settled in France upon those principles, and calculated for those ends, I believe there is no man in this country whose heart and voice would not go along with you. I am sure it will give me, for one, a heartfelt pleasure when I hear, that, in France, the great public assemblies, the natural securities for individual freedom, are perfectly free themselves; — when there can be no suspicion that they are under the coercion of a military power of any description; — when it may be truly said, that no armed force can be seen, which is not called into existence by their creative voice, and which must not instantly disappear at their dissolving word; — when such assemblies, after being freely chosen, shall proceed with the weight of magistracy, and not with the arts of candidates; — when they do not find themselves under the necessity of feeding one part of the community at the grievous charge of other parts, as necessitous as those who are so fed; — when they are not obliged (in order to flatter those who have their lives in their disposal) to tolerate acts of doubtful influence on commerce and on agriculture, and for the sake of a precarious relief under temporary scarcity, to sow (if I may be allowed the expression) the seeds of lasting want; — when they are not compelled daily to stimulate an irregular and juvenile imagination for supplies, which they are not in a condition firmly to demand; — when they are not obliged to diet the state from hand to mouth, upon the casual alms of choice, fancy, vanity, or caprice, on which plan the value of the object to the public which receives, often bears no sort of proportion to the loss of the individual who gives; — when they are not necessitated to call for contributions to be estimated on the conscience of the contributor, by which the most pernicious sorts of exemptions and immunities may be established, by which virtue is taxed and vice privileged, and honour and public spirit are obliged to bear the burdens of craft, selfishness, and avarice; — when they shall not be driven to be the instruments of the violence of others, from a sense of their own weakness, and from a want of authority to assess equal and proportioned charges upon all, they are not compelled to lay a strong hand upon the entire possessions of a part;—when, under the exigencies of the state, (aggravated, if not caused, by the imbecility of their own government, and of all government,) they are not obliged to resort to *confiscation* to supply the defect of *taxation*, and thereby to hold out a pernicious example, to teach the different descriptions of the community to prey upon one another;—when they abstain religiously from all general and extrajudicial declarations concerning the property of the subject;—when they look with horror upon all arbitrary decisions in their legislative capacity, striking at prescriptive right, long undisturbed possession, opposing an uninterrupted stream of regular judicial determinations, by which sort of decisions they are conscious no man's possession could be safe, and individual property, to the very idea, would be extinguished;—when I see your great sovereign bodies, your now supreme power, in this condition of deliberative freedom, and guided by these or similar principles in acting and forbearing, I shall be happy to behold in assemblies whose name is venerable to my understanding and dear to my heart, an authority, a dignity, and a moderation, which in all countries and governments, ought ever to accompany the collected reason and representative majesty of the commonwealth.

I shall rejoice no less in seeing a judicial power established in France, correspondent to such a legislature as I have presumed to hint at, and worthy to second it in its endeavours to secure the freedom and property of the subject. When your courts of justice shall obtain an ascertained condition, before they are made to decide on the condition of other men;—when they shall not be called upon to take cognizance of public offences, whilst they themselves are considered only to exist as a tolerated abuse;—when, under doubts of the legality of their rules of decision, their forms and modes of proceeding, and even of the validity of that system of authority to which they owe their existence;—when, amidst circumstances of suspense, fear, and humiliation, they shall not be put to judge on the lives, liberties, properties, or estimation of their fellow-citizens;—when they are not called upon to put any man to his trial upon undefined crimes of state, not ascertained by any previous rule, statute, or course of precedent; — when victims shall not be snatched from the fury of the people, to be brought before a tribunal, itself subject to the effects of the same fury, and where the acquittal of the parties accused might only place the judge in the situation of the criminal; — when I see tribunals placed in this state of independence of every thing but law, and with a clear law for their direction, — as a true lover of equal justice, (under the shadow of which alone true liberty can live,) I shall rejoice in seeing such a happy order established in France, as much as I do in my consciousness that an order of the same kind, or one not very remote from it, has been long settled, and I hope on a firm foundation, in England. I am not so narrowminded as to be unable to conceive that the same object may be attained in many ways, and perhaps in ways very different from those which we have followed in this country. If this real *practical* liberty, with a government powerful to protect, impotent to invade it, be established, or is in a fair train of being established in the democracy, or rather collection of democracies, which seem to be chosen for the future frame of society in France, it is not my having long enjoyed a sober share of freedom, under a qualified monarchy, that shall render me incapable of admiring and praising your system of republics. I shall rejoice, even though England should hereafter be reckoned only as one among the happy nations, and should no longer retain her proud distinction, her monopoly of fame for a practical constitution, in which the grand secret had been found of reconciling a government of real energy for all foreign and domestic purposes, with the most perfect security to the liberty and safety of individuals. The government, whatever its name or form may be, that shall be found substantially and practically to unite these advantages, will most merit the applause of all discerning men.

But if (for in my present want of information I must only speak hypothetically), neither your great assemblies, nor your judicatures, nor your municipalities, act, and forbear to act, in the particulars, upon the principles, and in the spirit that I have stated, I must delay my congratulations on your acquisition of liberty. You may have made a revolution, but not a reformation. You may have subverted monarchy, but not recovered freedom.

You see, sir, that I have merely confined myself in my few observations on what has been done and is doing in France, to the topics of the liberty, property, and safety of the subjects. I have not said much on the influence of the present measures upon your country as a state. It is not my business, as a citizen of the world; and it is unnecessary to take up much time about it, as it is sufficiently visible.

You are now to live in a new order of things, under a plan of government of which no man can speak from experience. Your talents, your public spirit, and your fortune, give you fair pretensions to a considerable share of it. Your settlement may be at hand; but that it is still at some distance, is more likely. The French may be yet to go through more transmigrations. They may pass, as one of our poets says, "through many varieties of untried being,"[1] before their state obtains its final form. In that progress through chaos and darkness, you will find it necessary (at all times it is more or less so) to fix rules to keep your life and conduct in some steady course. You have theories enough concerning the rights of men. It may not be amiss to add a small degree of attention to their nature and disposition. It is with man in the concrete, it is with common human life and human actions you are to be concerned. I have taken so many liberties with you, that I am almost got the length of venturing to suggest something which may appear in the assuming tone of advice. You will, however, be so good as to receive my very few hints with your usual indulgence, though some of them, I confess, are not in the taste of this enlightened age; and, indeed, are no better than the late ripe fruit of mere experience. — Never wholly separate in your mind the merits of any political question from the men who are concerned in it. You will be told, that if a measure is good, what have you to do with the character and views of those who bring it forward. But designing men never separate their plans from their

1 Addison, *Cato* 5.1.11.

interests; and if you assist them in their schemes, you will find the pretended good in the end thrown aside or perverted, and the interested object alone compassed, and that, perhaps, through your means. The power of bad men is no indifferent thing.

At this moment you may not perceive the full sense of this rule, but you will recollect it when the cases are before you; you will then see and find its use. It will often keep your virtue from becoming a tool of the ambition and ill designs of others. Let me add what I think has some connexion with the rule I mentioned: that you ought not to be so fond of any political object, as not to think the means of compassing it a serious consideration. No man is less disposed than I am to put you under the tuition of a petty pedantic scruple in the management of arduous affairs. All I recommend is, that whenever the sacrifice of any subordinate point of morality, or of honour, or even of common liberal sentiment and feeling is called for, one ought to be tolerably sure that the object is worth it. Nothing is good, but in proportion and with reference. There are several who give an air of consequence to very petty designs and actions, by the crimes through which they make their way to their objects. Whatever is obtained smoothly and by easy means appears of no value in their eyes. But when violent methods are in agitation, one ought to be pretty clear, that there are no others to which we can resort, and that a predilection from character to such methods is not the true cause of their being proposed. The state was reformed by Sylla and by Cæsar; but the Cornelian law and the Julian law were not worth the proscription. The pride of the Roman nobility deserved a check; but I cannot, for that reason, admire the conduct of Cinna, and Marius, and Saturninus.[2]

I admit that evils may be so very great and urgent that other evils are to be submitted to for the mere hope of their removal. A

2 Marius, "the People's general" and a notable military reformer; Saturninus, a demagogic tribune briefly successful in attempts to limit the power of the Senate; and Cinna, a consul not averse to corrupt methods who gave a larger share in the empire to newly enfranchised citizens — all here seen as currying favor with the populace in actions between 119 and 84 B.C.

war, for instance, may be necessary, and we know what are the
rights of war, but before we use those rights, we ought to be
clearly in the state which alone can justify them; and not, in the
very fold of peace and security, by a bloody sophistry, to act
towards any persons at once as citizens and as enemies, and,
without the necessary formalities and evident distinctive lines of
war, to exercise upon our countrymen the most dreadful of all
hostilities. Strong party contentions, and a very violent opposition to our desires and opinions, are not war, nor can justify any
one of its operations.

One form of government may be better than another; and
this difference may be worth a struggle. I think so. I do not mean
to treat any of those forms which are often the contrivances of
deep human wisdom (not the rights of men, as some people, in
my opinion, not very wisely, talk of them) with slight or disrespect; nor do I mean to level them.

A positively vicious and abusive government ought to be
changed, and if necessary, by violence, if it cannot be (as sometimes it is the case) reformed: but when the question is concerning the more or the less *perfection* in the organization of a government, the allowance to *means* is not of so much latitude. There is,
by the essential fundamental constitution of things, a radical
infirmity in all human contrivances, and the weakness is often so
attached to the very perfection of our political mechanism, that
some defect in it, something that stops short of its principle,
something that controls, that mitigates, that moderates it, becomes a necessary corrective to the evils that the theoretic perfection would produce. I am pretty sure it often is so, and this
truth may be exemplified abundantly.

It is true that every defect is not of course such a corrective as I
state; but supposing it is not, an imperfect good is still a good; the
defect may be tolerable, and may be removed at some future
time. In that case, prudence (in all things a virtue, in politics the
first of virtues,) will lead us rather to acquiesce in some qualified
plan that does not come up to the full perfection of the abstract
idea, than to push for the more perfect, which cannot be attained

without tearing to pieces the whole contexture of the common-wealth, and creating a heart-ache in a thousand worthy bosoms. In that case, combining the means and end, the less perfect is the more desirable. The *means* to any end being first in order, are *immediate* in their good or their evil, they are always, in a manner, *certainties*. The *end* is doubly problematical; first, whether it is to be attained; then, whether, supposing it attained, we obtain the true object we sought for.

But allow it in any degree probable, that theoretic and practi-cal perfection may differ, that an object pure and absolute may not be so good as one lowered, mixed, and qualified, then, what we abate in our demand in favour of moderation and justice and tenderness to individuals, would be neither more nor less than a real improvement which a wise legislator would make if he had no collateral motive whatsoever, and only looked in the formation of his scheme, to its own independent ends and purposes. Would it then be right to make way, through temerity and crime, to a form of things, which when obtained, evident reason, perhaps imperi-ous necessity would compel us to alter, with the disgrace of incon-sistency in our conduct, and of want of foresight in our designs?

Believe me, Sir, in all changes in the state, moderation is a virtue not only amiable but powerful. It is a disposing, arranging, conciliating, cementing virtue. In the formation of new constitu-tions, it is in its province. Great powers reside in those who can make great changes. Their own moderation is their only check; and if this virtue is not paramount in their minds, their acts will taste more of their power than of their wisdom or their benev-olence. Whatever they do will be in extremes; it will be crude, harsh, precipitate. It will be submitted to with grudging and reluctance. Revenge will be smothered and hoarded, and the duration of schemes made in that temper will be as precarious as their establishment was odious. This virtue of moderation (which times and situations will clearly distinguish from the counterfeits of pusillanimity and indecision) is the virtue only of superior minds. It requires a deep courage, and full of reflection, to be temperate, when the voice of multitudes (the specious mimic of fame and reputation) passes judgment against you; the impetuous desire of an unthinking public will endure no course, but what conducts to splendid and perilous extremes. Then to dare to be fearful, when all about you are full of presumption and confidence, and when those who are bold at the hazard of others, would punish your caution as disaffection, is to show a mind prepared for its trial; it discovers in the midst of general levity, a self-possessing and collected character which sooner or later bids fair to attract every thing to it, as to a centre. If, however, the tempest should prove to be so very violent, that it would make public prudence itself unseasonable, and therefore little less than madness for the individual and the public too, perhaps a young man could not do better than to retreat for a while into study — to leave the field to those whose duty or inclination, or the necessities of their condition, have put them in possession of it, and wait for the settlement of such a commonwealth as an honest man may act in with satisfaction and credit. This he can never do when those who counsel the public, or the prince, are under terror, let the authority under which they are made to speak other than the dictates of their conscience, be never so imposing in its name and attributes.

This moderation is no enemy to zeal and enthusiasm. There is room enough for them; for the restraint is no more than the restraint of principle, and the restraint of reason.

I have been led further than I intended. But every day's account shows more and more, in my opinion, the ill consequence of keeping good principles and good general views within no bounds. Pardon the liberty I have taken; though it seems somewhat singular, that I, whose opinions have so little weight in my own country, where I have some share in a public trust, should write as if it were possible that they should affect one man with regard to affairs in which I have no concern. But for the present, my time is my own, and to tire your patience is the only injury I can do you.

I am, &c.

EDM. BURKE.

A Letter to Richard Burke
on Protestant Ascendancy in Ireland (1792)

Along with free trade, the abolition of Catholic disabilities was the cause to which Burke returned most often on behalf of Ireland. His *Tracts on the Popery Laws*—written in 1765, possibly to assist in discussions with William Gerard Hamilton, his patron at that time and chief secretary to the lord lieutenant for Ireland—was an impassioned work of history and advocacy. Yet it was destined to remain an unpublished fragment, as Burke directed his energy to American and English affairs. He supported a Catholic relief bill introduced by the Irish House of Commons in 1778, but when it was sent to the House of Commons in England the bill was rendered more controversial by a provision added to relieve Protestant Dissenters of the burden of the Test Act. Burke did then favor the abolition of the test for Dissenters, but he thought it politic to surrender the second reform in order to secure the first, and his strategy worked.

On one other substantial occasion, Burke made his influence felt in the conduct of the empire toward Ireland. The agitation for free trade in 1778 had been partly the work of the Irish Volunteers, a movement originally pledged to support the British cause against the threat of a French invasion. In 1779 and 1780, at the height of the American war, the numbers of the Volunteers swelled by tens of thousands, and their loyalist and defensive character gradually altered in the direction of a pugnacious nationalism. Their demonstrations grew more heated after the British surrender at Yorktown in 1782—the same year in which a new bill was under consideration for the relief of Catholic disabilities. Burke, though he held the Volunteers in suspicion and deprecated the very idea of national independence, kept his counsel and eventually gave his support to legislative independence. He denounced meanwhile a suggestion that the crown pay for the education of priests and assume control of episcopal appointments. When that proposal was dropped and the reform measure passed into law during the Rockingham administration of 1782, Burke could claim a share of the credit; but in *A Letter to a Noble Lord,* remembering the disturbances of the time, he would recall that "government was unnerved, confounded, and in a manner suspended." By 1791, fear of a revolution throughout Europe had come to dominate his thinking on Ireland. Yet on Irish affairs he sometimes spoke like a revolutionary: the system that excluded Catholics from political office and from many common rights, if it could not be reformed at once, deserved to be overthrown.

In September 1791, his son Richard agreed to act as agent for the Irish Catholic Committee; in December, the committee petitioned Parliament to obtain the franchise for Catholics. The request was turned down without a pretense of conciliation in February 1792, just when Burke is known to have been working on his *Letter on Protestant Ascendancy.* This essay in political morality, never completed and first published posthumously, makes an interesting counterpoint to Burke's *Letter to Sir Hercules Langrishe,* a defense of the appeal for limited franchise that stirred considerable controversy when published in Ireland in 1792. The letter to Langrishe (an enlightened Whig, a Protestant, and a friend of Burke's) is about the history of Catholic rights. The letter to Richard is about the psychology of domination.

Its praise of the spirit of liberty takes us back almost to the Burke of the 1770s: "*Partial freedom is privilege and prerogative, and not liberty. Liberty, such as deserves the name, is an honest, equitable, diffusive, and impartial principle. . . . It is the portion of the mass of the citizens, and not the haughty license of some potent individual or some predominant faction.*" Yet, as a check against the violence of liberty, and to assure a degree of consensus, Burke affirms his preference for the established church: the Church of England and the Church of Ireland. "It is, as things now stand, the sole connecting *political* principle between the constitutions of the two independent kingdoms." Never did he reveal more clearly the grounds of his thinking about religious institutions. An establishment in religion is to be preferred for the sake of political stability; that is to say, the good of religion is instrumental rather than intrinsic: it assists in the cohesion of society. At the same time, the disabilities of those outside the established church should be kept to a minimum.

Burke here takes an essay writer's liberty in exploring the hidden springs and symptoms of tyranny. He allows himself, for example, a curious pause to linger over the meaning of the word *ascendancy*. There is ascendancy by nature, as when one speaks of an ascendant mind; or ascendancy that is acquired, as with the ascendant ideas of an epoch; yet ascendancy can also serve as a euphemism for brutal suppression. Beneath his charge of abuse of power against some Irish Protestants may lie a suspicion of Protestantism itself—as tending to the multiplication of sects and the atomization of faith, and as contributing to reduce society to "the dust and powder of individuality" which Burke associated with a tyranny of self-will. The suspicion was not entirely conscious, and it remained submerged during his Bristol years, when his defense of the rights of Dissenters was consistent with Burke's principles, while also meeting the democratic demand for liberty of conscience. But there was an amazement verging on irony when he spoke, in the American context, of "the dissidence of dissent, and the protestantism of the protestant religion." He would say in another place that the most perfect Protestant is he who protests against the whole of Christianity. This irony has become conscious, and is indeed generalized and corrosive, in Burke's writings on Ireland in the 1790s.

Religion, Burke felt, was the commonest basis of humane belief, and a necessary bulwark in justifying compassion and self-sacrifice. He often seems to doubt how far the various protestantisms are capable of filling the void produced in the mind by lack of faith. Their liberty, with their license, may make the void still wider: without the fear of God and without the fear of man, the creed of "the rights of man," which is another name for atheism, has shown itself capable of sanctioning the most relentless of persecutions.

His conclusion offers a delicate barter. The loyalty of Irish Catholics, which alone can secure the kingdom against the monstrous disorder of revolution, is vouched for on condition that they be granted political rights. Burke admits the utility of preserving a mainly tacit hierarchy. He accepts the ordinary inequalities of society, and trusts that most Catholics do as well. But because such a hierarchy always conceals the violence of an original coercion, the ascendant Protestants are making the most destructive of errors when they point with pride to their conquest: "One would think they would wish to let Time draw his oblivious veil over the unpleasant modes by which lordships and demesnes have been acquired in theirs, and almost in all other countries upon earth. It might be imagined, that, when the sufferer . . . had forgot the wrong, they would be pleased to forget it too." Acceptance of prescription, in property as in other matters, ought to be cool and matter-of-fact. It is a thing not to be inquired into. The price of the advantage that historical accident awards to the victors is generosity: to remove the sting of grievance, and render the sufferings of the victims merely historical.

Letter to Richard Burke, Esq.

My dear Son,

We are all again assembled in Town, to finish the last, but the most laborious, of the tasks, which have been imposed upon me during my Parliamentary service. We are as well as, at our time of life, we can expect to be. We have indeed some moments of anxiety about you. You are engaged in an undertaking similar in its principle to mine. You are engaged in the relief of an oppressed people. In that service you must necessarily excite the same sort of passions in those, who have exercised, and who wish to continue that oppression, that I have had to struggle with in this long labour. As your Father has done, you must make enemies of many of the rich, of the proud, and of the powerful. I and you began in the same way. I must confess, that, if our place was of our choice, I could wish it had been your lot to begin the career of your life with an endeavour to render some more moderate, and less invidious, service to the Publick. But being engaged in a great and critical work, I have not the least hesitation about your having hitherto done your duty as becomes you. If I had not an assurance not to be shaken from the character of your mind, I should be satisfied on that point by the cry, that is raised against you. If you had behaved, as they call it, discreetly, that is, faintly and treacherously in the execution of your trust, you would have had, for a while, the good word of all sorts of men, even of many of those, whose cause you had betrayed; and whilst your favour lasted, you might have coined that false reputation into a true and solid interest to yourself. This you are well apprized of; and you do not refuse to travel that beaten road from an ignorance, but from a contempt, of the objects it leads to.

When you choose an arduous and slippery path, God forbid that any weak feelings of my declining age, which calls for soothings and supports, and which can have none but from you, should make me wish that you should abandon what you are about, or should trifle with it. In this House we submit, though with troubled minds, to that order, which has connected all great duties with toils and with perils, which has conducted the road to glory through the regions of obloquy and reproach, and which will never suffer the disparaging alliance of spurious, false, and fugitive praise with genuine and permanent reputation. We know, that the Power, which has settled that order, and subjected you to it by placing you in the situation you are in, is able to bring you out of it with credit, and with safety. His will be done. All must come right. You may open the way with pain, and under reproach. Others will pursue it with ease and with applause.

I am sorry to find that pride and passion, and that sort of zeal for religion, which never shows any wonderful heat but when it afflicts and mortifies our neighbour, will not let the ruling description perceive that the privilege, for which your clients contend, is very nearly as much for the benefit of those, who refuse it, as those, who ask it. I am not to examine into the charges, that are daily made on the Administration of Ireland. I am not qualified to say how much in them is cold truth, and how much rhetorical exaggeration. Allowing some foundation to the complaint, it is to no purpose that these people allege that their Government is a job in its administration. I am sure it is a job in its constitution; nor is it possible, a scheme of polity, which, in total exclusion of the body of the community, confines (with little or no regard to their rank or condition in life) to a certain set of favoured citizens the rights, which formerly belonged to the whole, should not, by the operation of the same selfish and narrow principles, teach the persons, who administer in that Government, to prefer their own particular, but well understood private interest to the false and ill calculated private interest of the monopolizing Company they belong to. Eminent characters, to be sure, overrule places and circumstances. I have nothing to say to that virtue, which shoots up in full force by the native vigour of the seminal principle, in spite of the adverse soil and climate that it grows in. But speaking of things in their ordinary course, in a Country of monopoly there *can* be no patriotism. There may be a party spirit—but publick spirit there can be none. As to a spirit of liberty, still less can it exist, or any thing like it. A liberty made up of penalties! a liberty made up of incapacities! a liberty made up of exclusion and proscription, continued for ages, of four fifths, perhaps, of the inhabitants of all ranks and fortunes! In what does such liberty differ from the description of the most shocking kind of servitude?

But it will be said, in that Country some people are free—why this is the very description of despotism. *Partial freedom is privilege and prerogative, and not liberty.* Liberty, such as deserves the name, is an honest, equitable, diffusive, and impartial principle. It is a great and enlarged virtue, and not a sordid, selfish, and illiberal vice. It is the portion of the mass of the citizens; and not the haughty license of some potent individual, or some predominant faction.

If any thing ought to be despotick in a Country, it is its Government; because there is no cause, of constant operation, to make its yoke unequal. But the dominion of a party must continually, steadily, and by its very essence, lean upon the prostrate description. A Constitution formed so as to enable a party to overrule its very Government, and to overpower the people too, answers the purposes neither of Government nor of freedom. It compels that power, which ought, and often would be, disposed *equally* to protect the Subjects, to fail in its trust, to counteract its purposes, and to become no better than the instrument of the wrongs of a faction. Some degree of influence must exist in all Governments. But a Government, which has no interest to please the body of the people, and can neither support them, nor with safety call for their support, nor is of power to sway the domineering faction, can only exist by corruption; and taught by that monopolizing party, which usurps the title and qualities of the publick, to consider the body of the people as out of the Constitution, they will consider those, who are in it, in the light, in which they choose to consider themselves. The whole relation of Government and of freedom will be a battle, or a traffick.

This system in its real nature, and under its proper appellations, is odious and unnatural, especially when a Constitution is admitted, which not only, as all Constitutions do profess, has a regard to the good of the multitude, but in its theory makes profession of their power also. But of late this scheme of theirs has been new christened — *honestum nomen imponitur vitio.*[1] A word has been lately struck in the mint of the Castle of Dublin; thence it was conveyed to the Tholsel, or City-hall, where, having passed the touch of the Corporation, so respectably stamped and vouched, it soon became current in Parliament, and was carried back by the Speaker of the House of Commons in great pomp, as an offering of homage from whence it came. The word is *Ascendancy*. It is not absolutely new. But the sense, in which I have hitherto seen it used, was to signify an influence obtained over the minds of some other person by love and reverence, or by superiour management and dexterity. It had, therefore, to this its promotion no more than a moral, not a civil or political use. But I admit it is capable of being so applied; and if the Lord Mayor of Dublin, and the Speaker of the Irish Parliament, who recommend the preservation of the Protestant ascendency, mean to employ the word in that sense, that is, if they understand by it the preservation of the influence of that description of gentlemen over the Catholicks, by means of an authority derived from their wisdom and virtue, and from an opinion they raise in that people of a pious regard and affection for their freedom and happiness, it is impossible not to commend their adoption of so apt a term into the family of politicks. It may be truly said to enrich the language. Even if the Lord Mayor and Speaker mean to insinuate that this influence is to be obtained and held by flattering their people, by managing them, by skilfully adapting themselves to the humours and passions of those, whom they would govern, he must be a very untoward critick, who would cavil even at this use of the word, though such cajoleries would perhaps be more prudently practised than pro-

1 "A respectable name is given to vice."

fessed. These are all meanings laudable, or at least tolerable. But when we look a little more narrowly, and compare it with the plan to which it owes its present technical application, I find it has strayed far from its original sense. It goes much further than the privilege allowed by Horace. It is more than *parce detortum*.[2] This Protestant ascendency means nothing less than an influence obtained by virtue, by love, or even by artifice and seduction; full as little an influence derived from the means, by which Ministers have obtained an influence, which might be called, without straining, an *ascendency* in publick Assemblies in England, that is, by a liberal distribution of places and pensions, and other graces of Government. This last is wide indeed of the signification of the word. New *ascendency* is the old mastership. It is neither more nor less than the resolution of one set of people in Ireland to consider themselves as the sole citizens in the commonwealth; and to keep a dominion over the rest by reducing them to absolute slavery under a military power; and thus fortified in their power, to divide the publick estate, which is the result of general contribution, as a military booty solely amongst themselves.

The poor word ascendency, so soft and melodious in its sound, so lenitive and emollient in its first usage, is now employed to cover to the world the most rigid, and perhaps, not the most wise of all plans of policy. The word is large enough in its comprehension. I cannot conceive what mode of oppression in civil life or what mode of religious persecution, may not come within the methods of preserving an *ascendency*. In plain old English, as they apply it, it signifies *pride and dominion* on the one part of the relation, and on the other *subserviency and contempt*— and it signifies nothing else. The old words are as fit to be set to musick as the new; but use has long since affixed to them their true signification, and they sound, as the other will, harshly and odiously to the moral and intelligent ears of mankind.

---

2 Horace *Ars poetica* 53: "drawn sparingly from that source" (of Greek words imported into Latin).

This ascendency, by being a *Protestant* ascendency, does not better it from the combination of a note or two more in this antiharmonick scale. If Protestant ascendency means the proscription from citizenship of by far the major part of the people of any Country, then Protestant ascendency is a bad thing; and it ought to have no existence. But there is a deeper evil. By the use that is so frequently made of the term, and the policy, which is engrafted on it, the name Protestant becomes nothing more or better than the name of a persecuting faction, with a relation of some sort of theological hostility to others, but without any sort of ascertained tenets of its own, upon the ground of which it persecutes other men; for the patrons of this Protestant ascendency neither do, nor can, by any thing positive, define or describe what they mean by the word Protestant. It is defined, as Cowley defines wit, not by what it is, but by what it is not. It is not the Christian Religion as professed in the Churches holding communion with Rome, the majority of Christians; that is all, which in the latitude of the term is known about its signification. This makes such persecutors ten times worse than any of that description, that hitherto have been known in the world. The old persecutors, whether Pagan or Christian, whether Arian or Orthodox, whether Catholicks, Anglicans, or Calvinists, actually were, or at least had the decorum to pretend to be, strong Dogmatists. They pretended that their religious maxims were clear and ascertained, and so useful, that they were bound, for the eternal benefit of mankind, to defend or diffuse them, though by any sacrifices of the temporal good of those, who were the objects of their system of experiment.

The bottom of this theory of persecution is false. It is not permitted to us to sacrifice the temporal good of any body of men to our own ideas of the truth and falsehood of any religious opinions. By making men miserable in this life, they counteract one of the great ends of charity; which is, inasmuch as in us lies, to make men happy in every period of their existence, and most, in what most depends upon us. But give to these old persecutors their mistaken principle, in their reasoning they are consistent, and in their tempers they may be even kind and good natured.

But whenever a faction would render millions of mankind miserable, some millions of the race co-existent with themselves, and many millions in their succession, without knowing, or so much as pretending to ascertain, the doctrines of their own school (in which there is much of the lash and nothing of the lesson) the errours, which the persons in such a faction fall into, are not those, that are natural to human imbecility, nor is the least mixture of mistaken kindness to mankind an ingredient in the severities they inflict. The whole is nothing but pure and perfect malice. It is, indeed, a perfection in that kind belonging to beings of an higher order than man, and to them we ought to leave it.

This kind of persecutors, without zeal, without charity, know well enough that Religion, to pass by all questions of the truth or falsehood of any of its particular systems (a matter I abandon to the theologians on all sides) is a source of great comfort to us mortals in this our short but tedious journey through the world. They know, that to enjoy this consolation, men must believe their Religion upon some principle or other, whether of education, habit, theory, or authority. When men are driven from any of those principles, on which they have received Religion, without embracing with the same assurance and cordiality some other system, a dreadful void is left in their minds, and a terrible shock is given to their morals. They lose their guide, their comfort, their hope. None but the most cruel and hard-hearted of men, who had banished all natural tenderness from their minds, such as those beings of iron, the Atheists, could bring themselves to any persecution like this. Strange it is, but so it is, that men, driven by force from their habits in one mode of Religion, have, by contrary habits, under the same force, often quietly settled in another. They suborn their reason to declare in favour of their necessity. Man and his conscience cannot always be at war. If the first races have not been able to make a pacification between the conscience and the convenience, their descendants come generally to submit to the violence of the Laws, without violence to their minds. As things stood formerly, they possessed a *positive* scheme of direction, and of consolation. In this men may

acquiesce. The harsh methods in use with the old class of persecutors were to make converts, not apostates only. If they per-
versely hated other sects and factions, they loved their own in-
ordinately. But in this Protestant persecution there is any thing
but benevolence at work. What do the Irish Statutes? They do not
make a conformity to the *established* Religion, and to its doctrines
and practices, the condition of getting out of servitude. No such
thing. Let three millions of people but abandon all, that they and
their ancestors have been taught to believe sacred, and to for-
swear it publickly in terms the most degrading, scurrilous, and
indecent for men of integrity and virtue, and to abuse the whole
of their former lives, and to slander the education they have
received, and nothing more is required of them. There is no
system of folly, or impiety, or blasphemy, or Atheism, into which
they may not throw themselves, and which they may not profess
openly, and as a system, consistently with the enjoyment of all the
privileges of a free citizen in the happiest Constitution in the
world.

Some of the unhappy assertors of this strange scheme say,
they are not persecutors on account of Religion. In the first
place, they say what is not true. For what else do they disfran-
chise the people? If the man gets rid of a Religion, through
which their malice operates, he gets rid of all their penalties and
incapacities at once. They never afterwards inquire about him. I
speak here of their pretexts, and not of the true spirit of the
transaction, in which religious bigotry, I apprehend, has little
share. Every man has his taste; but I think, if I were so miserable
and undone as to be guilty of premeditated and continued violence towards any set of men, I had rather that my conduct was
supposed to arise from wild conceits concerning their religious
advantages, than from low and ungenerous motives relative to
my own selfish interest. I had rather be thought insane in my
charity than rational in my malice. This much, my dear Son, I
have to say of this Protestant persecution; that is, a persecution
of Religion itself.

A very great part of the mischiefs, that vex the world, arises from words. People soon forget the meaning, but the impression and the passion remain. The word Protestant is the charm, that locks up in the dungeon of servitude three millions of your people. It is not amiss to consider this spell of potency, this abracadabra, that is hung about the necks of the unhappy, not to heal, but to communicate disease. We sometimes hear of a Protestant *Religion*, frequently of a Protestant *interest*. We hear of the latter the most frequently, because it has a positive meaning. The other has none. We hear of it the most frequently, because it has a word in the phrase, which, well or ill understood, has animated to persecution and oppression at all times infinitely more than all the dogmas in dispute between religious factions. These are indeed well formed to perplex and torment the intellect; but not half so well calculated to inflame the passions and animosities of men.

I do readily admit, that a great deal of the wars, seditions, and troubles of the world, did formerly turn upon the contention between *interests*, that went by the names of Protestant and Catholick. But I imagined that at this time no one was weak enough to believe, or impudent enough to pretend, that questions of Popish and Protestant opinions, or interest, are the things, by which men are at present menaced with crusades by foreign invasion, or with seditions, which shake the foundations of the State at home. It is long since all this combination of things has vanished from the view of intelligent observers. The existence of quite another system of opinions and interests is now plain to the grossest sense. Are these the questions that raise a flame in the minds of men at this day? If ever the Church and the Constitution of England should fall in these Islands (and they will fall together), it is not Presbyterian discipline, nor Popish hierarchy, that will rise upon their ruins. It will not be the Church of Rome, nor the Church of Scotland — not the Church of Luther, nor the Church of Calvin. On the contrary, all these Churches are menaced, and menaced alike. It is the new fanatical Religion, now in the heat of its first ferment, of the Rights of Man, which rejects all Establishments, all discipline, all Ecclesiastical, and in truth all Civil order, which will triumph, and which will lay prostrate your

Church; which will destroy your distinctions, and which will put all your properties to auction, and disperse you over the Earth. If the present Establishment should fall, it is this Religion, which will triumph in Ireland and in England, as it has triumphed in France. This Religion, which laughs at creeds, and dogmas, and confessions of faith, may be fomented equally amongst all descriptions, and all sects; amongst nominal Catholicks, and amongst nominal Churchmen; and amongst those Dissenters, who know little, and care less, about a Presbytery, or any of its discipline, or any of its doctrine.

Against this new, this growing, this exterminatory system, all these Churches have a common concern to defend themselves. How the enthusiasts of this rising sect rejoice to see you of the old Churches play their game, and stir and rake the cinders of animosities sunk in their ashes, in order to keep up the execution of their plan for your common ruin!

I suppress all that is in my mind about the blindness of those of our Clergy, who will shut their eyes to a thing, which glares in such manifest day. If some wretches amongst an indigent and disorderly part of the populace raise a riot about tithes, there are of these gentlemen ready to cry out, that this is an overt act of a treasonable conspiracy. Here the bulls and the pardons, and the crusade, and the Pope, and the thunders of the Vatican, are every where at work. There is a plot to bring in a foreign power to destroy the Church. Alas! it is not about Popes, but about potatoes, that the minds of this unhappy people are agitated. It is not from the spirit of zeal, but the spirit of whiskey, that these wretches act. Is it then not conceived possible that a poor Clown can be unwilling, after paying three pounds rent to a gentleman in a brown coat, to pay fourteen shillings to one in a black coat, for his acre of potatoes, and tumultuously to desire some modification of the charge, without being supposed to have no other motive than a frantick zeal for being thus double taxed to another set of landholders, and another set of Priests? Have men no self-interest? no avarice? no repugnance to publick imposts? Have they no sturdy and restive minds? no undisciplined habits?

Is there nothing in the whole mob of irregular passions, which might precipitate some of the common people, in some places, to quarrel with a legal, because they feel it to be a burthensome, imposition? According to these gentlemen, no offence can be committed by Papists but from zeal to their Religion. To make room for the vices of Papists, they clear the House of all the vices of men. Some of the common people (not one however in ten thousand) commit disorders. Well! punish them as you do, and as you ought to punish them for their violence against the just property of each individual Clergyman, as each individual suffers. Support the injured Rector, or the injured Impropriator, in the enjoyment of the estate, of which (whether on the best plan or not) the Laws have put him in possession. Let the crime and the punishment stand upon their own bottom. But now we ought all of us, Clergymen most particularly, to avoid assigning another cause of quarrel, in order to infuse a new source of bitterness into a dispute, (which personal feelings on both sides will of themselves make bitter enough,) and thereby involve in it by religious descriptions men, who have individually no share whatsoever in those irregular acts. Let us not make the malignant fictions of our own imaginations, heated with factious controversies, reasons for keeping men, that are neither guilty, nor justly suspected of crime, in a servitude equally dishonourable and unsafe to Religion, and to the State. When men are constantly accused, but know themselves not to be guilty, they must naturally abhor their accusers. There is no character, when malignantly taken up and deliberately pursued, which more naturally excites indignation and abhorrence in mankind; especially in that part of mankind, which suffers from it.

I do not pretend to take pride in an extravagant attachment to any sect. Some gentlemen in Ireland affect that sort of glory. It is to their taste. Their piety, I take it for granted, justifies the fervour of their zeal, and may palliate the excess of it. Being myself no more than a common layman, commonly informed in controversies, leading only a very common life, and having only a common citizen's interest in the Church, or in the State, yet to you I will say, in justice to my own sentiments, that not one of those zealots for a Protestant interest wishes more sincerely than I do, perhaps not half so sincerely, for the support of the established Church in both these kingdoms. It is a great link towards holding fast the connexion of Religion with the State; and for keeping these two Islands, in their present critical independence of Constitution, in a close connexion of *opinion and affection*. I wish it well, as the Religion of the greater number of the primary land proprietors of the Kingdom, with whom all Establishments of Church and State, for strong political reasons, ought in my opinion to be firmly connected. I wish it well, because it is more closely combined than any other of the Church systems with the *Crown*, which is the stay of the mixed Constitution; because it is, as things now stand, the sole connecting *political* principle between the Constitutions of the two independent Kingdoms. I have another, and infinitely a stronger, reason for wishing it well; it is, that in the present time I consider it as one of the main pillars of the Christian Religion itself. The body and substance of every Religion I regard much more than any of the forms and dogmas of the particular sects. Its fall would leave a great void, which nothing else, of which I can form any distinct idea, might fill. I respect the Catholick hierarchy, and the Presbyterian republick. But I know that the hope or the fear of establishing either of them is, in these Kingdoms, equally chimerical, even if I preferred one or the other of them to the Establishment, which certainly I do not.

These are some of my reasons for wishing the support of the Church of Ireland as by Law established. These reasons are founded as well on the absolute as on the relative situation of that Kingdom. But is it because I love the Church, and the King, and the privileges of Parliament, that I am to be ready for any violence, or any injustice, or any absurdity in the means of supporting any of these powers, or all of them together? Instead of prating about Protestant ascendencies, Protestant Parliaments ought, in my opinion, to think at last of becoming Patriot Parliaments.

The Legislature of Ireland, like all Legislatures, ought to frame its Laws to suit the people and the circumstances of the Country, and not any longer to make it their whole business to force the nature, the temper, and the inveterate habits of a Nation to a conformity to speculative systems concerning any kind of Laws. Ireland has an established Government, and a Religion legally established, which are to be preserved. It has a people, who are to be preserved too, and to be led by reason, principle, sentiment and interest to acquiesce in that Government. Ireland is a Country under peculiar circumstances. The people of Ireland are a very mixed people; and the quantities of the several ingredients in the mixture are very much disproportioned to each other. Are we to govern this mixed body as if it were composed of the most simple elements, comprehending the whole in one system of benevolent legislation: or are we not rather to provide for the several parts according to the various and diversified necessities of the heterogeneous nature of the mass? Would not common reason and common honesty dictate to us the policy of regulating the people in the several descriptions, of which they are composed, according to the natural ranks and classes of an orderly civil society, under a common protecting Sovereign, and under a form of Constitution favourable at once to authority and to freedom; such as the British Constitution boasts to be, and such as it is, to those, who enjoy it?

You have an ecclesiastical Establishment, which, though the Religion of the Prince, and of most of the first class of landed proprietors, is not the Religion of the major part of the inhabitants, and which consequently does not answer to *them* any one purpose of a religious Establishment. This is a state of things, which no man in his senses can call perfectly happy. But it is the state of Ireland. Two hundred years of experiment show it to be unalterable. Many a fierce struggle has passed between the parties. The result is — you cannot make the people Protestants — and they cannot shake off a Protestant Government. This is what experience teaches, and what all men of sense, of all descriptions, know. To-day the question is this — are we to make the best of this situation, which we cannot alter? The question is — shall the condition of the body of the people be alleviated in other things, on account of their necessary suffering from their being subject to the burthens of two religious Establishments, from one of which they do not partake the least, living or dying, either of instruction or of consolation; or shall it be aggravated by stripping the people thus loaded of every thing, which might support and indemnify them in this state, so as to leave them naked of every sort of right, and of every name of franchise; to outlaw them from the Constitution, and to cut off (perhaps) three millions of plebian subjects, without reference to property, or any other qualification, from all connexion with the popular representation of the Kingdom?

As to Religion, it has nothing at all to do with the proceeding. Liberty is not sacrificed to a zeal for Religion; but a zeal for Religion is pretended and assumed, to destroy liberty. The Catholick Religion is completely free. It has no Establishment; but it is recognized, permitted, and, in a degree, protected by the Laws. If a man is satisfied to be a slave, he may be a Papist with perfect impunity. He may say mass, or hear it, as he pleases; but he must consider himself as an outlaw from the British Constitution. If the constitutional liberty of the subject were not the thing aimed at, the direct reverse course would be taken. The franchise would have been permitted, and the mass exterminated. But the conscience of a man left, and a tenderness for it hypocritically pretended, is to make it a trap to catch his liberty.

So much is this the design, that the violent partisans of this scheme fairly take up all the maxims and arguments, as well as the practices, by which tyranny has fortified itself at all times. Trusting wholly in their strength and power (and upon this they reckon, as always ready to strike wherever they wish to direct the storm) they abandon all pretext of the general good of the community. They say, that if the people, under any given modification, obtain the smallest portion or particle of constitutional freedom, it will be impossible for them to hold their property. They tell us, that they act only on the defensive. They inform the publick of Europe, that their estates are made up of forfeitures and confiscations from the Natives: — that, if the body of people obtain votes, any number of votes, however small, it will be a step to the choice of Members of their own Religion: — that the House of Commons, in spite of the influence of nineteen parts in twenty of the landed interest now in their hands, will be composed, in the whole, or in far the major part, of Papists; that this Popish House of Commons will instantly pass a Law to confiscate all their estates, which it will not be in their power to save even by entering into that Popish party themselves, because there are prior claimants to be satisfied: — that as to the House of Lords, though neither Papists nor Protestants have a share in electing them, the body of the Peerage will be so obliging and disinterested, as to fall in with this exterminatory scheme, which is to forfeit all their estates, the largest part of the Kingdom: and, to crown all, that His Majesty will give his cheerful assent to this causeless act of attainder of his innocent and faithful Protestant subjects: — that they will be, or are to be left, without house or land, to the dreadful resource of living by their wits, out of which they are already frightened by the apprehension of this spoliation, with which they are threatened: — that therefore they cannot so much as listen to any arguments drawn from equity or from national or constitutional policy: the sword is at their throats; beggary and famine at their door. See what it is to have a good look out, and to see danger at the end of a sufficiently long perspective!

This is indeed to speak plain, though to speak nothing very new. The same thing has been said in all times and in all languages. The language of tyranny has been invariable; the general good is inconsistent with my personal safety. Justice and liberty seem so alarming to these gentlemen, that they are not ashamed even to slander their own titles; to calumniate, and call in doubt, their right to their own estates, and to consider themselves as novel disseizors, usurpers, and intruders, rather than lose a pretext for becoming oppressors of their fellow citizens, whom they (not I) choose to describe themselves as having robbed.

Instead of putting themselves in this odious point of light, one would think they would wish to let Time draw his oblivious veil over the unpleasant modes, by which lordships and demesnes have been acquired in their's, and almost in all other countries upon earth. It might be imagined, that, when the sufferer (if a sufferer exists) had forgot the wrong, they would be pleased to forget it too; that they would permit the sacred name of possession to stand in the place of the melancholy and unpleasant title of grantees of confiscation; which, though firm and valid in Law, surely merits the name, that a great Roman Jurist gave to a title at least as valid in his nation, as confiscation would be either in his or in ours: — *Tristis et luctuosa successio.*[3]

Such is the situation of every man, who comes in upon the ruin of another—his succeeding, under this circumstance, is *tristis et luctuosa successio.* If it had been the fate of any gentleman to profit by the confiscation of his neighbour, one would think he would be more disposed to give him a valuable interest under him in his land; or to allow him a pension, as I understand one worthy person has done, without fear or apprehension that his benevolence to a ruined family would be construed into a recognition of the forfeited title. The publick of England the other day acted in this manner toward Lord Newburgh, a Catholick. Though the estate had been vested by Law in the greatest of the publick charities, they have given him a pension from his confiscation. They have gone further in other cases. On the last Rebellion in 1745, in Scotland, several forfeitures were incurred. They had been disposed of by Parliament to certain laudable uses. Parliament reversed the method, which they had adopted in Lord Newburgh's case, and in my opinion did better; they gave the forfeited estates to the successours of the forfeiting proprietors, chargeable in part with the uses. Is this, or any thing like this, asked in favour of any human creature in Ireland? It is bounty; it is charity; wise bounty and politick charity; but no man can claim it as a right. Here no such thing is claimed as right, or begged as charity. The demand has an object as distant from all

---

3 "Sad and sorrowful taking of possession, from the Theodosian Code."

considerations of this sort, as any two extremes can be. The people desire the privileges inseparably annexed, since Magna Charta, to the freehold, which they have by descent, or obtain as the fruits of their industry. They call for no man's estate: they desire not to be dispossessed of their own.

But this melancholy and invidious title is a favourite (and like favourites, always of the least merit) with those, who possess every other title upon earth along with it. For this purpose, they revive the bitter memory of every dissension, which has torn to pieces their miserable country for ages. After what has passed in 1782, one would not think that decorum, to say nothing of policy, would permit them to call up, by magick charms, the grounds, reasons, and principles of those terrible, confiscatory, and exterminatory periods. They would not set men upon calling from the quiet sleep of death any Samuel, to ask him, by what act of arbitrary Monarchs, by what inquisitions of corrupted tribunals, and tortured jurors; by what fictitious tenures, invented to dispossess whole unoffending tribes and their Chieftains! They would not conjure up the ghosts from the ruins of castles and churches, to tell for what attempt to struggle for the independence of an Irish Legislature, and to raise armies of volunteers, without regular commissions from the Crown, in support of that independence, the estates of the old Irish Nobility and Gentry had been confiscated. They would not wantonly call on those phantoms, to tell by what English Acts of Parliament, forced upon two reluctant Kings, the lands of their Country were put up to a mean and scandalous auction in every goldsmith's shop in London; or chopped to pieces, and cut into rations, to pay the mercenary soldiery of a regicide Usurper. They would not be so fond of titles under Cromwell,[4] who, if he avenged an Irish rebellion against the sovereign authority of the Parliament of England, had himself rebelled against the very Parliament, whose sovereignty he asserted, full as much as the Irish Nation, which he

---

4 Charles I and Charles II, abettors of a system of absentee ownership; and Cromwell, known to Irish Catholics as a confiscating tyrant.

was sent to subdue and confiscate, could rebel against that Parliament, or could rebel against the King, against whom both he and the Parliament, which he served, and which he betrayed, had both of them rebelled.

The gentlemen, who hold the language of the day, know perfectly well, that the Irish in 1641 pretended at least, that they did not rise against the King, nor in fact did they, whatever constructions Law might put upon their act. But full surely they rebelled against the authority of the Parliament of England, and they openly professed so to do. Admitting (I have now no time to discuss the matter) the enormous and unpardonable magnitude of this their crime, they rued it in their persons, and in those of their children and their grandchildren even to the fifth and sixth generations. Admitting, then, the enormity of this unnatural rebellion in favour of the independence of Ireland, will it follow, that it must be avenged for ever? Will it follow, that it must be avenged on thousands, and perhaps hundreds of thousands, of those, whom they can never trace, by the labours of the most subtle metaphysician of the traduction of crimes, or the most inquisitive genealogist of proscription, to the descendant of any one concerned in that nefarious Irish rebellion against the Parliament of England?

If, however, you could find out these pedigrees of guilt, I do not think the difference would be essential. History records many things, which ought to make us hate evil actions; but neither history nor morals, nor policy, can teach us to punish innocent men on that account. What lesson does the iniquity of prevalent factions read to us? It ought to lesson us into an abhorrence of the abuse of our own power in our own day: when we hate its excesses so much in other persons and in other times. To that school true Statesmen ought to be satisfied to leave mankind. They ought not to call from the dead all the discussions and litigations, which formerly inflamed the furious factions, which had torn their Country to pieces; they ought not to rake into the hideous and abominable things, which were done in the turbulent fury of an injured, robbed, and persecuted people, and which were afterwards cruelly revenged in the execution, and as outrageously and shamefully exaggerated in the representation, in order, an hundred and fifty years after, to find some colour for justifying them in the eternal proscription and civil excommunication of a whole people.

Let us come to a later period of those confiscations, with the memory of which the gentlemen, who triumph in the Acts of 1782, are so much delighted. The Irish again rebelled against the English Parliament in 1688, and the English Parliament again put up to sale the greatest part of their estates. I do not presume to defend the Irish for this rebellion; nor to blame the English Parliament for this confiscation. The Irish, it is true, did not revolt from King James's power. He threw himself upon their fidelity, and they supported him to the best of their feeble power. Be the crime of that obstinate adherence to an abdicated Sovereign against a prince, whom the Parliaments of Ireland and Scotland had recognized, what it may, I do not mean to justify this rebellion more than the former. It might, however, admit some palliation in them. In generous minds, some small degree of compassion might be excited for an errour, where they were misled, as Cicero says to a Conqueror, *quâdam specie et similitudine pacis*,[5] not without a mistaken appearance of duty, and for which the guilty have suffered by exile abroad, and slavery at home, to the extent of their folly or their offence. The best calculators compute that Ireland lost 200,000 of her inhabitants in that struggle. If the principle of the English and Scottish resistance at the Revolution is to be justified (as sure I am it is), the submission of Ireland must be somewhat extenuated. For if the Irish resisted King William, they resisted him on the very same principle that the English and Scotch resisted King James.[6] The Irish Catholicks must have been the very worst and the most truly unnatural of rebels, if they had not supported a Prince, whom they had seen

5 "Under an outward show and semblance of peace," adapting *Pro Caelio* vi. 14.
6 Irish resistance to William as a Protestant king is here analogous to English and Scottish resistance to James II as a Catholic.

attacked, not for any designs against *their* Religion, or *their* liberties, but for an extreme partiality for their sect; and who, far from trespassing on *their* liberties and properties, secured both them and the independence of their Country, in much the same manner that we have seen the same things done at the period of 1782 — I trust the last Revolution in Ireland.

That the Irish Parliament of King James did in some particulars, though feebly, imitate the rigour, which had been used towards the Irish, is true enough. Blamable enough they were for what they had done, though under the greatest possible provocation. I shall never praise confiscations or counter-confiscations as long as I live. When they happen by necessity, I shall think the necessity lamentable and odious: I shall think that any thing done under it ought not to pass into precedent, or to be adopted by choice, or to produce any of those shocking retaliations, which never suffer dissensions to subside. Least of all would I fix the transitory spirit of civil fury by perpetuating and methodising it in tyrannick government. If it were permitted to argue with power, might one not ask these gentlemen, whether it would not be more natural, instead of wantonly mooting these questions concerning their property, as if it were an exercise in Law, to found it on the solid rock of prescription; the soundest, the most general, and the most recognized title between man and man, that is known in municipal or in publick jurisprudence? a title, in which not arbitrary institutions, but the eternal order of things gives judgment; a title, which is not the creature, but the master, of positive Law; a title, which, though not fixed in its term, is rooted in its principle, in the law of nature itself, and is indeed the original ground of all known property; for all property in soil will always be traced back to that source, and will rest there. The miserable Natives of Ireland, who ninety-nine in an hundred are tormented with quite other cares, and are bowed down to labour for the bread of the hour, are not, as gentlemen pretend, plodding with antiquaries for titles of centuries ago to the estates of the great Lords and 'Squires, for whom they labour. But if they were thinking of the titles, which gentlemen labour to beat into their heads, where can they bottom their own claims but in a presumption and a proof, that these lands had at some time been possessed by their ancestors? These gentlemen, for they have Lawyers amongst them, know as well as I, that in England we have had always a prescription or limitation, as all nations have, against each other. The Crown was excepted; but that exception is destroyed, and we have lately established a sixty year's possession as against the Crown. All titles terminate in prescription; in which (differently from Time in the fabulous instances) the son devours the father, and the last prescription eats up all the former.

Preface to Brissot's Address
to His Constituents (1794)

Jacques-Pierre Brissot was a leader of the revolutionary party called the Gironde (from its supposed connection with the provincial departments of France), which in the early 1790s competed for authority against the Montagne (whose base of support was strongest in Paris). With the fall of the Girondins in June 1793, at the instigation of the Montagnards, the revolution was effectively placed under the command of Robespierre and the Committee of Public Safety. The regime of terror that followed did not slacken until the arrest of Robespierre in July 1794, and it is the leaders of this phase of the revolution who have come to be described as Jacobins.

An attack on the morals and manners of Jacobinism occupies all of Burke's later writings on France. Two definitions may be helpful. He would say in 1795, in *A Letter to William Smith*, that Jacobinism is "an attempt . . . to eradicate prejudice out of the minds of men." The first of his *Letters on a Regicide Peace*, in 1796, went further to connect the ideology with a social class: "Jacobinism is the revolt of the enterprising talents of a country against its property." Can one extend the same description to Brissot and his party? Between the flight of the king to Varennes (21 June 1791), which permanently discredited the advocates of a reformed monarchy, and the attack on the Tuileries (10 August 1792), when the Paris sections and their allies in the street took definitive control of the Revolution, the Girondins were distinguished by their belief that the Revolution had succeeded and ought therefore to be ended. The aim had been to bring about a republic and to establish a regime of liberty, equality, and fraternity. This had been secured above all by the abolition of seigneurial privileges and the approval of the constitution of 1791. The good of these reforms would be lost, the Girondins argued, if the Revolution now pressed on to the destruction of representative government and the abolition of property. With this assertion of principle Burke might have sympathized, up to a point. But he would not have cared for the distinction made by some later historians between the Girondins as moderates and the Jacobins as radicals. He knew that the Girondins had been among the chief evangelists for the spread of revolutionary doctrine to other nations. Brissot in particular had argued for war against Austria, partly in the belief that it would stablize the revolutionary economy. Yet it was the war, more than any other development, that created the climate for the Terror.

Burke seems to have recognized in Brissot, as he did in Mirabeau, the craft of a reforming politician who aspired to statesmanship. In the light of such an ambition, the "Preface to Brissot's Address" singles out for blame the conduct of Brissot's colleague Roland during the September massacres of 1792. Like most atrocities, the massacres arose from a plausible pretext: the suspicion that the foreign monarchs, poised for invasion, were operating a system of spies and agents in Paris, and that numbers of actual or potential traitors could be identified among the political prisoners. For almost a week starting on 2 September, a mob took over the prisons of Paris and killed about half their population — the ordeal being protracted by kangaroo courts, and by the sadistic assaults of the drunken crowd. Only a few of the many hundreds slain were "political"; more were priests and soldiers; most were drawn from the class of ordinary criminals. Roland's response to the event betrayed a desire to palliate its violence, to appease those who fomented it by praising their rough justice, and to invoke necessity as a plea on behalf of comparable actions in the future. An equivocal statement by a leader who would have preferred authority to reside in the Assembly, his letter was a helpless compromise between republican stability and the totalitarian doctrine that any deed is sanctified if done by the people.

This "Preface," seldom reprinted, is as close as Burke comes to a documentary treatment of the French Revolution, and it displays in a brief compass his exceptional gift for historical narrative. Since he left no full-scale response to the Terror, it also affords an indispensable clue to what he would have said about that episode. The long months of the judicial slaughter of suspects had begun with the arrest of Brissot himself—an irony of which Burke is fully aware—and his analysis here of revolutionary euphemism is among the earliest such explorations of the language of modern politics. In its pamphlet form, the "Preface" was followed by the text of Brissot's address to his constituents, translated by William Burke. Brissot there denounced the anarchy that came from supplanting equality of right by equality of fact, and the self-contradiction of a movement that stood for emancipation but governed other nations by despotism.

Preface to the Address of M. Brissot
to His Constituents

The French revolution has been the subject of various speculations, and various histories. As might be expected, the royalists and the republicans have differed a good deal in their accounts of the principles of that revolution, of the springs which have set it in motion, and of the true character of those who have been, or still are the principal actors on that astonishing scene.

They who are inclined to think favourably of that event, will undoubtedly object to every state of facts which comes only from the authority of a royalist. Thus much must be allowed by those who are the most firmly attached to the cause of religion, law, and order (for of such, and not of friends to despotism, the royal party is composed) that their very affection to this generous and manly cause, and their abhorrence of a revolution, not less fatal to liberty than to government, may possibly lead them in some particulars to a more harsh representation of the proceedings of their adversaries, than would be allowed by the cold neutrality of an impartial judge. This sort of errour arises from a source highly laudable; but the exactness of truth may suffer even from the feelings of virtue. History will do justice to the intentions of worthy men; but it will be on its guard against their infirmities; it will examine with great strictness of scrutiny, whatever appears from a writer in favour of his own cause. On the other hand, whatever escapes him, and makes against that cause, comes with the greatest weight.

In this important controversy, the translator of the following work brings forward to the English tribunal of opinion, the testimony of a witness beyond all exception. His competence is undoubted. He knows every thing which concerns this revolution to the bottom. He is a chief actor in all the scenes which he presents. No man can object to him as a royalist: the royal party, and the Christian religion, never had a more determined enemy. In a word, it is BRISSOT. — It is Brissot the republican, the jacobin, and the philosopher, who is brought to give an account of jacobinism, and of republicanism, and of philosophy.

It is worthy of observation, that this his account of the genius of jacobinism, and its effects, is not confined to the period in which that faction came to be divided within itself. In several, and those very important particulars, Brissot's observations apply to the whole of the preceding period, before the great schism, and whilst the jacobins acted as one body; insomuch, that the far greater part of the proceedings of the ruling powers, since the commencement of the revolution in France, so strikingly painted, so strongly and so justly reprobated by Brissot, were the acts of Brissot himself and his associates. All the members of the Girondin subdivision were as deeply concerned as any of the Mountain could possibly be, and some of them much more deeply, in those horrid transactions which have filled all the thinking part of Europe with the greatest detestation, and with the most serious apprehensions for the common liberty and safety.

A question will very naturally be asked, what could induce Brissot to draw such a picture? He must have been sensible it was his own. The answer is — the inducement was the same with that which led him to partake in the perpetration of all the crimes, the calamitous effects of which he describes with the pen of a master — ambition. His faction having obtained their stupendous and unnatural power, by rooting out of the minds of his unhappy countrymen, every principle of religion, morality, loyalty, fidelity, and honour, discovered, that when authority came into their hands, it would be a matter of no small difficulty for them to carry on government on the principles by which they had destroyed it.

The rights of men, and the new principles of liberty and equality, were very unhandy instruments for those who wished to establish a system of tranquillity and order. They who were taught to find nothing to respect in the title and the virtues of Louis the Sixteenth, a prince succeeding to the throne by the fundamental laws, in the line of a succession of monarchs continued for fourteen hundred years, found nothing which could bind them to an implicit fidelity, and dutiful allegiance to Mess. Brissot, Vergniaux, Condorcet, Anacharsis Cloots, and Thomas Paine.[1]

In this difficulty, they did as well as they could. To govern the people, they must incline the people to obey. The work was difficult, but it was necessary. They were to accomplish it by such materials and by such instruments as they had in their hands. They were to accomplish the purposes of order, morality, and submission to the laws, from the principles of atheism, profligacy, and sedition. Ill as the disguise became them, they began to assume the mask of an austere and rigid virtue; they exhausted all the stores of their eloquence (which in some of them were not inconsiderable) in declamations against tumult and confusion; they made daily harangues on the blessings of order, discipline, quiet, and obedience, to authority; they even shewed some sort of disposition to protect such property as had not been confiscated. They, who on every occasion had discovered a sort of furious thirst of blood, and a greedy appetite for slaughter, who avowed and gloried in the murders and massacres of the fourteenth of July, of the fifth and sixth of October, and of the tenth of August, now began to be squeamish and fastidious with regard to those of the second of September.[2]

In their pretended scruples on the sequel of the slaughter of the tenth of August, they imposed upon no living creature, and they obtained not the smallest credit for humanity. They

1 Pierre Victurnien Vergniaud (1753–93), deputy from the Gironde and an influential voice for Montesquieuan or "mixed" government in the constitutional debates, was guillotined with Brissot on 31 October 1793. Antoine Nicolas de Caritat (1743–94), Marquis de Condorcet, was the last of the *philosophes*. A sympathizer with the Girondins, the friend of La Fayette and Sieyès as well as of Brissot, he completed his *Sketch for a Historical Picture of the Progress of the Human Mind* shortly before going to meet his death in the Terror. Anacharsis Cloots (1755–94) joined Brissot and the Girondins in the attack on Robespierre. Both he and Thomas Paine (1737–1809) were excluded from the National Convention in December 1793. Cloots was executed in March 1794; Paine spent most of the year in prison.

2 Referring to the fall of the Bastille (14 July 1789), the march on Versailles (5–6 October 1789), the constitution of the Commune of Paris, the capture of the Tuileries (10 August 1792), and the September massacres (2–6 September 1792).

endeavoured to establish a distinction, by the belief of which they hoped to keep the spirit of murder safely bottled up, and sealed for their own purposes, without endangering themselves by the fumes of the poison which they prepared for their enemies.

Roland was the chief and the most accredited of the faction: — His morals had furnished little matter of exception against him; — old, domestick, and uxorious, he led a private life sufficiently blameless. He was therefore set up as the *Cato* of the republican party, which did not abound in such characters.[3]

This man like most of the chiefs, was the manager of a newspaper, in which he promoted the interest of his party. He was a fatal present made by the revolutionists, to the unhappy king, as one of his ministers under the new constitution. Amongst his colleagues were Claviere and Servan.[4] All the three have since that time, either lost their heads by the axe of their associates in rebellion, or to evade their own revolutionary justice have fallen by their own hands.

These ministers were regarded by the king as in a conspiracy to dethrone him. Nobody who considers the circumstances which preceded the deposition of Louis the Sixteenth; nobody who attends to the subsequent conduct of those ministers, can hesitate about the reality of such a conspiracy. The king certainly had no doubt of it; he found himself obliged to remove them; and the necessity which first obliged him to choose such regicide ministers, constrained him to replace them by Dumourier the Jacobin, and some others of little efficiency, though of a better description.[5]

3 The Roman statesman Cato (234–149 B.C.) was renowned for his virtue and sobriety.

4 Etienne Claviere (1735–93), Swiss banker and minister of finance from August 1792 to June 1793; Joseph Servan (1741–1808), minister of war from August to October 1792. Servan in fact did not perish though he was imprisoned from 1793 to 1795.

5 Charles François Dumouriez (1739–1823), general of the revolutionary army, was an ally of the Marquis de La Fayette, Mirabeau, and the Girondins, and became foreign minister in March 1792. When Marat accused him of treason, he did not return from the front but defected to Austria.

A little before this removal, and evidently as a part of the conspiracy, Roland put into the king's hands as a memorial, the most insolent, seditious, and atrocious libel, that has probably ever been penned. This paper Roland a few days after delivered to the National Assembly,[6] who instantly published and dispersed it over all France; and in order to give it the stronger operation they declared, that he and his brother ministers had carried with them the regret of the nation. None of the writings which have inflamed the Jacobin spirit to a savage fury, ever worked up a fiercer ferment through the whole mass of the republicans in every part of France.

Under the thin veil of *prediction*, he strongly *recommends* all the abominable practices which afterwards followed. In particular he inflamed the minds of the populace against the respectable and conscientious clergy, who became the chief objects of the massacre, and who were to him the chief objects of a malignity and rancour that one could hardly think to exist in an human heart.

We have the relicks of his fanatical persecution here. We are in a condition to judge of the merits of the persecutors and of the persecuted — I do not say the accusers and accused; because in all the furious declamations of the atheistick faction against these men, not one specifick charge has been made upon any one person of those who suffered in their massacre, or by their decree of exile.

The king had declared that he would sooner perish under their axe (he too well saw what was preparing for him) than give his sanction to the iniquitous act of proscription, under which those innocent people were to be transported.

On this proscription of the clergy, a principal part of the ostensible quarrel between the king and those ministers, had turned. From the time of the authorized publication of this libel, some of the manœuvres long and uniformly pursued for the king's deposition became more and more evident and declared.

---

6 Presented to the king June 13, delivered to him the preceding Monday. — Translator [*Burke's note*].

The tenth of August came on, and in the manner in which Roland had predicted: it was followed by the same consequences — The king was deposed, after cruel massacres, in the courts and the apartments of his palace, and in almost all parts of the city. In reward of his treason to his old master, Roland was by his new masters named minister of the home department.

The massacres of the second of September were begotten by the massacres of the tenth of August. They were universally foreseen and hourly expected. During this short interval between the two murderous scenes, the furies, male and female, cried out havock as loudly and as fiercely as ever. The ordinary jails were all filled with prepared victims; and when they overflowed, churches were turned into jails. At this time the relentless Roland had the care of the general police; he had for his colleague the bloody Danton, who was minister of justice: — the insidious Petion was mayor of Paris — the treacherous Manuel was procurator of the Common-hall.[7] The magistrates (some or all of them) were evidently the authors of this massacre. Lest the national guards should, by their very name, be reminded of their duty in preserving the lives of their fellow citizens, the common council of Paris, pretending that it was in vain to think of resisting the murderers (although in truth neither their numbers nor their arms were at all formidable) obliged those guards to draw the charges from their musquets, and took away their bayonets. One of their journalists, and according to their fashion, one of their leading states-

---

7 Jean-Marie Roland (1734–1793), Girondin ally, minister of the interior from March 1792, was arrested in May 1793. He committed suicide in November 1793 upon hearing of his wife's death by the guillotine. Georges Jacques Danton (1759–94), minister of justice from August 1792, was arrested in March 1794 and guillotined the following month. Jerôme Pétion (1756–94), mayor of Paris and president of the convention, was attacked by the Jacobins and fled in July 1792; a year later his body (partially devoured by wolves) was found in the countryside with that of another refugee. Both had died by poison. Louis Pierre Manuel (1751–93), prosecutor of the Commune, was suspended with Pétion in July 1792, but the Jacobins let them both into the government again. Manuel saved a number of prisoners who might otherwise have died in the September massacres, including Madame de Stael and Beaumarchais, and argued against the punishment of death for Louis XVI.

men, Gorsas mentions this fact in his newspaper, which he formerly called the Galley Journal. The title was well suited to the paper and its author. For some felonies he had been sentenced to the gallies; but by the benignity of the late king, this felon (to be one day advanced to the rank of a regicide) had been pardoned and released at the intercession of the ambassadors of Tippoo Sultan.[8] His gratitude was such as might naturally have been expected; and it has lately been rewarded as it deserved. This liberated galley-slave was raised, in mockery of all criminal law, to be minister of justice: he became from his elevation a more conspicuous object of accusation, and he has since received the punishment of his former crimes in proscription and death.

It will be asked, how the minister of the home department was employed at this crisis? The day after the massacre had commenced Roland appeared, but not with the powerful apparatus of a protecting magistrate, to rescue those who had survived the slaughter of the first day: nothing of this. On the third of September (that is, the day after the commencement of the massacre)[9] he writes a long, elaborate, verbose epistle to the assembly, in which, after magnifying, according to the *bon ton*[10] of the revolution, his own integrity, humanity, courage, and patriotism, he first directly justifies all the bloody proceedings of the tenth of August. He considers the slaughter of that day as a necessary measure for defeating a conspiracy, which (with a full knowledge of the falsehood of his assertion) he asserts to have been formed for a massacre of the people of Paris, and which he more than insinuates, was the work of his late unhappy master, who was universally known to carry his dread of shedding the blood of his most guilty subjects to an excess.

---

8 Antoine-Joseph Gorsas (1752–93), journalist and revolutionary, spoke of the September massacres of 1792 as "necessary days," but did not escape arrest with the other Girondins in June 1793. He fled, then returned to Paris and was recaptured and executed in October.

9 Letter to the National Assembly signed — *The Minister of the interior* ROLAND, dated Paris, Sept. 3d, 4*th year of Liberty* [*Burke's note*].

10 "Good form."

"Without the day of the tenth," says he, "it is evident that we should have been lost. The court, prepared for a long time, waited for the hour which was to accumulate all treasons, to display over Paris the standard of death, and to reign there by terrour. The sense of the people (le sentiment) always just and ready when their opinion is not corrupted, foresaw the epoch marked for their destruction, and rendered it fatal to the conspirators." He then proceeds, in the cant which has been applied to palliate all their atrocities from the fourteenth of July, 1789, to the present time;— "It is in the nature of things," continues he "and in that of the human heart, that victory should bring with it *some* excess. The sea, agitated by a violent storm, roars *long* after the tempest; but *every thing has bounds*, which ought *at length* to be observed."

In this memorable epistle, he considers such *excesses* as fatalities arising from the very nature of things, and consequently not to be punished. He allows a space of time for the duration of these agitations: and lest he should be thought rigid and too scanty in his measure, he thinks it may be *long*. But he would have things to cease *at length*. But when, and where?—When they may approach his own person.

"*Yesterday*," says he, "the Ministers *were denounced: vaguely* indeed as to the *matter*, because subjects of reproach were wanting; but with that warmth and force of assertion, which strike the imagination and seduce it for a moment, and which mislead and destroy confidence, without which no man should remain in place in a free government. *Yesterday, again*, in an assembly of the presidents of all the sections, convoked by the ministers, with a view of conciliating all minds, and of mutual explanation, I perceived that *distrust which suspects, interrogates, and fetters operations.*"

In this manner (that is, in mutual suspicions and interrogatories) this virtuous minister of the home department, and all the magistracy of Paris, spent the first day of the massacre, the atrocity of which has spread horrour and alarm throughout Europe. It does not appear that the putting a stop to the massacre, had any part in the object of their meeting, or in their consultations when they were met. Here was a minister tremblingly alive to his own safety, dead to that of his fellow citizens, eager to preserve his place, and worse than indifferent about its most important duties. Speaking of the people, he says, "that their hidden enemies may make use of this *agitation,*" (the tender appellation which he gives to horrid massacre) "to hurt *their best friends, and their most able defenders. Already the example begins*; let it restrain and arrest a *just* rage. Indignation carried to its height commences proscriptions which fall only on the *guilty,* but in which errour and particular passions may shortly involve the *honest man.*"

He saw that the able artificers in the trade and mystery of murder did not chuse that their skill should be unemployed after their first work; and that they were full as ready to cut off their rivals as their enemies. This gave him *one* alarm, that was serious. This letter of Roland in every part of it lets out the secret of all the parties in this revolution. *Plena rimarum est; hac, atque illac perfluit.*[11] We see that none of them condemn the occasional practice of murder; provided it is properly applied; provided it is kept within the bounds, which each of those parties think proper to prescribe. In this case Roland feared, that if what was occasionally useful, should become habitual, the practice might go further than was convenient. It might involve the best friends of the last revolution, as it had done the heroes of the first revolution: he feared that it would not be confined to the La Fayettes and Clermont-Tonnerres, the Duponts and Barnaves, but that it might extend to the Brissots and Vergniauxs, to the Condorcets, the Petions, and to himself.[12] Under this apprehension there is no doubt that his humane feelings were altogether unaffected.

---

11 Terence *Eunuchus* 1.105: "[With a lie to tell] I am full of holes, I leak all over."

12 The Marquis de La Fayette (1757–1834) supported the early stages of the Revolution and later adopted a stance of constitutional moderation. All of the other "heroes of the first revolution" were exiled, imprisoned, or executed: the Compte de Clermont-Tonnerre (1757–92); Pierre Samuel Dupont de Nemours (1739–1817); and Antoine Pierre Barnave (1761–93), hated by the Jacobins for defending the monarchy. The suggestion here is that the "best friends of the last [i.e., recent] revolution" will suffer a similar fate.

His observations on the massacre of the preceding day are such as cannot be passed over: — "Yesterday," said he, "was a day upon the events of which it is perhaps necessary to leave a *veil*; I know that the people with their vengeance *mingled a sort of justice*; they did not take for victims *all* who presented themselves to their fury; they directed it to *them who had for a long time been spared by the sword of the law*, and who they *believed*, from the peril of circumstances, should be sacrificed without delay. But I know that it is easy to *villains and traitors* to misrepresent this *effervescence*, and that it must be checked: I know that we owe to all France the declaration, that the *executive power* could not foresee or prevent this excess. I know that it is due to the constituted authorities to place a limit to it, or consider themselves as abolished."

In the midst of this carnage he thinks of nothing but throwing a veil over it; which was at once to cover the guilty from punishment, and to extinguish all compassion for the sufferers. He apologizes for it; in fact, he justifies it. He who (as the reader has just seen in what is quoted from this letter) feels so much indignation at "vague denunciations" when made against himself, and from which he then feared nothing more than the subversion of his power, is not ashamed to consider the charge of a conspiracy to massacre the Parisians brought against his master upon denunciations as vague as possible, or rather upon no denunciations, as a perfect justification of the monstrous proceedings against him. He is not ashamed to call the murder of the unhappy priests in the *Carmes*, who were under no criminal denunciation whatsoever, "a *vengeance* mingled with a *sort of justice*;" he observes that "they had been a long time spared by the sword of the law," and calls by anticipation all those who should represent this "*effeverscence*" in other colours, *villains and traitors*: he did not then foresee, how soon himself and his accomplices would be under the necessity of assuming the pretended character of this new sort of "*villainy and treason*," in the hope of obliterating the memory of their former real *villainies and treasons*: — he did not foresee, that in the course of six months a formal manifesto on the part of himself and his faction, written by his confederate

Brissot, was to represent this "*effervescence*" as another "*St. Bartholomew;*" and speak of it as "*having made humanity shudder, and sullied the Revolution for ever.*"[13]

It is very remarkable that he takes upon himself to know the motives of the assassins, their policy, and even what they "believed." How could this be if he had no connection with them? He praises the murderers for not having taken as yet *all* the lives of those who had, as he calls it, "*presented themselves* as victims to their fury." He paints the miserable prisoners who had been forcibly piled upon one another in the church of the Carmelites, by his faction, as *presenting themselves* as victims to their fury; as if death was their choice; or, (allowing the idiom of his language to make this equivocal) as if they were by some accident *presented* to the fury of their assassins: whereas he knew, that the leaders of the murderers fought these pure and innocent victims in the places where they had deposited them, and were sure to find them. The very selection, which he praises as a *sort of justice* tempering their fury, proves beyond a doubt, the foresight, deliberation, and method with which this massacre was made. He knew that circumstance on the very day of the commencement of the massacres, when, in all probability, he had begun this letter, for he presented it to the Assembly on the very next.

Whilst, however, he defends these acts, he is conscious that they will appear in another light to the world. He therefore acquits the executive power, that is, he acquits himself (but only by his own assertion) of those acts "of *vengeance mixed with a sort of justice,*" "as an *excess* which he could neither foresee nor prevent." He could not, he says, foresee these acts; when he tells us, the people of Paris had sagacity so well to foresee the designs of the court on the tenth of August; to foresee them so well, as to mark the precise epoch on which they were to be executed, and to contrive to anticipate them on the very day: he could not foresee these events, though he declares in this very letter that

13 See p. 12, and p. 13, of this translation [*Burke's note*]. The St. Bartholomew's Day Massacre in Paris (1572) was a mass murder of French Protestants.

victory *must* bring with it some *excess*; — "that the sea roars *long* after the tempest." So far as to his foresight. As to his disposition to prevent, if he had foreseen the massacres of that day; this will be judged by his care in putting a stop to the massacre then going on. This was no matter of foresight. He was in the very midst of it. He does not so much as pretend, that he had used any force to put a stop to it. But if he had used any, the sanction given under his hand, to a sort of justice in the murderers, was enough to disarm the protecting force.

That approbation of what they had already done, had its natural effect on the executive assassins, then in the paroxysm of their fury, as well as on their employers, then in the midst of the execution of their deliberate cold-blooded system of murder. He did not at all differ from either of them in the principle of those executions, but only in the time of their duration; and that only as it affected himself. This, though to him a great consideration, was none to his confederates, who were at the same time his rivals. They were encouraged to accomplish the work they had in hand. They did accomplish it; and whilst this grave moral epistle from a grave minister, recommending a cessation of their work of "vengeance mingled with a sort of justice" was before a grave assembly, the authors of the massacres proceeded without interruption in their business for four days together; that is, until the seventh of that month, and until all the victims of the first proscription in Paris and at Versailles, and several other places, were immolated at the shrine of the grim Moloch of liberty and equality. All the priests, all the loyalists, all the first essayists and novices of revolution in 1789, that could be found, were promiscuously put to death.

Through the whole of this long letter of Roland, it is curious to remark how the nerve and vigour of his style, which had spoken so potently to his sovereign, is relaxed, when he addresses himself to the *sans-culottes*; how that strength and dexterity of arm, with which he parries and beats down the scepter, is enfeebled and lost, when he comes to fence with the poignard! When he speaks to the populace he can no longer be direct. The whole compass of the language is tried to find synonimes and circumlocutions for massacre and murder. Things are never called by their common names. Massacre is sometimes *agitation*, sometimes *effervescence*, sometimes *excess*; sometimes too continued an exercise of a *revolutionary power.*

However, after what had passed had been praised, or excused, or pardoned, he declares loudly against such proceedings in *future*. Crimes had pioneered and made smooth the way for the march of the virtues; and from that time, order and justice, and a sacred regard for personal property, were to become the rules for the new democracy. Here Roland and the Brissotins leagued for their own preservation, by endeavouring to preserve peace. This short story will render many of the parts of Brissot's pamphlet, in which Roland's views and intentions are so often alluded to, the more intelligible in themselves, and the more useful in their application to the English reader.

Under the cover of these artifices, Roland, Brissot, and their party hoped to gain the bankers, merchants, substantial tradesmen, hoarders of assignats, and purchasers of the confiscated lands of the clergy and gentry, to join with their party, as holding out some sort of security to the effects which they possessed, whether these effects were the acquisitions of fair commerce, or the gains of jobbing in the misfortunes of their country, and the plunder of their fellow citizens. In this design the party of Roland and Brissot succeeded in a great degree. They obtained a majority in the National Convention. Composed however as that Assembly is, their majority was far from steady: but whilst they appeared to gain the Convention, and many of the outlying departments, they lost the city of Paris entirely and irrecoverably; it was fallen into the hands of Marat, Robespierre, and Danton. Their instruments were the *sans-culottes*, or rabble, who domineered in that capital, and were wholly at the devotion of those incendiaries, and received their daily pay. The people of property were of no consequence, and trembled before Marat and his janissaries.[14] As that great man had not obtained the helm of the state, it was not yet come to his turn to act the part of Brissot and his friends, in the assertion of subordination and regular government. But Robespierre has survived both these rival chiefs, and is now the great patron of Jacobin order.

To balance the exorbitant power of Paris (which threatened to leave nothing to the National Convention, but a character as insignificant as that which the first assembly had assigned to the unhappy Louis the Sixteenth) the faction of Brissot, whose leaders were Roland, Petion, Vergniaux, Isnard, Condorcet, &c. &c. &c. applied themselves to gain the great commercial towns, Lyons, Marseilles, Rouen, Nantz, and Bourdeaux. The republicans of the Brissotin description, to whom the concealed royalists, still very numerous, joined themselves, obtained a temporary superiority in all these places. In Bourdeaux, on account of the activity and eloquence of some of its representatives, this superiority was the most distinguished. This last city is seated on the Garonne, or Gironde; and being the centre of a department named from that river, the appellation of Girondists was given to the whole party. These and some other towns declared strongly against the principles of anarchy; and against the despotism of Paris. Numerous addresses were sent to the Convention, promising to maintain its authority, which the addressers were pleased to consider as legal and constitutional, though chosen, not to compose an executive government, but to form a plan for a constitution.

In the Convention measures were taken to obtain an armed force from the several departments to maintain the freedom of that body, and to provide for the personal safety of the members; neither of which, from the fourteenth of July 1789 to this hour, have been really enjoyed by their assemblies sitting under any denomination.

This scheme, which was well conceived, had not the desired

14 Originally, a Turkish soldier; by extension, someone who assists the forces of tyranny.

success. Paris, from which the Convention did not dare to move, though some threats of such a departure were from time to time thrown out, was too powerful for the party of the Gironde. Some of the proposed guards, but neither with regularity nor in force, did indeed arrive; they were debauched as fast as they came; or were sent to the frontiers. The game played by the revolutionists in 1789 with respect to the French guards of the unhappy king, was now played against the departmental guards, called together for the protection of the revolutionists. Every part of their own policy comes round, and strikes at their own power and their own lives.

The Parisians, on their part, were not slow in taking the alarm. They had just reason to apprehend, that if they permitted the smallest delay, they should see themselves besieged by an army collected from all parts of France. Violent threats were thrown out against that city in the assembly. Its total destruction was menaced. A very remarkable expression was used in these debates, "that in future times it might be inquired, on what part of the Seine Paris had stood." The faction which ruled in Paris, too bold to be intimidated, and too vigilant to be surprised, instantly armed themselves. In their turn they accused the Girondists of a treasonable design to break *the republick one and indivisible*, (whose unity they contended could only be preserved by the supremacy of Paris) into a number of *confederate* commonwealths. The Girondin faction on this account received also the name of *federalists*.

Things on both sides hastened fast to extremities. Paris, the mother of equality, was herself to be equalised. Matters were come to this alternative; either that city must be reduced to a mere member of the federative republick, or, the Convention, chosen, as they said, by all France, was to be brought regularly and systematically under the dominion of the common-hall, and even of any one of the sections of Paris.

In this awful context, thus brought to issue, the great mother club of the Jacobins was entirely in the Parisian interest. The Girondins no longer dared to shew their faces in that assembly.

Nine tenths at least of the jacobin clubs throughout France, adhered to the great patriarchal jacobiniere of Paris, to which they were (to use their own terms) *affiliated*. No authority of magistracy, judicial or executive, has the least weight, whenever these clubs chose to interfere; and they chose to interfere in every thing, and on every occasion. All hope of gaining them to the support of property, or to the acknowledgment of any law but their own will, was evidently vain, and hopeless. Nothing but an armed insurrection against their anarchical authority, could answer the purpose of the Girondins. Anarchy was to be cured by rebellion, as it had been caused by it.

As a preliminary to this attempt on the jacobins and the commons of Paris, which it was hoped would be supported by all the remaining property of France, it became absolutely necessary to prepare a manifesto, laying before the publick the whole policy, genius, character, and conduct of the partisans of club government. To make this exposition as fully and clearly as it ought to be made, it was of the same unavoidable necessity to go through a series of transactions, in which all those concerned in this revolution, were at the several periods of their activity, deeply involved. In consequence of this design, and under these difficulties, Brissot prepared the following declaration of his party, which he executed with no small ability; and in this manner the whole mystery of the French revolution was laid open in all its parts.

It is almost needless to mention to the reader the fate of the design to which this pamphlet was to be subservient. The Jacobins of Paris were more prompt than their adversaries. They were the readiest to resort to what La Fayette calls the *most sacred of all duties, that of insurrection*. Another æra of holy insurrection, commenced the thirty-first of last May. As the first fruits of that insurrection grafted on insurrection, and of that rebellion improving upon rebellion, the sacred irresponsible character of the members of the Convention was laughed to scorn. They had themselves shewn in their proceedings against the late king, how little the most fixed principles are to be relied upon, in their revolutionary constitution. The members of the Girondin party in the Convention, were seized upon or obliged to save themselves by flight. The unhappy author of this piece, with twenty of his associates, suffered together on the scaffold, after a trial, the iniquity of which puts all description to defiance.

The English reader will draw from this work of Brissot, and from the result of the last struggles of this party, some useful lessons. He will be enabled to judge of the information of those, who have undertaken to guide and enlighten us, and who, for reasons best known to themselves, have chosen to paint the French revolution and its consequences in brilliant and flattering colours. — They will know how to appreciate the liberty of France, which has been so much magnified in England. They will do justice to the wisdom, and goodness of their sovereign and his parliament, who have put them in a state of defence, in the war audaciously made upon us, in favour of that kind of liberty. When we see (as here we must see) in their true colours the character and policy of our enemies, our gratitude will become an active principle. It will produce a strong and zealous cooperation with the efforts of our government, in favour of a constitution under which we enjoy advantages, the full value of which, the querulous weakness of human nature requires sometimes the opportunity of a comparison, to understand and to relish.

Our confidence in those who watch for the publick will not be lessened. We shall be sensible that to alarm us in the late circumstances of our affairs, was not for our molestation, but for our security. We shall be sensible that this alarm was not ill-timed — and that it ought to have been given, as it was given, before the enemy had time fully to mature and accomplish their plans, for reducing us to the condition of France, as that condition is faithfully and without exaggeration described in the following work. We now have our arms in our hands; we have the means of opposing the sense, the courage, and the resources of England, to the deepest, the most craftily devised, the best combined, and the most extensive design, that ever was carried on since the beginning of the world, against all property, all order, all religion, all law, and all real freedom.

The reader is requested to attend to the part of this pamphlet which relates to the conduct of the Jacobins, with regard to the Austrian Netherlands, which they call Belgia, or Belgium.[15] It is from page seventy-two to page eighty-four of this translation. Here the views and designs upon all their neighbours are fully displayed. Here the whole mystery of their ferocious politicks is laid open with the utmost clearness. Here the manner in which they would treat every nation into which they could introduce their doctrines and influence is distinctly marked. We see that no nation was out of danger, and we see what the danger was with which every nation was threatened. The writer of this pamphlet throws the blame of several of the most violent of the proceedings on the other party. He and his friends, at the time alluded to, had a majority in the National Assembly. He admits that neither he nor they *ever publickly* opposed these measures; but he attributes their silence, to a fear of rendering themselves suspected. It is most certain, that whether from fear, or from approbation, they never discovered any dislike of those proceedings, till Dumourier was driven from the Netherlands.[16] But whatever their motive was, it is plain that the most violent is, and since the revolution has always been, the predominant party.

If Europe could not be saved without our interposition, (most certainly it could not) I am sure there is not an Englishman, who would not blush to be left out of the general effort made in favour of the general safety. But we are not secondary parties in this war; *we are principals in the danger, and ought to be principals in the exertion.* If any Englishman asks whether the designs of the French assassins are confined to the spot of Europe which they actually desolate, the citizen Brissot, the author of this book, and the

15 One of the first acts of the National Convention (which replaced the Legislative Assembly on 21 September 1792) was to order the invasion of Belgium.

16 Dumouriez lost the Austrian Netherlands, or Belgium, in 1793, and subsequently defected to Austria.

author of the declaration of war against England, will give him his answer. He will find in this book, that the republicans are divided into factions, full of the most furious and destructive animosity against each other: but he will find also that there is one point in which they perfectly agree — that they are all enemies alike, to the government of all other nations, and only contend with each other about the means of propagating their tenets, and extending their empire by conquest.

It is true, that in this present work, which the author professedly designed for an appeal to foreign nations and posterity, he has dressed up the philosophy of his own faction in as decent a garb as he could to make her appearance in publick; but through every disguise her hideous figure may be distinctly seen. If, however, the reader still wishes to see her in all her naked deformity, I would further refer him to a private letter of Brissot written towards the end of the last year, and quoted in a late very able pamphlet of Mallet du Pan. "We must," (says our philosopher) "*set fire to the four corners of Europe;*" in that alone is our safety. "*Dumourier cannot suit us.* I always distrusted him. Miranda is the general for us; he understands the *revolutionary power,* he has *courage, lights,* &c."[17] Here every thing is fairly avowed in plain language. The triumph of philosophy is the universal conflagration of Europe; the only real dissatisfaction with Dumourier is a suspicion of his moderation; and the secret motive of that preference which in this very pamphlet the author gives to Miranda, though without assigning his reasons, is declared to be the superior fitness of that foreign adventurer for the purposes of subversion and destruction. — On the other hand, if there can be any man in this country so hardy as to undertake the defence or the apology of the present monstrous usurpers of France; and if it should be said in their favour, that it is not just to credit the

17 See the translation of Mallet du Pan's work printed for Owen, page 53 [*Burke's note*]. Jacques Mallet du Pan (1749–1800) was a Protestant monarchist who wrote on French affairs; Francisco Miranda (1757–1815), an officer who served under Dumouriez. After Dumouriez's treason, Miranda was arrested by order of the Jacobins, tried, and acquitted by the Revolutionary Tribunal.

charges of their enemy Brissot against them, who have actually tried and condemned him on the very same charges among others; we are luckily supplied with the best possible evidence in support of this part of his book against them: it comes from among themselves. Camille Desmoulins published the "History of the Brissotins" in answer to this very address of Brissot. It was the counter-manifesto of the last Holy revolution of the thirty-first of May;[18] and the flagitious orthodoxy of his writings at that period has been admitted in the late scrutiny of him by the Jacobin club, when they saved him from that guillotine "which he grazed." In the beginning of his work he displays "the task of glory," as he calls it, which presented itself at the opening of the Convention. All is summed up in two points: "to create the French republick, and *to disorganize Europe; perhaps to purge it of its tyrants by the eruption of the volcanick principles of equality.*"[19] The coincidence is exact; the proof is complete and irresistible.

In a cause like this, and in a time like the present, there is no neutrality. They who are not actively, and with decision and energy, against jacobinism, are its partisans. They who do not dread it, love it. It cannot be viewed with indifference. It is a thing made to produce a powerful impression on the feelings. Such is the nature of jacobinism, such is the nature of man, that this system must be regarded either with enthusiastick admiration, or with the highest degree of detestation, resentment, and horrour.

Another great lesson may be taught by this book, and by the fortune of the author, and his party: I mean a lesson drawn from the consequences of engaging in daring innovations, from an hope that we may be able to limit their mischievous operation at our pleasure, and by our policy to secure ourselves against the effect of the evil examples we hold out to the world. This lesson is taught through almost all the important pages of history; but never has it been taught so clearly and so awfully as at this hour.

18 On 31 May 1793 the Jacobins in the National Convention rose up against the Girondins.

19 See the translation of the History of the Brissotins, by Camille Desmoulins, printed for Owen, p. 2 [*Burke's note*].

The revolutionists who have just suffered an ignominious death, under the sentence of the revolutionary tribunal (a tribunal composed of those with whom they had triumphed in the total destruction of the ancient government) were by no means ordinary men, or without very considerable talents and resources. But with all their talents and resources, and the apparent momentary extent of their power, we see the fate of their projects, their power, and their persons. We see before our eyes the absurdity of thinking to establish order upon principles of confusion, or with the materials and instruments of rebellion, to build up a solid and stable government.

Such partisans of a republick amongst us, as may not have the worst intentions, will see, that the principles, the plans, the manners, the morals, and the whole system of France, is altogether as adverse to the formation and duration of any rational scheme of a republick, as it is to that of a monarchy absolute or limited. It is indeed a system which can only answer the purposes of robbers and murderers.

The translator has only to say for himself, that he has found some difficulty in this version. His original author, through haste, perhaps, or through the perturbation of a mind filled with a great and arduous enterprise, is often obscure. There are some passages too, in which his language requires to be first translated into French, at least into such French as the academy would in former times have tolerated.[20] He writes with great force and vivacity; but the language, like every thing else in his country, has undergone a revolution. The translator thought it best to be as literal as possible; conceiving such a translation would perhaps be the most fit to convey the author's peculiar mode of thinking. In this way the translator has no credit for style; but he makes it up in fidelity. Indeed the facts and observations are so much more important than the style, that no apology is wanted for producing them in any intelligible manner.

20 The French Academy was celebrated for enforcing a standard of purity in language.

A Letter to a Noble Lord (1796)

In November 1795 Burke's pension was attacked in the House of Lords by the Earl of Lauderdale and the Duke of Bedford. There were plausible grounds for mockery. In his "Speech on Economical Reform" of 1780, Burke had accused George III of aggrandizing the power of the crown through excessive awards of sinecures and pensions to court favorites. He had shown hostility to the interests of the crown as recently as the winter of 1788–89, when the madness of the king prompted the Rockingham Whigs to mount a constitutional argument for a regency. This background lent a probable coloring to the charge that in opposing the French Revolution Burke was deserting his principles. Paine, in *The Rights of Man*, had denounced him as a courtier, "accustomed to kiss the aristocratical hand that hath purloined him from himself"; and when the Duke of Bedford made his unpleasant remarks on the pension, he must have thought his quarry fairly trapped. When, in the same ebullience, he stepped forward to embrace the French Revolution, he must have appeared to himself a generous-hearted man of privilege, quite out of reach for the upstart Irish adventurer Burke.

It was the low moment of Burke's life and fortunes. Five years earlier he had broken his friendship and political alliance with Fox, over the French Revolution, and by his vehemence had split the Rockingham Whigs. But though he crossed the floor to Pitt's side of the House, he remained a man without a party. His advice for a war against France was firmly rejected. In 1795, after fourteen years of work on Indian reforms, his efforts terminated in failure, with the acquittal of Warren Hastings by the House of Lords. At the comple-

tion of the trial a year earlier, Burke had retired from the House of
Commons, and in every public sense his career seemed to lie in
ruins. But he had a deeper and more private sorrow. His son Richard, elected MP from Malton in July 1794, had died in August. The
relationship between Edmund and Richard Burke had been altogether happy, with unbroken trust on both sides. Richard helped
to manage Burke's contacts with French refugees; he contributed
to the *Reflections* the passage containing the sentence "They have
learned to talk against monks with the spirit of a monk"; he acted —
though with more dubious results — as a faithful personal liaison to
Lord Fitzwilliam's administration in Ireland. The death of his son
had shattered Burke's hope for an heir and with it his dream of
becoming the first Lord Beaconsfield.

These circumstances explain a tone of elegiac regret, and a
fatalism uncommon in Burke's writing, which pervade the *Letter*
after its salute to Bedford as a member of the new sect in philosophy
and politics. Burke confesses: "I live in an inverted order. They
who ought to have succeeded me are gone before me. They who
should have been to me as posterity are in the place of ancestors."
Of his three decades of public service, he says in summary: "For
whatever I have been (I am now no more) I put myself on my
country." Yet the weaknesses of his situation are turned to strengths
by the power and cunning, the energy of rebuke and the sustained
ferocity of his counterattack. Confident of "my character as a reformer," one who, at a crisis of English society, had "a state to
preserve, as well as a state to reform," he presents himself as an
example of gratitude despite the ingratitude of his benefactors. The
young Duke of Bedford has done nothing to improve the system he
inherited, though it places him at its pinnacle; whereas Burke, from
his middle station, has done perhaps as much as anyone. He claims
a share of the credit for averting a national catastrophe in 1780–82,
a rebellion-in-the-making whose largest warning sign was the Gordon Riots. He knows what the spoilt nobility and the enthusiasts of
a leveling democracy cannot know from experience: the value of
qualified persons in a party or in government, who associate for the
purpose of assisting the state. Bedford glories in the charm of impiety and has buried without honor all the privileges that make him

what he is. Burke, by contrast, rounds off his letter with an act of unexpected piety toward a great man, Admiral Keppel — the uncle of Bedford but also an intimate friend of Burke's, and one whom he had successfully defended from an accusation of cowardice at a celebrated court martial several years before. That act of disinterested valor is never mentioned here. It is recalled implicitly, the antithesis of the jeering sarcasm of Bedford's attack.

Burke's invective against the "poor rich man" who abuses the privilege of nobility gives him a curious common impulse with the Jacobins. But the denunciation of an aristocrat was for him utterly consistent with a defense of aristocracy. Burke had long considered men of honor and noble reputation as the steadiest resource of liberty, whether the threat of tyranny came from the king or from the people. By their habit of reflecting on themselves in a line of succession, and the wish to deserve the pride that belongs to the character of their families, such persons are to be relied on more than any others for public spirit and self-sacrifice. In 1771, Burke wrote to the Duke of Richmond that the noble lords of the Rockingham party were "in general somewhat languid, scrupulous and unsystematick. But men of high birth and great property are rarely as enterprising as others, and for reasons that are very natural." He continued in his letter to that duke: "Persons in your station of life ought to have long views. You people of great families and hereditary trusts and fortunes are not like such as I am, who whatever we may be by the rapidity of our growth and of the fruit we bear, flatter ourselves that while we creep on the ground we belly into melons that are exquisite for size and flavour, yet still we are but annual plants that perish with our season and leave no sort of traces behind. You, if you are what you ought to be, are the great oaks that shade a country and perpetuate your benefits from generation to generation." The very houses of such men are "the publick repositories and offices of record for the constitution," and in times of national decay something is preserved where certain families "make it their business by the whole course of their lives, principally by their example to mould into the very vital stamina of their descendants those principles which ought to be transmitted pure and uncorrupted to posterity." Only in view of this generous wish can one understand Burke's hatred of the unworthy offspring of the aristocracy.

A *Letter to a Noble Lord* seems to have hurtled from its author as by compulsion. Yet it was pondered long, and extensively rewritten in proof, and the result is a compacted power with no precedent in his earlier writing. Burke here deploys a savage irony that is consistent with the dignity of self-vindication. Both moods issue in distinctive set pieces — the genealogies of Bedford and Burke; the panegyric on Windsor Castle; the fantastic daydream of the estates of "the low, fat, Bedford level" overrun by a tide of Jacobins — yet there is never a moment at which the two motives seem quite separable. Private letters from Burke, first published by F. P. Lock in the *English Historical Review* in 1997, have established conclusively what many scholars long suspected: that the *Letter* was addressed to Lord Grenville — the member of Pitt's cabinet who defended Burke against the attack in the House of Lords, in one of those gestures of gratuitous valor whose relation to gratitude is a deep subject of the *Letter* itself. Written as it is for an important ally in foreign policy, and more obliquely for the remnant of the Rockingham party that broke with Fox, the *Letter* offers a second review of Burke's career, after the speech at Bristol in 1780. Covering as it does his later services as statesman and adviser, this is the more personal document — romantic in its investment of public scenes with private pathos, and charged with an intimation of prophecy. For imaginative command and exuberance at its middle length, it has no equal in English prose.

A Letter from the Right Hon. Edmund Burke, to a Noble Lord,

on the Attacks Made upon Him and His Pension, in the House of Lords,

by the Duke of Bedford and the Earl of Lauderdale

My Lord,

I could hardly flatter myself with the hope, that so very early in the season I should have to acknowledge obligations to the duke of Bedford and to the earl of Lauderdale. These noble persons have lost no time in conferring upon me, that sort of honour, which it is alone within their competence, and which it is certainly most congenial to their nature and their manners to bestow.

To be ill spoken of, in whatever language they speak, by the zealots of the new sect in philosophy and politicks, of which these noble persons think so charitably, and of which others think so justly, to me, is no matter of uneasiness or surprise. To have incurred the displeasure of the duke of Orleans or the duke of Bedford, to fall under the censure of citizen Brissot or of his friend the earl of Lauderdale, I ought to consider as proofs, not the least satisfactory, that I have produced some part of the effect I proposed by my endeavours. I have laboured hard to earn, what the noble Lords are generous enough to pay. Personal offence I have given them none. The part they take against me is from zeal to the cause. It is well! It is perfectly well! I have to do homage to their justice. I have to thank the Bedfords and the Lauderdales for having so faithfully and so fully acquitted towards me whatever arrear of debt was left undischarged by the Priestleys and the Paines.

Some, perhaps, may think them executors in their own wrong: I at least have nothing to complain of. They have gone beyond the demands of justice. They have been (a little perhaps beyond their intention) favourable to me. They have been the means of bringing out, by their invectives, the handsome things which lord Grenville[1] has had the goodness and condescension to say in my behalf. Retired as I am from the world, and from all its affairs and all its pleasures, I confess it does kindle, in my nearly extinguished feelings, a very vivid satisfaction to be so attacked and so commended. It is soothing to my wounded mind, to be commended by an able, vigorous, and well informed statesman, and at the very moment when he stands forth with a manliness and resolution, worthy of himself and of his cause, for the preservation of the person and government of our sovereign, and therein for the security of the laws, the liberties, the morals, and the lives of his people. To be in any fair way connected with such things, is indeed a distinction. No philosophy can make me above it: no melancholy can depress me so low, as to make me wholly insensible to such an honour.

Why will they not let me remain in obscurity and inaction? Are they apprehensive, that if an atom of me remains, the sect has something to fear? Must I be annihilated, lest, like old *John Zisca*'s,[2] my skin might be made into a drum, to animate Europe

1 In the same debate on the Treasonable Practices Bill (13 November 1795) in which the Duke of Bedford and the Earl of Lauderdale attacked Burke's pension in the House of Lords, William Wyndham, first Lord Grenville (1759–1834), who was Pitt's foreign secretary, defended it as the honorable reward of an extraordinary career of public service. The son of George Grenville, whose American policy Burke opposed, he had succeeded Burke as paymaster, and after a brief period as Speaker of the House joined the cabinet in 1789. His brief but wholly laudatory letter about the *Reflections* was among the first responses to the book that Burke received. The passing mention of Grenville makes him appear tangential to the argument here — as he would not be had Burke identified him as the lord to whom the *Letter* is addressed — and Grenville's own politics may give a clue to the sort of commitments Burke wished to evoke by implication in his final self-reckoning. Like Burke, he supported Wilberforce's abolitionist aims. He also supported war with France, and the repressive domestic legislation of Pitt, but in later years he would form a coalition that allowed Fox back into the cabinet. His last parliamentary speech in 1822 concerned Catholic emancipation.

2 John Zisca (ca. 1379–1429), Hussite general, who was said to have ordered that his skin be made into a drumhead after his death.

to eternal battle, against a tyranny that threatens to overwhelm all Europe, and all the human race?

My lord, it is a subject of awful meditation. Before this of France, the annals of all time have not furnished an instance of a *complete* revolution. That revolution seems to have extended even to the constitution of the mind of man. It has this of wonderful in it, that it resembles what lord Verulam[3] says of the operations of nature: It was perfect, not only in its elements and principles, but in all its members and its organs from the very beginning. The moral scheme of France furnishes the only pattern ever known, which they who admire will *instantly* resemble. It is indeed an inexhaustible repertory of one kind of examples. In my wretched condition, though hardly to be classed with the living, I am not safe from them. They have tygers to fall upon animated strength. They have hyenas to prey upon carcasses. The national menagerie is collected by the first physiologists of the time; and it is defective in no description of savage nature. They pursue, even such as me, into the obscurest retreats, and haul them before their revolutionary tribunals. Neither sex, nor age — nor the sanctuary of the tomb, is sacred to them. They have so determined a hatred to all privileged orders, that they deny even to the departed, the sad immunities of the grave. They are not wholly without an object. Their turpitude purveys to their malice; and they unplumb the dead for bullets to assassinate the living. If all revolutionists were not proof against all caution, I should recommend it to their consideration, that no persons were ever known in history, either sacred or profane, to vex the sepulchre, and by their sorceries, to call up the prophetick dead, with any other event, than the prediction of their own disastrous fate. — "Leave me, oh leave me to repose!"[4]

In one thing I can excuse the duke of Bedford for his attack upon me and my mortuary pension. He cannot readily comprehend the transaction he condemns. What I have obtained was

---

3 Francis Bacon, first Baron Verulam and Viscount St. Albans (1561– 1626), author of the *Advancement of Learning* and founder of the method of inquiry that treats nature as an external entity to be probed by scientific research.

4 Thomas Gray, *The Descent of Odin*, line 50.

the fruit of no bargain; the production of no intrigue; the result of no compromise; the effect of no solicitation. The first suggestion of it never came from me, mediately or immediately, to his majesty or any of his ministers. It was long known that the instant my engagements would permit it, and before the heaviest of all calamities had for ever condemned me to obscurity and sorrow, I had resolved on a total retreat. I had executed that design. I was entirely out of the way of serving or of hurting any statesman, or any party, when the ministers so generously and so nobly carried into effect the spontaneous bounty of the crown. Both descriptions have acted as became them. When I could no longer serve them, the ministers have considered my situation. When I could no longer hurt them, the revolutionists have trampled on my infirmity. My gratitude, I trust, is equal to the manner in which the benefit was conferred. It came to me indeed, at a time of life, and in a state of mind and body, in which no circumstance of fortune could afford me any real pleasure. But this was no fault in the royal donor, or in his ministers, who were pleased, in acknowledging the merits of an invalid servant of the publick, to assuage the sorrows of a desolate old man.

It would ill become me to boast of any thing. It would as ill become me, thus called upon, to depreciate the value of a long life, spent with unexampled toil in the service of my country. Since the total body of my services, on account of the industry which was shewn in them, and the fairness of my intentions, have obtained the acceptance of my sovereign, it would be absurd in me to range myself on the side of the duke of Bedford and the corresponding society, or, as far as in me lies, to permit a dispute on the rate at which the authority appointed by *our* constitution to estimate such things, has been pleased to set them.

Loose libels ought to be passed by in silence and contempt. By me they have been so always. I knew that as long as I remained in publick, I should live down the calumnies of malice, and the judgments of ignorance. If I happened to be now and then in the wrong, as who is not, like all other men, I must bear the consequence of my faults and my mistakes. The libels of the present day, are just of the same stuff as the libels of the past. But they derive an importance from the rank of the persons they come from, and the gravity of the place where they were uttered. In some way or other I ought to take some notice of them. To assert myself thus traduced is not vanity or arrogance. It is a demand of justice; it is a demonstration of gratitude. If I am unworthy, the ministers are worse than prodigal. On that hypothesis, I perfectly agree with the duke of Bedford.

For whatever I have been (I am now no more) I put myself on my country. I ought to be allowed a reasonable freedom, because I stand upon my deliverance; and no culprit ought to plead in irons. Even in the utmost latitude of defensive liberty, I wish to preserve all possible decorum. Whatever it may be in the eyes of these noble persons themselves, to me, their situation calls for the most profound respect. If I should happen to trespass a little, which I trust I shall not, let it always be supposed, that a confusion of characters may produce mistakes; that in the masquerades of the grand carnival of our age, whimsical adventures happen; odd things are said and pass off. If I should fail a single point in the high respect I owe to those illustrious persons, I cannot be supposed to mean the duke of Bedford and the earl of Lauderdale of the house of peers, but the duke of Bedford and the earl of Lauderdale of palace-yard; — The dukes and earls of Brentford.[5] There they are on the pavement; there they seem to come nearer to my humble level; and, virtually at least, to have waived their high privilege.

Making this protestation, I refuse all revolutionary tribunals, where men have been put to death for no other reason, than that they had obtained favours from the crown. I claim, not the letter, but the spirit of the old English law, that is, to be tried by my peers. I decline his grace's jurisdiction as a judge. I challenge the duke of Bedford as a juror to pass upon the value of my services. Whatever his natural parts may be, I cannot recognize in his few and idle years, the competence to judge of my long and labori-

---

5 The two kings of Brentford—alike in their dandyism and adoptive French manners—appear in Buckingham's satirical play *The Rehearsal* (1672).

ous life. If I can help it, he shall not be on the inquest of my *quantum meruit*.[6] Poor rich man! He can hardly know any thing of publick industry in its exertions, or can estimate its compensations when its work is done. I have no doubt of his grace's readiness in all the calculations of vulgar arithmetick; but I shrewdly suspect, that he is little studied in the theory of moral proportions; and has never learned the rule of three in the arithmetick of policy and state.[7]

His grace thinks I have obtained too much. I answer, that my exertions, whatever they have been, were such as no hopes of pecuniary reward could possibly excite; and no pecuniary compensation can possibly reward them. Between money and such services, if done by abler men than I am, there is no common principle of comparison: they are quantities incommensurable. Money is made for the comfort and convenience of animal life. It cannot be a reward for what, mere animal life must indeed sustain, but never can inspire. With submission to his grace, I have not had more than sufficient. As to any noble use, I trust I know how to employ, as well as he, a much greater fortune than he possesses. In a more confined application, I certainly stand in need of every kind of relief and easement much more than he does. When I say I have not received more than I deserve, is this the language I hold to majesty? No! Far, very far, from it! Before that presence, I claim no merit at all. Every thing towards me is favour, and bounty. One style to a gracious benefactor; another to a proud and insulting foe.

His grace is pleased to aggravate my guilt, by charging my acceptance of his majesty's grant as a departure from my ideas, and the spirit of my conduct with regard to œconomy. If it be, my ideas of œconomy were false and ill founded. But they are the duke of Bedford's ideas of œconomy I have contradicted, and not my own. If he means to allude to certain bills brought in by

6 "As much as he deserves."

7 Rule for deriving the fourth member of a double ratio from the first three: as, for example, 2 is to 3 as 4 is to x, where x is 6.

me on a message from the throne in 1782, I tell him, that there is
nothing in my conduct that can contradict either the letter or
the spirit of those acts. Does he mean the pay-office act? I take it
for granted he does not. The act to which he alludes is, I suppose, the establishment act. I greatly doubt whether his grace
has ever read the one or the other. The first of these systems cost
me, with every assistance which my then situation gave me, pains
incredible. I found an opinion common through all the offices,
and general in the publick at large, that it would prove impossible to reform and methodize the office of paymaster general.
I undertook it, however; and I succeeded in my undertaking.
Whether the military service, or whether the general œconomy
of our finances have profited by that act, I leave to those who are
acquainted with the army, and with the treasury, to judge.

An opinion full as general prevailed also at the same time,
that nothing could be done for the regulation of the civil-list
establishment. The very attempt to introduce method into it,
and any limitations of its services, was held absurd. I had not
seen the man, who so much as suggested one œconomical principle, or an œconomical expedient, upon that subject. Nothing
but coarse amputation, or coarser taxation, were then talked of,
both of them without design, combination, or the least shadow
of principle. Blind and headlong zeal, or factious fury, were the
whole contribution brought by the most noisy on that occasion,
towards the satisfaction of the publick, or the relief of the crown.

Let me tell my youthful censor, that the necessities of that
time required something very different from what others then
suggested, or what his grace now conceives. Let me inform him,
that it was one of the most critical periods in our annals.

Astronomers have supposed, that if a certain comet, whose
path intersected the ecliptick, had met the earth in some (I
forget what) sign, it would have whirled us along with it, in its
eccentrick course, into God knows what regions of heat and
cold. Had the portentous comet of the rights of man, (which
"from its horrid hair shakes pestilence, and war," and "with fear

of change perplexes monarchs")[8] had that comet crossed upon us in that internal state of England, nothing human could have prevented our being irresistibly hurried, out of the highway of heaven, into all the vices, crimes, horrours and miseries of the French revolution.

Happily, France was not then jacobinised. Her hostility was at a good distance. We had a limb cut off; but we preserved the body: We lost our colonies; but we kept our constitution. There was, indeed, much intestine heat; there was a dreadful fermentation. Wild and savage insurrection quitted the woods, and prowled about our streets in the name of reform. Such was the distemper of the publick mind, that there was no madman, in his maddest ideas, and maddest projects, who might not count upon numbers to support his principles and execute his designs.

Many of the changes, by a great misnomer called parliamentary reforms, went, not in the intention of all the professors and supporters of them, undoubtedly, but went in their certain, and, in my opinion, not very remote effect, home to the utter destruction of the constitution of this kingdom. Had they taken place, not France, but England, would have had the honour of leading up the death-dance of democratick revolution. Other projects, exactly coincident in time with those, struck at the very existence of the kingdom under any constitution. There are who remember the blind fury of some, and the lamentable helplessness of others; here, a torpid confusion, from a panick fear of the danger; there, the same inaction from a stupid insensibility to it; here, wellwishers to the mischief; there, indifferent lookers-on. At the same time, a sort of national convention, dubious in its nature, and perilous in its example, nosed parliament in the very seat of its authority; sat with a sort of superintendance over it; and little less than dictated to it, not only laws, but the very form and essence of legislature itself. In Ireland things ran in a still more eccentrick course. Government was unnerved, confounded, and

8 *Paradise Lost* 2:710–11, 1:598–99.

in a manner suspended. Its equipoise was totally gone. I do not mean to speak disrespectfully of lord North. He was a man of admirable parts; of general knowledge; of a versatile understanding fitted for every sort of business; of infinite wit and pleasantry; of a delightful temper; and with a mind most perfectly disinterested. But it would be only to degrade myself by a weak adulation, and not to honour the memory of a great man, to deny that he wanted something of the vigilance and spirit of command, that the time required. Indeed, a darkness, next to the fog of this awful day, loured over the whole region. For a little time the helm appeared abandoned —

Ipse diem noctemque negat discernere cœlo
Nec meminisse viœ mediâ Palinurus in undâ.[9]

At that time I was connected with men of high place in the community. They loved liberty as much as the duke of Bedford can do; and they understood it at least as well. Perhaps their politicks, as usual took a tincture from their character, and they cultivated what they loved. The liberty they pursued was a liberty inseparable from order, from virtue, from morals, and from religion, and was neither hypocritically nor fanatically followed. They did not wish, that liberty, in itself, one of the first of blessings, should in its perversion become the greatest curse which could fall upon mankind. To preserve the constitution entire, and practically equal to all the great ends of its formation, not in one single part, but in all its parts, was to them the first object. Popularity and power they regarded alike. These were with them only different means of obtaining that object; and had no preference over each other in their minds, but as one or the other might afford a surer or a less certain prospect of arriving at that end. It is some consolation to me in the cheerless gloom, which darkens the evening of my life, that with them I commenced my political career, and never for a moment, in reality, nor in ap-

9 *Aeneid* 3:201–2: "Even Palinurus says he cannot tell the day from the night sky, or think of a middle way through the billowing waves."

pearance, for any length of time, was separated from their good wishes and good opinion.

By what accident it matters not, nor upon what desert, but just then, and in the midst of that hunt of obloquy, which ever has pursued me with a full cry through life, I had obtained a very considerable degree of publick confidence. I know well enough how equivocal a test this kind of popular opinion forms of the merit that obtained it. I am no stranger to the insecurity of its tenure. I do not boast of it. It is mentioned, to shew, not how highly I prize the thing, but my right to value the use I made of it. I endeavoured to turn that short-lived advantage to myself into a permanent benefit to my country. Far am I from detracting from the merit of some gentlemen, out of office or in it, on that occasion. No! — It is not my way to refuse a full and heaped measure of justice to the aids that I receive. I have, through life, been willing to give every thing to others; and to reserve nothing for myself, but the inward conscience, that I had omitted no pains, to discover, to animate, to discipline, to direct the abilities of the country for its service, and to place them in the best light to improve their age, or to adorn it. This conscience I have. I have never suppressed any man; never checked him for a moment in his course, by any jealousy, or by any policy. I was always ready, to the height of my means (and they were always infinitely below my desires) to forward those abilities which overpowered my own. He is an ill-furnished undertaker, who has no machinery but his own hands to work with. Poor in my own faculties, I ever thought myself rich in theirs. In that period of difficulty and danger, more especially, I consulted, and sincerely co-operated with men of all parties, who seemed disposed to the same ends, or to any main part of them. Nothing, to prevent disorder, was omitted: when it appeared, nothing to subdue it was left un-counselled, nor unexecuted, as far as I could prevail. At the time I speak of, and having a momentary lead, so aided and so encouraged, and as a feeble instrument in a mighty hand — I do not say, I saved my country; I am sure I did my country important service. There were few, indeed, that did not at that time acknowledge it, and that time was thirteen years ago. It was but one voice, that no man in the kingdom better deserved an honourable provision should be made for him.

So much for my general conduct through the whole of the portentous crisis from 1780 to 1782, and the general sense then entertained of that conduct by my country. But my character, as a reformer, in the particular instances which the duke of Bedford refers to, is so connected in principle with my opinions on the hideous changes, which have since barbarized France, and spreading thence, threaten the political and moral order of the whole world, that it seems to demand something of a more detailed discussion.

My œconomical reforms were not, as his grace may think, the suppression of a paltry pension or employment, more or less. Œconomy in my plans was, as it ought to be, secondary, subordinate, instrumental. I acted on state principles. I found a great distemper in the commonwealth; and, according to the nature of the evil and of the object, I treated it. The malady was deep; it was complicated, in the causes and in the symptoms. Throughout it was full of contra-indicants. On one hand government, daily growing more invidious from an apparent increase of the means of strength, was every day growing more contemptible by real weakness. Nor was this dissolution confined to government commonly so called. It extended to parliament; which was losing not a little in its dignity and estimation, by an opinion of its not acting on worthy motives. On the other hand, the desires of the people, (partly natural and partly infused into them by art) appeared in so wild and inconsiderate a manner, with regard to the œconomical object (for I set aside for a moment the dreadful tampering with the body of the constitution itself) that if their petitions had literally been complied with, the state would have been convulsed; and a gate would have been opened, through which all property might be sacked and ravaged. Nothing could have saved the publick from the mischiefs of the false reform but its absurdity; which would soon have brought itself, and with it all real reform, into discredit. This would have left a rankling wound in the hearts of the people, who would know they had failed in the accomplishment of their wishes, but who, like the rest of mankind in all ages, would impute the blame to any thing rather than to their own proceedings. But there were then persons in the world, who nourished complaint; and would have been thoroughly disappointed if the people were ever satisfied. I was not of that humour. I wished that they *should* be satisfied. It was my aim to give to the people the substance of what I knew they desired, and what I thought was right whether they desired it or not, before it had been modified for them into senseless petitions. I knew that there is a manifest marked distinction, which ill men, with ill designs, or weak men incapable of any design, will constantly be confounding, that is, a marked distinction between change and reformation. The former alters the substance of the objects themselves; and gets rid of all their essential good, as well as of all the accidental evil annexed to them. Change is novelty; and whether it is to operate any one of the effects of reformation at all, or whether it may not contradict the very principle upon which reformation is desired, cannot be certainly known before hand. Reform is, not a change in the substance, or in the primary modification of the object, but a direct application of a remedy to the grievance complained of. So far as that is removed, all is sure. It stops there; and if it fails, the substance which underwent the operation, at the very worst, is but where it was.

All this, in effect, I think, but am not sure, I have said elsewhere. It cannot at this time be too often repeated; line upon line; precept upon precept; until it comes into the currency of a proverb, *to innovate is not to reform.* The French revolutionists complained of every thing; they refused to reform any thing; and they left nothing, no, nothing at all *unchanged.* The consequences are *before* us, — not in remote history; not in future prognostication: they are about us; they are upon us. They shake the publick security; they menace private enjoyment. They dwarf the growth of the young; they break the quiet of the old. If we travel, they stop our way. They infest us in town; they pursue us to the country. Our business is interrupted; our repose is troubled; our pleasures are saddened; our very studies are poisoned and perverted, and knowledge is rendered worse than ignorance, by the enormous evils of this dreadful innovation. The revolution harpies of France, sprung from night and hell, or from that chaotick anarchy, which generates equivocally "all monstrous, all prodigious things,"[10] cuckoo-like, adulterously lay their eggs, and brood over, and hatch them in the nest of every neighbouring state. These obscene harpies, who deck themselves, in I know not what divine attributes, but who in reality are foul and ravenous birds of prey (both mothers and daughters) flutter over our heads, and souse down upon our tables, and leave nothing unrent, unrifled, unravaged, or unpolluted with the slime of their filthy offal.[11]

If his grace can contemplate the result of this complete innovation, or, as some friends of his will call it, *reform*, in the whole body of its solidity and compound mass, at which, as Hamlet says, the face of heaven glows with horrour and indignation,[12] and which, in truth, makes every reflecting mind, and every feeling heart, perfectly thought-sick, without a thorough abhorrence of

10 *Paradise Lost* 2:625.
11 Tristius haud illis monstrum, nec faevior ulla
     Pestis, & ira Deûm Stygiis sese extulit undis.
     Virginei volucrum vultus; faedissima ventris.
     Proluvies; uncaeque manus; & pallida semper
     Ora fame——.
Here the Poet breaks the line, because he (and that He is Virgil) had not verse or language to describe that monster even as he had conceived her. Had he lived to our time, he would have been more overpowered with the reality than he was with the imagination. Virgil only knew the horrour of the times before him. Had he lived to see the revolutionists and constitutionalists of France, he would have had more horrid and disgusting features of his harpies to describe, and more frequent failures in the attempt to describe them [*Burke's note*].
     Aeneid 214–18: "No monster more terrible than these, no plague or punishment of the Gods more savage, ever rose up from the Stygian waves. Virgins above, vultures beneath, spraying out grossest filth, with sharp-clawed hands and faces always pallid from extreme hunger."
12 *Hamlet* 3.4.49.

every thing they say, and every thing they do, I am amazed at the morbid strength, or the natural infirmity of his mind.

It was then not my love, but my hatred to innovation, that produced my plan of reform. Without troubling myself with the exactness of the logical diagram, I considered them as things substantially opposite. It was to prevent that evil, that I proposed the measures, which his grace is pleased, and I am not sorry he is pleased, to recal to my recollection. I had (what I hope that noble duke will remember in all his operations) a state to preserve, as well as a state to reform. I had a people to gratify, but not to inflame, or to mislead. I do not claim half the credit for what I did, as for what I prevented from being done. In that situation of the publick mind, I did not undertake, as was then proposed, to new model the house of commons or the house of lords; or to change the authority under which any officer of the crown acted, who was suffered at all to exist. Crown, lords, commons, judicial system, system of administration, existed as they had existed before; and in the mode and manner in which they had always existed. My measures were, what I then truly stated them to the house to be, in their intent, healing and mediatorial. A complaint was made of too much influence in the house of commons; I reduced it in both houses; and I gave my reasons article by article for every reduction, and shewed why I thought it safe for the service of the state. I heaved the lead every inch of way I made. A disposition to expence was complained of; to that I opposed, not mere retrenchment, but a system of œconomy, which would make a random expence without plan or foresight, in future not easily practicable. I proceeded upon principles of research to put me in possession of my matter; on principles of method to regulate it; and on principles in the human mind and in civil affairs to secure and perpetuate the operation. I conceived nothing arbitrarily; nor proposed any thing to be done by the will and pleasure of others, or my own; but by reason, and by reason only. I have ever abhorred, since the first dawn of my understanding to this its obscure twilight, all the operations of opinion, fancy, inclination, and will, in the affairs of government, where only a sovereign reason, paramount to all forms of legislation and administration, should dictate. Government is made for the very purpose of opposing that reason to will and to caprice, in the reformers or in the reformed, in the governors or in the governed, in kings, in senates, or in people.

On a careful review, therefore, and analysis of all the component parts of the civil list, and on weighing them against each other, in order to make, as much as possible, all of them a subject of estimate (the foundation and corner-stone of all regular provident œconomy) it appeared to me evident, that this was impracticable, whilst that part, called the pension list, was totally discretionary in its amount. For this reason, and for this only, I proposed to reduce it, both in its gross quantity, and in its larger individual proportions, to a certainty: lest, if it were left without a *general* limit, it might eat up the civil list service; if suffered to be granted in portions too great for the fund, it might defeat its own end; and by unlimited allowances to some, it might disable the crown in means of providing for others. The pension list was to be kept as a sacred fund; but it could not be kept as a constant open fund, sufficient for growing demands, if some demands would wholly devour it. The tenour of the act will shew that it regarded the civil list *only*, the reduction of which to some sort of estimate was my great object.

No other of the crown funds did I meddle with, because they had not the same relations. This of the four and a half per cents does his grace imagine had escaped me, or had escaped all the men of business, who acted with me in those regulations? I knew that such a fund existed, and that pensions had been always granted on it, before his grace was born. This fund was full in my eye. It was full in the eyes of those who worked with me. It was left on principle. On principle I did what was then done; and on principle what was left undone was omitted. I did not dare to rob the nation of all funds to reward merit. If I pressed this point too close, I acted contrary to the avowed principles on which I went. Gentlemen are very fond of quoting me; but if any one thinks it worth his while to know the rules that guided me in my plan of reform, he will read my printed speech on that subject; at least what is contained from page 230 to page 241 in the second volume of the collection which a friend has given himself the trouble to make of my publications. Be this as it may, these two bills (though achieved with the greatest labour, and management of every sort, both within and without the house) were only a part, and but a small part, of a very large system, comprehending all the objects I stated in opening my proposition, and indeed many more, which I just hinted at in my speech to the electors of Bristol, when I was put out of that representation. All these, in some state or other of forwardness, I have long had by me.

But do I justify his majesty's grace on these grounds? I think them the least of my services! The time gave them an occasional value: What I have done in the way of political œconomy was far from confined to this body of measures. I did not come into parliament to con my lesson. I had earned my pension before I set my foot in St. Stephen's chapel.[13] I was prepared and disciplined to this political warfare. The first session I sat in parliament, I found it necessary to analyze the whole commercial, financial, constitutional and foreign interests of Great Britain and its empire. A great deal was then done; and more, far more would have been done, if more had been permitted by events. Then in the vigour of my manhood, my constitution sunk under my labour. Had I then died, (and I seemed to myself very near death) I had then earned for those who belonged to me, more than the duke of Bedford's ideas of service are of power to estimate. But in truth, these services I am called to account for, are not those on which I value myself the most. If I were to call for a reward (which I have never done) it should be for those in which for fourteen years, without intermission, I shewed the most industry, and had the least success; I mean in the affairs of India. They are those on which I value myself the most; most for the

13 Where the House of Commons met until 1834.

importance; most for the labour; most for the judgment; most for constancy and perseverance in the pursuit. Others may value them most for the *intention*. In that, surely, they are not mistaken.

Does his grace think, that they who advised the crown to make my retreat easy, considered me only as an œconomist? That, well understood, however, is a good deal. If I had not deemed it of some value, I should not have made political œconomy an object of my humble studies, from my very early youth to near the end of my service in parliament, even before (at least to any knowledge of mine) it had employed the thoughts of speculative men in other parts of Europe. At that time it was still in its infancy in England, where, in the last century, it had its origin. Great and learned men thought my studies were not wholly thrown away, and deigned to communicate with me now and then on some particulars of their immortal works. Something of these studies may appear incidentally in some of the earliest things I published. The house has been witness to their effect, and has profited of them more or less, for above eight and twenty years.

To their estimate I leave the matter. I was not, like his grace of Bedford, swaddled, and rocked, and dandled into a legislator; "*Nitor in adversum*" is the motto for a man like me.[14] I possessed not one of the qualities, nor cultivated one of the arts, that recommend men to the favour and protection of the great. I was not made for a minion or a tool. As little did I follow the trade of winning the hearts, by imposing on the understandings, of the people. At every step of my progress in life (for in every step was I traversed and opposed), and at every turnpike I met, I was obliged to shew my passport, and again and again to prove my sole title to the honour of being useful to my country, by a proof that I was not wholly unacquainted with its laws, and the whole system of its interests both abroad and at home. Otherwise no rank, no toleration even, for me. I had no arts, but manly arts.

---

14 Ovid *Metamorphoses* 2:72: "I strive against adversity" (from Phoebus's speech to Phaeton on the skill and strength required to drive his chariot over the heavens).

On them I have stood, and, please God, in spite of the duke of Bedford and the earl of Lauderdale, to the last gasp will I stand.

Had his grace condescended to inquire concerning the person, whom he has not thought it below him to reproach, he might have found, that in the whole course of my life, I have never, on any pretence of œconomy, or on any other pretence, so much as in a single instance, stood between any man and his reward of service, or his encouragement in useful talent and pursuit, from the highest of those services and pursuits to the lowest. On the contrary I have, on a hundred occasions, exerted myself with singular zeal to forward every man's even tolerable pretensions. I have more than once had good-natured reprehensions from my friends for carrying the matter to something bordering on abuse. This line of conduct, whatever its merits might be, was partly owing to natural disposition; but I think full as much to reason and principle. I looked on the consideration of publick service, or publick ornament, to be real and very justice: and I ever held a scanty and penurious justice to partake of the nature of a wrong. I held it to be, in its consequences, the worst economy in the world. In saving money, I soon can count up all the good I do; but when by a cold penury, I blast the abilities of a nation, and stunt the growth of its active energies, the ill I may do is beyond all calculation. Whether it be too much or too little, whatever I have done has been general and systematick. I have never entered into those trifling vexations and oppressive details, that have been falsely, and most ridiculously laid to my charge.

Did I blame the pensions given to Mr. Barré and Mr. Dunning between the proposition and execution of my plan? No! surely no! Those pensions were within my principles. I assert it, those gentlemen deserved their pensions, their titles — all they had; and more had they had, I should have been but pleased the more. They were men of talents; they were men of service. I put the profession of the law out of the question in one of them. It is a service that rewards itself. But their *publick service*, though, from their abilities unquestionably of more value than mine, in its quantity and in its duration was not to be mentioned with it. But I never could drive a hard bargain in my life, concerning any matter whatever; and least of all do I know how to haggle and huckster with merit. Pension for myself I obtained none; nor did I solicit any. Yet I was loaded with hatred for every thing that was withheld, and with obloquy for every thing that was given. I was thus left to support the grants of a name ever dear to me,[15] and ever venerable to the world, in favour of those, who were no friends of mine or of his, against the rude attacks of those who were at that time friends to the grantees, and their own zealous partisans. I have never heard the earl of Lauderdale complain of these pensions. He finds nothing wrong till he comes to me. This is impartiality, in the true modern revolutionary style.

Whatever I did at that time, so far as it regarded order and œconomy, is stable and eternal; as all principles must be. A particular order of things may be altered; order itself cannot lose its value. As to other particulars, they are variable by time and by circumstances. Laws of regulation are not fundamental laws. The publick exigencies are the masters of all such laws. They rule the laws, and are not to be ruled by them. They who exercise the legislative power at the time must judge.

It may be new to his grace, but I beg leave to tell him, that mere parsimony is not œconomy. It is separable in theory from it; and in fact it may, or it may not, be a *part* of œconomy, according to circumstances. Expence, and great expence, may be an essential part in true œconomy. If parsimony were to be considered as one of the kinds of that virtue, there is however another and an higher œconomy. Œconomy is a distributive virtue, and consists not in saving, but in selection. Parsimony requires no providence, no sagacity, no powers of combination, no comparison, no judgment. Mere instinct, and that not an instinct of the noblest kind, may produce this false economy in perfection. The

15 Charles Watson Wentworth (1730–82), second Marquis of Rockingham, who until his death was the leader of Burke's party.

other œconomy has larger views. It demands a discriminating judgment, and a firm sagacious mind. It shuts one door to impudent importunity, only to open another, and a wider, to unpresuming merit. If none but meritorious service or real talent were to be rewarded, this nation has not wanted, and this nation will not want, the means of rewarding all the service it ever will receive, and encouraging all the merit it ever will produce. No state, since the foundation of society, has been impoverished by that species of profusion. Had the œconomy of selection and proportion been at all times observed, we should not now have had an overgrown duke of Bedford, to oppress the industry of humble men, and to limit by the standard of his own conceptions, the justice, the bounty, or, if he pleases, the charity of the crown.

His grace may think as meanly as he will of my deserts in the far greater part of my conduct in life. It is free for him to do so. There will always be some difference of opinion in the value of political services. But there is one merit of mine, which he, of all men living, ought to be the last to call in question. I have supported with very great zeal, and I am told with some degree of success, those opinions, or if his grace likes another expression better, those old prejudices which buoy up the ponderous mass of his nobility, wealth, and titles. I have omitted no exertion to prevent him and them from sinking to that level, to which the meretricious French faction, his grace at least coquets with, omit no exertion to reduce both. I have done all I could to discountenance their inquiries into the fortunes of those, who hold large portions of wealth without any apparent merit of their own. I have strained every nerve to keep the duke of Bedford in that situation, which alone makes him my superiour. Your lordship has been a witness of the use he makes of that pre-eminence.

But be it, that this is virtue! Be it, that there is virtue in this well selected rigour; yet all virtues are not equally becoming to all men and at all times. There are crimes, undoubtedly there are crimes, which in all seasons of our existence, ought to put a generous antipathy in action; crimes that provoke an indignant justice, and call forth a warm and animated pursuit. But all things, that

concern, what I may call, the preventive police of morality, all
things merely rigid, harsh and censorial, the antiquated moral-
ists, at whose feet I was brought up, would not have thought these
the fittest matter to form the favourite virtues of young men of
rank. What might have been well enough, and have been received with a veneration mixed with awe and terrour, from an
old, severe, crabbed Cato, would have wanted something of propriety in the young Scipios, the ornament of the Roman nobility,
in the flower of their life. But the times, the morals, the masters,
the scholars have all undergone a thorough revolution. It is a vile
illiberal school, this new French academy of the *sans culottes*.
There is nothing in it that is fit for a gentleman to learn.

Whatever its vogue may be, I still flatter myself, that the parents of the growing generation will be satisfied with what is to be
taught to their children in Westminster, in Eton, or in Winches-
ter: I still indulge the hope that no *grown* gentleman or nobleman
of our time will think of finishing at Mr. Thelwall's lecture whatever may have been left incomplete at the old universities of his
country.[16] I would give to lord Grenville and Mr. Pitt for a motto,
what was said of a Roman censor or praetor (or what was he), who
in virtue of a Senatus consultum shut up certain academies,

> " *Cludere ludum impudentiæ jussit.* "[17]

Every honest father of a family in the kingdom will rejoice at the
breaking up for the holidays, and will pray that there may be a
very long vacation in all such schools.

The awful state of the time, and not myself or my own justification, is my true object in what I now write; or in what I shall
ever write or say. It little signifies to the world what becomes of
such things as me, or even as the duke of Bedford. What I say

---

16 John Thelwall (1764–1834), a radical reformer and member of the Society
of the Friends of the People and the Corresponding Society. Tried for sedition and
acquitted in December 1794, Thelwall gave a popular series of lectures on classical
history as a coded version of his views of contemporary politics, to evade government
censorship under the Convention Act of 1795.

17 *Senatus consultum,* or "resolution of the Senate." Tacitus *De Oratoribus* 35: "He
ordered the training ground of impudence to be closed."

about either of us is nothing more than a vehicle, as you, my lord, will easily perceive, to convey my sentiments on matters far more worthy of your attention. It is when I stick to my apparent first subject that I ought to apologize, not when I depart from it. I therefore must beg your lordship's pardon for again resuming it after this very short digression; assuring you that I shall never altogether lose sight of such matter as persons abler than I am may turn to some profit.

The duke of Bedford conceives, that he is obliged to call the attention of the house of peers to his majesty's grant to me, which he considers as excessive and out of all bounds.

I know not how it has happened, but it really seems, that, whilst his grace was meditating his well-considered censure upon me, he fell into a sort of sleep. Homer nods; and the duke of Bedford may dream; and as dreams (even his golden dreams) are apt to be ill-pieced and incongruously put together, his grace preserved his idea of reproach to *me*, but took the subject-matter from the crown-grants *to his own family*. This is "the stuff of which his dreams are made."[18] In that way of putting things together his grace is perfectly in the right. The grants to the house of Russel were so enormous, as not only to outrage economy, but even to stagger credibility. The duke of Bedford is the leviathan among all the creatures of the crown. He tumbles about his unwieldy bulk; he plays and frolicks in the ocean of the royal bounty. Huge as he is, and whilst "he lies floating many a rood,"[19] he is still a creature. His ribs, his fins, his whalebone, his blubber, the very spiracles through which he spouts a torrent of brine against his origin, and covers me all over with the spray, — every thing of him and about him is from the throne. Is it for *him* to question the dispensation of the royal favour?

I really am at a loss to draw any sort of parallel between the publick merits of his grace, by which he justifies the grants he holds, and these services of mine, on the favourable construction

18 *The Tempest* 4.1.156–57.
19 *Paradise Lost* 1:196.

of which I have obtained what his grace so much disapproves. In private life, I have not at all the honour of acquaintance with the noble duke. But I ought to presume, and it costs me nothing to do so, that he abundantly deserves the esteem and love of all who live with him. But as to publick service, why truly it would not be more ridiculous for me to compare myself in rank, in fortune, in splendid descent, in youth, strength, or figure, with the duke of Bedford, than to make a parallel between his services, and my attempts to be useful to my country. It would not be gross adulation, but uncivil irony, to say, that he has any publick merit of his own to keep alive the idea of the services by which his vast landed pensions were obtained. My merits, whatever they are, are original and personal; his are derivative. It is his ancestor, the original pensioner, that has laid up this inexhaustible fund of merit, which makes his grace so very delicate and exceptious about the merit of all other grantees of the crown. Had he permitted me to remain in quiet, I should have said 'tis his estate; that's enough. It is his by law; what have I to do with it or its history? He would naturally have said on his side, 'tis this man's fortune. — He is as good now, as my ancestor was two hundred and fifty years ago. I am a young man with very old pensions; he is an old man with very young pensions, — that's all.

Why will his grace, by attacking me, force me reluctantly to compare my little merit with that which obtained from the crown those prodigies of profuse donation by which he tramples on the mediocrity of humble and laborious individuals? I would willingly leave him to the herald's college, which the philosophy of the sans culottes, (prouder by far than all the Garters, and Norroys and Clarencieux, and Rouge Dragons that ever pranced in a procession of what his friends call aristocrats and despots) will abolish with contumely and scorn. These historians, recorders, and blazoners of virtues and arms, differ wholly from that other description of historians, who never assign any act of politicians to a good motive. These gentle historians, on the contrary, dip their pens in nothing but the milk of human kindness. They seek no further for merit than the preamble of a patent, or the inscription on a tomb. With them every man created a peer is first an hero ready made. They judge of every man's capacity for office by the offices he has filled; and the more offices the more ability. Every general-officer with them is a Marlborough; every statesman a Burleigh; every judge a Murray or a Yorke. They, who alive, were laughed at or pitied by all their acquaintance, make as good a figure as the best of them in the pages of Guillim, Edmondson, and Collins.

To these recorders, so full of good nature to the great and prosperous, I would willingly leave the first baron Russel, and earl of Bedford, and the merits of his grants. But the aulnager,[20] the weigher, the meter of grants, will not suffer us to acquiesce in the judgment of the prince reigning at the time when they were made. They are never good to those who earn them. Well then; since the new grantees have war made on them by the old, and that the word of the sovereign is not to be taken, let us turn our eyes to history, in which great men have always a pleasure in contemplating the heroick origin of their house.

The first peer of the name, the first purchaser of the grants, was a Mr. Russel, a person of an ancient gentleman's family raised by being a minion of Henry the Eighth. As there generally is some resemblance of character to create these relations, the favourite was in all likelihood much such another as his master. The first of those immoderate grants was not taken from the ancient demesne of the crown, but from the recent confiscation of the ancient nobility of the land. The lion having sucked the blood of his prey, threw the offal carcase to the jackall in waiting. Having tasted once the food of confiscation, the favourites became fierce and ravenous. This worthy favourite's first grant was from the lay nobility. The second, infinitely improving on the enormity of the first, was from the plunder of the church. In truth his grace is somewhat excusable for his dislike to a grant like mine, not only in its quantity, but in its kind so different from his own.

20 An officer who measures and judges the quality of woolen goods.

Mine was from a mild and benevolent sovereign; his from Henry the Eighth.

Mine had not its fund in the murder of any innocent person of illustrious rank,[21] or in the pillage of any body of unoffending men. His grants were from the aggregate and consolidated funds of judgments iniquitously legal, and from possessions voluntarily surrendered by the lawful proprietors with the gibbet at their door.

The merit of the grantee whom he derives from, was that of being a prompt and greedy instrument of a *levelling* tyrant, who oppressed all descriptions of his people, but who fell with particular fury on every thing that was *great and noble*. Mine has been, in endeavouring to screen every man, in every class, from oppression, and particularly in defending the high and eminent, who in the bad times of confiscating princes, confiscating chief governours, or confiscating demagogues, are the most exposed to jealousy, avarice and envy.

The merit of the original grantee of his grace's pensions, was in giving his hand to the work, and partaking the spoil with a prince, who plundered a part of the national church of his time and country. Mine was in defending the whole of the national church of my own time and my own country, and the whole of the national churches of all countries, from the principles and the examples which lead to ecclesiastical pillage, thence to a contempt of *all* prescriptive titles, thence to the pillage of *all* property, and thence to universal desolation.

The merit of the origin of his grace's fortune was in being a favourite and chief adviser to a prince, who left no liberty to their native country. My endeavour was to obtain liberty for the municipal country in which I was born, and for all descriptions and denominations in it. Mine was to support with unrelaxing vigilance every right, every privilege, every franchise, in this my

21 See the history of the melancholy catastrophe of the Duke of Buckingham. Temp. Hen. 8 [*Burke's note*]. Edward Stafford, third Duke of Buckingham (1478–1521), privy councillor to Henry VIII, tried and executed for treason in 1521 on trivial charges.

adopted, my dearer and more comprehensive country; and not only to preserve those rights in this chief feat of empire, but in every nation, in every land, in every climate, language and religion, in the vast domain that still is under the protection, and the larger that was once under the protection, of the British crown.

His founder's merits were, by arts in which he served his master and made his fortune, to bring poverty, wretchedness and depopulation on his country. Mine were under a benevolent prince, in promoting the commerce, manufactures and agriculture of his kingdom; in which his majesty shews an eminent example, who even in his amusements is a patriot, and in hours of leisure an improver of his native soil.

His founder's merit, was the merit of a gentleman raised by the arts of a court, and the protection of a Wolsey, to the eminence of a great and potent lord. His merit in that eminence was by instigating a tyrant to injustice, to provoke a people to rebellion. — My merit was, to awaken the sober part of the country, that they might put themselves on their guard against any one potent lord, or any greater number of potent lords, or any combination of great leading men of any sort, if ever they should attempt to proceed in the same courses, but in the reverse order, that is, by instigating a corrupted populace to rebellion, and, through that rebellion, introducing a tyranny yet worse than the tyranny which his grace's ancestor supported, and of which he profited in the manner we behold in the despotism of Henry the Eighth.

The political merit of the first pensioner of his grace's house, was that of being concerned as a counsellor of state in advising, and in his person executing the conditions of a dishonourable peace with France; the surrendering the fortress of Boulogne, then our out-guard on the continent. By that surrender, Calais, the key of France, and the bridle in the mouth of that power, was, not many years afterwards, finally lost. My merit has been in resisting the power and pride of France, under any form of its rule; but in opposing it with the greatest zeal and earnestness, when that rule appeared in the worst form it could assume; the worst indeed which the prime cause and principle of all evil could possibly give it. It was my endeavour by every means to excite a spirit in the house, where I had the honour of a seat, for carrying on with early vigour and decision, the most clearly just and necessary war, that this or any nation ever carried on; in order to save my country from the iron yoke of its power, and from the more dreadful contagion of its principles; to preserve, while they can be preserved, pure and untainted, the ancient, inbred integrity, piety, good nature, and good humour of the people of England, from the dreadful pestilence which beginning in France, threatens to lay waste the whole moral, and in a great degree the whole physical world, having done both in the focus of its most intense malignity.

The labours of his grace's founder merited the curses, not loud but deep, of the commons of England, on whom *he* and his master had effected a *complete parliamentary reform*, by making them in their slavery and humiliation, the true and adequate representatives of a debased, degraded, and undone people. My merits were, in having had an active, though not always an ostentatious share, in every one act, without exception, of undisputed constitutional utility in my time, and in having supported on all occasions, the authority, the efficiency, and the privileges of the commons of Great Britain. I ended my services by a recorded and fully reasoned assertion on their own journals of their constitutional rights, and a vindication of their constitutional conduct. I laboured in all things to merit their inward approbation, and (along with the assistance of the largest, the greatest, and best of my endeavours) I received their free, unbiassed, publick, and solemn thanks.

Thus stands the account of the comparative merits of the crown grants which compose the duke of Bedford's fortune as balanced against mine. In the name of common sense, why should the duke of Bedford think, that none but of the house of Russel are entitled to the favour of the crown? Why should he imagine that no king of England has been capable of judging of merit but king Henry the Eighth? Indeed, he will pardon me; he is a little mistaken; all virtue did not end in the first earl of Bedford. All discernment did not lose its vision when his creator closed his eyes. Let him remit his rigour on the disproportion between merit and reward in others, and they will make no inquiry into the origin of his fortune. They will regard with much more satisfaction, as he will contemplate with infinitely more advantage, whatever in his pedigree has been dulcified by an exposure to the influence of heaven in a long flow of generations, from the hard, acidulous, metallick tincture of the spring. It is little to be doubted, that several of his forefathers in that long series, have degenerated into honour and virtue. Let the duke of Bedford (I am sure he will) reject with scorn and horrour, the counsels of the lecturers, those wicked panders to avarice and ambition, who would tempt him in the troubles of his country, to seek another enormous fortune from the forfeitures of another nobility, and the plunder of another church. Let him (and I trust that yet he will) employ all the energy of his youth, and all the resources of his wealth, to crush rebellious principles which have no foundation in morals, and rebellious movements that have no provocation in tyranny.

Then will be forgot the rebellions, which, by a doubtful priority in crime, his ancestor had provoked and extinguished. On such a conduct in the noble duke, many of his countrymen might, and with some excuse might, give way to the enthusiasm of their gratitude, and in the dashing style of some of the old declaimers, cry out, that if the fates had found no other way in which they could give a [22] duke of Bedford and his opulence as props to a tottering world, then the butchery of the duke of Buckingham might be tolerated; it might be regarded even with complacency, whilst in the heir of confiscation they saw the sympathizing comforter of the martyrs, who suffer under the cruel confiscation of this day; whilst they behold with admiration his

22 At si non aliam venturo fata Neroni, &c [*Burke's note*]. Lucan *Pharsalia* 1:33: "And if the fates could find no other way to bring in Nero, etc."

zealous protection of the virtuous and loyal nobility of France, and his manly support of his brethren, the yet standing nobility and gentry of his native land. Then his grace's merit would be pure and new, and sharp, as fresh from the mint of honour. As he pleased he might reflect honour on his predecessors, or throw it forward on those who were to succeed him. He might be the propagator of the stock of honour, or the root of it, as he thought proper.

Had it pleased God to continue to me the hopes of succession, I should have been according to my mediocrity, and the mediocrity of the age I live in, a sort of founder of a family; I should have left a son, who, in all the points in which personal merit can be viewed, in science, in erudition, in genius, in taste, in honour, in generosity, in humanity, in every liberal sentiment, and every liberal accomplishment, would not have shewn himself inferiour to the duke of Bedford, or to any of those whom he traces in his line. His grace very soon would have wanted all plausibility in his attack upon that provision which belonged more to mine than to me. HE would soon have supplied every deficiency, and symmetrized every disproportion. It would not have been for that successor to resort to any stagnant wasting reservoir of merit in me, or in any ancestry. He had in himself a salient, living spring, of generous and manly action. Every day he lived he would have re-purchased the bounty of the crown, and ten times more, if ten times more he had received. He was made a publick creature; and had no enjoyment whatever, but in the performance of some duty. At this exigent moment, the loss of a finished man is not easily supplied.

But a disposer whose power we are little able to resist, and whose wisdom it behoves us not at all to dispute; has ordained it in another manner, and (whatever my querulous weakness might suggest) a far better. The storm has gone over me; and I lie like one of those old oaks which the late hurricane has scattered about me. I am stripped of all my honours; I am torn up by the roots, and lie prostrate on the earth! There, and prostrate there, I most unfeignedly recognize the divine justice, and in some degree submit to it. But whilst I humble myself before God, I do not know that it is forbidden to repel the attacks of unjust and inconsiderate men. The patience of Job is proverbial. After some of the convulsive struggles of our irritable nature, he submitted himself, and repented in dust and ashes. But even so, I do not find him blamed for reprehending, and with a considerable degree of verbal asperity, those ill-natured neighbours of his, who visited his dunghill to read moral, political, and economical lectures on his misery. I am alone. I have none to meet my enemies in the gate. Indeed, my lord, I greatly deceive myself, if in this hard season I would give a peck of refuse wheat for all that is called fame and honour in the world. This is the appetite but of a few. It is a luxury; it is a privilege: it is an indulgence for those who are at their ease. But we are all of us made to shun disgrace, as we are made to shrink from pain, and poverty, and disease. It is an instinct; and under the direction of reason, instinct is always in the right. I live in an inverted order. They who ought to have succeeded me are gone before me. They who should have been to me as posterity are in the place of ancestors. I owe to the dearest relation (which ever must subsist in memory) that act of piety, which he would have performed to me; I owe it to him to shew that he was not descended, as the duke of Bedford would have it, from an unworthy parent.

The crown has considered me after long service: the crown has paid the duke of Bedford by advance. He has had a long credit for any service which he may perform hereafter. He is secure, and long may he be secure, in his advance, whether he performs any services or not. But let him take care how he endangers the safety of that constitution which secures his own utility or his own insignificance; or how he discourages those, who take up, even puny arms, to defend an order of things, which, like the sun of heaven, shines alike on the useful and the worthless. His grants are engrafted on the publick law of Europe, covered with the awful hoar of innumerable ages. They are guarded by the sacred rules of prescription, found in that full treasury of jurisprudence from which the jejuneness and penury of our municipal law has, by degrees, been enriched and strengthened. This prescription I had my share (a very full share) in bringing to its perfection.[23] The duke of Bedford will stand as long as prescriptive law endures; as long as the great stable laws of property common to us with all civilized nations, are kept in their integrity, and without the smallest intermixture of laws, maxims, principles, or precedents of the grand revolution. They are secure against all changes but one. The whole revolutionary system, institutes, digest, code, novels, text, gloss, comment, are, not only the same, but they are the very reverse, and the reverse fundamentally, of all the laws, on which civil life has hitherto been upheld in all the governments of the world. The learned professors of the rights of man regard prescription, not as a title to bar all claim, set up against old possession — but they look on prescription as itself a bar against the possessor and proprietor. They hold an immemorial possession to be no more than a long continued, and therefore an aggravated injustice.

Such are *their* ideas; such *their* religion, and such *their* law. But as to *our* country and *our* race, as long as the well compacted structure of our church and state, the sanctuary, the holy of holies of that ancient law, defended by reverence, defended by power, a fortress at once and a temple,[24] shall stand inviolate on the brow of the British Sion — as long as the British monarchy, not more limited than fenced by the orders of the state, shall, like the proud Keep of Windsor, rising in the majesty of proportion, and girt with the double belt of its kindred and coeval towers, as long as this awful structure shall oversee and guard the subjected land — so long the mounds and dykes of the low, fat, Bedford level will have nothing to fear from all the pickaxes of all the levellers of France. As long as our sovereign lord the king, and his faithful subjects, the lords and commons of this realm, — the triple cord, which no man can break; the solemn, sworn,

---

23 Sir George Savile's Act, called the *Nullum Tempus* Act [*Burke's note*].

24 *Templum in modum arcis.* Tacitus of the temple of Jerusalem [*Burke's note*]. Tacitus *Histories* 5:12: "A temple in the shape of a fortress."

constitutional frank-pledge of this nation; the firm guarantees of each others being, and each others rights; the joint and several securities, each in its place and order, for every kind and every quality, of property and of dignity—As long as these endure, so long the duke of Bedford is safe: and we are all safe together—the high from the blights of envy and the spoliations of rapacity; the low from the iron hand of oppression and the insolent spurn of contempt. Amen! and so be it: and so it will be,

> *Dum domus Æneæ Capitoli immobile faxum*
> *Accolet; imperiumque pater Romanus habebit.* —[25]

But if the rude inroad of Gallick tumult, with its sophistical rights of man, to falsify the account, and its sword as a make-weight to throw into the scale, shall be introduced into our city by a misguided populace, set on by proud great men, themselves blinded and intoxicated by a frantick ambition, we shall, all of us, perish and be overwhelmed in a common ruin. If a great storm blow on our coast, it will cast the whales on the strand as well as the periwinkles. His Grace will not survive the poor grantee he despises, no not for a twelvemonth. If the great look for safety in the services they render to this Gallick cause, it is to be foolish, even above the weight of privilege allowed to wealth. If his Grace be one of these whom they endeavour to proselytize, he ought to be aware of the character of the sect, whose doctrines he is invited to embrace. With them, insurrection is the most sacred of revolutionary duties to the state. Ingratitude to benefactors is the first of revolutionary virtues. Ingratitude is indeed their four cardinal virtues compacted and amalgamated into one; and he will find it in every thing that has happened since the commencement of the philosophick revolution to this hour. If he pleads the merit of having performed the duty of insurrection against the order he lives in (God forbid he ever should), the merit of others will be to perform the duty of insurrection against him. If he pleads (again God forbid he should, and I do not

---

25 *Aeneid* 9:448–49: "So long as the house of Aeneas stands on the immoveable rock of the Capitol, and the father of Rome holds sway."

suspect he will) his ingratitude to the crown for its creation of his family, others will plead their right and duty to pay him in kind. They will laugh, indeed they will laugh, at his parchment and his wax. His deeds will be drawn out with the rest of the lumber of his evidence room, and burnt to the tune of *ça ira*[26] in the courts of Bedford (then Equality) house.

Am I to blame, if I attempt to pay his Grace's hostile re-proaches to me with a friendly admonition to himself? Can I be blamed, for pointing out to him in what manner he is like to be affected, if the sect of the cannibal philosophers of France should proselytize any considerable part of this people, and, by their joint proselytizing arms, should conquer that government, to which his Grace does not seem to me to give all the support his own security demands? Surely it is proper, that he, and that others like him, should know the true genius of this sect; what their opinions are, what they have done; and to whom; and what, (if a prognostick is to be formed from the dispositions and actions of men) it is certain they will do hereafter. He ought to know, that they have sworn assistance, the only engagements they ever will keep, to all in this country, who bear a resemblance to them-selves, and who think as such, that *The whole duty of man*[27] consists in destruction. They are a misallied and disparaged branch of the house of Nimrod. They are the duke of Bedford's natural hunt-ers; and he is their natural game. Because he is not very pro-foundly reflecting, he sleeps in profound security: they, on the contrary, are always vigilant, active, enterprising, and, though far removed from any knowledge which makes men estimable or useful, in all the instruments and resources of evil, their leaders are not meanly instructed, or insufficiently furnished. In the French revolution every thing is new; and, from want of prepara-tion to meet so unlooked-for an evil, every thing is dangerous. Never, before this time, was a set of literary men, converted into a gang of robbers and assassins. Never before, did a den of bra-

26 A popular Jacobin song.
27 Anglican devotional work published anonymously in 1658.

voes and banditti, assume the garb and tone of an academy of philosophers.

Let me tell his Grace, that an union of such characters, monstrous as it seems, is not made for producing despicable enemies. But if they are formidable as foes, as friends they are dreadful indeed. The men of property in France confiding in a force, which seemed to be irresistible, because it had never been tried, neglected to prepare for a conflict with their enemies at their own weapons. They were found in such a situation as the Mexicans were, when they were attacked by the dogs, the cavalry, the iron, and the gunpowder of an handful of bearded men, whom they did not know to exist in nature. This is a comparison that some, I think, have made; and it is just. In France they had their enemies within their houses. They were even in the bosoms of many of them. But they had not sagacity to discern their savage character. They seemed tame, and even caressing. They had nothing but *douce humanité* in their mouth. They could not bear the punishment of the mildest laws on the greatest criminals. The slightest severity of justice made their flesh creep. The very idea that war existed in the world disturbed their repose. Military glory was no more, with them, than a splendid infamy. Hardly would they hear of self-defence, which they reduced within such bounds, as to leave it no defence at all. All this while they meditated the confiscations and massacres we have seen. Had any one told these unfortunate noblemen and gentlemen, how, and by whom, the grand fabrick of the French monarchy under which they flourished would be subverted, they would not have pitied him as a visionary, but would have turned from him as what they call a *mauvais plaisant.*[28] Yet we have seen what has happened. The persons who have suffered from the cannibal philosophy of France, are so like the duke of Bedford, that nothing but his Grace's probably not speaking quite so good French, could enable us to find out any difference. A great many of them had as pompous titles as he, and were of full as illustrious a race: some

28 Sorry jester.

few of them had fortunes as ample; several of them, without meaning the least disparagement to the duke of Bedford, were as wise, and as virtuous, and as valiant, and as well educated, and as complete in all the lineaments of men of honour as he is: And to all this they had added the powerful outguard of a military profession, which, in its nature, renders men somewhat more cautious than those, who have nothing to attend to but the lazy enjoyment of undisturbed possessions. But security was their ruin. They are dashed to pieces in the storm, and our shores are covered with the wrecks. If they had been aware that such a thing might happen, such a thing never could have happened.

I assure his Grace, that if I state to him the designs of his enemies, in a manner which may appear to him ludicrous and impossible, I tell him nothing that has not exactly happened, point by point, but twenty-four miles from our own shore. I assure him that the Frenchified faction, more encouraged, than others are warned, by what has happened in France, looks at him and his landed possessions, as an object at once of curiosity and rapacity. He is made for them in every part of their double character. As robbers, to them he is a noble booty: as speculatists, he is a glorious subject for their experimental philosophy. He affords matter for an extensive analysis, in all the branches of their science, geometrical, physical, civil and political. These philosophers are fanaticks; independent of any interest, which if it operated alone would make them much more tractable, they are carried with such an headlong rage towards every desperate trial, that they would sacrifice the whole human race to the slightest of their experiments. I am better able to enter into the character of this description of men than the noble Duke can be. I have lived long and variously in the world. Without any considerable pretensions to literature in myself, I have aspired to the love of letters. I have lived for a great many years in habitudes with those who professed them. I can form a tolerable estimate of what is likely to happen from a character, chiefly dependent for fame and fortune, on knowledge and talent, as well in its morbid and perverted state, as in that which is sound and natural. Naturally men so formed and finished are the first gifts of Providence to the world. But when they have once thrown off the fear of God, which was in all ages too often the case, and the fear of man, which is now the case, and when in that state they come to understand one another, and to act in corps, a more dreadful calamity cannot arise out of hell to scourge mankind. Nothing can be conceived more hard than the heart of a thoroughbred metaphysician. It comes nearer to the cold malignity of a wicked spirit than to the frailty and passion of a man. It is like that of the principle of evil himself, incorporeal, pure, unmixed, dephlegmated, defecated evil. It is no easy operation to eradicate humanity from the human breast. What Shakespeare calls "the compunctious visitings of nature,"[29] will sometimes knock at their hearts, and protest against their murderous speculations. But they have a means of compounding with their nature. Their humanity is not dissolved. They only give it a long prorogation. They are ready to declare that they do not think two thousand years too long a period for the good that they pursue. It is remarkable, that they never see any way to their projected good but by the road of some evil. Their imagination is not fatigued with the contemplation of human suffering through the wild waste of centuries added to centuries of misery and desolation. Their humanity is at their horizon — and, like the horizon, it always flies before them. The geometricians, and the chymists bring, the one from the dry bones of their diagrams, and the other from the foot of their furnaces, dispositions that make them worse than indifferent about those feelings and habitudes, which are the supports of the moral world. Ambition is come upon them suddenly; they are intoxicated with it, and it has rendered them fearless of the danger, which may from thence arise to others or to themselves. These philosophers, consider men in their experiments, no more than they do mice in an air pump, or in a recipient of mephitick gas. Whatever his Grace may think of himself, they look upon him, and every thing that belongs

29 *Macbeth* 1.5.45.

to him, with no more regard than they do upon the whiskers of that little long-tailed animal, that has been long the game of the grave, demure, insidious, spring-nailed, velvet-pawed, green-eyed philosophers, whether going upon two legs, or upon four.

His Grace's landed possessions are irresistibly inviting to an *agrarian* experiment. They are a downright insult upon the rights of man. They are more extensive than the territory of many of the Grecian republicks; and they are without comparison more fertile than most of them. There are now republicks in Italy, in Germany, and in Switzerland, which do not possess any thing like so fair and ample a domain. There is scope for seven philosophers to proceed in their analytical experiments, upon Harrington's seven different forms of republicks, in the acres of this one Duke.[30] Hitherto they have been wholly unproductive to speculation; fitted for nothing but to fatten bullocks, and to produce grain for beer, still more to stupify the dull English understanding. Abbé Sieyes[31] has whole nests of pigeon-holes full of constitutions ready made, ticketed, sorted, and numbered; suited to every season and every fancy; some with the top of the pattern at the bottom, and some with the bottom at the top; some plain, some flowered; some distinguished for their simplicity; others for their complexity; some of blood colour; some of *boue de Paris*; some with directories, others without a direction; some with councils of elders, and councils of youngsters; some without any council at all. Some where the electors choose the representatives; others, where the representatives choose the electors. Some in long coats, and some in short cloaks; some with pantaloons; some without breeches. Some with five shilling qualifications; some totally unqualified. So that no constitution-fancier may go unsuited from his shop, provided he loves a pattern of pillage,

30 James Harrington (1611–77) in *The Commonwealth of Oceana* (1656), a visionary work of republican theory dedicated to Oliver Cromwell, described in elaborate detail the proper ordering of a commonwealth and its constitution.

31 Emmanuel-Joseph Sieyès (1748–1836), theorist of revolutionary liberty whose pamphlet *What Is the Third Estate?* (1789) helped embolden the third estate to declare itself the nation.

oppression, arbitrary imprisonment, confiscation, exile, revolutionary judgment, and legalized premeditated murder, in any shapes into which they can be put. What a pity it is, that the progress of experimental philosophy should be checked by his Grace's monopoly! Such are their sentiments, I assure him; such is their language, when they dare to speak; and such are their proceedings, when they have the means to act.

Their geographers, and geometricians, have been some time out of practice. It is some time since they have divided their own country into squares. That figure has lost the charms of its novelty. They want new lands for new trials. It is not only the geometricians of the republick that find him a good subject, the chymists have bespoke him after the geometricians have done with him. As the first set have an eye on his Grace's lands, the chymists are not less taken with his buildings. They consider mortar as a very anti-revolutionary invention in its present state; but properly employed, an admirable material for overturning all establishments. They have found that the gunpowder of *ruins* is far the fittest for making other *ruins*, and so *ad infinitum*. They have calculated what quantity of matter convertible into nitre is to be found in Bedford house, in Wooburn Abbey, and in what his Grace and his trustees have still suffered to stand of that foolish royalist Inigo Jones, in Covent Garden. Churches, play-houses, coffee-houses, all alike are destined to be mingled, and equalised, and blended into one common rubbish; and well sifted, and lixiviated, to crystallize into true democratick explosive insurrectionary nitre. Their academy del *Cimento*[32] (per antiphrasin) with Morveau and Hassenfrats at its head, have computed that the brave sans-culottes may make war on all the aristrocracy of Europe for a twelvemonth, out of the rubbish of the duke of Bedford's buildings.[33]

32 L'Accademia del Cimento (Academy of Experiment) was founded in 1657 to promote experimental science; the reference here concerns two French chemists who were supporters of the revolution.

33 There is nothing, on which the leaders of the republick, one and indivisible, value themselves, more than on the chymical operations, by which, through science,

While the Morveaux and Priestleys are proceeding with these experiments upon the duke of Bedford's houses, the Sieyes, and the rest of the analytical legislators, and constitution-vendors, are quite as busy in their trade of decomposing organization, in forming his Grace's vassals into primary assemblies, national guards, first, second and third requisitioners, committees of research, conductors of the travelling guillotine, judges of revolutionary tribunals, legislative hangmen, supervisors of domiciliary visitation, exactors of forced loans, and assessors of the maximum.

The din of all this smithery may some time or other possibly wake this noble Duke, and push him to an endeavour to save some little matter from their experimental philosophy. If he pleads his grants from the crown, he is ruined at the outset. If he pleads he has received them from the pillage of superstitious corporations, this indeed will stagger them a little, because they are enemies to all corporations, and to all religion. However, they will soon recover themselves, and will tell his Grace, or his learned council, that all such property belongs to the *nation*; and that it would be more wise for him, if he wishes to live the natural term of a *citizen*, (that is, according to Condorcet's calculation, six months on an average) not to pass for an usurper upon the national property. This is what the *serjeants* at law of the

---

they convert the pride of aristocracy to an instrument of its own destruction — on the operations by which they reduce the magnificent ancient country seats of the nobility, decorated with the *feudal* titles of Duke, Marquis, or Earl, into magazines of what they call *revolutionary* gunpowder. They tell us, that hitherto things "had not yet been properly and in a *revolutionary* manner explored." — "The strong *chateaus*, those *feudal* fortresses, that *were ordered to be demolished*, attracted next the attention of your committee. *Nature* there had *secretly* regained her *rights*, and had produced saltpetre for the *purpose*, as it should seem, *of facilitating the execution of your decree by preparing the means of destruction*. From these *ruins*, which *still frown* on the liberties of the republick, we have extracted the means of producing good; and those piles, which have hitherto glutted the *pride of despots*, and covered the plots of La Vendée, will soon furnish wherewithal to tame the traitors, and to overwhelm the disaffected." — "The *rebellious cities* also, have afforded a large quantity of saltpetre. *Commune Affranchie*, (that is, the noble city of Lyons reduced in many parts to a heap of ruins) and Toulon will pay a *second* tribute to our artillery." Report 1st. February 1794 [*Burke's note*].

rights of man, will say to the puny *apprentices* of the common law of England.

Is the genius of philosophy not yet known? You may as well think the garden of the Thuilleries was well protected with the cords of ribbon insultingly stretched by the national assembly to keep the sovereign canaille from intruding on the retirement of the poor king of the French, as that such flimsy cobwebs will stand between the savages of the revolution and their natural prey. Deep philosophers are no triflers; brave sans-culottes are no formalists. They will no more regard a Marquis of Tavistock than an Abbot of Tavistock; the Lord of Wooburn will not be more respectable in their eyes than the Prior of Wooburn: they will make no difference between the superiour of a Covent Garden of nuns and of a Covent Garden of another description.[34] They will not care a rush whether his coat is long or short; whether the colour be purple or blue and buff. They will not trouble *their* heads, with what part of *his* head, his hair is cut from; and they will look with equal respect on a tonsure and a crop. Their only question will be that of their *Legendre*, or some other of their legislative butchers, how he cuts up? how he tallows in the cawl or on the kidneys?

Is it not a singular phenomenon, that whilst the sans-culotte carcase butchers, and the philosophers of the shambles, are pricking their dotted lines upon his hide, and like the print of the poor ox that we see in the shop-windows at Charing-cross, alive as he is, and thinking no harm in the world, he is divided into rumps, and sirloins, and briskets, and into all sorts of pieces for roasting, boiling, and stewing, that all the while they are measuring *him*, his Grace is measuring *me*; is invidiously comparing the bounty of the crown with the deserts of the defender of his order, and in the same moment fawning on those who have the knife half out of the sheath — poor innocent!

34 Covent Garden, previously the Convent Garden of Westminster, passed into the hands of the Russell family after the destruction of the monasteries in the sixteenth century, and by the eighteenth century was well known for its brothels.

Pleas'd to the last, he crops the flow'ry food,
And licks the hand just rais'd to shed his blood.[35]

No man lives too long, who lives to do with spirit, and suffer with resignation, what Providence pleases to command or inflict: but indeed they are sharp incommodities which beset old age. It was but the other day, that on putting in order some things which had been brought here on my taking leave of London for ever, I looked over a number of fine portraits, most of them of persons now dead, but whose society, in my better days, made this a proud and happy place. Amongst these was the picture of Lord Keppel. It was painted by an artist worthy of the subject, the excellent friend of that excellent man from their earliest youth, and a common friend of us both, with whom we lived for many years without a moment of coldness, of peevishness, of jealousy, or of jar, to the day of our final separation.[36]

I ever looked on Lord Keppel as one of the greatest and best men of his age; and I loved, and cultivated him accordingly. He was much in my heart, and I believe I was in his to the very last beat. It was after his trial at Portsmouth that he gave me this picture. With what zeal and anxious affection I attended him through that his agony of glory, what part my son in the early flush and enthusiasm of his virtue, and the pious passion with which he attached himself to all my connections, with what pro-digality we both squandered ourselves in courting almost every sort of enmity for his sake, I believe he felt, just as I should have felt, such friendship on such an occasion. I partook indeed of this honour, with several of the first, and best, and ablest in the kingdom, but I was behind hand with none of them; and I am sure, that if to the eternal disgrace of this nation, and to the total annihilation of every trace of honour and virtue in it, things had

35 Pope *Essay on Man* 1:83–84.
36 Admiral Keppel (1725–86) faced a court-martial in 1779 on charges arising from his alleged failure to engage with the French fleet in the Battle of Ushant. Sir Joshua Reynolds made six copies of a portrait of Keppel on the occasion of his acquittal, one of which was given to Burke in recognition of his service in Keppel's defense.

taken a different turn from what they did, I should have attended him to the quarter-deck with no less good will and more pride, though with far other feelings, than I partook of the general flow of national joy that attended the justice that was done to his virtue.

Pardon, my Lord, the feeble garrulity of age, which loves to diffuse itself in discourse of the departed great. At my years we live in retrospect alone: and, wholly unfitted for the society of vigorous life, we enjoy, the best balm to all wounds, the consolation of friendship, in those only whom we have lost for ever. Feeling the loss of Lord Keppel at all times, at no time did I feel it so much as on the first day when I was attacked in the house of lords.

Had he lived, that reverend form would have risen in its place, and with a mild, parental reprehension to his nephew the duke of Bedford, he would have told him that the favour of that gracious prince, who had honoured his virtues with the government of the navy of Great Britain, and with a seat in the hereditary great council of his kingdom, was not undeservedly shewn to the friend of the best portion of his life, and his faithful companion and counsellor under his rudest trials. He would have told him, that to whomever else these reproaches might be becoming, they were not decorous in his near kindred. He would have told him that when men in that rank lose decorum, they lose every thing.

On that day I had a loss in Lord Keppel; but the publick loss of him in this awful crisis—! I speak from much knowledge of the person, he never would have listened to any compromise with the rabble rout of this sans culotterie of France. His goodness of heart, his reason, his taste, his publick duty, his principles, his prejudices, would have repelled him for ever from all connection with that horrid medley of madness, vice, impiety, and crime.

Lord Keppel had two countries; one of descent, and one of birth. Their interest and their glory are the same; and his mind was capacious of both. His family was noble, and it was Dutch:

that is, he was of the oldest and purest nobility that Europe can boast, among a people renowned above all others for love of their native land. Though it was never shewn in insult to any human being, Lord Keppel was something high. It was a wild stock of pride, on which the tenderest of all hearts had grafted the milder virtues. He valued ancient nobility; and he was not disinclined to augment it with new honours. He valued the old nobility and the new, not as an excuse for inglorious sloth, but as an incitement to virtuous activity. He considered it as a sort of cure for selfishness and a narrow mind; conceiving that a man born in an elevated place, in himself was nothing, but every thing in what went before, and what was to come after him. Without much speculation, but by the sure instinct of ingenuous feelings, and by the dictates of plain unsophisticated natural understanding, he felt, that no great commonwealth could by any possibility long subsist, without a body of some kind or other of nobility, decorated with honour, and fortified by privilege. This nobility forms the chain that connects the ages of a nation, which otherwise (with Mr. Paine) would soon be taught that no one generation can bind another. He felt that no political fabrick could be well made without some such order of things as might, through a series of time, afford a rational hope of securing unity, coherence, consistency, and stability to the state. He felt that nothing else can protect it against the levity of courts, and the greater levity of the multitude. That to talk of hereditary monarchy without any thing else of hereditary reverence in the commonwealth, was a low-minded absurdity; fit only for those detestable "fools aspiring to be knaves,"[37] who began to forge in 1789, the false money of the French constitution — That it is one fatal objection to all *new* fancied and *new fabricated* republicks, (among a people, who, once possessing such an advantage, have wickedly and insolently rejected it,) that the *prejudice* of an old nobility is a thing that *cannot* be made. It may be improved, it

---

37 Pope *Epilogue to the Satires* 1:164; intended to recall the preceding line: "See all our Nobles begging to be slaves!"

may be corrected, it may be replenished: men may be taken from it, or aggregated to it, but the *thing itself* is matter of *inveterate* opinion, and therefore *cannot* be matter of mere positive institution. He felt, that this nobility, in fact does not exist in wrong of other orders of the state, but by them, and for them.

I knew the man I speak of; and, if we can divine the future, out of what we collect from the past, no person living would look with more scorn and horrour on the impious parricide committed on all their ancestry, and on the desperate attainder passed on all their posterity, by the Orleans, and the Rochefoucaults, and the Fayettes, and the Viscomtes de Noailles, and the false Perigords, and the long *et cætera* of the perfidious sans culottes of the court, who like demoniacks, possessed with a spirit of fallen pride, and inverted ambition, abdicated their dignities, disowned their families, betrayed the most sacred of all trusts, and by breaking to pieces a great link of society, and all the cramps and holdings of the state, brought eternal confusion and desolation on their country. For the fate of the miscreant parricides themselves he would have had no pity. Compassion for the myriads of men, of whom the world was not worthy, who by their means have perished in prisons, or on scaffolds, or are pining in beggary and exile, would leave no room in his, or in any well-formed mind, for any such sensation. We are not made at once to pity the oppressor and the oppressed.

Looking to his Batavian descent, how could he bear to behold his kindred, the descendants of the brave nobility of Holland, whose blood prodigally poured out, had, more than all the canals, meers, and inundations of their country, protected their independence, to behold them bowed in the basest servitude, to the basest and vilest of the human race; in servitude to those who in no respect were superiour in dignity, or could aspire to a better place than that of hangmen to the tyrants, to whose sceptered pride they had opposed an elevation of soul, that surmounted, and overpowered the loftiness of Castile, the haughtiness of Austria, and the overbearing arrogance of France?

Could he with patience bear, that the children of that nobility, who would have deluged their country and given it to the sea, rather than submit to Louis XIV. who was then in his meridian glory, when his arms were conducted by the Turennes, by the Luxembourgs, by the Bousslers; when his councils were directed by the Colberts, and the Louvois; when his tribunals were filled by the Lamoignons and the Daguessaus — that these should be given up to the cruel sport of the Pichegru's, the Jourdans, the Santerres, under the Rolands, and Brissots, and Gorsas, and Robespierres, the Reubels, the Carnots, and Talliens, and Dantons, and the whole tribe of regicides, robbers, and revolutionary judges, that, from the rotten carcase of their own murdered country, have poured out innumerable swarms of the lowest, and at once the most destructive of the classes of animated nature, which, like columns of locusts, have laid waste the fairest part of the world?

Would Keppel have borne to see the ruin of the virtuous patricians, that happy union of the noble and the burgher, who with signal prudence and integrity, had long governed the cities of the confederate republick, the cherishing fathers of their country, who, denying commerce to themselves, made it flourish in a manner unexampled under their protection? Could Keppel have borne that a vile faction should totally destroy this harmonious construction, in favour of a robbing democracy, founded on the spurious rights of man?

He was no great clerk, but he was perfectly well versed in the interests of Europe, and he could not have heard with patience, that the country of Grotius, the cradle of the law of nations, and one of the richest repositories of all law, should be taught a new code by the ignorant flippancy of Thomas Paine, the presumptuous foppery of La Fayette, with his stolen rights of man in his hand, the wild profligate intrigue and turbulency of Marat, and the impious sophistry of Condorcet, in his insolent address to the Batavian republick?

Could Keppel, who idolized the house of Nassau, who was himself given to England, along with the blessings of the British and Dutch revolutions; with revolutions of stability; with revolu-

tions which consolidated and married the liberties and the interests of the two nations for ever, could he see the fountain of
British liberty itself in servitude to France? Could he see with
patience a prince of Orange expelled as a sort of diminutive
despot, with every kind of contumely, from the country, which
that family of deliverers had so often rescued from slavery, and
obliged to live in exile in another country, which owes its liberty
to his house?

Would Keppel have heard with patience, that the conduct to
be held on such occasions was to become short by the knees to
the faction of the homicides, to intreat them quietly to retire? or
if the fortune of war should drive them from their first wicked
and unprovoked invasion, that no security should be taken, no
arrangement made, no barrier formed, no alliance entered into
for the security of that, which under a foreign name is the most
precious part of England? What would he have said, if it was ever
proposed that the Austrian Netherlands (which ought to be a
barrier to Holland, and the tie of an alliance, to protect her
against any species of rule that might be erected, or even restored in France) should be formed into a republick under her
influence, and dependent upon her power?

But above all, what would he have said, if he had heard it
made a matter of accusation against me, by his nephew the duke
of Bedford, that I was the author of the war? Had I a mind to
keep that high distinction to myself, as from pride I might, but
from justice I dare not, he would have snatched his share of it
from my hand, and held it with the grasp of a dying convulsion to
his end.

It would be a most arrogant presumption in me to assume to
myself the glory of what belongs to his majesty, and to his ministers, and to his parliament, and to the far greater majority of his
faithful people: But had I stood alone to counsel, and that all
were determined to be guided by my advice, and to follow it
implicitly — then I should have been the sole author of a war. But
it should have been a war on my ideas and my principles. However, let his Grace think as he may of my demerits with regard to

the war with regicide, he will find my guilt confined to that alone. He never shall, with the smallest colour of reason, accuse me of being the author of a peace with regicide. But that is high matter; and ought not to be mixed with any thing of so little moment, as what may belong to me, or even to the duke of Bedford.

I have the honour to be, &c.

EDMUND BURKE.

Select Bibliography

PRINCIPAL WORKS OF BURKE

A Vindication of Natural Society (1756).
A Philosophical Enquiry into the Origin of our Ideas of the Sublime and Beautiful (1757; with additions, 1759).
An Essay towards an Abridgement of the English History (1757).
Thoughts on the Cause of the Present Discontents (1770).
Speech on American Taxation (delivered 1774; published 1775).
Speech on Conciliation with the Colonies (1775).
A Letter to the Sheriffs of Bristol on the Affairs of America (1777).
Speech on Oeconomical Reformation (1780).
Speech at the Guildhall in Bristol (1780).
Ninth Report from the Select Committee on India (1783).
Speech on Fox's East India Bill (delivered 1783; published 1784).
Speech on the Nabob of Arcot's Debts (1785).
Reflections on the Revolution in France (1790).
A Letter to a Member of the National Assembly (1791).
An Appeal from the New to the Old Whigs (1791).
A Letter to Sir Hercules Langrishe on the Roman Catholics of Ireland (1792).
A Letter to a Noble Lord (1796).
Two Letters on Peace with the Regicide Directory of France (1797).

SCHOLARLY EDITIONS AND SELECTIONS

Further Reflections on the Revolution in France, ed. Daniel Ritchie (Indianapolis, 1992).

A Philosophical Enquiry into the Origin of our Ideas of the Sublime and Beauti-
ful, ed. J. T. Boulton (London, 1958).
Pre-Revolutionary Writings, ed. Ian Harris (Cambridge, 1993).
Reflections on the Revolution in France, ed. Conor Cruise O'Brien (Har-
mondsworth, 1968).
Selected Letters of Edmund Burke, ed. Harvey C. Mansfield, Jr. (Chicago,
1984).

CRITICISM AND BIOGRAPHY

Blakemore, Steven. *Burke and the Fall of Language* (Hanover, N.H.,
1988).
Bromwich, David. "Burke, Wordsworth, and the Defense of History."
In *A Choice of Inheritance* (Cambridge, Mass., 1989).
Canavan, Francis P. *The Political Reason of Edmund Burke* (Durham, N.C.,
1960).
Chapman, Gerald W. *Edmund Burke: The Practical Imagination* (Cam-
bridge, Mass., 1967).
Cobban, Alfred. *Edmund Burke and the Revolt against the Eighteenth Cen-
tury* (London, 1929).
Cone, Carl B. *Burke and the Nature of Politics,* 2 vols. (1957, 1964).
Conniff, James. *The Useful Cobbler: Edmund Burke and the Politics of Progress*
(Albany, 1994).
Copeland, Thomas W. *Edmund Burke: Six Essays* (London, 1960).
Faulkner, John. "Edmund Burke's Early Conception of Poetry and
Rhetoric." *Studies in Burke and His Time* 12 (1970–71): 1747–63.
Freeman, Michael. *Edmund Burke and the Critique of Political Radicalism*
(Chicago, 1980).
Janes, Regina. "Edmund Burke's Flying Leap from India to France."
History of European Ideas 7 (1986): 509–27.
Kramnick, Isaac. *The Rage of Edmund Burke* (New York, 1977).
Lock, F. P. *Burke's Reflections on the Revolution in France* (London, 1985).
Magnus, Sir Philip. *Edmund Burke: A Life* (London, 1939).
Morley, John. *Edmund Burke* (London, 1887).
O'Brien, Conor Cruise. *The Great Melody: A Thematic Biography of Ed-
mund Burke* (Chicago, 1992).
Parkin, Charles. *The Moral Basis of Burke's Political Thought* (Cambridge,
1956).

Reid, Christopher. *Edmund Burke and the Practice of Political Writing* (London, 1985).

Robinson, Nicholas K. *Edmund Burke: A Life in Caricature* (New Haven, 1996).

Sack, J. J. "The Memory of Burke and the Memory of Pitt." *Historical Journal* 30 (1987): 623–40.

Samuels, Arthur P. I. *The Early Life Correspondence and Writings of Edmund Burke* (Cambridge, 1923).

Stanlis, Peter J. *Edmund Burke and the Natural Law* (Ann Arbor, 1957).

Whelan, Frederick G. *Edmund Burke and India* (Pittsburgh, 1996).

White, Steven K. *Edmund Burke: Modernity, Politics, and Aesthetics* (Thousand Oaks, 1994).

HISTORICAL STUDIES

Bailyn, Bernard. *The Ideological Origins of the American Revolution* (Cambridge, Mass., 1967).

Boulton, James. *The Language of Politics in the Age of Wilkes and Burke* (Oxford, 1963).

Burrow, J. W. *A Liberal Descent: Victorian Historians and the English Past* (Cambridge, 1981).

Butler, Marilyn, ed. *Burke, Paine, Godwin, and the Revolution Controversy* (Cambridge, 1984).

Butterfield, Herbert. *George III and the Historians* (London, 1957).

Cannon, John. *The Fox-North Coalition* (Cambridge, 1969).

Christie, Ian. *Myth and Reality in Late Eighteenth-Century British Politics* (Berkeley, 1970).

Clark, J. C. D. *English Society, 1688–1832* (Cambridge, 1985).

Cobban, Alfred, ed. *The Debate on the French Revolution* (London, 1950).

Colley, Linda. *Britons: Forging the Nation, 1797–1837* (New Haven, 1992).

Derry, John. *The Regency Crisis and the Whigs, 1788–9.* (Cambridge, 1963).

Elliott, Marianne. *Partners in Revolution: The United Irishmen and France* (New Haven, 1982).

Gilmour, Ian. *Riot, Risings and Revolution* (London, 1991).

Goodwin, Albert. *The Friends of Liberty* (Cambridge, Mass., 1979).

Hoffman, Ross J. S. *The Marquis: A Study of Lord Rockingham, 1730–1782* (New York, 1973).

Langford, Paul. *A Polite and Commercial People: England, 1727–1783* (Oxford, 1989).

Lecky, W. E. H. *A History of England in the Eighteenth Century,* vols. 3–5 (London, 1883–90).

Macaulay, Thomas Babington. "Warren Hastings." In *Critical and Historical Essays,* Everyman edition, vol. 1 (London, 1907).

Marshall, P. J. *The Impeachment of Warren Hastings* (Oxford, 1965).

Morgan, Edmund. *Inventing the People* (New York, 1988).

Morris, Marilyn. *The British Monarchy and the French Revolution* (New Haven, 1998).

Namier, Sir Lewis. *England in the Age of the American Revolution* (London, 1930).

O'Gorman, Frank. *The Whig Party and the French Revolution* (London, 1967).

Pares, Richard. *King George III and the Politicians* (Oxford, 1953).

Pocock, J. G. A. *Virtue, Commerce, and History* (Cambridge, 1985).

Thompson, E. P. *Customs in Common* (London, 1992).

Trevelyan, G. O. *George III and Charles Fox,* 2 vols. (London, 1911).

Underdown, P. T. "Henry Cruger and Edmund Burke." *William and Mary Quarterly* 15, no. 1 (1958): 14–34.

BURKE AND POLITICAL THOUGHT

Arendt, Hannah. *On Revolution* (New York, 1963).

Barker, Ernest. *Essays on Government* (Oxford, 1945).

Burrow, J. W. *Whigs and Liberals* (Oxford, 1988).

Butterfield, Herbert. *The Englishman and His History* (Cambridge, 1944).

Deane, Seamus. *The French Revolution and Enlightenment in England, 1789–1832* (Cambridge, Mass., 1988).

Dunn, Susan. *Sister Revolutions* (New York, 1999).

Halévy, Elie. *The Growth of Philosophic Radicalism,* trans. Mary Morris (Boston, 1955).

Lerner, Ralph. *Revolutions Revisited* (Chapel Hill, 1994).

Letwin, Shirley Robin. *The Pursuit of Certainty* (Cambridge, 1965).

Mansfield, Harvey. *Statesmanship and Party Government: A Study of Burke and Bolingbroke* (Chicago, 1965).

McConnell, Michael. "Establishment and Toleration in Edmund

Burke's 'Constitution of Freedom.' " *Supreme Court Review* (1995): 393–462.

Mosher, Michael. "The Skeptic's Burke." *Political Theory* 19 (1991): 391–418.

Oakeshott, Michael. *Rationalism in Politics and Other Essays* (Indianapolis, 1991).

Pitkin, Fenichel Hanna. *The Concept of Representation* (Berkeley, 1967).

Pocock, J. G. A. "Burke and the Ancient Constitution." In *Politics, Language, and Time* (New York, 1971).

Robbins, Caroline. *The Eighteenth Century Commonwealthman* (Cambridge, Mass., 1961).

Ruggiero, Guido de. *The History of European Liberalism,* trans. R. G. Collingwood (Oxford, 1927).

Stephen, Sir Leslie. *History of English Thought in the Eighteenth Century,* vol. 2 (London, 1876).

Stokes, Eric. *The English Utilitarians and India* (Oxford, 1959).

Strauss, Leo. *Natural Right and History* (Chicago, 1953).

Suleri, Sara. *The Rhetoric of English India* (Chicago, 1992).

Talmon, J. L. *The Origins of Totalitarian Democracy* (New York, 1952).

Williams, Raymond. *Culture and Society, 1780–1950* (London, 1958).

Winch, Donald. *Riches and Poverty* (Cambridge, 1996).

Wood, Neal. "The Aesthetic Dimension of Burke's Political Thought." *Journal of British Studies 4* (1964): 41–64.

Index

C.

D.

E.

F.

G.